"The world needs more brave whistleb[...]ists in the service of reclaiming demo[...] of power. Project Censored stands o[...] [...] such work." —Deepa Kumar, author of *Islamophobia and the Politics of Empire* and associate professor of media studies at Rutgers University

"Project Censored provides the kind of fearless and honest journalism we so desperately need in these dangerous times." —Peter Kuznick, professor of history at American University and coauthor with Oliver Stone of *The Untold History of the United States*

"For ages, I've dreamed of a United States where Project Censored isn't necessary, where these crucial stories and defining issues are on the front page of the *New York Times*, the cover of *Time*, and in heavy rotation on CNN. That world still doesn't exist, but we always have Project Censored's yearly book to pull together the most important things the corporate media ignored, missed, or botched." —Russ Kick, author of *You Are Being Lied To*, *Everything You Know Is Wrong*, and the *New York Times* bestselling series *The Graphic Canon*

"[Project Censored] is a clarion call for truth telling. Not only does this volume highlight fearless speech in fateful times, it connect the dots between the key issues we face, lauds our whistleblowers and amplifies their voices, and shines light in the dark places of our government that most need exposure." —Daniel Ellsberg, *The Pentagon Papers*

"Project Censored brings to light some of the most important stories of the year that you never saw or heard about. This is your chance to find out what got buried." —Diane Ravitch, author of *The Death and Life of the Great American School System*

"[Project Censored] shows how the American public has been bamboozled, snookered, and dumbed down by the corporate media. It is chock-full of 'ah-ha' moments where we understand just how we've been fleeced by banksters, stripped of our civil liberties, and blindly led down a path of never-ending war." —Medea Benjamin, author of *Drone Warfare*, and cofounder of Global Exchange and CODEPINK.

"At a time when the need for independent journalism and for media outlets unaffiliated with and untainted by the government and corporate sponsors is greater than ever . . . we are fortunate to have an ally like Project Censored." —Dahr Jamail

"Most journalists in the United States believe the press here is free. That grand illusion only helps obscure the fact that, by and large, the US corporate press does not report what's really going on, while tuning out, or laughing off, all those who try to do just that. Americans—now more than ever—need those outlets that do labor to report some truth. Project Censored is not just among the bravest, smartest, and most rigorous of those outlets, but the only one that's wholly focused on those stories that the corporate press ignores, downplays, and/or distorts." —Mark Crispin Miller, author, professor of media ecology, New York University.

"This book is evidence of Project Censored's profoundly important work in educating readers on current events and the skills needed to be a critical thinker." —*Publishers Weekly*, on *Censored 2014*

"Activist groups like Project Censored . . . are helping to build the media democracy movement. We have to challenge the powers that be and rebuild media from the bottom up."—Amy Goodman

"Project Censored is one of the organizations that we should listen to, to be assured that our newspapers and our broadcasting outlets are practicing thorough and ethical journalism."—Walter Cronkite

"[*Censored*] should be affixed to the bulletin boards in every newsroom in America. And, perhaps read aloud to a few publishers and television executives."—Ralph Nader

"[*Censored*] offers devastating evidence of the dumbing-down of mainstream news in America. . . . Required reading for broadcasters, journalists, and well-informed citizens."—*Los Angeles Times*

"One of the most significant media research projects in the country." —I. F. Stone

"A terrific resource, especially for its directory of alternative media and organizations. . . . Recommended for media collections." —*Library Journal*

CENSORED 2015

INSPIRING WE THE PEOPLE

The Top Censored Stories and Media Analysis of 2013–14

Andy Lee Roth, Mickey Huff
with Project Censored

Foreword by
Ralph Nader

Cartoons by
Khalil Bendib

Seven Stories Press
New York • Oakland

Seven Stories Press
140 Watts Street
New York, NY 10013
www.sevenstories.com

ISBN 978-1-60980-565-4 (paperback)

ISBN 978-1-60980-566-1 (electronic)

ISSN 1074-5998

9 8 7 6 5 4 3 2 1

Book design by Jon Gilbert

Printed in the USA

Contents

CHAPTER 2: Déjà Vu: What Happened to Previous *Censored* Stories?
by Susan Rahman, with research and writing from College of Marin
students Scott Arrow, McLaren Berhendt, Jonah Birnbaum, Justin
Burkhalter, Alex Cutler, Delvante Galon, Christy Gelardi, Lea Islemann,
Devon Johnson, Lauren Markel, Alexandria McDowell, Raffi Oughourlian,
Shannon Reed, Alex Ritchie, Paige Shave, and Pippa Whelan; with
additional contributions by Mickey Huff and Andy Lee Roth; and a
special update on Fukushima by Brian Covert

CHAPTER 3: Mea Culpa, Mi Amore: Sorry for All the Junk Food News and
News Abuse . . . Now Here's Some More
by Nolan Higdon and Mickey Huff, with contributions by Lauren Freeman,
Alexandra Blair, Bryan Reid, Sam Park, Crystal Bedford, Emilee Mann,
Daniel Mizzi, Jess Lopez, Josie Ensley, Jessica Sander, and Darian Keeps

CHAPTER 4: Media Democracy in Action: Inspiring We the People
compiled by Andy Lee Roth and Mickey Huff, with contributions by Patrice
McDermott of OpenTheGovernment.org, Davey D of Hard Knock Radio,
Shahid Buttar of the Bill of Rights Defense Committee, Rob Williams and
Julie Frechette of the Action Coalition for Media Education, David Cobb of
Move to Amend, and Dave Maass of Electronic Frontier Foundation

CHAPTER 5: Service Learning: The SUNY–Buffalo State and Project Censored
Partnership by Michael I. Niman

CHAPTER 6: Rewriting Apartheid: News Media Whitewashing of South Africa
and the Legacy of Nelson Mandela
by Brian Covert

CHAPTER 7: "We Can Live without Gold, but We Can't Live without Water":
Contesting Big Mining in the Americas
by Dorothy Kidd

CHAPTER 8: Law Enforcement–Related Deaths in the US: "Justified
Homicides" and Their Impacts on Victims' Families
by Peter Phillips, Diana Grant, and Greg Sewell

Stuart Hall
(February 3, 1932–February 10, 2014)

Sociologist, founder of the New Left Review,
champion for media democracy, and "familiar stranger"

Hall's work reminds us that the audience for mass media messages need not passively accept the creators' intended meanings; audiences can also interpret those messages in ways that subvert their intended meanings and challenge the social order that they legitimize.

An attempt to keep representation open is a way of constantly wanting new kinds of knowledges to be produced in the world, new kinds of subjectivities to be explored, and new dimensions of meaning which have not been foreclosed by the systems of power which are in operation.

STUART HALL
at the Media Education Foundation

Foreword

Ralph Nader

Project Censored, founded thirty-eight years ago by Professor Carl Jensen of Sonoma State University, has evolved into a deep, wide and utterly engrossing exercise to unmask censorship, self-censorship, and propaganda in the mass media. Jensen enlisted Professor Peter Phillips to succeed him, and later Phillips brought in professors Mickey Huff and Andy Lee Roth, who have worked to expand the project to its current size of approximately two dozen college and university campuses across the country. In this capacity, faculty and students continue to scrutinize the media for fact-based stories that have been censored or underreported in the corporate media. Students also follow up on censored stories from past years and engage in efforts to raise awareness among their peers and the general public. This widening initiative has sparked a veritable student movement against all the things that stand in the way of the "peoples' right to know."

Information is the currency of democracy. If citizens and civic organizations do not use readily available information, there is less pressure to report important news stories. When courageous reporters get alarming facts into print or on TV/radio without any reaction from the public, or follow-up by officials, or civic commentary or action, there is little more discouraging. This happens often. It's a problem that Project Censored has attempted to address through its annual yearbooks and other work, but the fact is that we are not responding adequately to the great reporting that already exists—or to the findings of investigations by government inspectors general, prosecutors, attorneys general, and legislative and regulatory institutions—in order to improve our society. In a phrase, too often, we as a society fail to follow up.

Citizens, nongovernmental organizations, and other civic institutions also play a key role in countering censorship when they use the state and federal Freedom of Information Acts (FOIA). These laws are designed so that citizens themselves can make requests for government files, reports, documents, and memoranda, and, if denied, they can pursue their rights to this information in court. Project Censored regularly highlights some of the groups putting these tools into action, especially in its annual "Media Democracy in Action" chapter, but if there were even more civic advocacy groups, for example, in the fields of nanotechnology and genetic engineering, atomic energy, the exploitation of public lands, massive billing frauds in the health care industry, or corporate fraud on federal programs such as Medicare or Pentagon contracts, there would be more information coming out from all quarters. Certainly there would be more FOIA requests and litigation to exact a price for censorship or self-censorship: the two very often go together. The same is true for whistleblowing protection groups such as the Government Accountability Project (GAP), which has proven to be remarkably effective over the years.

Pressures to self-censor in order to avoid offending advertisers are another problem. The July/August 2014 issue of *Columbia Journalism Review* gives a hint at what may be occurring with the corporate media, beholden more than ever to their advertisers for revenue. In 1982, 60 percent of US journalists said they had "almost complete freedom" in selecting their stories. In 2013, 33 percent of US journalists said they had "almost complete freedom" in selecting their stories. As Project Censored has documented year after year, media concentration by publicly held corporate giants like Disney, Time Warner, Comcast, Gannett, and the Murdoch empire tends to generate a climate of control.

Reporters exposed to this climate of control, these cultures of self-censorship, proceed to comply—as is often the case with the White House press corps. The same inhibitions operate on the campaign trails for presidential and congressional candidates. Establishment reporters wallow in a rut of self-restraint or boredom and wait for gaffes—even when third-party candidates or citizens point out crucial questions that should be asked, including why candidates unreasonably restrict access by reporters. Indeed, after explaining the newsworthiness of my own 2008 presidential campaign agenda, I asked *Washington Post* editor, Fred Hiatt, why there was almost no coverage of my ongoing campaign in his paper. I had campaigned in Washington DC and highlighted the city's pressing issues that the other major candidates were not touching. He blurted out: "Because you can't win." I replied, well then why are you covering, daily, the Washington Nationals baseball team, which wasn't winning many games. He smiled. When the media accept the game as the two major parties want it played, whole segments of a society's needs are blacked out from ever being discussed.

The blackouts are immense and expanding. If organizations or savvy individuals do not push for full disclosure of newsworthy stories or trends, or if they ignore major developments such as the capture of academic science by corporate interests—as in the cases of Monsanto and Syngenta, described in this year's *Censored* story #19—or if readers do not respond favorably to "good news" stories, the results are the same. The general public remains uninformed. It is for this reason, as I have previously remarked, the annual volumes of *Censored* figuratively should be affixed to the bulletin boards in every newsroom in America.

"Important stories" are often viewed as dull by reporters and therefore unworthy of coverage, unless there is overt conflict—and in that case, the more clashing the better. It is almost as if there is a precondition of conflict, which is not always a good incentive to expand public notice. The fourth estate should have a more sensible definition of newsworthiness that does not require riots, civil disobedience, or other disruptions. The growing movement to protect "the commons"—a phenomenon steadily covered in yearly volumes of *Censored*—would benefit from that sensibility. (Another good source for current writing about the commons is David Bollier's website, www.bollier.org.)

Corporate/governmental secrecy persists due to more than negligence, indifference, bureaucratic bungling, inadequate resources, procrastination, or official classification of state secrets and corporate trade secrets. Lying, prevarication, and dissembling also facilitate deliberate obfuscation and cover-ups, as in the 2002–03 run-up to the Bush/Cheney criminal invasion of Iraq. British novelist Dresden James, quoted in this volume, put it well: "When a well-packaged web of lies has been sold gradually to the masses over generations, the truth will seem utterly preposterous and its speaker a raving lunatic."

Many valiant reformers in American history could have attested to that pithy insight!

Journalism programs can advance critical thinking and civic improvements by courses or seminars such as Congress 101 or White House Press Corps 101 that each year could study, monitor, and publically reveal observations about coverage of Congress and the President. With such attention being put on our elected officials by journalism schools, I can assure you that members of Congress and the executive branch will take notice of the studies and findings provided by these courses. And every year, the aggregate experience and impact will create fresh, focused information and reports on the dark corners of Capitol Hill and the White House, which will reach the voters. Similar efforts can be focused on executive and legislative branches at the state and local levels.

The annual *Censored* series should be used both to motivate and inform citizens to carry forward the illumination of acquired knowledge—a precursor to action for a better society. But precursors are not enough as a fourteenth-century Chinese philosopher wrote: "To know and not do is not to know."

RALPH NADER is America's leading consumer's and citizen's advocate, a lawyer and an author who has co-founded numerous public interest groups including Public Citizen, the Center for Auto Safety, Clean Water Action Project, the Disability Rights Center, the Pension Rights Center, Commercial Alert, the Public Interest Research Group (PIRG), and the Center for Study of Responsive Law. For the past forty-five years Ralph Nader has challenged abuses by corporate and government officials and urged citizens to use their time, energy and democratic rights to demand greater institutional accountability. In 1965, Nader's landmark book *Unsafe at Any Speed* changed the face of the automobile industry. *The Atlantic* named Nader as one of the 100 most influential figures in American history, and *Time* and *LIFE* magazines honored him as one of the most influential Americans of the twentieth century. As a result of his efforts, cars are safer, food is healthier, our environment is less polluted, and our democracy is more robust.

Introduction

Andy Lee Roth and Mickey Huff

Bing! Bing! the light bulb of an idea
Buzz! Buzz! talking it over with neighbors or co-workers
Pow! Pow! telling truth to power

—Peter Linebaugh[1]

The First Amendment of the United States Constitution links freedom of speech and press with the rights to assemble and petition, as historian Peter Linebaugh's verse succinctly expresses. Freedom of speech and the press provide the illumination of new ideas. In the absence of these freedoms, people have little or no basis on which to challenge the status quo. That task, however, is a collective endeavor. And, as both the First Amendment and Linebaugh's poem affirm, it is through communication with each other and shared public effort that we make new possibilities into reality. The First Amendment affirms these freedoms and rights as fundamental to democracy, and in the Declaration of Independence, these key elements of life and liberty are more broadly referred to in the phrase "the pursuit of happiness."

Notably, then, the Preamble to the Constitution makes no mention of judges, politicians, or corporate executives. Instead it identifies "We the People" as, in one commentator's words, the "true and ultimate authority" in American government.[2]

From Josh MacPhee's art on the cover to its last page, *Censored 2015: Inspiring We the People* shows how the goal of bettering the human condition, in our communities and around the world, depends on personal inspiration, galvanized by communication into socially conscious collective effort. Inspiration, communication, participation: Bing! Buzz! Pow!

As citizens and community members, what are we to make of the First Amendment and the Preamble to the Constitution in an era characterized, on one hand, by the extraordinary whistleblowing of national security insiders, and, on the other hand, the Central Intelligence Agency using Twitter and Facebook to put CIA content "right at your fingertips"?[3] "We stand at a historic crossroads," journalist Glenn Greenwald wrote in *No Place to Hide*. "Will the digital age usher in the individual liberation and political freedoms that the Internet is uniquely capable of unleashing? Or will it bring about a system of omnipresent monitoring and control, beyond the dreams of even the greatest tyrants of the past. Right now, either path is possible. Our actions will determine where we end up."[4]

Censored 2015 illuminates topics and issues—left altogether dark or duskily obscured by the corporate media—where *collaborative* action is necessary. From ocean acidification, to the aftermath of Fukushima, and the Trans-Pacific Partnership—to name just a few of the under-reported stories featured in this volume—it is increasingly clear that individual action, though crucial, is by itself insufficient. Insofar as these are "public issues," to employ sociologist C. Wright Mills's useful concept, they require collective, public engagement.[5] Individual insights (the *Bing! Bing!* of new ideas) must be galvanized into collective effort (*Buzz! Buzz! Pow! Pow!*), if action to address public issues is to be effective. Thus, *Censored 2015* also highlights the good work of individuals and organizations that are already acting to resist would-be tyrants' monitoring and control, telling truth to power in order to champion liberation and freedom.

RESISTING ENCLOSURES, PAST AND PRESENT: ILLUMINATING AN OPEN FUTURE

We live in an era characterized by privatization and inequality. In tracing the history of the commons, its privatization, and resistance, Peter Linebaugh describes a process in which enclosure of the commons and inequality operate in a feedback loop: "Expropriation intensifies exploitation: X^2 has been our experience."[6] Most obviously, expropriation involves the enclosure of land, but it also includes the privatization of handicrafts, transport, and the "complete separation of the worker from the means of production."[7]

Of course, censorship of press and speech is another fundamental form of closure.[8] Enclosures lead to the destruction of independence and the rise of terror in the community.[9] This fear is reactive, while informed democratic participation is proactive. The antidote to the political and social maladies of enclosure lies in creating and maintaining an open society. Secrecy and censorship are enemies of such a society. In fact, dating back 800 years to 1215, the Magna Carta illuminated rights of due process, which influenced the founders of the United States some 550 years later, such that they believed in protecting habeas corpus for all persons, evidenced by the Fifth Amendment to the Constitution. The First Amendment protects a free press, speech and expression, assembly and petition, while the Fourth Amendment essentially protects our right to privacy, the right to be left alone. As Linebaugh said, "History gives us . . . ground to stand on."[10] This is our history, and we should stand on this solid ground as we collectively resist secrecy and censorship in their many guises, and we should protest vigorously when we are witness to the loss of these aforementioned fundamental principles and rights.

Secrecy is a specific form of government regulation, involving the enclosure of information. As Daniel Patrick Moynihan, chairman of the 1997 Commission on Protecting and Reducing Government Secrecy, wrote, "Normal regulation concerns how citizens must behave, and so regulations are widely promulgated. Secrecy, by contrast, concerns what citizens may know; and the citizen is not told what may not be known."[11] This renders informed democratic self-government impossible. Further, historian Antoon De Baets, who writes about censorship of history as well as the history of censorship, identifies epistemological problems in the study of censorship. Unsurprisingly, they involve the nature of suppressed information itself, namely, the difficulty in accessing secret material. Were it not for whistleblowers and other reporting actors, we literally would not know the degree of censorship that actually exists in a society, like the US, that purports to be open and free. However, De Baets argues that the urge to censor can actually backfire, inadvertently highlighting that which it aims to suppress:

> [W]henever the silenced and silent historians are not able to refute the heralded truths of official historical propaganda, philosophers, poets, novelists, playwrights, filmmakers, journalists, storytellers, and singers take care of the historical truth and keep it alive. Paradoxically, the ostensible vulnerability of many of these substitutes is their power.... Thus, censorship may not suppress alternative views but rather generate them, and, by doing so, become counterproductive. Censorship backfires."[12]

Perhaps this will be the case with the Chelsea Manning and Edward Snowden stories. In spring 2014, the concurrence of two news stories exemplified how the framing of current events today may shape our sense of history in the future. On April 15, 2014, US corporate media informed us that a US army general had upheld the conviction and thirty-five-year prison sentence of whistleblower Chelsea Manning, while on the same day, the Pulitzer Prize in public service had been awarded to Barton Gellman at the *Washington Post* and Glenn Greenwald, Laura Poitras, and Ewan MacAskill of the *Guardian* for their coverage of the US government's sweeping surveillance programs.[13] Of course, the *Post* and the *Guardian*'s award-winning coverage was based on secret documents leaked by NSA whistleblower Edward Snowden.

Like Manning before him, Snowden has been pilloried by the corporate media (as was Daniel Ellsberg dating back to the Pentagon Papers) even as these establishment outlets have opportunistically used documents leaked by Manning and Snowden for news scoops of their own. To wit, Secretary of State John Kerry called Ellsberg a hero while in the same sentence denouncing Snowden. To call this political theater may be too polite.

As contrasts like this make clear, US corporate news remains in a sordid state of affairs—further motivating Project Censored to continue to do all that we can to promote independent journalism, media literacy, and critical thinking skills as essential components of democracy. As Peter Linebaugh has remarked, nodding to the more affirmative, "common people who have been enclosed and foreclosed . . . are beginning to disclose an alternative, open future."[14]

THE WORLD DOESN'T STOP FOR US TO TAKE ITS TEMPERATURE

While we do our best to help create this open future and cover the most up-to-date issues of media censorship, the 24/7 news cycle, coupled with the proliferation of information technology, makes this increasingly challenging. We write, after all, at a time when even the CIA has its own Facebook and Twitter accounts.[15] Even with our amazing publishing team, it still takes months to produce the *Censored* yearbook. Every year, between the time when we wrap the manuscript and when the book hits the shelves, the world does not stop, news continues to develop, and some things we may remark upon in spring seem outdated by fall. Such was the case last year with Chelsea Manning, and certainly with the Edward Snowden NSA affair.

Readers may notice an occasional repeated phrase, "as this book goes to press" prefacing several stories in this volume. For example, as this book goes to press, indeed, as we write this introduction, the *New York Times* published an important article, "The Fog Machine of

War, Chelsea Manning on the US Military and Media Freedom." In this opinion piece, Manning described a culture of censorship in war reporting. She wrote, "the current limits on press freedom and excessive government secrecy make it impossible for Americans to grasp fully what is happening in the wars we finance."[16]

Manning noted that embedded reporting was so controlled in Iraq, that it was not simply difficult for journalists to report from within Iraq in a critical way; in fact, most reporters were unable to gain access at all. She wrote about numerous instances in which reporters had their access revoked upon publication of controversial articles. The late Michael Hastings, writing for *Rolling Stone*, lost his credentials after publishing a critical report about General Stanley McChrystal in Afghanistan that eventually led to McChrystal's dismissal. Though Hastings's report showed how a free press could hold those in power accountable for their actions, he was demonized for his coverage of the incident. Even after his untimely death in June 2013, government officials and the press, notably the *New York Times*, continued to trash Hastings.[17] It seems that even in death no one is safe from establishment attacks and the ongoing war on journalism. Hastings reported what he saw, and he did not violate state secrets, yet was attacked for not complying with the rules of "embedded journalism." Apparently the rules forbid critical, fact-based coverage.

According to Manning,

> A Pentagon spokesman said, "Embeds are a privilege, not a right." If a reporter's embed status is terminated, typically she or he is blacklisted. This program of limiting press access was challenged in court in 2013 by a freelance reporter, Wayne Anderson, who claimed to have followed his agreement but to have been terminated after publishing adverse reports about the conflict in Afghanistan. The ruling on his case upheld the military's position that there was no constitutionally protected right to be an embedded journalist.[18]

Manning further shared her utter dismay regarding the US military's role meddling in Iraqi elections, disrupting antigovernment Iraqi activists, and shaping and suppressing intelligence reports.

Further support for Manning's critique can be found in a June 2014 study by the Media Credentialing Working Group. The study, titled "Who Gets a Press Pass? Media Credentialing Practices in the United States," found that:

> [O]ne out of every five respondents who applied for a credential was denied by a credentialing organization at least once. Moreover, certain categories of applicants are more likely to be denied than others: freelance journalists were significantly less likely to receive media credentials than employed journalists; photographers were more likely to be denied than non-photographers; and respondents who identified themselves as activists were more likely to be denied than those respondents who did not.[19]

Government restrictions on press credentialing, as documented in the June 2014 study, and the government's *de facto* position that embedded journalists have reduced First Amendment rights, as highlighted by Manning's editorial, point to a crisis of the free press, one of the most fundamental institutions in a democratic society. The most effective check on this kind of abuse of power hinges on We the People challenging our elected representatives to demand transparency in reporting, the rapid declassification of government documents that in no way endanger military missions, and an end to the persecution—whether informal as in the case of Hastings, or official as in the prosecution of Manning and the pursuit of Snowden—of journalists and whistleblowers that aim to inform the public. Given public opinion polls indicating that American's faith in government is near an all-time low and that their distrust of (corporate) media is near an historic high mark (as detailed in chapter 3), Americans are increasingly expressing their collective sense that the cherished values of open government and reliable journalism are threatened to a breaking point.

Manning's editorial is just one current, developing story as *Censored 2015* goes to press. We would be remiss to not address it, but in cases such as this, the world doesn't stop for us to take its temperature. We have more information at our fingertips than ever before, and information literally can travel the globe in mere seconds. However, speed and clarity are not always synonymous. As in past *Censored* yearbooks, we reiterate here the importance of taking time for thoughtful analysis of such information. Critical thinking skills have not kept up with the speed of the digital revolution. This is why Project Censored attempts not only to highlight underreported stories that get lost in the din of information superhighways, but also aims to provide a long-range beacon, illuminating background issues, historical context, and critical-thinking skills necessary to becoming independently minded, media-literate citizens.

INSIDE *CENSORED 2015*

This year's volume opens with a foreword by Ralph Nader, whose public life has been dedicated to service of We the People. He reminds us of the importance of a free press in maintaining our liberties. We are honored and inspired by his contribution here.

Chapter 1 features Project Censored's listing and analysis of the Top 25 underreported news stories from 2013 to 2014. "The News that Didn't Make the News" this year includes independent press dispatches on public issues affecting the environment (e.g. story #1, "Ocean Acidification Increasing at Unprecedented Rate"), the economy (e.g. story #5, "Bankers Back on Wall Street Despite Major Crimes"), US Empire (including story #10, "Top Ten US Aid Recipients All Practice Torture") and the power of We the People to actively resist abuses of power (e.g. stories #21, "Questioning the Charter School Hype," and #24, "Restorative Justice Turns Violent School Around"). The Top 25 list also features several stories from the independent press highlighting systemic news slant in the corporate press (including, for example, stories #8, "Corporate News Ignores Connections between Extreme Weather and Global Warming," and #22, "Corporate News Media Understate Rape, Sexual Violence"). Once again we call attention to the truth telling of independent journalists and celebrate not only their individual commitments, but also the independent news organizations and constitutional protections that make their reporting possible. As always, we hope for a day when Project Censored's annual list of censored and underreported news stories would be unnecessary. Until then, we continue to produce our annual Top 25 list.

Chapter 2, "Déjà Vu," tracks what happened to a select handful of previous years' Top 25 stories. Researched by students of Susan Rahman at the College of Marin, this year's chapter revisits the aforementioned coverage of the Manning and Snowden cases (stories #1 and #4 in *Censored 2014*); as well as *Censored 2014*'s story #3, on the Trans-Pacific Partnership threatening global corporate governance; story #14, on the looming health crisis posed by wireless technology; and story #25, on Israel forcing birth control on Ethiopian immigrants. The chapter also features a special update on Fukushima by frequent Project Censored contributor Brian Covert.

Chapter 3 showcases Junk Food News and News Abuse from the past year. Nolan Higdon and Mickey Huff, along with students from Diablo Valley College, provide snapshots of the inanity and propaganda mill that is the corporate press and look at what alternative stories they could have covered to better serve the public interest. This year's lowlights include a celebrity bigotry mea culpa tour, Barbie's unapologetic follow up, twerking and DUI growing pains, plus an exposé of the propaganda war in the Ukraine and Syria; spies vs. spies, US–USSR style; TPP coverage that's MIA, and, sadly, much more.

Chapter 4, Media Democracy in Action, highlights some of the individuals and organizations that radically inspire We the People, from the grassroots and up. This year we proudly feature OpenTheGovernment.org, Hard Knock Radio, the Bill of Rights Defense Committee, the Action Coalition for Media Education (ACME), Move to Amend, and Electronic Frontier Foundation. It is no surprise the corporate media oft ignore these groups' efforts, for they truly go to the heart of what it means to affirm openness and democracy. Each of these organizations leads by example, epitomizing the observation that democracy is not a spectator sport.

In chapter 5, Professor Michael I. Niman writes about the development of the Project Censored Service Learning Partnership at State University of New York–Buffalo State. His pioneering efforts in establishing a service learning course based on Project Censored's work further the Project's educational outreach. As Project Censored expands its campus affiliates program, providing college and university students with hands-on training in media literacy and critical thinking, across different fields of study, Niman and his students demonstrate how productive—and transformative—such learning can be.

Journalist Brian Covert contributes another important piece to this year's *Censored* in chapter 6, "Rewriting Apartheid: News Media Whitewashing of South Africa and the Legacy of Nelson Mandela." While President Barack Obama was taking selfies at Mandela's funeral and establishment media piled on, key elements of who Mandela was and what he stood for, including his views on contemporary apartheid issues in the Middle East and the longtime hypocrisy of American leaders on these matters, were conspicuously absent from corporate news coverage in the US. Covert's chapter provides readers an opportunity to learn more, not only about Mandela, but also regarding US involvement in the African continent and broader, global patterns of US hegemony.

In chapter 7, Dorothy Kidd tracks the largely untold history of a global rush in mining exploration and extraction, ushered in over the last three decades by the passage in nearly one hundred countries of neoliberal laws that favor corporate mining interests with reduced taxes, and with weakened environmental, labor, and human rights regulations. "If you were to depend on commercial news," Kidd writes, "you would know little about this." Equally underreported, however, is how the affected communities—and especially indigenous peoples—are connecting with legal and environmental organizations to "change the rules of the game" and are using social media to tell their own stories, while circumventing the dominant corporate media.

Violence in the US has always been a big story, unfortunately, but the story of police violence and its impact on communities is a neglected topic in the corporate media, as evidenced by this year's story #18, "National Database of Police Killings Aims for Accountability." In chapter 8, Peter Phillips, Diana Grant, and Greg Sewell report the findings of a decade-long study of law enforcement–related deaths in the US. Their report contrasts family members' accounts of the deaths of their loved ones with official police reports and news stories, shining necessary light on a crucial social justice issue that affects too many communities across the nation.

In Chapter 9, Zara Zimbardo argues, "It is easier to imagine the Zombie Apocalypse than to imagine the end of capitalism." Her analysis of our contemporary infatuation with the undead provides a cultural history of zombies in the American imagination. She traces representations of zombies in movies, novels, and television across three stages of global capitalist expansion, "from New World slavery in Haiti, to American consumerism and militarism, to the networked neoliberal era," explaining why apocalyptic scenarios featuring zombies have become an era-defining genre of mass-mediated storytelling.

In the book's final chapter, "Play It Again, (Uncle) Sam: A Brief History of US Imperialism, Propaganda, and the News," Deepa Kumar provides a cogent and remarkably clear historical overview of how propaganda shapes public debate on US foreign policy and warfare. "War propaganda," she writes, "has a habit of repeating itself." From the Spanish–American War, through the two world wars, to Vietnam, Iraq, and beyond, she identifies a fundamental, longstanding pattern of government-disseminated deception that operates to this day. Identifying patterns in pro-war propaganda is a crucial step, she writes, in "uncovering the truth" about American Empire and bringing it to the public.

INCLUDING WE THE PEOPLE

Taking into account the diverse contributions to *Censored 2015*—and how each one suggests different ways to convert individual inspiration into effective collaborative effort—we find evidence of what French social theorist Michel Foucault once described as a "plurality of resistances." Instead of a singular "great Refusal," Foucault forecast "a plurality of resistances, each of them a special case."[20] Or, as Glenn Greenwald has expressed it, "[I]t is human beings collectively, not a small number of elites working in secret, who can decide what kind of world we want to live in. Promoting the human capacity to reason and make decisions: that is the purpose of whistleblowing, of activism, of political journalism."[21] In terms of Josh MacPhee's vivid cover image, we might imagine darkness transformed to light—not by a single, great spotlight under the control of some central power, but rather by thousands, even millions, of handheld lights, lanterns, and candles.

The Constitution expressed its cherished and enduring political ideals in the name of "We the People of the United States." However, the public issues that confront the members of today's world require a broader, more inclusive understanding of "We the People."

As ocean acidification, the Trans-Pacific Partnership, and global war make clear, we can no longer understand ourselves fully through the limited category of "citizen"—unless we redefine that term to refer to global, rather than national, identities.

The power of We the People is evident throughout *Censored 2015*. We invite you to read further and to find inspiration, as we do, in the promise that, when we extend "We the People" to transcend national identities, we will see clearly the value of all that we share in common and the power to be tapped in organizing to act on that basis.

Notes

1. Peter Linebaugh, *Stop, Thief!: The Commons, Enclosures and Resistance* (Oakland, CA: PM Press, 2014), 15.
2. Jeffrey Toobin, "Our Broken Constitution," *New Yorker*, December 9, 2013, 73.
3. "CIA Goes Social," Central Intelligence Agency, News & Information, June 6, 2014, https://www.cia.gov/news-information/featured-story-archive/2014-featured-story-archive/cia-goes-social.html.
4. Glenn Greenwald, *No Place to Hide: Edward Snowden, the NSA, and the U.S. Surveillance State* (New York: Metropolitan Books, 2014), 6.

5. In *The Sociological Imagination* (New York: Oxford University Press, 1959), C. Wright Mills distinguished between "personal troubles" and "public issues." The former occur within "the character of the individual" and the sphere of the individual's "immediate relations with others" (8). By contrast, *public issues* involve a crisis in the "institutional arrangements" of the society, in ways that transcend individuals' local environments and inner lives. Public issues, Mills suggested, arise when "some value cherished by *publics* is felt to be threatened" (8, emphasis added).

6. Linebaugh, *Stop, Thief!*, 74.

7. Ibid., 32.

8. Ibid., 81.

9. Ibid., 142.

10. Linebaugh, *Stop Thief!*, 3. On the Magna Carta, see also Peter Linebaugh, *The Magna Carta Manifesto: Liberty and Commons for All* (Berkeley and Los Angeles: University of California Press, 2008).

11. David Patrick Moynihan, "Chairman's Foreword," *Report of the Commission on Protecting and Reducing Government Secrecy*, S. Doc. 105-2 (December 31, 1997), http://www.gpo.gov/fdsys/pkg/GPO-CDOC-105sdoc2/pdf/GPO-CDOC-105sdoc2-4.pdf, xxxvi. On the Moynihan Commission report, see also Susan Maret, "Introduction: Government Secrecy," *Research in Social Problems and Public Policy* 19 (2011), xi-xxx.

12. Antoon De Baets, "Censorship Backfires: A Taxonomy of Concepts Related to Censorship," in *Censored 2013: Dispatches from the Media Revolution*, eds. Mickey Huff and Andy Lee Roth (New York: Seven Stories Press), 232.

13. See, for example, Associated Press, "WikiLeaks Case: Manning's Conviction, 35-Year Sentence Upheld," *San Francisco Chronicle*, April 15, 2014, A8; and Associated Press, "Pulitzers Honor Reporting on Government Surveillance," *San Francisco Chronicle*, April 15, 2014, A5.

14. Linebaugh, *Stop Thief!*, 212.

15. "CIA Goes Social"; see also Nick Fielding and Ian Cobain, "Revealed: US Spy Operation that Manipulates Social Media," *Guardian*, March 17, 2011, http://www.guardian.co.uk/technology/2011/mar/17/us-spy-operation-social-networks. This was story #2 in *Censored 2012: Sourcebook for the Media Revolution* (New York: Seven Stories Press, 2011), accessible online at http://www.projectcensored.org/2-us-military-manipulates-the-social-media. With the launch of the CIA's social media sites on June 6, 2014, the anniversary of World War II's D-Day, we can't help but wonder, is their target the American people?

16. Chelsea Manning, "The Fog Machine of War: Chelsea Manning on the U.S. Military and Media Freedom," *New York Times*, June 14, 2014, http://www.nytimes.com/2014/06/15/opinion/sunday/chelsea-manning-the-us-militarys-campaign-against-media-freedom.html?_r=0.

17. For example, see Jim Naureckas, "NYT Pays Tribute to Hastings by Attacking Him after Death," Fairness and Accuracy in Reporting, June, 20, 2013, http://www.fair.org/blog/2013/06/20/nyt-pays-tribute-to-hastings-by-attacking-him-after-death/; and Ryan Grim and Jason Linkins, "Michael Hastings' Wife Obliterates New York Times For Dismissive Obituary," *Huffington Post*, June 19, 2013, http://www.huffingtonpost.com/2013/06/19/michael-hastings-wife_n_3469095.html.

18. Manning, "Fog Machine of War."

19. Jeffrey Hermes et al., "Who Gets a Press Pass? Media Credentialing Practices in the United States," Media Credentialing Working Group, June 2014, http://www.dmlp.org/sites/dmlp.org/files/Who%20Gets%20a%20Press%20Pass_0.pdf. We are grateful to Susan Maret for drawing this study to our attention.

20. Michel Foucault, *The History of Sexuality. An Introduction*, vol. 1, trans. Robert Hurley (New York: Vintage Books, 1990[1978]), 96.

21. Greenwald, *No Place to Hide*, 253.

CHAPTER 1

The Top *Censored* Stories and Media Analysis of 2013–14

Andy Lee Roth, Mickey Huff, and Project Censored

INTRODUCTION

The operation of unwitting bias is difficult either to locate or prove. Its manifestations are always indirect. It comes through in terms of who is or who is not accorded the status of an accredited witness: in the tones of voice: in the set-up of studio confrontations: in the assumptions which underlie the questions asked or not asked: in terms of the analytical concepts which serve informally to link events to causes: in what passes for explanation.

—Stuart Hall[1]

In a succinct and stimulating but overlooked essay from 1970, the late Stuart Hall (to whom we dedicate *Censored 2015*) posed a powerful pair of questions. "A World at One with Itself" played with the title of an influential BBC news program, *World at One*, as Hall critiqued contemporary British news coverage of violence in Trinidad, Guatemala, and his adopted homeland, England. In each of these cases, news coverage attributed violence to groups that, in Hall's words, consistently challenged "the built-in definitions and values enshrined in the political culture of broadcasters and audiences alike."[2] Without systematic, in-depth background, British journalists provided *"actuality without context"* (a phrase Hall emphasized with italics) thus contributing to a "general sense of a meaningless explosion of meaningless and violent acts—'out there' somewhere, in an unintelligible world."[3]

Thus, Hall challenged his readers to consider two questions: "Do/

can the media help us to understand these significant real events in the real world? Do the media clarify them or mystify us about them?"

Like so many of his political interventions, Hall's questions continue to challenge us to stake a position by digging analytically deeper.[4] In considering the possibility that media—and journalism, in particular—might *mystify* our understanding of the real world, rather than *clarify* it, Hall sought to address deeper themes than the usual debates regarding, for example, the boundaries between "hard" and "soft" news, or "biased" versus "objective" coverage. For Hall, such questions were "relevant" but "technical." These "routine ways of setting up the problem" were "drawn from the press" itself, reflecting both their shared worldviews as news professionals and the "powerful hold" of journalistic conventions.

Instead, by asking us to consider the media's capacity to clarify, Hall challenged us to face another, even deeper question: "What constitutes the definition of news currently employed?"[5] Questioning the conventional definition of news draws our attention to what Hall termed "unwitting" bias; that is, "the institutional slanting, built-in not by the devious inclination of editors to the political right or left, but by the steady and unexamined play of attitudes which, via the mediating structure of professionally defined news values, inclines all media towards the status quo."[6]

The first of Hall's questions—"Do/can the media help us to understand these significant real events in the real world?"—used what might first seem like an awkward construction, "Do/can." As is often the case in Hall's work, slowing down to consider the specific choice yields rewards. Asking whether some condition produces a given outcome is different from asking whether it *could* do so. Hall leaves open the possibility that, even if the news to which we have access today mystifies the world more than clarifies it, we may nonetheless hope for better.

Four decades later, the unwitting bias that concerned Hall in 1970 remains characteristic of most news that originates from corporate media. This chapter, presenting synopses of Project Censored's Top 25 censored news stories from 2013 to 2014, bears witness to Hall's analysis of unwitting news bias in three important ways.

First, and most obviously: in 2014, corporate media continue to reproduce what Hall termed "official ideologies of the status quo"—not simply reflecting a "consensual" style of politics, but also reinforcing it by blocking certain kinds of events and actors from achieving newsworthy status. Though "objectivity" is an oft-invoked journalistic value, standards of treatment vary when journalists cover groups or events that conflict with the political culture's foundational assumptions and sacred values. As Hall noted, "these are precisely the forms of political and civil action which the media, by virtue of their submission to the consensus, are consistently unable to deal with, comprehend or interpret."[7] The stories covered in this chapter closely fit this description.

Second—and here we hope that Hall's legacy is duly honored—the journalism represented in the following Top 25 stories makes good on the possibility suggested by his first question; in other words, journalism not only has the *potential* to clarify our understanding of significant real world events, but it actually does so. Although many of the stories that follow may seem critical—and even discouraging—in tenor, we must remember and appreciate that, but for the work of these intrepid and independent investigative journalists, we would know and understand very little or nothing at all about these important stories. Their dispatches provide the context that is crucial for more complete understanding, and they raise the bar for what counts as explanation.

Peter Phillips captured this point succinctly in his introduction to *Censored 1998*: "Being named as an author of a 'most censored' story is a high honor, as it distinguishes quality investigative journalism from the entertainment news so prevalent in today's media. The 25 news stories in this chapter are timely, factual accounts of important subjects" that the corporate media have "ignored, under-covered, or diminished."[8] As the stories in this list show, not all journalism inclines toward the status quo. Effectively censored from corporate news media coverage, these stories have only been dealt with, comprehended, and interpreted effectively by independent journalists.

Third, and finally, this year's Top 25 list bears subtle but significant evidence of one cause for hope regarding the future of journalism and its crucial role in making democracy possible. As the Project's founder Carl Jensen noted in his preface to *Censored: The 1994 Project*

Censored Yearbook, it is *students* who have identified, researched, and written the synopses of the Top 25 stories.[9] In 1994, these students were all participants in a seminar on media censorship taught by Professor Jensen at Sonoma State University. In 2014, twenty volumes later, Project Censored's campus affiliates program links students and faculty from approximately two dozen college and university campuses across the country in this ongoing collective effort. The Top 25 stories featured in *Censored* 2015—plus a handful of honorable mentions—represent the best efforts of some 260 students and 49 faculty members from 18 college and university campuses, who together identified and vetted 237 Validated Independent News stories during our 2013–14 cycle.[10]

This direct, hands-on training in critical thinking and media literacy is a crucial aspect of Project Censored's mission to prepare a next generation—including many who are already or will become community leaders, and some who may even pursue journalism as a vocation—to cultivate a wary attitude toward corporate media, to support independent journalism, and to recognize the crucial role of a truly free press for democracy. For each story synopsis, we identify not only the names and publication sources of the original news stories, but also the names and campus affiliations of the students and faculty members who both investigated whether the story received any coverage in the corporate media and wrote the original synopsis of it. We identify the student researchers and faculty evaluators, not only to give credit where credit is due—the independent press is so diverse and extensive today that no single small group of people can keep track of it—but also to inspire other students and teachers, who might want to do this kind of work themselves, to join us. Those interested can learn more about how to do so in this volume or on the Project Censored website.[11]

The brief synopses that follow are not meant to replace the original news reports on which they are based. Instead, they summarize the stories' key points, hopefully in ways that lead interested readers back to the original reports themselves. The "Note on Research and Evaluation of *Censored* News Stories," which follows immediately, provides more detail on the vetting process and how stories are ranked. Following the Top 25 list, the chapter concludes with analytic comments on several overarching themes that cannot be captured in the format of a list.

We hope you will find that this year's Top 25 stories, by refusing to conform to the status quo assumptions of the corporate media, provide remarkable clarity about significant real-world events in ways that inspire us to meaningful engagement.

We would like to acknowledge Noah Tenney, James F. Tracy, Susan Maret, and Lori Schwarz for providing crucial assistance in the final stage of reviewing all of the Top 25 stories for any corporate coverage. We are grateful for their invaluable contributions.

Notes

1. Stuart Hall, "A World at One with Itself," in *The Manufacture of News: Deviance, Social Problems and the Mass Media*, eds. Stanley Cohen and Jock Young, (London: Constable, 1973), 85–94. [Originally published in *New Society*, June 18, 1970, 1056–58.]
2. Ibid, 91.
3. Ibid, 91, 92.
4. As one remembrance of Hall observed, "He was committed to intervening publically on key political questions: he never followed a narrow academic path but knew theory was an essential lens for critique." Les Back, "Stuart Hall: A Bright Star," openDemocracy, February 16, 2014, http://www.opendemocracy.net/les-back/stuart-hall-bright-star.
5. Hall, "World at One," 85.
6. Ibid., 87–88.
7. Ibid., 90.
8. Peter Phillips, *Censored 1998: The News that Didn't Make the News* (New York: Seven Stories Press, 1997), 25.
9. Carl Jensen, *Censored: The 1994 Project Censored Yearbook* (New York: Four Walls Eight Windows, 1994), 8. Note: Four previous yearbooks (1989–92) had been self-published in spiral-bound format; Shelburne Press in Chapel Hill, North Carolina, published the 1993 yearbook.
10. Synopses for all 237 of these stories, including citations and links to the original news reports, can be found on the Project Censored website, under the heading "Validated News." See http://www.projectcensored.org/category/validated-independent-news, which we update regularly through each annual cycle with new Validated Independent News stories from our campus affiliates. For the early history of the campus affiliates program, see Peter Phillips and Mickey Huff, "Colleges and Universities Validate Independent News and Challenge Censorship," in *Censored 2011*, eds. Mickey Huff, Peter Phillips, and Project Censored (New York: Seven Stories Press, 2010), 355–69.
11. See "How to Support Project Censored" on page 327 and online see "Project Censored in the Classroom," http://www.projectcensored.org/project-censoreds-commitment-to-independent-news-in-the-classroom.

A NOTE ON RESEARCH AND EVALUATION OF *CENSORED* NEWS STORIES

How do we at Project Censored identify and evaluate independent news stories, and how do we know that the Top 25 stories that we bring forward each year are not only relevant and significant, but also trustworthy? The answer is that each candidate news story undergoes rigorous review, which takes place in multiple stages during each annual cycle. Although adapted to take advantage of both the Project's expanding affiliates program and current technologies, the vetting process is quite similar to the one Project Censored founder Carl Jensen established thirty-eight years ago.

Candidate stories are initially identified by Project Censored professors and students, or are nominated by members of the general public, who bring them to the Project's attention through our website.[1] Together, faculty and students vet each candidate story in terms of its importance, timeliness, quality of sources, and corporate news coverage. If it fails on any one of these criteria, the story does not go forward.

Once Project Censored receives the candidate story, we undertake a second round of judgment, using the same criteria and updating the review of any competing corporate coverage. Stories that pass this round of review get posted on our website as Validated Independent News stories (VINs).[2]

In early spring, we present all VINs in the current cycle to the faculty and students at all of our affiliate campuses, and to our national and international panel of judges, who cast votes to winnow the candidate stories from nearly 300 down to 25.

Once the Top 25 have been determined, students in Peter Phillip's Media Censorship course at Sonoma State University, and Project Censored student interns working with Mickey Huff at Diablo Valley College, begin another intensive review of each story using LexisNexis and ProQuest databases. Additional faculty and students contribute to this final stage of review.

The Top 25 finalists are then sent to our panel of judges, who vote to rank them in numerical order. At the same time, these experts—

including media studies professors, professional journalists, and a former commissioner of the Federal Communications Commission, among others—offer their insights on the stories' strengths and weaknesses.[3]

Thus, by the time a story appears in the pages of *Censored*, it has undergone at least five distinct rounds of review and evaluation.

Although the stories that Project Censored brings forward may be socially and politically controversial—and sometimes even psychologically challenging—we are confident that each is the result of serious journalistic effort and, so, deserves greater public attention.

Notes

1.   For information on how to nominate a story, see "How To Support Project Censored," at the back of this volume.
2.   Validated Independent News stories are archived on the Project Censored website at http://www.projectcensored.org/category/validated-independent-news.
3.   For a complete list of the national and international judges and their brief biographies, see the acknowledgments section of this book.

THE TOP CENSORED STORIES AND
MEDIA ANALYSIS OF 2013–2014

1. Ocean Acidification Increasing at Unprecedented Rate

Julia Whitty, "10 Key Findings From a Rapidly Acidifying Arctic Ocean," *Mother Jones*, May 7, 2013, http://www.motherjones.com/blue-marble/2013/05/arctic-ocean-rapidly-getting-more-acidic.
Craig Welch, "Sea Change, The Pacific's Perilous Turn," *Seattle Times*, September 12, 2013, http://apps.seattletimes.com/reports/sea-change/2013/sep/11/pacific-ocean-perilous-turn-overview.
Eli Kintisch, "Snails Are Dissolving in Pacific Ocean," *ScienceNOW*, May 1, 2014, http://news.sciencemag.org/biology/2014/05/snails-are-dissolving-pacific-ocean.

Student Researcher: Amanda Baxter (Sonoma State University)

Faculty Evaluator: Elaine Wellin (Sonoma State University)

It's well known that burning fossil fuels in the form of coal, oil, and natural gas releases carbon dioxide (CO_2) into the air. Less understood is that a quarter of this carbon dioxide—about twenty trillion pounds, every year—is absorbed by oceans. Writing for the *Seattle Times*, Craig Welch invited us to "imagine every person on earth tossing a hunk of CO_2 as heavy as a bowling ball into the sea. That's what we do to the oceans every day." As Welch and others reported, this carbon dioxide is changing the ocean's chemistry faster than at any time in human history, in ways that have potentially devastating consequences for both ocean life and for humans who depend on the world's fisheries as vital sources of protein and livelihood.

When CO_2 mixes with seawater, it lowers the pH levels of the water, making it more acidic and sour. In turn this erodes some animals' shells and skeletons and robs the water of ingredients that those animals require for healthy development. Known as ocean acidification, this phenomenon, Welch wrote, "is helping push the seas toward a great unraveling that threatens to scramble marine life on a scale almost too big to fathom, and far faster than first expected."

The impacts of ocean acidification have been most pronounced in the Arctic and Antarctic, because cold, deep seas absorb more carbon dioxide. Julia Whitty reported for *Mother Jones* that we've enjoyed a free ride so far: "The ocean has swallowed our atmospheric carbon dioxide emissions and slowed global warming during the past few critical decades while we dithered in disbelief." Now, however, the average acidity of surface ocean waters worldwide is more than 30

percent greater than at the start of the Industrial Revolution. Whitty's coverage draws on findings from the 2013 Arctic Ocean Acidification Assessment.[1] The Arctic Ocean is especially vulnerable, she wrote, because short, simple food webs are characteristic of Arctic marine ecosystems. "Energy is channeled in just a few steps from small plants and animals to large predators like seabirds and seals." As a result, the integrity of the entire system depends heavily on keystone species, including pteropods (also known as sea butterflies) and echinoderms (more commonly known as sea stars and urchins). Although larger creatures like birds and mammals may not be directly affected by ocean acidification, Whitty reported, they will be indirectly affected if their food sources "decline, expand, relocate, or otherwise change in response to ocean acidification." As ocean acidification impacts the abundance, productivity, and distribution of Arctic marine species, these changes are likely to affect the culture, diet, and livelihoods of indigenous Arctic peoples and other Arctic residents.

The impacts of ocean acidification are not limited to the Arctic and Antarctic Oceans, however. As Eli Klintisch reported for *Science* magazine, researchers have documented impacts to tiny marine snails in the Pacific Ocean along the west coast of North America. Normally pteropods have smooth shells. As Klintisch described, a study led by Nina Bednaršek of the National Oceanic and Atmospheric Administration (NOAA) and her colleagues found that pteropods from thirteen coastal sites between Washington state and southern California had pitted shells. In an article published in the *Proceedings of the Royal Society B*,[2] Bednaršek and her colleagues reported that more than half of the shells they collected showed signs of dissolving, which made the shells look like "cauliflower" or "sandpaper." These findings were consistent with previous laboratory studies, which showed that, as seawater becomes more acidic, the change disrupts the shell formation process in young pteropods and dissolves already formed shells in mature ones. Previous studies, Klintisch reported, document that shell damage makes it harder for pteropods and other invertebrates to "fight infection, maintain metabolic chemistry, defend (themselves) against predators, and control buoyancy."

The impacts of the pteropods' fast dissolving shells are difficult to predict, but they could be profound. On one hand, pteropods are among the most abundant organisms on the earth; on the other hand, like other small creatures at the bottom of the ocean food chain that have not been closely studied, their role in the ecosystem is not completely understood. We do know that the pteropods examined in the *Royal Society* study are a key food source for pink salmon. Pink salmon, in turn, are crucial to the North Pacific fishery.

Scientists initially believed that fish would not be directly affected by ocean acidification, but recent research indicates otherwise.[3] From clownfish off the coast of Papua New Guinea (remember Nemo?) to walleye pollock (got fish sticks?), scientists have found that exposure to high levels of carbon dioxide scramble fish's sense of smell, hearing, and sight. Though fish are excellent at altering their blood chemistry to accommodate changing seas, elevated CO_2 levels disrupt many fish's brain signaling. Baby clownfish exposed to high levels of CO_2 were five times more likely to die when placed back in the wild. At first scientists thought clownfish were unusually vulnerable to high levels of CO_2, but subsequent research showed that many reef fish are similarly affected. Early results, Craig Welch reported, suggest that walleye pollock experience some of the same behavioral problems as reef fish when exposed to high levels of CO_2. That, in turn, raises concerns about the North Pacific's $1 billion-a-year pollock fishery, which accounts for half the nation's catch of fish.

As Welch wrote in his "Sea Change" article for the *Seattle Times*, "The most-studied animals remain those we catch. Little is known about the things they eat." This points to another problematic dimension of ocean acidification. Despite the potential magnitude of the problem—remember, ocean acidification is changing the chemistry of the world's oceans faster than ever before, and faster than the world's leading scientists had predicted—there is little funding for research on ocean acidification and its affects. As Welch reported, "Combined nationwide spending on acidification research for eight federal agencies, including grants to university scientists by the National Science Foundation, totals about $30 million a year—less than the annual budget for the coastal Washington city of Hoquiam, population 10,000."

2. Top Ten US Aid Recipients All Practice Torture

Daniel Wickham, "Top 10 US Aid Recipients All Practice Torture," *Left Foot Forward,* January 30, 2014, http://www.leftfootforward.org/2014/01/top-ten-us-aid-recipients-all-practice-torture.

Student Researcher: Alyssa Tufaro (Florida Atlantic University)

Faculty Evaluator: James F. Tracy (Florida Atlantic University)

The top ten nations slated to receive US foreign assistance in fiscal year 2014 all practice torture and are responsible for major human rights abuses, Daniel Wickham has reported. Wickham based this conclusion on a combination of projected foreign assistance figures from a January 2013 report by the Congressional Research Service, and from findings on torture reported independently by Amnesty International, Human Rights Watch, and other major human rights organizations.

A Congressional Research Service report, prepared for the members and committees of Congress, indicated the projected fiscal year 2014 budgets for US foreign assistance by country.[4] According to this report, the top ten countries and their expected assistance (in millions of current US dollars) are as follows:

Israel	3,100
Afghanistan	2,200
Egypt	1,600
Pakistan	1,200
Nigeria	693
Jordan	671
Iraq	573
Kenya	564
Tanzania	553
Uganda	456

Wickham reported that, according to Amnesty International, Human Rights Watch, and other leading human rights organizations, each of the listed countries is accused of torturing people in the last year, and at least half are reported to be doing so on a massive scale.

For example, Israel, the top recipient of US financial assistance, has been accused of committing major human rights abuses over the last year, including the torture of Palestinian children. A recent report by the Public Committee Against Torture in Israel described how detained children "suspected of minor crimes" have been sexually assaulted by Israeli security forces and kept in outdoor cages during the winter. It found that "74 per cent of Palestinian child detainees experience physical violence during arrest, transfer or interrogation."[5] A United Nations report indicated that torture is "widespread" in Afghanistan, while Amnesty International documented torture as a "common" practice in Iraq and an "abysmal" human rights situation in Egypt.[6] Human Rights Watch reported that torture is practiced with "near-total impunity" in Jordan.[7]

As Wickham reported, financial assistance to such governments could violate existing US law, which mandates that little or no funding be granted to a country that "engages in a consistent pattern of gross violations of internationally recognized human rights, including torture."[8] The United States remains a signatory of the United Nations Convention against Torture and Other Cruel, Inhuman or Degrading Treatment or Punishment, ratified in October 1994.[9] That the top ten recipients of U.S. foreign assistance "all practice torture raises serious questions," Wickham wrote, "about the Obama administration's stance on human rights. If the United States wants to be taken seriously on these issues, a serious re-evaluation of its foreign assistance programme is needed."

3. WikiLeaks Revelations on Trans-Pacific Partnership Ignored by Corporate Media

Zachary Keck, "Congress May Have Just Killed the Trans-Pacific Partnership," *Diplomat*, November 18, 2013, http://thediplomat.com/2013/11/congress-may-have-killed-the-trans-pacific-partnership.

John Robles, "The TPP Is a Corporate Coup D'état—Kristinn Hrafnsson," Voice of Russia, November 15, 2013, http://voiceofrussia.com/2013_11_15/The-TPP-is-a-corporate-coup-d-tat-Kristinn-Hrafnsson-5798.

John Robles, "Trans Pacific Partnership is Like SOPA on Steroids—Kristinn Hrafnsson," Voice of Russia, November 23, 2013, http://voiceofrussia.com/2013_11_23/Trans-Pacific-Partnership-is-like-SOPA-on-steroids-Kristinn-Hrafnsson-1552.

"Secret Trans-Pacific Partnership Agreement (TPP)," WikiLeaks, November 13, 2013, https://wikileaks.org/tpp.

Shannon Tiezzi, "The TPP's Not Dead Yet (But It's Close)," *Diplomat*, December 7, 2013, http://thediplomat.com/2013/12/the-tpps-not-dead-yet-but-its-close.

James Trimarco, "Will a Secretive International Trade Deal Ban GMO Labeling?," *YES! Magazine*, October 18 2013, http://www.yesmagazine.org/planet/will-secretive-international-trade-deal-ban-gmo-labeling-trans-pacific-partnership.

Student Researchers: Dylan Scherpf (Frostburg State University) and Brandon Karns (Sonoma State University)

Faculty and Community Evaluators: Andy Duncan (Frostburg State University) and Thadeus Dean Humphrey (community evaluator)

On November 13, 2013, WikiLeaks published a section of a trade agreement called the Trans-Pacific Partnership Treaty, or TPP. On the surface, the treaty is meant to facilitate trade among Australia, Brunei, Canada, Chile, Japan, Malaysia, Mexico, New Zealand, Peru, Singapore, the United States, and Vietnam. However, there are a number of red flags surrounding the agreement.

Eight hundred million people, and one-third of all world trade, stand to be affected by the treaty—and yet only three people from each member nation have access to the entire document. Meanwhile, six hundred "corporate advisors," representing big oil, pharmaceutical, and entertainment companies, are involved in the writing and negotiations of the treaty.

The influence of these companies is clear, as large sections of the proposal involve corporate law and intellectual property rights, rather than free trade. Corporations could gain the ability to sue govern-

ments not only for loss, but prospective loss. At the same time, patents and copyrights would see more protection. This means longer patents, leading to less access to generic drugs, and a lockdown on Internet content. Commenting on the leaked TPP chapter, which details how corporations could seek financial compensation for non-tariff barriers to trade, Arthur Stamoulis of the Citizens Trade Campaign observed, "The Tribunals that adjudicate these cases don't have the power to literally demand that a government change its policies, but they can award payments worth millions and even billions of dollars, such that if a country doesn't want additional cases brought against it, it gets the line."

Furthermore, as James Trimarco wrote in *YES! Magazine*, observers believe the TPP "could pull the rug out from under national and local governments trying to regulate the sale and import of GMO [genetically modified organism] foods." Tony Corbo of Food and Water Watch pointed out that because the TPP is being negotiated in secret, it is hard to say whether it would outlaw the labeling or banning of

GMO foods. However, the chief US negotiator on agriculture is Islam Siddiqui, a former Monsanto lobbyist, and the US Food and Drug Administration does not currently recognize GMO foods as any different from non-GMO foods and therefore do not see a reason that products containing GMO ingredients should be specially labeled.

Though the WikiLeaks exposure was followed quickly by an anti-TPP push in Congress, the lack of coverage in corporate US media is disconcerting. Japanese, Australian, and even Russian media discuss the TPP openly, while American news sources remained silent—even as the Obama administration attempted to fast-track it through Congress. *The Washington Post* was alone among the major establishment press in covering the WikiLeak's revelations about the TPP. For example, Timothy B. Lee reported that the intellectual property section of the treaty is "a wish list for Hollywood and the pharmaceutical industry" and speculated whether the leak might "derail Obama's trade agenda."[10] However, the *Post* relegated even this relatively superficial and US-focused perspective to its online blog. Other major papers, including the *New York Times*, the *Los Angeles Times*, and the *Wall Street Journal* passed on this story of far-reaching global import.

4. Corporate Internet Providers Threaten Net Neutrality

Paul Ausick, "Verizon Goes After FCC in Court Monday," 24/7 Wall St., September 9, 2013, http://247wallst.com/telecom-wireless/2013/09/09/verizon-goes-after-fcc-in-court-monday.

Cole Stangler, "Your Internet's in Danger," In These Times, October 2, 2013, http://inthesetimes.com/article/15689/your_internets_in_danger.

Jennifer Yeh, "Legal Gymnastics Ensue in Oral Arguments for Verizon vs. FCC," Free Press, September 10, 2013, http://www.freepress.net/blog/2013/09/10/legal-gymnastics-ensue-oral-arguments-verizon-vs-fcc.

Student Researcher: Petra Dillman (College of Marin)

Faculty Evaluator Susan Rahman (College of Marin)

As *Censored 2015* went to press, the Federal Communications Commission (FCC) had just publicly revealed its proposed new rules for Internet traffic. A 3–2 vote by the FCC opened a four-month window for formal public comments on how strict those rules should be, and galvanized corporate media attention on the issue of net neutrality.[11] By contrast, for months leading up to this development, independent journalists, including Paul Ausick, Cole Stangler and Jennifer Yeh,

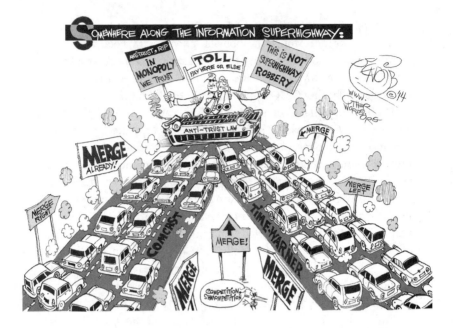

informed the public about the anticipated showdown over net neutrality and the stakes in that battle.

In September of 2013, the federal appeals court of Washington DC began a crucial case brought by Verizon Communications Inc., challenging the Federal Communications Commission's (FCC) authority to regulate Internet service providers. Under the FCC's current Open Internet Order, service providers such as Verizon cannot charge varying prices or give priority to users that access certain websites or may be able to pay more for faster speeds compared to competitors. Verizon claims the FCC violates their First Amendment right and they should have the ability to manage and promote the content they see fit. The FCC has continually ruled that controlling communications is not in the best interest of the public. If the court decides in favor of Verizon and revokes the Open Internet Order, the FCC will have no way to regulate unbiased data access, changing the future for everyday Internet users in the twenty-first century.

Cole Stangler, a reporter for *In These Times*, described how many open Internet advocates fear that service providers "could ultimately enable the construction of a multi-tiered Internet landscape resembling something like cable television—where wealthy conglomerates have access to a mass consumer base and other providers, such as independent media, struggle to reach an audience." Today the Internet is a critical medium for public communication. Amalia Deloney, grassroots policy director at the Center for Media Justice, pointed out that corporate oversight would pose a threat to public discourse and organizing efforts. The consequent trepidation seems to be that service providers could make specific websites impossibly slow to load, successfully regulating communication among would-be activists. It seems Internet service providers would do more to limit free speech than advocate for it.

Verizon v. FCC has been well covered by both corporate and independent media. However, corporate outlets such as the *New York Times* and *Forbes* tend to highlight the business aspects of the case, skimming over vital particulars affecting the public and the Internet's future.[12]

5. Bankers Back on Wall Street Despite Major Crimes

Max Stendahl, "Former GE Execs Freed from Prison after Convictions Nixed," *Law360*, November 27, 2013, http://www.law360.com/articles/492222/former-ge-execs-freed-from-prison-after-convictions-nixed.

Matt Taibbi, "Another Batch of Wall Street Villains Freed on Technicality," *Rolling Stone*, December 4, 2013, http://www.rollingstone.com/politics/blogs/taibblog/another-batch-of-wall-street-villains-freed-on-technicality-20131204.

Janine Jackson, "Why Aren't Big Bankers in Jail?" *Extra!* (Fairness and Accuracy in Reporting), January 1, 2014, http://fair.org/extra-online-articles/why-arent-big-bankers-in-jail.

Matt Taibbi, "Gangster Bankers: Too Big to Jail," *Rolling Stone*, February 14, 2013, http://www.rollingstone.com/politics/news/gangster-bankers-too-big-to-jail-20130214.

Student Researchers: Markisha Barber (Frostburg State University), and Noah Tenney and Tania Sanchez (Sonoma State University)

Faculty Evaluators: Andy Duncan (Frostburg State University) and Peter Phillips (Sonoma State University)

A story spanning a decade has come to an unfortunate yet unsurprising end. Three former General Electric bankers—Dominick Carollo, Steven Goldberg, and Peter Grimm—had been convicted in 2012 for rigging auctions of municipal bonds, essentially stealing from projects intended to build public schools, hospitals, libraries, and nursing homes in virtually every US state.[13] However, in November 2013, those convictions were reversed on a technicality: Because it took federal prosecutors so long to build the massive case, the statute of limitations ran out. The three men were released from prison the

next day—just in time, as a defense attorney noted, to be home for Thanksgiving dinner.

These men were part of a decade-long scheme that bilked cities and towns of funds for public-works projects by paying kickbacks to brokers and manipulating bids. Between August 1999 and November 2006, Carollo, Goldberg, and Grimm participated in countless rigged bids via telephone. Like mafiosi, they used a secret language and code words to keep their underground business low-key. Prosecutors accumulated over 570,000 recorded phone conversations that directly linked the men to fraudulent activity. Evidence at trial established that they cost municipalities around the country millions of dollars.

This type of white-collar immorality is a major issue because cash-strapped municipalities could have used the stolen money to provide essential services. Matt Taibbi of *Rolling Stone* called this fraud the equivalent of robbing a church fund to pay for lap dances. Taibbi, however, is among a few reporters—including Paul Burton and Jonathan Hemmerdinger of the *Bond Buyer*—to consistently inform the public on these crimes and to point out the perhaps insurmountable obstacles faced by even an activist US Department of Justice in getting convictions. "It really is hard to put these guys away," Taibbi wrote. "It's even harder to keep them there."

Meanwhile, as Janine Jackson reported for Fairness and Accuracy in Reporting's *Extra!*, "While there have been substantive inquiries into the wrongdoing of investment banks and auditors, those calling for jail time are often dismissed as irrational, driven by 'blood lust' (*Washington Post*, 9/12/13), 'anger' (*Chicago Tribune*, 11/30/13) or 'vengeance' (*Washington Post*, 11/18/13)." Various media outlets have explained that, while bad business decisions are not crimes, knowingly selling fraudulent mortgages and other dubious financial products is punishable by jail time. People have pointed to multiple reasons for the lack of prosecutions, such as regulatory agencies stopping key functions and non-deterrent settlements from government watchdogs. Media outlets have also made the case that imprisonment and increased liability would be ineffective, and many press accounts appear to be arguing for the legality of CEO actions. As Jackson reported, "Many press accounts seem more intent on explaining why what CEOs did wasn't a crime than on asking whether it should be."

However, outlets acknowledging the human victims of Wall Street wrongdoing have been less dismissive of imprisonment. Calls for jail time can be seen as demands for equal treatment under law. For example, in February 2013, Matt Taibbi of *Rolling Stone* argued against the emerging distinction between "an arrestable class and an unarrestable class."

6. The Deep State: Government "without Reference to the Consent of the Governed"

Mike Lofgren, "Anatomy of the Deep State," Moyers & Company, February 21, 2014, http://billmoyers.com/2014/02/21/anatomy-of-the-deep-state.

Student Researcher: Alexander P. Ruhe (Burlington College)

Faculty Evaluator: Rob Williams (Burlington College)

It is no secret that concerned citizens are condemning the United States government's lack of transparency, accountability, and honest constituent representation. Reporting for Moyers & Company, Mike Lofgren, a congressional staff member for twenty-eight years specializing in national security, addressed the issue of the "deep state" that undemocratically orchestrates unchecked private agendas, while corporate media distract the public's attention by focusing on traditional Washington partisan politics. Lofgren contended that, although the deep state is "neither omniscient nor invincible," it is a "relentlessly well entrenched," "hybrid association of elements of government and parts of top-level finance and industry that is effectively able to govern the United States without reference to the consent of the governed."

Exploiting the world's resources and governments with criminal impunity, a wealthy elite—sporting an estimated $32 trillion in tax-exempt offshore havens—are the deep dark secret of plutocratic imperialism, operating behind more visible, privately controlled government representatives. Rep. Spencer Bachus (R-AL), the House Financial Services Committee incoming chairman in 2010, openly flouted constitutional rights when he stated, "My view is that Washington and the regulators are there to serve the banks."

The establishment news media labels Congress as the most hopelessly deadlocked since the 1850s, the violently rancorous decade preceding the American Civil War. However, corporate media do little to draw attention to the hidden wealthy elites who undemocratically control our government, because these elites own the major media. It is only the deep state's protectiveness toward its higher-ranking personnel that allows them to escape the consequences of their frequent ineptitude. The US needs brave, determined, and well-supported leaders to demand implementation of "loophole" proof laws in a restructured system of checks and balances in order to effectively halt the unethical influence of wealthy powers on our democratic representatives.

7. FBI Dismisses Murder Plot against Occupy Leaders as NSA and Big Business Crack Down on Dissent

Dave Lindorff, "FBI Document—'[DELETED]' Plots to Kill Occupy Leaders 'If Deemed Necessary,'" *WhoWhatWhy*, June 27, 2013, http://whowhatwhy.com/2013/06/27/fbi-document-deleted-plots-to-kill-occupy-leaders-if-deemed-necessary.

Beau Hodai, "Dissent or Terror: How the Nation's Counter Terrorism Apparatus, in Partnership with Corporate America, Turned on Occupy Wall Street," Center for Media and Democracy's SourceWatch/DBA Press, May 2013, http://www.prwatch.org/files/Dissent or Terror FINAL.pdf.

Alex Kane, "How America's National Security Apparatus—in Partnership With Big Corporations—Cracked Down on Dissent," AlterNet, May 21, 2013, http://www.alternet.org/print/news-amp-politics/how-americas-national-security-apparatus-partnership-big-corporations-cracked-down.

Student Researchers: Danielle Davis and Andie Bugajski (Sonoma State University)
Faculty Evaluators: Robert Switky and Melinda Milligan (Sonoma State University)

In October 2011, when the Occupy movement arrived in Houston, protesters were subject to local and federal surveillance, infiltration by police provocateurs, and police assault. Months later, Dave Lindorff reported that a document obtained in December 2012 from the Houston FBI office shows that the agency was aware of a plot to assassinate Occupy movement leaders—and did nothing about it.

The document, obtained as part of a Freedom of Information Act (FOIA) request filed by the Washington DC–based Partnership for Civil Justice Fund, reads in part:

> An identified [DELETED] as of October planned to engage in sniper attacks against protestors (sic) in Houston, Texas if deemed necessary. An identified [DELETED] had received intelligence that indicated the protesters in New York and Seattle planned similar protests in Houston, Dallas, San Antonio and Austin, Texas. [DELETED] planned to gather intelligence against the leaders of the protest groups and obtain photographs, then formulate a plan to kill the leadership via suppressed sniper rifles.

As of June 2013, Lindorff reported, the FBI knew the identity of the person(s) who planned the sniper attacks, but had not released any names. The head of the FBI's media office, Paul Bresson, explained, "The FOIA documents that you reference are redacted in several places pursuant to FOIA and privacy laws that govern the release of such information so therefore I am unable to help fill in the blanks. . . . [I]f the FBI was aware of credible and specific information involving a murder plot, law enforcement would have responded with appropriate action."

Occupy Houston activists have speculated that the wording "if deemed necessary" might indicate that the unidentified plotter was an organization, such as the police or a private security group. Documents from the FBI and the Department of Homeland Security identify Occupy as a "terrorist" activity.

The FBI has a record of orchestrating attacks on citizen organizations deemed to be threats. For example, the Church Committee hearings of the 1970s revealed that the FBI orchestrated local police attacks (in Chicago, San Francisco, and New York) on leaders of the Black Panther Party.

Alex Kane of AlterNet wrote that Beau Hodai's SourceWatch report provided "an eye-opening look into how US counter-terrorism agencies monitored the Occupy movement in 2011 and 2012." Government documents, obtained by the Center for Media and Democracy and DBA Press from the National Security Agency and other government offices, revealed "a grim mosaic of 'counter-terrorism' operations" and negative attitudes toward activists and other citizens.

For instance, the largest Occupy Phoenix action took place in early December 2011, outside of meetings held there by the American Legislative Exchange Council (ALEC). ALEC hired forty-nine active but off-duty Phoenix Police Department (PPD) officers and nine retired PPD officers to act as private security during ALEC's meetings.

The upshot, Hodai reported, is "the wholesale criminalization of tens of thousands, if not hundreds of thousands, of American citizens who have dared to voice opposition to what is increasingly viewed as the undue influence of private corporate/financial interests in the functions of public government."

8. Corporate News Ignores Connections between Extreme Weather and Global Warming

Peter Hart, "Weather—Without Climate," *Extra!* (Fairness and Accuracy in Reporting), December 2, 2013, http://fair.org/extra-online-articles/weather-without-climate.

Dahr Jamail, "The Climate Change Scorecard," *Tomdispatch*, December 17, 2013, http://www.tomdispatch.com/post/175785/tomgram%3A_dahr_jamail,_the_climate_change_scorecard.

Jamie Henn, "In the Wake of Haiyan, We Must Divest from Fossil Fuels," *YES! Magazine*, November 12, 2013, http://www.yesmagazine.org/planet/divesting-from-disaster.

Student Researchers: Noah Tenney, Kayla Silva, Cydney Shorkend, and Carla Cardenas (Sonoma State University), and Nicholas DePietro (Florida Atlantic University)

Faculty Evaluators: Peter Phillips, Ervand Peterson, and Andy Lee Roth (Sonoma State University), and James F. Tracy (Florida Atlantic University)

As extreme weather becomes increasingly common, it has received a fair share of coverage during network news broadcasts. Often missing from these reports, however, is any mention of climate change and its connection to extreme weather events. As Peter Hart reported for *Extra!*, the nightly news covers extreme weather events as unusual

and newsworthy, but usually without explanation of climate change as an underlying cause.

A study by Fairness and Accuracy in Reporting (FAIR) found that extreme weather events in 2013 resulted in 450 news segments, of which only sixteen mentioned climate change. As for specific evening news shows, *CBS Evening News* only used terms like "global warming" and "greenhouse gases" in two of 114 extreme weather reports. *ABC World News* only mentioned climate change in eight reports out of 200, and *NBC Nightly News* only mentioned it in six reports out of 136. There was also a CBS report on the unsupported notion that there had been a "pause" in global warming.

There continues to be serious scientific debate on the extent to which current weather events and climate change should be linked. Nonetheless, a majority of the American public still makes the connection between climate and weather despite the media's failure to report on it.

Writing for *Tomdispatch*, Dahr Jamail reported on the increasingly high stakes of ignoring the scientific evidence for climate change. Jamail reported the perspectives of scientific experts who do not figure in corporate news coverage of our "extreme weather." Concerns range from the costs of Arctic methane releases to a December 2013 study by eighteen eminent scientists concluding that "continuation of high fossil fuel emissions, given current knowledge of the consequences, would be an act of extraordinary witting intergenerational injustice."[14]

Although Typhoon Haiyan, which devastated the Philippines in November 2013, received ample corporate news coverage, Jamie Henn reported for *YES! Magazine* that it should not be thought of as a "natural" disaster but, instead, as a "climate disaster"—driven by coal, oil, and gas companies that "continue to pour billions of tons of carbon dioxide into our atmosphere, disrupting our climate." Henn reported on the growing fossil fuel divestment campaign that now includes over 500 universities, cities, and religious institutions across Europe, North America, Australia and New Zealand. "It's time," Henn wrote, "to tell our public institutions to divest from disaster."

Though climate engineering is often touted as a technological answer to climate change, German researchers have argued that attempts to artificially engineer the earth's climate would likely cause worse effects than presently forecasted climate change trends. David Keller and colleagues from the Helmholtz Center for Ocean Research in Kiel, Germany, reported findings based on an earth system model that replicated five different strategies to reduce global warming and help prevent wide-scale climate change. Climate engineering, or reducing the levels of sunlight hitting the planet's surface through "solar radiation management," could change rainfall patterns, worsen conditions in arid zones, or cause irreversible harm once the technology's use ceased. After considering other technological fixes, the study's authors concluded that any such measures would have limited effectiveness without further cutbacks in carbon-based greenhouse emissions.

9. US Media Hypocrisy in Covering Ukraine Crisis

Robert Parry, "America's Staggering Hypocrisy," Consortium News, March 4, 2014, http://consortiumnews.com/2014/03/04/americas-staggering-hypocrisy.

Stephen F. Cohen, "Distorting Russia: How the American Media Misrepresent Putin, Sochi and Ukraine," *Nation*, March 3, 2014, http://www.thenation.com/article/178344/distorting-russia.

Nafeez Ahmed, "Ukraine Crisis is about Great Power Oil, Gas Pipeline Rivalry," *Guardian*, March 6, 2014, http://www.theguardian.com/environment/earth-insight/2014/mar/06/ukraine-crisis-great-power-oil-gas-rivals-pipelines.

Student Researcher: Bryan Brennan (Diablo Valley College)

Faculty Evaluator: Mickey Huff (Diablo Valley College)

Russia's occupation of Crimea has caused US corporate media and government officials to call for a stern US response. Secretary of State John Kerry declaimed the Russian intervention as "a nineteenth-century act in the twenty-first century." What Russia's US critics seem to forget, Robert Parry reported, is the United States' own history of overthrowing democratic governments, including the illegal invasion of Iraq, which Kerry supported.

Corporate media also fail to acknowledge that Putin ordered the occupation of Kiev after a coup, led at least partly by neo-Nazis—conditions arguably less criminal than the US invasion of Iraq, which the US legitimized with false claims. "If Putin is violating international law by sending Russian troops into the Crimea after a violent coup spearheaded by neo-Nazi militias ousted Ukraine's democratically elected president," wrote Parry, "then why hasn't the US government turned over George W. Bush, Dick Cheney and indeed John Kerry to the International Criminal Court for their far more criminal invasion of Iraq?"[5]

Further, Ukraine's democratically elected president, Viktor Yanukovych, fled Kiev for his life after the coup and sought Russia's help quelling the neo-Nazi groups in Ukraine, citing their oppression of the country's native Russian population. It was only after this that Putin requested the Russian parliament's permission to deploy Russian troops in to stop the expansion of neo-Nazi control to areas that have deep historical ties to Russia.

Nevertheless, while downplaying these details, US corporate media accuse Russia of violating international law. "The overriding hypocrisy of the *Washington Post*, Secretary Kerry and indeed nearly all of Official Washington, is their insistence that the United States actually promotes the principle of democracy or, for that matter, the rule

of international law," wrote Parry. "Those are at best situational ethics when it comes to advancing US interests around the world." In a subsequent report, Parry wrote that, despite evidence to the contrary, US policy makers and corporate media have intentionally neglected to report that neo-Nazi militias played a central role in the February 22, 2014, overthrow of President Viktor Yanukovych. Parry reported, "The US media's take on the Ukraine crisis is that a 'democratic revolution' ousted President Viktor Yanukovych, followed by a 'legitimate' change of government. So, to mention the key role played by neo-Nazi militias in the putsch or to note that Yanukovych was democratically elected—and then illegally deposed—gets you dismissed as a 'Russian propagandist.'"[16]

Parry is not alone in the view that US media outlets exacerbate conflict with propaganda to vilify Russia and its president, Vladimir Putin. As Stephen Cohen reported, from coverage of living conditions and high terror tension at the Sochi Olympics to the bullying cruel regime of Putin and its strong arming of Ukraine, the US corporate media have painted Putin and Russia as public enemy number one, thereby reviving Cold War rhetoric and tactics. Putin and Russia are depicted as militant bullies, rather than a leader and a country trying to preserve control over strategic oil assets to maintain the country's sphere of influence.

The corporate media's coverage of Putin and the Ukraine is part of a larger pattern of bias identified by Cohen. He has described the positive US press coverage enjoyed by President Boris Yeltsin in the 1990s, at a time when "the US media adopted Washington's narrative that almost everything President Boris Yeltsin did was a 'transition from communism to democracy' and thus in America's best interests." Whereas the US media presented Yeltsin as pursuing legitimate politics and national interests, the frame that US media now use to portray Putin and Russia is that Putin's Russia has no legitimate politics and national interests, even on its own borders, as in Ukraine. "American media on Russia today," Cohen wrote, "are less objective, less balanced, more conformist and scarcely less ideological than when they covered Soviet Russia during the Cold War."

A resurgence of cold war rhetoric may make better sense against the backdrop of geopolitical oil interests, as analyzed by Nafeez Ahmed. As he reported, Ukraine finds itself between the two superpowers and their ongoing struggle for influence in the Eurasian oil market. Russia's Gazprom Company already controls roughly one-fifth of the world's oil supply. In 2013, Ukraine signed a $10 billion shale gas deal with US-based Chevron in hopes of ending its dependency on Russian gas by 2020. Professor R. Craig Nation, director of Russian and Eurasian Studies at the US Army War College, stated in a North Atlantic Treaty Organization (NATO) publication, "Ukraine is increasingly perceived to be critically situated in the emerging battle to dominate energy transport corridors linking the oil and natural gas reserves of the Caspian basin to European markets." The Obama administration has since spent over $5 billion to "ensure a secure and prosperous and democratic Ukraine." For those who are pondering whether we face the prospect of a New Cold War," Ahmed concluded, "a better question might be—did the Cold War ever really end?"

10. World Health Organization Suppresses Report on Iraqi Cancers and Birth Defects

Denis Halliday, "WHO Refuses to Publish Report on Cancers and Birth Defects in Iraq Caused by Depleted Uranium Ammunition," Global Research, September 13, 2013, http://www.globalresearch.ca/who-refuses-to-publish-report-on-cancers-and-birth-defects-in-iraq-caused-by-depleted-uranium-ammunition/5349556.

Mozhgan Savabieasfahani, "What's Delaying the WHO Report on Iraqi Birth Defects?" ZNet, June 12, 2013, http://zcomm.org/znetarticle/whats-delaying-the-who-report-on-iraqi-birth-defects-by-mozhgan-savabieasfahani.

Student Researcher: Jessica Clark (Sonoma State University)

Faculty Evaluator: Andy Lee Roth (Sonoma State University)

In contradiction with its own mandate, the World Health Organization (WHO) continues to suppress evidence uncovered in Iraq that US military use of depleted uranium (DU) and other weapons have not only killed many civilians but are also the cause of an epidemic of birth defects and other public health issues. By refusing to release the report publicly, the WHO effectively protects the US military and its government from accountability for the resulting public health catastrophe.

A WHO and Iraq Ministry of Health report on cancers and birth defects was set to be released in November 2012, but officials have indefinitely delayed that report's release. To this date, Denis Halliday wrote, the WHO report remains "classified." According to the WHO, the report's release has been delayed because its analysis needs to be evaluated by a "team of independent scientists."

Halliday's report drew comparisons between the Iraqi case and the legacy of health issues arising from US use of Agent Orange in Vietnam.

Meanwhile, the reality in Iraq, Mozhgan Savabieasfahani contended, is that "Iraq is poisoned." For example, she wrote, "[T]hirty-five million Iraqis wake up every morning to a living nightmare of childhood cancers, adult cancers and birth defects. Familial cancers, cluster cancers and multiple cancers in the same individual have become frequent in Iraq."[17] Why, then, does the WHO refuse to release its study? "One possible answer," she wrote, "was suggested on May 26 by the *Guardian.*"[18]

It reported the recent comments of Hans von Sponeck, the former assistant secretary general of the United Nations: "The US government sought to prevent WHO from surveying areas in southern Iraq where depleted uranium had been used and caused serious health and environmental dangers."

Containing information that is "essential" to inform public health policy in Iraq, the WHO report, Savabieasfahani wrote, "will enable researchers to collaborate, ask the most relevant questions and spearhead research to remedy this health emergency."

11. Wealthy Donors and Corporations Set Think Tanks' Agendas

Rick Carp, "Who Pays for Think Tanks? Corporate and Foundation Money Often Comes with an Agenda," *Extra!* (Fairness and Accuracy in Reporting), July 1, 2013, http://fair.org/home/who-pays-for-think-tanks.

"Not Just Koch Brothers: New Study Reveals Funders behind Climate Change Denial Effort," *Science Daily*, December 20, 2013, http://www.sciencedaily.com/releases/2013/12/131220154511.htm.

Robert J. Brulle, "Institutionalizing Delay: Foundation Funding and the Creation of US Climate Change Counter-Movement Organizations," *Climatic Change* 122, no. 4 (February 2014): 681–94, http://link.springer.com/article/10.1007%2Fs10584-013-1018-7.

Student Researchers: Devin Elliott and Mitchell Monack (Sonoma State University)

Faculty Evaluators: Joseph Anderson (Monterey Peninsula College), James J. Dean (Sonoma State University), and Stanley Falkow (Stanford University)

Think tanks provide information and analysis to policy makers and the public, making them increasingly influential institutions in our political process. However, many think tanks—including the Brookings Institution, Heritage Foundation, American Enterprise Institute, Cato Institute, and the RAND Corporation, among others—receive significant financial backing from extremely wealthy corporations and/or individuals. Because the law does not require public disclosure of donors' identities, these relationships raise the issue of whether think tanks' analyses and recommendations are "tainted by donor agendas," according to a July 2013 report by FAIR (Fairness and Accuracy in Reporting).

For example, the Center for American Progress instructs its analysts to consult the organization's development staff (who maintain the closest contacts with donors and potential donors) before publishing findings that might upset its contributors.

In its study of the nation's top twenty-five think tanks, FAIR finds that all have received money from corporations, foundations, government, or major individual donors. In many cases, these donors not only get a tax deduction for their contributions, they also can influence the think tank's formulation of policy.

FAIR found that almost two-thirds of the top twenty-five think tanks have taken money from oil companies, with thirteen funded by ExxonMobil, nine by Chevron, and four by Shell. Representatives of Big Energy also serve as members of many think tanks' boards. Similarly, half of the top twenty-five think tanks receive money from weapon manufacturers. And, overall, all the think tanks in the FAIR study appear to be influenced by the corporations, foundations, and billionaires who fund them and who seek government policies that favor their own private interests.

In a separate study, Robert J. Brulle, an environmental sociologist at Drexel University, exposed "the organizational underpinnings and funding behind the powerful climate change countermovement." According to Brulle's study, conservative foundations (including the Searle Freedom Trust, the John William Pope Foundation, the Howard Charitable Foundation, and the Sarah Scaife Foundation) have bankrolled climate change denial. However, since 2008, major foundations, including the Koch-affiliated foundations and the ExxonMobil Foundation, have pulled back from publicly visible funding; instead, funding has been channeled through untraceable sources, including organizations such as the DonorsTrust foundation. According to Brulle's data, approximately 75 percent of the income of climate change–denying organizations now comes from "unidentifiable sources." Brulle explained:

> Like a play on Broadway, the countermovement has stars in the spotlight—often prominent contrarian scientists or conservative politicians—but behind the stars is an organizational structure of directors, script writers and producers, in the form of conservative foundations. If you want to understand what's driving this movement, you have to look at what's going on behind the scenes. . . . The real issue here is one of democracy. . . . Without a free flow of accurate information, democratic politics and government accountability become impossible. . . . Powerful funders are supporting the campaign to deny scientific findings about global warming and raise public doubts about the roots and remedies of this massive global threat. At the very least, American voters deserve to know who is behind these efforts.

12. Pentagon Awash in Money Despite Serious Audit Problems

Dave Gilson, "Can't Touch This," *Mother Jones*, December 2013, http://www.motherjones.com/politics/2013/12/pentagon-budget-deal-charts-cuts.

Student Researcher: Jeannette Acevedo (Sonoma State University)

Faculty Evaluator: Peter Phillips (Sonoma State University)

Congress is expanding the Pentagon's 2014 budget by $32 billion. The Pentagon currently receives over $600 billion, when its current budget is combined with supplemental war funding. One out of every five US tax dollars is spent on defense, cumulatively more than the total of the next ten countries' defense budgets combined. Where does the money go? "The exact answer is a mystery," wrote Dave Gilson for *Mother Jones*. "That's because the Pentagon's books are a complete mess." As the Government Accountability Office dryly noted, the Pentagon has "serious financial management problems" that render its financial statements "inauditable."

Despite a 1997 requirement that federal agencies submit to annual audits, the Pentagon, Gilson reported, claims it will not "achieve audit readiness" until 2017.

Lack of budgetary accountability has led to risky investments by the Pentagon, Gilson reported, including the F-35 Joint Strike Fighter, for example. As Gilson summarizes, the F-35 program is "years behind schedule, hugely over budget, and plagued with problems that have earned it a reputation as the biggest defense boondoggle in history."

The *Mother Jones* report also analyzed how congressional interests and coalitions contributed to the protection of the Pentagon budget, even at a time when Congress was imposing spending reductions to food stamps and other mandatory social programs. Though fiscal conservatives in Congress favored defense cuts (like their liberal dove counterparts), they aligned with conservative hawks to impose social cuts, rather than reduce the Pentagon's budget. Similarly, those conservative hawks found allies among liberal hawks, who were not supportive of domestic cuts, but also wanted more money for military spending. As Gilson observed, military spending was "the glue holding the budget deal together."

13. Lawsuit Challenges Nuclear Power Industry Immunity from Liability in Nuclear Accidents

"Fukushima: Landmark Lawsuit Filed against General Electric, Toshiba and Hitachi," News Network and Broadcasting Collective (NSNBC) International, January 30, 2014, http://nsnbc. me/2014/01/30/fukushima-landmark-lawsuit-filed-general-electric-toshiba-hitachi.

Faith Aquino, "Senior Advisor for Fukushima Cleanup Says Foreign Assistance Needed," Japan Daily Press, October 17, 2013, http://japandailypress.com/senior-adviser-for-fukushima-clean-up-says-foreign-assistance-needed-1738025.

Chris Carrington, "Why the Obama Administration Will Not Admit that Fukushima Radiation is Poisoning Americans," Global Research, http://www.globalresearch.ca/why-the-obama-administration-will-not-admit-that-fukushima-radiation-is-poisoning-americans/5365626.

Student Researchers: Alfredo Rivas (San Francisco State University) and Paige Vreeburg (Sonoma State University)

Faculty Evaluators: Kenn Burrows (San Francisco State University) and Emily Acosta Lewis (Sonoma State University)

A lawsuit filed by lawyers on behalf of 1,415 plaintiffs, including 38 residents of Fukushima and 357 persons from outside Japan, holds not only the Tokyo Electric Power Company (TEPCO) but also Toshiba, Hitachi, and General Electric responsible for the 2011 meltdown of the Fukushima Daiichi nuclear power plant. Historically, manufacturers and operators of nuclear power plants have been granted immunities in liability for accidents, because no insurance company anywhere in the world would agree to insure the power plants when the industry first developed. As NSNBC International reported, the Fukushima case is a "landmark challenge" to nuclear power plant manufacturers' immunity from liability in nuclear accidents.

Toshiba, Hitachi, and General Electric manufactured the tanks developed to hold radioactive fluids back in the 1970s. Among the evidence in support of the plaintiffs' case is a report by Japan's Fisheries Research Agency that found radiation levels in sea life south of the plant to be 124 times more than the threshold considered safe for human consumption.

The Japanese government and TEPCO have sought to keep the situation under wraps, and the public is largely unaware of the nuclear power industry's irresponsible actions. Inaccurate reports of the radiation damage from TEPCO, along with inadequate manpower to deal with the crisis, have resulted in poor attempts to reverse the radiation damage that resulted from the meltdown of TEPCO's Fukushima Daiichi nuclear power plant following the March 2011 tsunami.

A senior advisor of the Fukushima cleanup, Barbara Judge, has said that foreign assistance in dealing with the nuclear cleanup is needed; however, TEPCO has withheld accurate radiation readings of the leaks, making foreign assistance impossible. The resulting poor cleanup efforts have further damaged ecosystems around Fukushima without proper supportive action to repair them.

General Electric (GE) is not being held accountable for its role in the Fukushima disaster, Chris Carrington reported, because of its ties to the Obama administration. General Electric CEO Jeffrey Immelt was appointed to lead the United States Economic Recovery Advisory Board by President Barack Obama in 2009. Five of the six nuclear reactors used at Fukushima were GE Mark I Boiling Water Reactor vessels; three of these were not only supplied but also built by General Electric. Since 1972, nuclear reactors of the type have been considered safety risks due to their particular vulnerability to explosion and rupture from hydrogen buildup.

14. Accumulating Evidence of Ongoing Wireless Technology Health Hazards

"Two Important New Papers Show Mobile Phone Use Does Cause an Increase in Brain Tumours," Powerwatch (UK), October 16, 2013, http://www.powerwatch.org.uk/news/20131016-hardell-carlberg-papers.asp.

James F. Tracy, "Health Impacts of RF Radiation: Media Blackout on Smart Meter Danger," Global Research, January 21, 2014, http://www.globalresearch.ca/health-impacts-of-rf-radiation-us-media-blackout-on-smart-meter-dangers/5365598.

Student Researchers: Julian Klein (San Francisco State University) and Casey Lewis (Sonoma State University)

Faculty Evaluators: Kenn Burrows (San Francisco State University) and Peter Phillips (Sonoma State University)

Wireless phones emit radio-frequency electromagnetic fields (RF-EMFs) when in use. In May 2011, after the consideration of laboratory studies, studies of long-term use of wireless phones, and data on the incidence of brain tumors, the World Health Organization (WHO) concluded RF-EMFs to be a "possible" human carcinogen.[19] Other studies have shown an association between long-term mobile and cordless phone use with glioma and acoustic neuroma. In October 2013, Powerwatch, a United Kingdom–based watchdog focused on the health risks posed by electromagnetic fields, reported that two new research articles provide further evidence of mobile phone use as a cause of increased brain tumors.

The first paper showed that RF-EMF exposure from mobile (and cordless) phones should be regarded as a class 1 human carcinogen (cancer-causing agent), as defined by the WHO's cancer research arm. The study's authors concluded that current exposure guidelines are in urgent need of revision.[20]

The second study aimed to assess the relationship between "especially long-term (>10 years) use of wireless phones" and the development of malignant brain tumors. According to the authors, this study "confirmed previous results" of the association between mobile phone use and malignant brain tumors, and supported the hypothesis that RF-EMFs "play a role both in the initiation and promotion stages of carcinogenesis"—in other words, the process by which normal cells are transformed into cancer cells.[21]

Mobile phones are not the only wireless technology that poses health threats. As James F. Tracy reported, the US has seen a virtual media blackout on the radiation dangers of smart meters. In January 2014, Tracy reported that the WHO's International Agency for Research on Cancer stated that "radio-frequency (RF) electromagnetic fields are possibly carcinogenic to humans based on an increased risk for glioma, a malignant type of brain cancer, associated with wireless cell phone use."

Smart meters are a central element in the creation of a "smart grid" that President Obama has made a priority.[22] In his article, Tracy wrote that the media blackout is likely intended to keep the public unaware of not only the health dangers associated with smart meters, but also potentially hidden agendas, including the meters' potential for "social control" through "energy rationing and surveillance." A "more immediate" motivation, he wrote, is "simply profit and continued media monopoly control of public opinion and discourse."

Tracy reported on a content analysis of US newspapers between May 31, 2011, the date that the WHO declared RF a class 2B carcinogen, and June 2014. Of the 839 articles on the topic published in that time, less than 10 percent (eighty-two articles) mention both "smart meters" and "carcinogen" or "carcinogenic" in the same report. Of these, sixty-five articles appeared in Canadian, Australian, or UK papers. Meanwhile, corporate news coverage in the US reassured the public that the Federal Communications Commission (FCC) had found smart meters to be within its safety standards, that they impose no danger to one's health, and that they are "environmental friendly." "With potential continued revenue growth," Tracy concluded, the telecommunications industry shows little interest in "raising questions and relaying information that can safeguard public health and allow citizens to ask intelligent questions concerning the health of themselves and their loved ones."[23]

15. Reporting Miscarriages, Criminalizing Pregnant Women's Bodies

Tara Culp-Ressler, "Kansas May Force Doctors to Report Women's Miscarriages to the State Health Department," *ThinkProgress*, March 24, 2014, http://thinkprogress.org/health/2014/03/24/3418085/kansas-miscarriage-reporting.

Student Researcher: Alandra Brown (Indian River State College)

Faculty Evaluator: Elliot D. Cohen (Indian River State College)

A proposed bill before the Kansas state legislature would require women to report miscarriages at any stage in pregnancy. This has been described as the first step along the path to criminalizing pregnant women's bodies. Under an amendment attached to House Bill 2613, doctors would be required to report all of their patients' miscarriages to the state health department, Tara Culp-Ressler reported for *ThinkProgress*.

The initial purpose of HB 2613 was to provide an alternative to the state's current stillbirth certificate. Some parents believe the existing law overemphasizes their child's death in a way that is emotionally painful. Senator Mary Pilcher-Cook, who happens to be among the state's most active and enthusiastic abortion opponents, added the miscarriage-reporting requirement. The bill's original author, Kansas representative John Doll, subsequently withdrew his support from the legislation: "I can't support the bill as it was amended. I think it waters it down and makes it into a political statement. I wanted a bill to help give closure to some families—I didn't want it to have anything to do with pro-life or pro-choice issues."

No other state has enacted a mandatory miscarriage reporting law, Culp-Ressler reported, although Virginia considered similar legislation in 2009. "We never see these bills," said Elizabeth Nash, the states issue manager for the Guttmacher Institute, a nonprofit organization that works to advance reproductive health including abortion rights. "The whole point," Nash explained, "is to further the idea of the fetus as a person. It's a way of establishing the groundwork for making abortion harder to get, and eventually illegal."

In addition to adding the mandatory miscarriage reporting amendment to HB 2613, Sen. Pilcher-Cook has also sought to weaken the state's sex education laws, levy a sales tax on abortion procedures, and prevent the state's abortion restrictions from including exceptions for rape and incest.

Culp-Ressler reported that National Advocates for Pregnant Women (NAPW) has documented "hundreds of cases of women being held criminally liable for decisions they made while pregnant, particularly if they later suffered a miscarriage or stillbirth."[24] Ultimately, Culp-Ressler concluded, enacting additional regulations related to the end of a pregnancy, like Kansas HB 2613, "turn pregnant women into suspects in the eyes of the law."

16. The Beef Industry's "Feedlot Feedback Loop"

Brad Jacobson, "They're Feeding WHAT to Cows?" *OnEarth*, December 12, 2013, http://www.onearth.org/articles/2013/12/you-wont-believe-the-crap-literally-that-factory-farms-feed-to-cattle.

Paul Solotaroff, "In the Belly of the Beast," *Rolling Stone*, December 10, 2013, http://www.rollingstone.com/feature/belly-beast-meat-factory-farms-animal-activists.

Carey L. Biron, "US Plans to Speed Poultry Slaughtering, Cut Inspections," Inter Press Service, March 7, 2014, http://www.ipsnews.net/2014/03/u-s-planning-speed-poultry-slaughtering-cut-inspections.

Student Researchers: Brendan Barber and Mitsi Patino (College of Marin), and Jazmine Flores (Indian River State College)

Faculty Evaluators: Susan Rahman (College of Marin) and Elliot D. Cohen (Indian River State College)

The beef industry increasingly feeds cattle "poultry litter," scraped from chicken coop floors, a practice that, as Brad Jacobson reported for *OnEarth*, "risks the spread of mad cow disease—yet the Food and Drug Administration [FDA] has done nothing to stop it."

After a string of bovine spongiform encephalopathy ("mad cow disease") scares in the 1980s and '90s, many precautions were taken to prevent further outbreaks. Mad cow disease affects humans

MAD COW DISEASE

slowly but fatally, and cooking beef thoroughly does not get rid of the bacteria.

In 1997, the FDA made it illegal to feed dead cows to living cows, the main cause of the disease. In response to those laws, the beef industry teamed up with the poultry industry to exploit a major loophole in the 1997 law. Jacobson describes a "Feedlot Feedback Loop": first, the poultry industry feeds the dead remains of cattle to chickens and other poultry; the mess created by poultry, known as "litter," is then sold to the cattle producer who feed it to cattle that the public eventually consumes as beef.

In early 2003, the FDA proposed to ban the use of poultry litter as cattle feed. Big Agriculture opposed this, and the FDA revised its policy. Instead of a permanent ban, the FDA required chicken-feed manufacturers to agree that they would leave out the riskiest, most infectious bovine tissues.

Industry officials assert that there has been no rise in recorded cases of mad cow disease, but the US Department of Agriculture (USDA) tests less than 1 percent of the thirty-five million cattle slaughtered annually for the bacterium that causes mad cow disease, making industry claims especially difficult to assess.

Aggravating the lack of adequate third-party inspection of industry practices, the government is now finalizing the decision on whether or not a proposed USDA plan for speeding and cutting the inspection of poultry should be passed. The poultry industry has been seeking these changes for years. The proposed rule would allow the speed in chicken processing to increase from 140 birds per minute to 175 birds per minute. Faster speeds reduce the extent of inspection. In addition, the number of federal inspectors in processing plants would be cut by 75 percent. In place of federal inspectors, company employees—who do not receive the same level of training or have independence—would take on inspection duties.

The proposed plan not only jeopardizes consumer health but also worker safety. With high processing speeds, the probability of accidents and worker injuries also increase. The increased speed will only make the job more dangerous.

At the time of this report, the Obama administration seems to be in favor of the proposed rule.

17. 2016 Will Find Gaza out of Drinking Water

Zander Swinburne, "The Water Is Running out in Gaza: Humanitarian Catastrophe Looms as Territory's Only Aquifer Fails," *Independent*, June 30, 2013, http://www.independent.co.uk/news/world/middle-east/the-water-is-running-out-in-gaza-humanitarian-catastrophe-looms-as-territorys-only-aquifer-fails-8679987.html.
Wissam Nassar, "In Pictures: Gaza Water Crisis Worsens," Al Jazeera, May 12, 2014, http://www.aljazeera.com/indepth/inpictures/2014/03/pictures-gaza-water-crisis-wors-201432673053211982.html.
"Over 90% of Water in Gaza Unfit for Drinking," B'Tselem (Israeli Information Center for Human Rights in the Occupied Territories), February 9, 2014, http://www.btselem.org/gaza_strip/20140209_gaza_water_crisis.

Student Researcher: Pippa Whelan (College of Marin)

Faculty Evaluator: Susan Rahman (College of Marin)

In Gaza, 1.7 million Palestinians currently live without clean drinking water. With no perennial streams and low rainfall, Gaza relies on a single aquifer for all of its fresh water. The coastal aquifer, Zander Swinburne reported, is contaminated with sewage, chemicals, and seawater. The Palestinian Water Authority recently determined that 95 percent of the water in Gaza does not meet World Health Organization (WHO) standards for human consumption. The polluted water causes chronic health problems and contributes to high rates of child mortality. One study estimated that 26 percent of disease in Gaza results from contaminated water supplies.[25] "A crippling Egyptian-Israeli blockade on Gaza has exacerbated the problem," Al Jazeera reported.

A recent United Nations report warned that the water situation for Palestinians in Gaza was "critical." According to that report, "the aquifer could become unusable as early as 2016, with the damage irreversible by 2020."[26] Even with immediate remedial action, the 2012 report stated, the aquifer will take decades to recover; otherwise it would "take centuries for the aquifer to recover."

As a result of the contaminated water supply, Al Jazeera reported, the Palestinian Ministry of Health recommends that residents boil water before using it for drinking or cooking. However, residents contend that even with boiling, tap water is "not fit to drink," and, in many cases, is simply unavailable. According to people in the territory, Zander Swinburne reported, "during the summer months water might spurt out of their taps every other day . . . pressure is often so low that those living on upper floors might see just a trickle."[27]

Instead, according to United Nations estimates, over 80 percent of Gazans buy their drinking water, with some families paying as much as a third of their household income, according to June Kunugi, a special representative of the UN children's fund UNICEF. Palestinians purchase more than a quarter of their water from Israel's national water company, Mekorot, Al Jazeera reported. Mekorot sells Gaza 4.2 million cubic meters of water annually.

Contaminated water also affects agriculture in Gaza. For example, high levels of salinity mean that most citrus crops can no longer be grown.

The Egyptian–Israeli blockade of Gaza intensifies the water problems. Materials needed for repairs of water and waste facilities cannot be imported. Lack of reliable electricity has forced 85 percent of agricultural wells out of operation, contributing to the risk of drought for more than 30,000 square acres of crops.

As B'Tselem—the Israeli Information Center for Human Rights in the Occupied Territories—reported, there is discrimination in water allocation: "Israeli citizens receive much more water than Palestinian residents of the West Bank and the Gaza Strip."[28] Water from shared resources is unequally divided, and in the Gaza Strip, Palestinians have access to only seventy to ninety liters per person per day—fewer than both the WHO-recommended minimum of one hundred liters per person per day and the average Israeli allocation of 100 to 230 liters per person each day.

18. National Database of Police Killings Aims for Accountability

Bethania Palma Markus, "Journalist Calls for Accountability in Police Killings," *Truthout*, March 18, 2014, http://www.truth-out.org/news/item/22538-journalist-calls-for-accountability-in-police-killings.

Student Researcher: Shasha-Gaye Santiago (Indian River State College)

Faculty Evaluator: Elliot D. Cohen (Indian River State College)

Although the Federal Bureau of Investigation tracks how many police officers die in the line of duty, it keeps no such record for how many civilians are killed by police each year. Recognizing a significant gap in the public records of civilian deaths at the hands of law enforcement officers, D. Brian Burghart, the editor of the *Reno News & Review* and a journalism instructor at University of Nevada, decided to create a public database. "In 2014, how could we not know how many people our government kills on our streets every year?" And he launched Fatal Encounters, a website that, as Bethania Palma Markus reported for *Truthout*, "tracks and tallies when cops take lives" and "invites the public to help build the database." Burghart has compiled a list of police agencies across the country to facilitate public record requests about fatal incidents.

19. Agribusiness Giants Attempt to Silence and Discredit Scientists Whose Research Reveals Herbicides' Health Threats

E. Ann Clark, "Orwellian Airbrushing of Scientific Record," GMWatch, November 30, 2013, http://gmwatch.org/index.php/news/archive/2013/15192-orwellian-airbrushing-ofscientific-record.

James Corbett, "Genetic Fallacy: How Monsanto Silences Scientific Dissent," *Corbett Report*, December 3, 2013, http://www.corbettreport.com/genetic-fallacy-how-monsanto-silences-scientific-dissent.

Rachel Aviv, "A Valuable Reputation," *New Yorker*, February 10, 2014, http://www.newyorker.com/reporting/2014/02/10/140210fa_fact_aviv.

"Silencing the Scientist: Tyrone Hayes on Being Targeted by Herbicide Firm Syngenta," *Democracy Now!*, February 21, 2014, http://www.democracynow.org/2014/2/21/silencing_the_scientist_tyrone_hayes_on.

Student Researcher: Katelyn Parks (San Francisco State University)

Faculty Evaluator: Kenn Burrows (San Francisco State University)

Independent journalists, including E. Ann Clark, James Corbett, Rachel Aviv, and *Democracy Now!*, document how Big Agriculture giants Monsanto and Syngenta have attempted to silence the findings and destroy the reputations of scientists whose research shows that the companies' herbicides pose serious threats to human health.

In September 2012, Dr. Gilles-Éric Séralini published research findings in the peer-reviewed *Journal of Food and Chemical Toxicology*. These findings showed the toxic impact of Monsanto's herbicide and genetically modified corn—including adverse health effects on rats. However, after publication, the journal made the unprecedented decision to retract the study.

Journal editor Dr. A. Wallace Hayes admitted that none of the established criteria for retracting a study applied to the Séralini paper. However, as Clark and Corbett reported, a new connection between the journal and Monsanto might account for the retraction, as well as another retraction of a similar study from Brazil that demonstrated the toxic effects on mice of an insecticide that forms the basis of the Bt GMO crops. After these papers were published, the *Journal of Food and Chemical Toxicology* created a new position: the associate editor for biotechnology. The journal then selected Richard E. Goodman, from the University of Nebraska, to fill the position and preside over such retractions. As it turns out, Goodman worked in regulatory sciences for Monsanto from 1997 to 2004.

Neither the journal's retraction of Séralini's research nor its implications were covered by corporate media, reflecting a trend in which

science critical of GMOs is sidelined and dismissed by the special interests promoting them.

Monsanto is not alone in trying to silence its critics. As Rachel Aviv of the *New Yorker* and Amy Goodman of *Democracy Now!* reported, after fifteen years of research, Tyrone Hayes, University of California–Berkeley professor of integrative biology, determined that Syngenta's herbicide atrazine causes sexual abnormalities in frogs and could cause the same problems for humans. The company now known as Syngenta hired Hayes to research atrazine in 1997. But when his findings ran contrary to their interests, they refused to allow him to publish and instead worked to discredit him. He left Syngenta in 2001, but continued to research the harmful effects of atrazine on the endocrine system.

Court documents from a class action lawsuit against Syngenta show how the company sought to smear Hayes's reputation and to prevent the Environmental Protection Agency from banning the profitable chemical, which is already banned by the European Union. The company's public relations team drafted a list of four goals. Reporter Rachel Aviv wrote, "The first was 'discredit Hayes.' In a spiral-bound notebook, Syngenta's communications manager, Sherry Ford, who referred to Hayes by his initials, wrote that the company could 'prevent citing of TH data by revealing him as noncredible.' He was a frequent topic of conversation at company meetings. Syngenta looked for ways to 'exploit Hayes' faults/problems.' 'If TH involved in scandal, enviros will drop him,' Ford wrote."

Despite its documented threats to environmental health and public health, atrazine remains on the market.

20. Estonia a Global Example of E-Government, Digital Freedom, Privacy, and Security

Ben Horowitz and Sten Tamkivi, "Estonia: The Little Country that Cloud," *Ben's Blog*, January 27, 2014, http://www.bhorowitz.com/estonia_the_little_country_that_cloud.

Student Researcher: Ashley Ibarra (San Francisco State University)

Faculty Evaluator: Kenn Burrows (San Francisco State University)

Since Estonia regained independence in 1991, its government has sought to redesign the nation's entire information infrastructure with goals of openness, privacy, and security. The technology platform that Estonia built to serve its citizens sets an example for the rest of the world. Each citizen has one identification number to use across all systems, from paper passport and bank records to any government office or medical care. This includes giving electronic signatures, filing taxes, and voting. Estonians elect their parliament online, and get their taxes back in two days.

The liquid movement of data, along with privacy and security measures, are of primary importance. Citizens have the ability to choose who can see their information. A citizen cannot block the state from seeing their data, but they can see who has accessed their data and file an inquiry to have an official fired if their information is accessed without valid reason.

Estonia is a world leader in cybersecurity and home of the North Atlantic Treaty Organization (NATO) Cyber Defense Center. The

United States can learn a lot from Estonia, Ben Horowitz and Sten Tamkivi have suggested: get the key infrastructure right, instead of building websites to try to manage large public projects (e.g. Heath-Care.gov), and respect citizens' privacy while being transparent and innovative. Estonia shows how this is possible.

21. Questioning the Charter School Hype

Jeff Bryant, "The Truth about Charter Schools: Padded Cells, Corruption, Lousy Instruction and Worse results," *Salon*, January 10, 2014, http://www.salon.com/2014/01/10/the_truth_about_charter_schools_padded_cells_corruption_lousy_instruction_and_worse_results.

James Horn, "KIPP Forces 5th Graders to 'Earn' Desks by Sitting on the Floor for a Week," Alter-Net, Education blog, December 17, 2013, http://www.alternet.org/education/kipp-forces-5th-graders-earn-desks-sitting-floor-week.

Stan Karp, "How Charter Schools Are Undermining the Future of Public Education," AlterNet, November 14, 2013, http://www.alternet.org/education/how-charter-schools-are-undermining-future-public-education.

Ben Chapman and Rachel Monahan, "Padded 'Calm-Down' Room at Charter School Drives Kids to Anxiety Attacks," *New York Daily News*, December 11, 2013, http://www.nydailynews.com/new-york/padded-calm-down-room-causing-anxiety-kids-article-1.1543983.

Stan Karp, "Charter Schools and the Future of Public Education," *Rethinking Schools* 28, no. 1 (Fall 2013), http://www.rethinkingschools.org/archive/28_01/28_01_karp.shtml.

Student Researchers: Jessie Lina De La O (Sonoma State University) and Jordan Monterosso (Indian River State College)

Faculty Evaluators: Lynn Lowery (Sonoma State University) and Elliot D. Cohen (Indian River State College)

Charter schools have been heralded as the antidote to "failed" public schools, especially in poor urban communities with many African-American and Latino/a students. Politicians and celebrities alike now advocate charters schools and preside over their openings. However, as *Salon*, AlterNet, and other independent media outlets have reported, charter schools have come under fire for not fulfilling the roles or achieving the results that their proponents have claimed. Instead of providing positive teaching and preparing children for the future, recent news reports have indicated that charter schools are subjecting students to padded cells, public shaming and embarrassment, poor instruction, and the negative consequences of financial corruption.

In January 2014, *Salon*'s Jeff Bryant reported on a five-year-old New York charter school where a student was "occasionally thrown in a padded cell and detained alone for stretches as long as 20 minutes." Bryant also described students who were made to "earn" their desks by sitting on their classroom floor. Similarly, AlterNet's James Horn reported on the Knowledge Is Power Program (KIPP), which is the largest corporate public charter school program in the United States. "KIPP requires the poorest urban children, those who have received the least in life, to earn everything," Horn reported. The harsh practices implemented by some charter school instructors result in negative repercussions for all children involved, obstructing their learning and undermining their sense of security in what is supposed to be a positive environment.

KIPP is just one example of the growing number of large, national chains of educational management organizations (or EMOs) that run many of the new charter schools. As Bryant reported, along with the development of EMOs themselves, "nationwide organizations have rapidly developed to lobby for these schools." One such organization, the Alliance for School Choice, recently received a $6 million gift from the Walton Family Foundation, of Wal-Mart fame.

Stan Karp of *Rethinking Schools* wrote, "The charter school movement has changed dramatically in recent years in ways that have undermined its original intentions. . . . It's time to put the brakes on charter expansion and refocus public policy on providing excellent public schools for all."

22. Corporate News Media Understate Rape, Sexual Violence

Rania Khalek, "Calling Rape by its Right Name," *Extra!* (Fairness and Accuracy in Reporting), February 1, 2014, http://fair.org/extra-online-articles/calling-rape-by-its-right-name.
Wasi Daniju, "Dear Mainstream Media: I Believe the Word You're Looking for is 'Rape,'" *Ceasefire*, November 10, 2013, http://ceasefiremagazine.co.uk/dear-mainstream-media-word-rape.
Eleanor J. Bader, "Stoking Fire: How News Outlets, Prosecutors Minimize Sexual Violence with Language," RH Reality Check, December 9, 2013, http://rhrealitycheck.org/article/2013/12/09/stoking-fire-how-news-outlets-prosecutors-minimize-sexual-violence-with-language.

Student Researchers: Cealia Brannan (Florida Atlantic University), and Laura A. Parada and Christina Sabia (Indian River State College)

Faculty Evaluators: James F. Tracy (Florida Atlantic University) and Elliot D. Cohen (Indian River State College)

Media analysts observe how journalists refrain from using the word "rape" to describe incidents of sexual assault. Instead, news outlets downplay the humiliation and cruelty entailed in these acts by referring to them as "sex crimes," "inappropriate sexual activity," or "forced sex," even though such acts are legally recognized as "rape."

"'Rape,' along with the images it conjures, is an ugly, nasty word," artist and writer Wasi Daniju observed. "Uglier and nastier still, though, is the experience of each and every person that experiences it. Their experience warrants, at the very least, the respect and truth of being accurately labeled and recognized."

A report released by Legal Momentum, a New York City–based feminist advocacy law group, titled *Raped or "Seduced"? How Language Helps Shape Our Response to Sexual Violence*, addressed what it terms the "linguistic avoidance" of such concerns. For example, when the media uses the language of consensual sex—terms like "recruited" rather than "kidnapped" or "took by force," and phrases like "performed oral sex" or "engaged in sexual activity" instead of writing that "he forcefully penetrated her vagina with his penis"—they do more than use euphemisms to distort reality; they essentially mislead, misdirect, and diminish the violation. Such accounts also suggest that both parties were willing participants.

Fairness and Accuracy in Reporting (FAIR) pointed to the *Los Angeles Times* to illustrate one example of this phenomenon. In January 2013, the *Times* published an important story addressing how two Los Angeles police officers were accused of using the threat of imprisonment to force several women they previously arrested to have sex with them. This is recognized under law as "rape." "But the *Times* avoided using that term," FAIR noted, "inexplicably employing every other word and phrase imaginable—including 'sex crimes,' 'sexual favors' and 'forced sex'—to describe what the officers were accused of."

23. Number of US Prison Inmates Serving Life Sentences Hits New Record

David J. Krajicek, "Hard Time: Prisons Are Packed With More Lifers Than Ever," *WhoWhatWhy*, September 18, 2013, http://whowhatwhy.com/2013/09/18/hard-time-prisons-are-packed-with-more-lifers-than-ever.

Ed Pilkington, "More Than 3000 U.S. Prisoners Locked Up for Life Without Parole for Non-Violent Crimes," *Guardian*, November 13, 2013, http://www.theguardian.com/world/2013/nov/13/us-prisoners-sentences-life-non-violent-crimes.

"A Living Death: Life without Parole for Nonviolent Offenses," American Civil Liberties Union, November 2013, https://www.aclu.org/files/assets/111813-lwop-complete-report.pdf.

Jessica M. Pasco, "Three Strikes, He's Out," *Good Times* (Santa Cruz, CA), November 6, 2013, http://www.gtweekly.com/index.php/santa-cruz-news/santa-cruz-local-news/5182-three-strikes-hes-out.html.

Felicia Gustin, "Can Restorative Justice Save Us? A Look at an Alternative to Mass Incarceration," *War Times*, November 4, 2013, http://www.war-times.org/can-restorative-justice-save-us-look-alternative-mass-incarceration.

Student Researchers: Isabella Diaz (Florida Atlantic University), Chelsea Pulver (College of Marin), and Pietro Pizzani, Mia Hulbert, and Fabiola Garcia (Indian River State College)

Faculty Evaluators: James F. Tracy (Florida Atlantic University), Susan Rahman (College of Marin) and Elliot D. Cohen (Indian River State College)

A report released by the Sentencing Project, a Washington DC–based nonprofit criminal justice advocacy group, revealed that the number of prisoners serving life sentences in the US state and federal prisons reached a new record of close to 160,000 in 2012.[29] Of these, 49,000 are serving life without possibility of parole, an increase of 22.2 percent since 2008. The study's findings place in striking context the figures promoted by the federal government, which indicate a reduction in the overall number of prisoners in federal and state facilities, from 1.62 million to 1.57 million between 2009 and 2012.

Ashley Nellis, senior research analyst with the Sentencing Project, argued that the rise in prisoners serving life sentences has to do with political posturing over "tough on crime" measures. "Unfortunately, lifers are typically excluded from most sentencing reform conversations because there's this sense that it's not going to sell, politically or with the public," Nellis said. "Legislators are saying, 'We have to throw somebody under the bus.'"

California is the leader in lifers, with one-quarter of the country's life-sentenced population (40,362), followed by Florida (12,549) and New York (10,245), Texas (9,031), Georgia (7,938), Ohio (6,075), Michigan (5,137), Pennsylvania (5,104), and Louisiana (4,657).

There are currently 3,281 prisoners in the US serving a life sentence—with no chance of parole—for minor, nonviolent crimes, according to a November 2013 report by the American Civil Liberties Union (ACLU). Louisiana, one of nine states where inmates currently serve life sentences for nonviolent crimes, has the nation's strictest three-strike law, which states that after three offenses the guilty person is imprisoned for life without parole.

As Ed Pilkington reported in the *Guardian*, the ACLU study documented "thousands of lives ruined and families destroyed" by this practice. Among those is Timothy Jackson, now fifty-three, who in

1996 was caught stealing a jacket from a New Orleans department store. "It has been very hard for me," Jackson wrote the ACLU. "I know that for my crime I had to do some time, but a life sentence for a jacket valued at $159."

The ACLU study reported that keeping these prisoners locked up for life costs taxpayers around $1.8 billion annually. The study stated that the US is "virtually alone in its willingness to sentence non-violent offenders to die behind bars." Life without parole for nonviolent sentences has been ruled a violation of human rights by the European Court of Human Rights.

With 2.3 million people imprisoned in the US today, Felicia Gustin of *War Times* has asked, is locking people away the answer to creating safer communities? She reported on the work of the Restorative Community Conferencing Program, based in Oakland, California. According to the program's coordinator, Denise Curtis, "restorative justice is a different approach to crime. . . . Our current justice system asks: What law was broken? Who broke it? and How should they be punished? Restorative justice asks: Who has been harmed? What needs have arisen because of the harm? and Whose responsibility is it to make things as right as they can?"

As Gustin reported, the program works with youth cases referred by the district attorney. Some involve felonies such as assault, robbery, and burglary. The Oakland Unified School District has also successfully incorporated restorative justice practices as an alternative to expelling and suspending youth which, according to Curtis, "impact Black and Brown youth disproportionately much more than white youth."

Variations of restorative justice programs currently operate in Baltimore, Minneapolis, New York, Chicago and New Orleans, among other cities, and at least one study has shown such programs have been effective in reducing recidivism. Nevertheless, few are aware of restorative justice as a real alternative to mass incarceration and this positive development deserves more news coverage.

24. Restorative Justice Turns Violent Schools Around

Jeff Deeney, "A Philadelphia School's Big Bet on Nonviolence," *Atlantic*, July 18, 2013, http://www.theatlantic.com/national/archive/2013/07/a-philadelphia-schools-big-bet-on-nonviolence/277893.

Fania Davis, "Discipline with Dignity: Oakland Classrooms Try Healing Instead of Punishment," *YES! Magazine*, February 19, 2014, http://www.yesmagazine.org/issues/education-uprising/where-dignity-is-part-of-the-school-day.

Student Researchers: Katie Barretta and Slava Eltchev (San Francisco State University)

Faculty Evaluator: Kenn Burrows (San Francisco State University)

Last year when American Paradigm Schools took over Philadelphia's infamous, failing John Paul Jones Middle School, they did something a lot of people would find inconceivable. Rather than beef up the already heavy security to ensure safety and restore order, American Paradigm stripped it away. During renovations, they removed both metal detectors and barred windows. The police predicted chaos. But, instead, new numbers seem to show that in a single year the number of serious incidents fell by 90 percent.

The school was known as "Jones Jail" for its reputation of violence and disorder, and because the building physically resembled a youth correctional facility. Situated in the Kensington section of the city, it drew students from the heart of a desperately poor hub of injection drug users and street-level prostitution where gun violence rates are off the charts.

School officials stated it wasn't just the humanizing physical makeover of the facility that helped. They also credit the Alternatives to Violence Project (AVP), a noncoercive, nonviolent conflict resolution regimen originally used in prison settings, which was later adapted to violent schools. AVP, when tailored to school settings, emphasizes student empowerment, relationship building, and anger management over institutional control and surveillance.

There are no aggressive security guards in schools using the AVP model; instead they have engagement coaches, who provide support, encouragement, and a sense of safety. AVP recruited its engagement coaches from Troops to Teachers, a program that trains veterans as educators. Trained in nonviolent conflict resolution, the engagement coaches "help mediate disputes rather than dole out punishment," Jeff Deeney reported in the *Atlantic*. Because students come to trust their engagement coaches, the school has been able to forestall potential conflicts: For example, "Coaches often get advance word," Deeney wrote, "when something's about to go down in the hallways."

From Oakland, Fania Davis reported for *YES! Magazine* about Restorative Justice for Oakland Youth (RJOY), which has successfully influenced the local school district to replace "zero-tolerance" policies with restorative justice—and with impressive, positive results. Under the program, high school students with failing grades and multiple incarcerations who were not even expected to graduate now do not simply graduate but also achieve 3.0+ GPAs and earn honors as valedictorians.

As Davis, RJOY's executive director, wrote, "Today hundreds of Oakland students are learning a new habit." Instead of resorting to violence, they are being empowered to engage in restorative processes that promote "dialogue, accountability, a deeper sense of community, and healing." The hallmark of restorative justice is "intentionally bringing together people with seemingly diametrically opposed viewpoints—particularly people who have harmed with people who have been harmed—in a carefully prepared face-to-face encounter where everyone listens and speaks with respect and from the heart no matter their differences."

A University of California–Berkeley study found that RJOY's middle school program reduced school suspension rates by 87 percent and referrals for violence by 77 percent.[30] Racial disparity in discipline was eliminated, while graduation rates and test scores rose.

25. "Chaptered Out": US Military Seeks to Balance Budget on Backs of Disabled Veterans

Dave Philipps, "Left Behind, No Break for the Wounded," *Colorado Springs Gazette*, May 20, 2013, http://cdn.csgazette.biz/soldiers/day2.html.

Sheila MacVicar, "76,000 Soldiers 'Chaptered Out' of Veterans' Benefits Since 2006," Al Jazeera America, November 9, 2013, http://america.aljazeera.com/watch/shows/america-tonight/america-tonight-blog/2013/11/11/exclusive-76-000soldierschapteredoutofmilitarybene-fitssince06.html.

Student Researchers: Carter Gaskill and Crystal Lau (DePauw University)

Faculty Evaluator: Brett R. O'Bannon and Kevin Howley (DePauw University)

The US military has been engaged in a policy of forcing wounded and disabled veterans out of service to avoid paying benefits and to make room for new able-bodied recruits. Identifying injured combat soldiers as delinquent and negligent has lead to a practice called "chap-

tering out" which results in those soldiers being forced to leave the military without an honorable discharge. Because of this, thousands of soldiers have been chaptered out, losing federally sponsored benefits including health care, unemployment, and educational programs.

Dave Philipps, a reporter for the *Colorado Springs Gazette*, exposed this practice through his story of Purple Heart recipient Sergeant Jerrald Jensen.

Jensen, a decorated two-tour Afghanistan war veteran and recovering active-duty sergeant, was forced from the army without benefits for what army officials called "a pattern of misconduct." Jensen failed to pass a urine test after being prescribed drugs for his injuries. He was also written up for being late to an appointment. Jensen made numerous attempts to be retested but was chaptered out by his superiors. "They told me that I didn't deserve to wear the uniform now, nor did I ever deserve to wear it," Jensen told Al Jazeera America.

Philipps has followed several stories of wounded soldiers who have been kicked out of the military and left with nothing. "Many have been diagnosed with post traumatic stress disorder (PTSD) and some also have traumatic brain injuries (TBI), both of which can influence behavior and judgment," said Philipps. He estimates that 76,000 soldiers have been chaptered out since 2006, and that number has increased every year since the war in Iraq began.

Although the military declined to be interviewed, denying any policy that targeted disabled soldiers to be forced out without benefits, an insider from the US Army Medical Command confirmed that this does happen. According to Philipps, "These commanders are stuck in this position where if they try to get them out medically, they are still stuck with them, maybe for a long time. If they decide to kick them out for misconduct instead, they could be out in weeks." Some soldiers like Jensen have had success appealing their discharges, but many others are left without any support from the nation they served.

CENSORED 2015 HONORABLE MENTIONS

Corporate Media Sources on Syrian Crisis Tied to Defense and Intelligence Industries

Gin Armstrong, Whitney Yax, and Kevin Connor, "Conflicts of Interest in the Syria Debate," Public Accountability Initiative, October 11, 2013, http://public-accountability.org/2013/10/conflicts-of-interest-in-the-syria-debate.

"The Military Industrial Pundits", *Democracy Now!*, October 18, 2013, http://www.democracynow.org/2013/10/18/the_military_industrial_pundits_conflicts_of.

Student Researchers: Grace Quinn and Anne Connelly (DePauw University)

Faculty Evaluators: Kevin Howley and Jeff McCall (DePauw University)

The debate of whether or not America should militarily intervene in Syria was widely covered by corporate American news outlets for several weeks in August and September 2013. This public discourse took place in major news outlets including CNN, MSNBC, Fox News, Bloomberg, and the *Washington Post*. However, as a reported by the Public Accountability Initiative, individuals who perhaps should not have been speaking on these delicate issues dominated the corporate media's coverage of the debate.

The interviewed guests on news broadcasts and authors of newspaper articles regarding military intervention in Syria were presented to the American public as diplomats, generals, and experts with unbiased credibility on the issue. However, the majority of these sources were connected to contracting, investment, or consulting firms with a primary focus on defense and intelligence. These ties were left out of the reporting, despite being clear conflicts of interest due to the personal benefits these sources might derive from US military intervention.

The report made a few key points. It identified twenty-two commentators who spoke on military intervention in Syria, all of whom were linked to defense and intelligence contractors or investment firms. These twenty-two contractors made a total of 111 appearances in newspapers and broadcasts, though only thirteen reports disclosed these links. Some of these "experts" would receive direct financial gain from military intervention, while others had clients who would benefit financially from intervention. Not surprisingly, the majority of the commentators overwhelmingly supported military action in Syria and identified it as an issue of US national security.

By filling the dialogue with individuals holding personal and financial interests in military intervention in Syria, corporate news outlets corrupted public debate over military intervention in the Syria conflict. The corporate media's failure to disclose such vital information to the American people calls into question its duties. The press has an obligation to truthfully inform the public. They ought to be held accountable for giving individuals with such sizable conflicts of interest the platform to speak on such momentous matters.

Minority Patients Sustain Higher Trauma Center Death Rates

"Trauma Centers Serving Mostly White Patients Have Lower Death Rates for Patients of All Races," *Science Daily*, September 11, 2013, http://www.sciencedaily.com/releases/2013/09/130911125005.htm.

Student Researchers: Maria Gutierrez Muñoz, J. P. Carrillo, Ashley O'Brien, Jessica Lozano, and Ian Levy (Santa Rosa Junior College)

Faculty Evaluator: Susan Rahman (Santa Rosa Junior College)

A study by researchers at Johns Hopkins University School of Medicine analyzed data from 181 trauma centers within the US and showed a correlation between trauma centers that serve mainly minority patients and higher than average death rates of those patients they serve.[31] Trauma centers that serve mainly white patients have newer and more efficient technology, better trained staff, and more access to specialists and services; these trauma centers have better outcomes and more of their patients are insured or are able to afford the health care costs. In contrast, trauma centers that serve mainly minority patients have fewer economic resources available to them for use in the improvement of equipment, quality of staff, and maintenance; this discrepancy in funding among trauma centers in different neighborhoods leads to unnecessary deaths that could be prevented were trauma centers sufficiently funded.

Adil Haider, an associate professor of surgery at the Johns Hopkins University School of Medicine and lead author of the study, said that the new research may help answer a long-standing question: is the reason for the disparity found in the biology or history of the patient, or in the hospital treating that patient? The study, he said, suggests that hospitals play the bigger role. "It's not just differences in the patients," says Haider. "All patients of all races do better at the trauma centers treating white majority populations, so this research tells us we need to direct attention to hospitals with higher mortality rates to help them improve their outcomes, or we won't ever be able to turn this around."[32]

Haider stated, "It can't continue to be the case that the color of a patient's skin determines whether he or she survives a serious injury." Trauma centers in areas that have a majority of patients who cannot afford the insurance or medical bills—typically people of color—are not discriminating against patients based on race or privilege, but rather they are improperly funded and because of this, patients are dying—deaths that could be prevented with the proper funding.

"Epidemic" of Wage Theft Plagues American Workers

Josh Eidelson, "84 Percent of NYC Fast Food Workers Report Wage Theft in a New Survey," *Nation*, May 16, 2013, http://www.thenation.com/blog/174375/84-percent-nyc-fast-food-workers-report-wage-theft-new-survey#.

Caroline Fairchild, "Low-Wage Workers Are Robbed More than Banks, Gas Stations and Convenience Stores Combined," *Huffington Post*, October 31, 2013, http://www.huffingtonpost.com/2013/10/30/low-wage-workers-robbed_n_4178706.html.

Ramy Srour, "Corporations Rewriting US Labor Laws," Inter Press Service, Nov 1, 2013, http://www.ipsnews.net/2013/11/corporations-rewriting-u-s-labour-laws.

Student Researcher: Ryan Kemp (Florida Atlantic University)

Faculty Evaluator: James F. Tracy (Florida Atlantic University)

A report from the Economic Policy Institute (EPI) finds that low-wage workers are robbed far more often than banks, gas stations, and convenience stores combined, by employers who fail to adhere to minimum wage laws or pay overtime. "The country suffers an epidemic of wage theft, as large numbers of employers violate minimum-wage, overtime, and other wage and hour laws with virtual impunity," University of Oregon economist Gordon Lafer wrote in the report.[33]

Such workplace abuses are occurring as some of the most powerful corporate lobbies attack labor standards and workplace protections, including minimum wage laws, paid sick leave, and even child labor protections. As Ramy Srour reported, EPI researchers found that corporate lobbies have engaged in "an intense attack" on labor standards and workplace protections. According to John Schmitt, a senior economist at the Center for Economic and Policy Research, "what is particularly important about this new report is that it emphasizes the recent legislative developments at the state and local levels, which unfortunately have been largely ignored."

Wage theft is on the increase even in the context of greater worker productivity. According to EPI statistics, from 1983 to 2010 the bottom 60 percent of Americans lost wealth, despite the fact that the overall US economy has grown over this same time period. According to EPI Vice President Ross Eisenbrey, "this is a remarkable indictment of how the economy is not working for everybody."

Public Radio International Obscures US Involvement in Guatemalan Massacre

Keane Bhatt, "This American Life Whitewashes U.S. Crimes in Central America, Wins Peabody Award," *North American Congress on Latin America* (*NACLA*), July 29, 2013, http://nacla.org/blog/2013/7/29/this-american-life-whitewashes-us-crimes-central-america-wins-peabody-award.

Keane Bhatt, "How the Media Got Guatemala's Dos Erres Massacre Wrong," Real News, August 4, 2013, http://therealnews.com/t2/index.php?Itemid=74&id=31&jumival=10519&option=com_content&task=view.

Student Researcher: Karen Griffith (Sonoma State University)

Faculty Evaluators: Nora Wilkins and Andy Lee Roth (Sonoma State University)

In May 2012, Public Radio International's *This American Life* partnered with ProPublica and Fundación MEPI to produce a broadcast titled, "What Happened at Dos Erres," which gave a new account of a 1982 military massacre in that Guatemalan village.[34] In March 2013, the broadcast received a prestigious Peabody Award for excellence in electronic journalism. What *This American Life* failed to mention in its account of "What Happened at Dos Erres," and what the Peabody board overlooked, Keane Bhatt reported, was prior documentation of the United States' direct involvement in supporting the murder of over two hundred innocent Guatemalan civilians in that event.

Although *This American Life*'s Ira Glass reported that state-led massacres "happened in over six hundred villages" and cited a 1999 United Nations–sponsored truth commission report that found "the number of Guatemalans killed or disappeared by their own government was over 180,000," Glass failed to report that the same commission also concluded that the "government of the United States, through various agencies including the CIA, provided direct and indirect support for some state operations," which resulted in atrocities like those at Dos Erres. As Bhatt noted in his report, the *Washington Post* and PBS both reported this aspect of the commission's report at the time.[35]

Bhatt's report also clarifies the deep historical context of Guatemalan state-sponsored violence against its civilian population, in ways that the *This American Life* story failed to explain. In 1954, the US organized a coup d'état against Guatemala's first democratically elected President Jacobo Árbenz. Consequently, a series of US-backed dictators ruled Guatemala. The Dos Erres massacre was part of the Guatemalan military's ongoing campaign, which the US had supported at least indirectly since the 1954 coup. Under the direction of Efraín Ríos Montt, who ruled Guatemala for seventeen months from 1982 to 1983, the state's security forces escalated their attacks on leftist insurgents. The US helped to train and arm Montt's troops. Declassified US intelligence documents revealed CIA and Pentagon involvement in the massacre.

During his rule, Montt counted President Ronald Reagan as a close ally. As Bhatt documented, the Reagan administration deliberately obscured "Guatemala's record of atrocities" under Montt. Although the *This American Life* episode included commentary by Kate Doyle, an expert on declassified documents at the National Security Archives, as Bhatt also reported the broadcast version of "What Happened at Dos Erres" omitted the portions of Doyle's in-studio discussion where she spoke about US complicity in the massacre. Similarly, Bhatt noted that the *This American Life* broadcast also "excluded content from its own media partner, ProPublica," which would have corroborated US involvement in the massacre.

"One would be hard-pressed," Bhatt wrote, "to encounter another contemporary mainstream account of that period so thoroughly sanitized of Washington's involvement in crimes against humanity."

Notes

1. Arctic Monitoring and Assessment Program (AMAP), "AMAP Arctic Ocean Acidification Assessment: Summary for Policy-Makers," AMAP, Oslo, Norway, May 13, 2013, http://www.amap.no/documents/doc/amap-arctic-ocean-acidification-assessment-summary-for-policy-makers/808. This document presents the executive summary of the 2013 Arctic Ocean Acidification (AOA) Assessment, which can be accessed here: http://www.amap.no/documents/doc/AMAP-Assessment-2013-Arctic-Ocean-Acidification/881.

2. Nina Bednaršek et al., "*Limacina helicina* Shell Dissolution as an Indicator of Declining Habitat Suitability Owing to Ocean Acidification in the California Current Ecosystem," *Proceedings of the Royal Society B* 281, no. 1785 (April 30, 2014), http://rspb.royalsocietypublishing.org/content/281/1785/20140123.abstract.

3. See, for example, Astrid C. Wittmann and Hans-O. Pörtner, "Sensitivities of Extant Animal Taxa to Ocean Acidification," *Nature Climate Change*, August 25, 2013, http://www.nature.com/nclimate/journal/vaop/ncurrent/full/nclimate1982.html.

4. Susan B. Epstein, Alex Tiersky, and Marian L. Lawson, "State, Foreign Operations, and Related Programs: FY2014 Budget and Appropriations," Congressional Research Office, January 16, 2014, http://www.fas.org/sgp/crs/row/R43043.pdf. See, in particular, Table 4, "Top 10 Recipients of U.S. Foreign Assistance, FY2012 Actual and FY2014 Request," 14.

5. Adam Withnall, "Israel Government 'Tortures' Children by Keeping Them in Cages, Human Rights Group Says," *Independent* (UK), January 1, 2014, http://www.independent.co.uk/news/world/middle-east/israel-government-tortures-children-by-keeping-them-in-cages-human-rights-group-says-9032826.html.

6. Amnesty International, "Annual Report 2013: Iraq," http://www.amnesty.org/en/region/iraq/report-2013 - section-67-4; "Egypt three years on, wide-scale repression continues unabated," Amnesty International, January 23, 2014, http://www.amnesty.org/en/news/egypt-three-years-wide-scale-repression-continues-unabated-2014-01-23.

7. Human Rights Watch, "World Report 2014: Jordan," http://www.hrw.org/world-report/2014/country-chapters/jordan?page=3.

8. 22 U.S. Code § 2151n, Human rights and development assistance, http://www.law.cornell.edu/uscode/text/22/2151n.

9. See, e.g., http://www.state.gov/documents/organization/100296.pdf.

10. Timothy B. Lee, "Leaked Treaty Is a Hollywood Wish List. Could it Derail Obama's Trade Agenda?," *The Switch* (blog), *Washington Post*, November 13, 2013, http://www.washingtonpost.com/blogs/the-switch/wp/2013/11/13/leaked-treaty-is-a-hollywood-wish-list-could-it-derail-obamas-trade-agenda.

11. See, for example, Jim Puzzanghera, "FCC Floats its Net Plan," *Los Angeles Times*, May 16, 2014, B1; http://www.latimes.com/business/la-fi-fcc-net-neutrality-20140516-story.html - page=1.

12. See, for example, Bret Swanson, "Why Broadband Consumers Are the Likely Winners in Verizon v. FCC," *Forbes*, September 25, 2013, http://www.forbes.com/sites/bretswanson/2013/09/25/why-broadband-consumers-are-the-likely-winners-in-verizon-v-fcc.

13. Department of Justice, Antitrust Division, "Three Former Financial Services Executives Sentenced to Serve Time in Prison for Roles in Conspiracies Involving Investment Contracts for the Proceeds of Municipal Bonds," October 18, 2012, http://www.stopfraud.gov/iso/opa/stopfraud/2012/12-at-1258.html.

14. James Hansen et al., "Assessing 'Dangerous Climate Change': Required Reduction of Carbon Emissions to Protect Young People, Future Generations and Nature," *PLOSOne*, December 3, 2013, http://www.plosone.org/article/info%3Adoi%2F10.1371%2Fjournal.pone.0081648.

15. Noam Chomsky has written about the US occupation of Guantánamo in Cuba as another instance of the contradiction between the US position toward Russia and its own lack of respect for national sovereignty. See Chomsky, "The Politics of Red Lines," *In These Times*, May 1, 2014, http://inthesetimes.com/article/16631/russia_ukraine_noam_chomsky.

16. Robert Perry, "Ukraine's Inconvenient Neo-Nazis," Consortium News, March 30, 2014, http://consortiumnews.com/2014/03/30/ukraines-inconvenient-neo-nazis.

17. Savabieasfahani's ZNet article cites this study, of which she is the corresponding author, as evidence for the claim that "Iraq is poisoned": M. Al-Sabbak et al., "Metal Contamination and the Epidemic of Congenital Birth Defects in Iraqi Cities," *Bulletin of Environmental Contamination and Toxology* 89, no. 5 (November 2012): 937–44; http://www.ncbi.nlm.nih.gov/pmc/articles/PMC3464374/pdf/128_2012_Article_817.pdf.

18. *The Guardian* article that Savabieasfahani cited is by John Pilger. See Pilger, "We've Moved on from the Iraq War—but Iraqis Don't Have that Choice," *Guardian*, May 26, 2013, http://www.theguardian.com/commentisfree/2013/may/26/iraqis-cant-turn-backs-on-deadly-legacy.

19. "IARC Classifies Radiofrequency Electromagnetic Fields as Possibly Carcinogenic to Humans," press release no. 208, International Agency for Research on Cancer, World Health Organization, May 31, 2011, http://www.iarc.fr/en/media-centre/pr/2011/pdfs/pr208_E.pdf.

20. Lennart Hardell and Michael Carlberg, "Using the Hill Viewpoints from 1965 for Evaluating Strengths of Evidence of the Risk for Brain Tumors Associated with Use of Mobile and Cordless Phones," *Rev. Environmental Health* 28, no. 3 (November 2013): 97–106.

21. Lennart Hardell et al., "Case-Control Study of the Association between Malignant Brain Tumors Diagnosed between 2007 and 2009 and Mobile and Cordless Phone Use," *International Journal of Oncology* 43, no. 6 (September 2013): 1833–45, http://www.ncbi.nlm.nih.gov/pmc/articles/PMC3834325.

22. "President Obama Announces $3.4 Billion Investment to Spur Transition to Smart Energy Grid," White House, October 27, 2009, http://www.whitehouse.gov/the-press-office/president-obama-announces-34-billion-investment-spur-transition-smart-energy-grid.

23. For previous coverage by Project Censored of this topic, see both chapter 2 of this volume and "Wireless Technology a Looming Health Crisis," *Censored 2014: Fearless Speech in Fateful Times*, eds. Mickey Huff and Andy Lee Roth (New York: Seven Stories Press, 2013), 54–55, 131–32.

24. Lynn M. Paltrow and Jeanne Flavin, "Arrests of and Forced Interventions on Pregnant Women in the United States, 1973–2005: Implications for Women's Legal Status and Public Health," *Journal of Health Politics, Policy and Law* 38, no. 2 (2013): 299–343, http://advocatesforpregnantwomen.org/main/publications/articles_and_reports/executive_summary_paltrow_flavin_jhppl_article.php.

25. ANERA, "Water in the West Bank and Gaza," ANERA Reports on the Ground in the Middle East 2 (March 2012), http://www.anera.org/wp-content/uploads/2013/03/ANERAWaterReport.pdf.

26. United Nations Country Team, "Gaza in 2020: A Liveable Place?," August 2012, http://www.unrwa.org/newsroom/press-releases/gaza-2020-liveable-place

27. For detailed testimony by Gaza residents, see "Over 90% of Water in Gaza Unfit for Drinking," B'Tselem, February 9, 2014, http://www.btselem.org/gaza_strip/20140209_gaza_water_crisis.

28. Ibid. See also "Undeniable Discrimination in the Amount of Water Allocated to Israelis and Palestinians," B'Tselem, February 12, 2014, http://www.btselem.org/press_releases/20140212_discrimination_in_water_allocation.

29. Ashley Nellis, "Life Goes On: The Historic Rise in Life Sentences in America," Sentencing Project, September 2013, http://sentencingproject.org/doc/publications/inc_Life Goes On 2013.pdf.

30. Michael D. Sumner, Carol J. Silverman, and Mary Louise Frampton, "School-Based Restorative Justice as an Alternative to Zero-Tolerance Policies: Lessons from West Oakland," Thelton E. Henderson Center for Social Justice, University of California–Berkeley School of Law, November 2010, http://www.law.berkeley.edu/files/11-2010_School-based_Restorative_Justice_As_an_Alternative_to_Zero-Tolerance_Policies.pdf.

31. Adil H. Haider et al., "Minority Trauma Patients Tend to Cluster at Trauma Centers with Worse-Than-Expected Mortality: Can This Phenomenon Help Explain Racial Disparities in Trauma Outcomes?," *Annals of Surgery* 258, issue 4 (October 2013): 572–81, http://journals.lww.com/annalsofsurgery/Abstract/2013/10000/Minority_Trauma_Patients_Tend_to_Cluster_at_Trauma.7.aspx. See also "Higher Death Rates in Centers Treating More Minority Patients May be Due to Financial Strains," *Johns Hopkins Medicine*, September, 12, 2013,

http://www.hopkinsmedicine.org/news/media/releases/study_shows_trauma_centers_serving_mostly_white_patients_have_lower_death_rates_for_patients_of_all_races.

32. Ibid.

33. Gordon Lafer, "The Legislative Attack on American Wages and Labor Standards, 2011–2012," Economic Policy Institute, October 31, 2013, http://www.epi.org/publication/attack-on-american-labor-standards.

34. "What Happened at Dos Erres," *This American Life*, May 25, 2012, http://www.thisamericanlife.org/radio-archives/episode/465/what-happened-at-dos-erres. See also Sebastian Rotella and Ana Arana, "Finding Oscar: Massacre, Memory and Justice in Guatemala," ProPublica, May 25, 2012, http://www.propublica.org/article/finding-oscar-massacre-memory-and-justice-in-guatemala.

35. Douglas Farah, "War Study Censures Military in Guatemala," *Washington Post*, February 26, 1999, http://www.washingtonpost.com/wp-srv/inatl/daily/feb99/guatemala26.htm.

TOP 25 STORY ANALYSES: STORY CATEGORIES AND HISTORICAL THEMES

The careful reader has likely noticed that many of the social problems and public issues featured in the Top 25 stories interrelate. Indeed, drawing connections among groups of stories can be an instructive exercise. What common themes link the Top 25 stories of 2013–14? Here is one possible organization of the stories by theme:

▸ *Environment and Health:* #1, Ocean Acidification; #14, Wireless Technology Health Hazards; and #16, Beef Industry's "Feedlot Feedback Loop."

▸ *US Empire:* #2, Top Ten US Aid Recipients All Practice Torture; #11, WHO Suppresses Report on Iraqi Cancers and Birth Defects; #12, Pentagon Awash in Money Despite Serious Audit Problems; #25, "Chaptered Out."

▸ *Economy:* #3, WikiLeaks Revelations on Trans-Pacific Partnership; #5, Bankers Back on Wall Street Despite Major Crimes; and a story receiving an Honorable Mention, "Epidemic" of Wage Theft Plagues American Workers.

▸ *Democracy at Home:* #6, The Deep State; #7, FBI Dismisses Murder Plot against Occupy Leaders; #11, Wealthy Donors and Corporations Set Think Tank's Agendas; and #23, Number of US Inmates Serving Life Sentences Hits New Record.

▸ *News Stories about the News:* #8, Corporate News Ignores Connections between Extreme Weather and Global Warming; #9,

US Media Hypocrisy on Ukraine; and #22, Corporate News Media Understate Rape, Sexual Violence.

> *People and Communities Organizing:* #13, Lawsuit Challenges Nuclear Power Industry Immunity; #18, National Database of Police Killings Aims for Accountability; #20, Estonia a Global Example of E-Government, Digital Freedom, Privacy and Security; #21, Questioning the Charter School Hype; and #24, Restorative Justice Turns Violent School Around.

Obviously, some stories could fit in other categories. For example, is the story of wealthy donors and corporations setting think tanks' agendas (#11) about democracy or the economy? Of course, the two intertwine: so long as there is economic injustice, democracy is eroded. The same could be said for the environment and health. The story of the class action lawsuit challenging the nuclear power industry's immunity from liability in nuclear power accidents—such as Fukushima (#13)—is at once a story of the environment and health, corporate power and democracy, *and* people organizing in order to address a gross social injustice. It fits in all of those three categories, but is not completely covered by any one of them.

Creating news categories is an imaginative activity that exposes underlying values and makes clear tacit assumptions. We present one example to illustrate what we mean. As we assembled this year's Top 25 list, one of the Project's esteemed judges questioned whether stories such as those included above in the "News Stories about the News" category really belonged in Project Censored's Top 25 list. Could the corporate media really be expected to report on its own inadequacies? The judge's insightful question made clear a value judgment on our part about what journalism ought to provide members of a society. Obviously, since they appear in the Top 25 list, we believe that news stories from independent journalists about institutional slant in corporate news coverage are essential to an informed public and, thus, to democracy.[1] These stories challenge an assertion so often made by establishment news professionals when faced with charges of excluding important stories: if a story *was* important or newsworthy, we would have covered it, they say.

This is a form of boundary work, through which corporate news professionals define what counts as news and (more or less explicitly) position themselves as the judges and guardians of those boundaries.[2] Think, for example, of the venerable *New York Times* slogan, "All the news that's fit to print," and the boundary work it does. The slogan stipulates what can be understood as an *incorrigible* proposition, one about which it is impossible to be mistaken. How do corporate journalists—and, more importantly, the public—preserve their trust in corporate news, even when critics can point to facts and events that belie this trust? The process hinges on what the pioneering anthropologist E. E. Evans-Pritchard termed "secondary elaboration of belief." Believers invoke exceptional circumstances in order to explain away apparent failures.[3] In this context, (independent) news stories about the shortcomings of (corporate) news act as crucial counter-evidence when defenders of establishment media and the status quo resort to arguments that effectively stipulate corporate press infallibility.

The goal of grouping the stories into categories is not to arrive at some ultimate scheme that rigidly locates each story; instead, the exercise encourages critical thinking about the underlying dynamics— the social institutions, the cultural values, and the otherwise taken-for-granted assumptions—that link groups of stories. This exercise is important because these dynamics not only connect important but underreported news stories, they also shape US society, its social structure, and its place in the larger world. Spending some time with friends, family, or classmates, and playing with how different stories connect to one another, advocating for different groupings, imagining new categories—these are ways to transform ourselves from passive consumers of media content into active participants in the interpretation of their meanings. If an informed populace is crucial to democracy, then actively interpreting connections among news stories is arguably one way of engaging news that will leave us inspired to act, rather than bored or demoralized.

Readers of past *Censored* yearbooks may already have observed that, of course, Project Censored has been playing with categorizing and drawing connections among stories in our Top 25 lists for some time. Most recently, in *Censored* yearbooks from 2012 through 2014, this has taken the form of "Censored News Clusters," which provided more detailed analyses, based on each year's Top 25 stories, of topics such as: "Whistleblowers and Gag Laws" and "Human Rights and Civil Liberties" (*Censored 2014: Fearless Speech in Fateful Times*); "The Police State and Civil Liberties" and "Human Costs of War and Violence" (in *Censored 2013: Dispatches from the Media Revolution*); and "Social Media and Internet Freedom" and "Collaboration and the Common Good" (from *Censored 2012: Sourcebook for the Media Revolution*). But reaching further back, as early as 1994, Carl Jensen and Project Censored were drawing attention to the deeper themes that connected stories featured in the Project's annual Top 25 lists. The 1994 *Censored* yearbook identified stories in the following categories: Corporate, Environment, International, Crime, Military, Politics, Education, Health, and Civil Rights.[4]

Another instructive exercise is to compare stories from *Censored 2015*'s Top 25 with those from previous decades' lists. Although some of the bylines and sources change, the topics are remarkably similar and continuous. Examine the lists below to see just how often some of our most censored stories have recurred.

COMPARISON OF TOP 25 STORY TOPICS, 1995 AND 2015

Censored 1995	*Censored 2015*
#3 Secret Pentagon Plan to Subsidize Defense Contractor Mergers	#12 Pentagon Awash in Money Despite Serious Audit Problems-
#5 Clinton Administration Retreats on Ozone Crisis	#1 Ocean Acidification Increasing at Unprecedented Rate
#10 News Media Mask Spousal Violence in the "Language of Love"	#22 Corporate News Media Understate Rape, Sexual Violence
#11 The Treasury Department Ignores S&L Crimes	#5 Bankers Back on Wall Street Despite Major Crimes
#13 The Nuclear Regulatory Commission's Dirty Secret *and* #14 Faulty Nuclear Fuel Rods Spell Potential Disaster	#13 Lawsuit Challenges Nuclear Power Industry Immunity from Liability in Nuclear Accidents
#18 Nationwide Collusion Between Drug Companies and Pharmacists	#19 Agribusiness Giants Attempt to Silence and Discredit Scientists Whose Research Reveals Herbicides' Health Threats
#25 Deadly "Mad Cow" Disease Spreads to North America	#16 The Beef Industry's "Feedlot Feedback Loop"

From 1995 to 2015, the *Censored* yearbooks alert us to deep continuities in both the social problems that challenge us as a society, and the crucial role that a truly independent press plays in alerting the public to these problems when corporate media fail to do so.

For readers who want to trace for themselves the historical legacies of some of the Project's recurrent censored news story topics, Project Censored maintains a complete archive of past years' Top 25 story lists on our website. Older *Censored* yearbooks are also available in public libraries and can be ordered directly from Project Censored or Seven Stories Press.

Stepping back to take a broader view of the stories covered by this year's Top 25 list and how they compare with previous *Censored* yearbooks' coverage, a simple but powerful pair of themes unites them all. With overwhelming consistency, the stories featured by Project Censored hinge on a combination of (1) abuses of power that run contrary to the authentic spirit and actual practice of democratic government ("We the People") and (2) organized resistance to those abuses, aimed at creating a more just, inclusive society.

On this point it is worth reflecting briefly on the theme of "People and Communities Organizing," as proposed above. As noted in previous *Censored* yearbooks, corporate news media often marginalize, diminish, or ignore what we might consider to be "good" news stories—where "good" refers not to trivial, superficial segments at the end of the evening's TV news broadcast, but rather to substantive coverage of people and communities organizing in order to resist systemic social injustice or to remedy longstanding social problems.[5]

It is important for journalism to treat people organizing to create positive change as newsworthy. Of course, news coverage such as this year's #21 story, "Questioning the Charter School Hype" could easily—and accurately—be identified as a story about education. But it may be more consequential to link it with other stories that are not necessarily limited to the domain of education, but in which groups of people, within and across communities, have organized to protect common interests and public goods from private predation. Because corporate news so often reflects and, more or less subtly, promotes corporate interests, it should come as no surprise that establishment news either marginalizes or excludes stories suggesting that people might live more fulfilling lives when they decline the limiting, default roles of "consumer" and "spectator" in favor of more meaningful alternatives, such as "community member" or "activist."

A good example of this comes from *Censored 2013*, which featured "2012: The International Year of Cooperatives" as its #7 story.[6] It is not surprising that corporate-owned news media might be reluctant to cover a story indicating that worker-owned and worker-run businesses not only promise to become the fastest growing business model by the year 2025, but that they also promote more equitable distribution of wealth and genuine connection to the workplace, two key components of a sustainable economy. The story, originally reported by Jessica Reeder for *YES! Magazine*, made clear that an alternative to the corporate model was not only possible, but also quickly becoming a robust challenger. Promoting awareness of that reality runs contrary to corporate interests, of course.

As we hope *Censored 2015*'s Top 25 story list makes powerfully clear, independent news media expand our conceptions of what is newsworthy and who counts as an authoritative source of information and opinion. In terms of Stuart Hall's analysis, as discussed in the introduction to this chapter, at its best the independent press provides an alternative to the status quo assumptions and ideologies of the corporate media. The areas of consensus that the corporate media take for granted and reinforce come under question by independent journalists; and independent media redefine the areas of conflict, in which establishment journalists safely marginalize and even vilify any group whose members challenge the political culture's built-in definitions and sacred values.[7]

Through their courageous openness, independent journalists—and, of course, the organizations that publish and broadcast their dispatches—provide us with new kinds of knowledge, and new dimensions of meaning, beyond those sanctioned by current systems of power. New kinds of knowledge, new dimensions of meaning—these, we respectfully suggest, are wellsprings that should inspire We the People to continue to strive together for the free development of our best capacities.

Notes

1. We also deem it newsworthy when the independent press exhibits institutional biases of its own. See, for example, Peter Phillips, "Left Progressive Media Inside the Propaganda Model," Project Censored, May 2, 2010, http://www.projectcensored.org/left-progressive-media-inside-the-propaganda-model.

2. Sociologist Thomas F. Gieryn developed the concept of boundary work to analyze how scientists create, advocate, dispute, and maintain divisions among different (and sometimes competing) fields of knowledge, including, especially, distinctions between "science" and "non-science." Subsequently, scholars have extended the concept of boundary work to examine other professions, including journalism. See, for example, Samuel P. Winch, *Mapping the Cultural Space of Journalism: How Journalists Distinguish News from Entertainment* (Westport CT: Praeger, 1998).

3. E. E. Evans-Pritchard, *Witchcraft, Oracles and Magic Among the Azande* (Oxford: Oxford University Press, 1937). For those who would restrict incorrigible propositions and secondary elaboration of belief to "primitive" or "superstitious" people and cultures only, Melvin Pollner's *Mundane Reason: Reality in Everyday Life and Sociological Discourse* (Cambridge: Cambridge University Press, 1987) provides challenging examples and analyses, drawn from everyday contemporary life. For a cogent overview of Pollner's revolutionary work, see John Heritage and Steven Clayman, "Mel Pollner: A View from the Suburbs," *American Sociologist* 43, no. 1 (March 2012), 99–108; http://www.sscnet.ucla.edu/soc/faculty/heritage/Site/Publications_files/MELVIN_POLLNER.pdf.

4. Carl Jensen and Project Censored, *Censored: The News That Didn't Make the News: The 1994 Project Censored Yearbook* (New York: Four Walls Eight Windows, 1994), 32–33.

5. See, for example, the foreword by Sarah van Gelder on "solutions journalism," the introduction by Andy Lee Roth and Mickey Huff, and "The New Story: Why We Need One and How to Create It" by Michael Nagler in *Censored 2014: Fearless Speech in Fateful Times* (New York: Seven Stories Press, 2013); Kenn Burrows and Michael Nagler's chapter, "The Creative Tension of the Emerging Future: Facing the Seven Challenges of Humanity," in *Censored 2013: Dispatches from the Media Revolution* (New York: Seven Stories Press, 2012); and the "Stories of Hope and Change" chapters, produced by Kate Sims in collaboration with YES! Magazine in the 2008–10 *Censored* yearbooks, and authored by Kenn Burrows in *Censored 2011* and *2012*.

6. See *Censored 2013*, 79–81, and, online, http://www.projectcensored.org/7-2012-the-international-year-of-cooperatives.

7. On identifying areas of *consensus, conflict*, and *toleration* as a means of mapping unwitting bias in news coverage, see Stuart Hall, "A World at One with Itself," in *The Manufacture of News: Deviance, Social Problems and the Mass Media*, eds. Stanley Cohen and Jock Young, (London: Constable, 1973), 88.

CHAPTER 2

Déjà Vu

What Happened to Previous *Censored* Stories?

Susan Rahman, with research and writing from College of Marin students Scott Arrow, McLaren Berhendt, Jonah Birnbaum, Justin Burkhalter, Alex Cutler, Delvante Galon, Christy Gelardi, Lea Islemann, Devon Johnson, Lauren Markel, Alexandria McDowell, Raffi Oughourlian, Shannon Reed, Alex Ritchie, Paige Shave, and Pippa Whelan; with additional contributions by Mickey Huff and Andy Lee Roth; and a special update on Fukushima by Brian Covert

History, despite its wrenching pain,
Cannot be unlived, but if faced
With courage, need not be lived again.

—Maya Angelou (April 4, 1928–May 28, 2014)

As in previous *Censored* yearbooks, this year's Déjà Vu chapter reviews a handful of stories featured in prior years' Top 25 lists. These reviews focus on the stories' subsequent coverage, assessing the extent to which they have become part of broader public discourse, or whether they remain "censored" by establishment media and marginal to public attention. Drawing on the insights of Maya Angelou, we revisit previous years' censored and underreported news stories in the belief that, with adequate public understanding, they "need not be lived again."

Typically, the stories featured in Project Censored's Top 25 list have one of two fates, as far as corporate media coverage goes. Either the corporate media continue to ignore these important news stories, or there is a time lag of approximately eighteen to twenty-four months from when independent journalists break the story and the corporate news media catch up and begin to cover it themselves.[1] For those stories that do finally receive corporate coverage, we typically find a significant degree of "spin" or framing, as will be highlighted in analyses of several of this year's featured Déjà Vu stories.[2]

Project Censored seeks to "uncensor" topics that remain elusive—or illusive—in corporate coverage of news. Were it not for independent journalists choosing to cover important stories, even when they know that aspects of those stories may bar them from achieving prominence in corporate outlets, we at Project Censored would have nothing to report. However, due to the committed—and often courageous—efforts of independent journalists, Project Censored has been flooded with a wealth of crucial, independent news stories over the past thirty-eight years. And, in turn, Project Censored has provided its readers with a steady flow of underreported news stories, presented fairly, researched and validated by students, faculty, and a diverse panel of media scholars across the United States. This year's Déjà Vu chapter features stories on whistleblowing, the Trans-Pacific Partnership, the looming health risks of wireless technologies, Israel forcing birth control on Ethiopian immigrants, and a special update on Fukushima by Brian Covert.

DÉJÀ VU ALL OVER AGAIN: SUPPORTING OFFICIAL NARRATIVES BY ATTACKING THE COUNTER-NARRATORS

Two of this year's Déjà Vu stories address what we at Project Censored have called a war on journalism and whistleblowers. The clouds of propaganda emanating from corporate media on these topics underscore the importance of reviewing and updating stories that expose government secrecy and illustrate corporate media shortcomings. In essence, this entails a meta-critique, as we examine how the corporate news media report stories that involve free press issues, and how government officials and policies influence that coverage. Unfortunately for the free press, both government and corporate media continue their assault on those who challenge status quo notions of what counts as "news," how it gets reported, and by whom.

Given that those in the so-called Fourth Estate (corporate media journalists who rely on government and establishment sources) tend to shape and disseminate official narratives, it should not be surprising that these outlets and their sources are often biased against those posing counter-narratives (independent journalists and whistleblowers). On occasion, government and corporate media representatives resort to attacking the messengers rather than addressing their actual messages. Before we turn to this year's Déjà Vu stories themselves, it is instructive to take a closer look at government and corporate media behavior on the matter of independent journalism and whistleblowing as a news story itself.

As we wrapped last year's book, *Censored 2014: Fearless Speech in Fateful Times*, Chelsea Manning had not yet been sentenced, and the Edward Snowden story was just hitting the press. In recapping *Censored 2014* story #1, "Bradley [now Chelsea] Manning and the Failure of Corporate Media," and #4, "Obama's War on Whistleblowers," we look at how Manning has continued to be underreported, but we pay particular attention to the ongoing Snowden case, his revelations about government secrecy, spying and data collection, and the ensuing public outcry, as this is one of the most significant stories of the past year. His story has garnered much media attention, including a spring interview on primetime network television (NBC). Although the problem with a lack of coverage of a particular story is obvious, when there *is* coverage by the corporate media, like with Snowden, it is important to assess *how* the story is covered.

The Manning story was ignored in large part, and much of the coverage looked at gender politics and other personal issues when not rhetorically asking if Manning was guilty of "aiding and abetting the enemy" (she was not). Snowden's story has received far more coverage in comparison. However, as in Manning's case, corporate frames have focused attention on Snowden himself, including his personality and motivations, rather than on the original documents about the National Security Agency (NSA) spying programs, their questionable legality, and how both the Bush and Obama administrations lied about them. Instead, the corporate media punditocracy reduced these complex issues to a simplistic either/or decision: hero or traitor? Some corporate coverage framed debate even more narrowly, musing as to whether Snowden was either traitor or criminal, excluding all other alternatives.[3] Apparently any other consideration is unfit to be heard—in other words, censored from public view. The Big Brother society has been normalized in a post-9/11 world.

By now, it should be no secret that whistleblowers have been under attack by the Obama administration.[4] During the Obama presidency, there have been eight government employees prosecuted under the Espionage Act, more than under every previous administration combined.[5] That said, in addition to government officials attacking whistleblowers, they've also targeted those who report whistleblower information like Glenn Greenwald, Julian Assange of WikiLeaks, and others that support transparency and a free press. In fact, several high profile members of the corporate media have helped lead the charge.

Indeed, in terms of shooting the messengers, this past year was like Déjà Vu all over again for attackers and victims alike. Greenwald's partner, David Miranda, was detained and searched when traveling abroad and, because of their journalistic pursuits, they have lived under constant scrutiny.[6] Greenwald was publicly shamed on NBC's *Meet the Press* for his role in helping to publish Snowden's revelations. Host David Gregory thought it appropriate to ask Greenwald if he was in fact a "real" journalist.[7] The fact that Greenwald has won the prestigious Pulitzer Prize and Polk Award for public service and national security reporting should put to rest the question of whether or not he is a "real" journalist, though that doesn't seem to stop those trying to discredit him. Ironically, Greenwald had previously collaborated with NBC News to help write four stories using the very information Snowden leaked, which NBC seemed to have no trouble using despite its attacks on both men.

Upon receiving the Pulitzer, Greenwald remarked to the *Huffington Post* about the attacks against him, "That's just part of, I think, what journalism is, is if you want to be adversarial to those who wield power, you have to expect that those who wield power aren't gonna like what you're doing very much . . . And not only doesn't that bother me, I see that as a vindication that what I'm doing is the right thing."[8]

Highlighting how corporate news media cover free press issues—including the ongoing war on journalism and whistleblowers—matters deeply because the issues at stake in these stories impact how we find out about all other news stories: at their core, press freedom stories are about journalism and protecting the commons of human knowledge. Given the press freedoms identified in the First Amendment, these issues ought to be both readily available to all citizens and prominent in our public discourse.[9] Why, then, at every turn do we find policy created to stifle the public's access to information and decision-making? Why do those who claim to represent the free press lead attacks against their more independent colleagues who want to report the most crucial information of our times? Perhaps those in government and the corporate press would rather Americans be kept in the dark: compliant, distracted, and easily controlled.

An educated public is capable of stronger collective action—better able to face those wrenching aspects of our shared history, which Maya Angelou and others remind us must be faced courageously if we aim to create a better future. We at Project Censored consider it our duty to continue to speak out against censorship and the injustices that those who employ it seek to hide, and we encourage readers to do the same.[10] In this spirit, we offer updates to these previously censored stories.

> *If you are neutral in situations of injustice,*
> *you have chosen the side of the oppressor.*
>
> —Desmond Tutu

Censored 2014 #1
Chelsea Manning and the Failure of Corporate Media

SUMMARY: United States military intelligence analyst Chelsea Manning confessed in court to providing vast archives of military and diplomatic files to the anti-secrecy group WikiLeaks.[11] Manning wanted the information to become public "to make the world a better place" and hoped to "spark a domestic debate on the role of the military in (US) foreign policy." The 700,000 released documents revealed a multitude of previously secret crimes and acts of deceit and corruption by US military and government officials. Among these was the infamous "collateral murder" video from July 2007, which showed US personnel in Iraq killing innocent civilians, including two Reuters reporters, and wounding two children. The soldiers mocked their victims during the unprovoked attack.[12]

According to Manning's testimony in February 2013, she tried

to release the Afghanistan and Iraq War Logs through conventional sources. In winter 2010, Manning contacted the *Washington Post*, the *New York Times*, and *Politico* in hopes that they would publish the materials. They refused, so Manning began uploading documents to WikiLeaks. Al Jazeera reported that Manning's testimony "raises the question of whether the mainstream press was prepared to host the debate on US interventions and foreign policy that Manning had in mind."

Corporate media largely focused on Manning's decision to change gender, disregarding her First Amendment rights or the abusive nature of her imprisonment, which included almost three years without trial and nearly one year in "administrative segregation," the military equivalent of solitary confinement. In a February 2013 court appearance, Manning pled guilty to twelve of the twenty-two charges. One of the remaining ten charges was the capital offense of "aiding and abetting the enemy." At the time, Manning faced the possibility of a life sentence without parole.

UPDATE: The Manning trial came to an end on July 30, 2013. Pvt. Manning was convicted of twenty of the twenty-two charges she faced. She was sentenced to thirty-five years in prison for leaking

750,000 classified documents to the public via WikiLeaks, but was not convicted of one of the most serious charges against her, "aiding and abetting the enemy." This is known as one of the largest caches of classified documents in US history. Manning was imprisoned for over three years before trial, subjected to illegal pretrial punishment, and put in solitary confinement. These and other mistreatments provide Manning's legal team with significant grounds for appealing the convictions, though the military has preliminarily upheld Manning's sentencing.

A day after sentencing, Manning announced that she wanted to live as a woman. Her attorney David Coombs told the Associated Press that Chelsea had known for some time that she wanted to live as a woman but did not want to release the statement during the trial and have it seem insincere. "People might think it was an effort to get further attention," said Coombs. Manning knew that the army might not provide hormone treatments but was hoping that United States Penitentiary, Leavenworth, where she will serve her sentence, would allow it since she was diagnosed with gender identity disorder by an army psychiatrist who testified to this during her trial. Manning will be eligible for her first parole review after serving ten years of her sentence. However, she may be eligible after seven years because of the 1,294 days credited by the judge toward her sentence for mistreatment during her stay in prison before and during the trial.

Edward Snowden and Chelsea Manning both came under scrutiny for leaking top-secret government documents and are often compared to one another in the media, yet they face different battles. Manning has been sentenced to thirty-five years in federal prison, while Snowden lives in an undisclosed location in Russia on (temporary) asylum. Both have been labeled whistleblowers, and both were awarded the Sam Adams Award. The award is given annually by the Sam Adams Associates for Integrity in Intelligence, a group of retired Central Intelligence Agency (CIA) officers, to an intelligence professional who has taken a stand for integrity and ethics. Edward Snowden was publicly acknowledged and accepted his award. Snowden also acknowledged Chelsea and congratulated her in a YouTube video. Manning wrote a letter in acceptance and had her childhood friend Aaron Kirkhouse accept the award on her behalf.

In January 2014, the *New York Times* editorial board advocated that President Obama should grant clemency to Snowden. *Firedoglake*'s Kevin Gosztola's praised the *Times*' editorial board for its position but also challenged them, raising the question, "If Snowden is a whistle-blower, what is Chelsea Manning?" *The Times* editorial said Snowden could not have gone through the "proper channels"—which, Gosztola wrote, had also been impossible for Manning. Manning offered documents to the *New York Times* and other establishment news organizations, but they never responded to these offers. Snowden has been hailed as a hero, a whistleblower, a dissident, a traitor, a criminal, and a patriot, ultimately receiving much more press coverage than Manning.

As Fairness and Accuracy in Reporting (FAIR) showed, media outlets such as *Time* magazine tended to take for granted—or outright ignore—the important information that Manning and Snowden leaked, while vilifying them through comparisons to figures such as Fort Hood shooter Nidal Hasan and Navy Yard shooter Aaron Alexis. Rather than discussing how the information Manning leaked has shifted our understanding of governmental procedures and actions, corporate news coverage details her gender identity and emphasizes the debate over whether she should receive hormones and/or a sex change while imprisoned, as ways to distract attention from the serious issues raised by the documents she revealed. It's an example of what Project Censored calls News Abuse (discussed in the next chapter).

In addition to the Chelsea Manning Support Network, Manning has also been assisted by Courage to Resist, which has raised $50,000 toward her defense. She is now represented by Nancy Hollander and Vincent Ward in a case before the US Court of Appeals for the Armed Forces. Attorney David Coombs, who represented Manning throughout her trial, will continue to assist her in legal matters regarding her official name change and her fight to receive hormone therapy. Coombs had previously filed a pardon request with President Obama and a clemency request with the secretary of the army but was told that action needed to be taken by the convening authority and appellate courts before any consideration would be made regarding a pardon or clemency. Major General Jeffrey Buchanan, who under military law has the power to approve or deny the decision of the trial judge, announced in April that he has denied the request for clemency and upheld the thirty-five-year sentence. Even though Manning supporters have sent over 3,000 letters in her support, this result came as no surprise.

The Chelsea Manning Support Network's website hosts a petition that can be signed by anyone who wishes to express support for Manning to the White House and the court martial convening authority. Supporters have also marched in a peace parade in Boston each of the past three years to raise awareness of the need to continue to fight for Manning's freedom. Manning was named the honorary grand marshal in San Francisco's 2014 lesbian gay bisexual transgender parade. Her case, its aftermath, and the WikiLeaks documents themselves, have received less coverage overall than the more recent Edward Snowden case, which we examine next.

SOURCES:

Associated Press, "Bradley Manning Explains Gender Change," *Politico*, August 26, 2013, http://www.politico.com/story/2013/08/bradley-chelsea-manning-gender-change-95928.html.

Emma Cape, "New Legal Team with Fight for Chelsea on Appeal," Chelsea Manning Support Network, March 17, 2014, http://www.privatemanning.org/news/new-legal-team-will-fight-for-chelsea-on-appeal.

David Coombs, "Update on PFC Chelsea Manning," Chelsea Manning Support Network, March 26, 2014, http://www.privatemanning.org/featured/david-coombs-update-on-pfc-chelsea-manning.

"Chelsea Manning Awarded 2014 Sam Adams Prize for Integrity in Intelligence," RT News, January 16, 2014, http://rt.com/news/manning-sam-adams-award-697.

Nick Denver, "Snowden Congratulates Chelsea Manning," *Time*, February 19, 2014, http://swampland.time.com/2014/02/19/edward-snowden-congratulates-chelsea-manning.

Editorial Board, "Edward Snowden, Whistle-Blower," *New York Times*, January 2, 2014, A18, http://www.nytimes.com/2014/01/02/opinion/edward-snowden-whistle-blower.html.

Kevin Gosztola, "Dear New York Times Editors: If Snowden is a Whistleblower, What is Chelsea Manning?," *Firedoglake*, January 2, 2014, http://dissenter.firedoglake.com/2014/01/02/dear-new-york-times-editors-if-snowden-is-a-whistleblower-what-is-chelsea-manning.

Fairness and Accuracy in Reporting, "Whistleblowers and Other Threats," *Extra!*, November 2013, 3.

Censored 2014 #4

Obama's War on Whistleblowers

SUMMARY: President Barack Obama signed both the Whistleblower Protection Enhancement Act, expanding whistleblower protections, in November 2012, and the National Defense Authorization Act

(NDAA) furthering these protections in January 2013. However, his NDAA signing statement also undermined these protections, stating that those expanded protections "could be interpreted in a manner that would interfere with my authority to manage and direct executive branch officials." Thus, in his signing statement, Obama promised to ignore expanded whistleblower protections if they conflicted with his power to "supervise, control, and correct employees' communications with the Congress in cases where such communications would be unlawful or would reveal information that is properly privileged or otherwise confidential."

Despite rhetoric to the contrary, the Obama administration is targeting government whistleblowers, having invoked the otherwise dormant Espionage Act of 1917 at least eight times. Under President Obama, the Department of Justice has also used the Intelligence Identities Protection Act to obtain a conviction against Central Intelligence Agency (CIA) whistleblower John Kiriakou for exposing the waterboarding of prisoners, ironically making Kiriakou the first CIA official to be sentenced to prison in connection with the torture program (but for exposing it, not for participating in it). And the justice department charged former National Security Agency (NSA) senior executive Thomas Drake with espionage for exposing hundreds of millions of dollars of waste.

The highly visible prosecution of Chelsea Manning has become what is arguably the most effective deterrent against government whistleblowers. Manning admitted to leaking troves of classified documents to WikiLeaks, but pleaded not guilty on counts of espionage. Since the Manning case, another whistleblower has been in the limelight, Edward Snowden, for leaking documents about NSA spying. The Snowden affair has eclipsed recent previous whistleblowing cases in media coverage, though that coverage, as we will see, has been quite skewed.

UPDATE: In late May 2013, Edward Snowden became the biggest name associated with whistleblowers since Chelsea Manning. After the release of NSA documents, he was called many things—a patriot, a traitor, a hero, a criminal, and a dissident, to name a few. Snowden, a computer specialist and former CIA employee who worked as an NSA contractor, believed it was his duty to alert the American public to gross constitutional violations by the US government.

On May 20, 2013, Snowden flew from Hawaii to Hong Kong, where he later met with journalists Glenn Greenwald and Laura Poitras and shared numerous classified documents. These documents exposed Internet surveillance programs such as PRISM, MUSCULAR, XKeyscore, and Tempora, and the bulk collection of US and European telephone metadata.

On June 14, 2013, federal prosecutors charged Snowden with espionage and theft of government property. After publicly denouncing the NSA's practices of violating citizens' privacy rights, Snowden left the country and, on June 23, was granted temporary asylum in Russia.

The 2012 change in the Whistleblower Protection Act complicated the ability of government intelligence employees to bring forward information without fear of prosecution. Although Snowden worked on behalf of the United States government, Booz Allen Hamilton, a company that fulfilled NSA contracts, was his direct employer. As an employee of a private company, Snowden's right to protection under the Whistleblower Protection Act was significantly limited. Although most federal workers fall under the Whistleblower Protection Act of 1989, a separate law aptly named the Intelligence Community Whistleblower Protection Act is generally regarded as a fairly weak protection act and is ambiguous. It allows for national security whistleblowers to release classified information to an inspector general or member of a congressional intelligence committee, but does not protect whistleblowers from retaliation. Snowden commented on his status as a employee of a private company (from the *Washington Post*): "As an employee of a private company rather than a direct employee of the US government, I was not protected by US whistleblower laws, and I would not have been protected from retaliation and legal sanction for revealing classified information about law-breaking in accordance with the recommended process." Snowden explained (from the *Washington Post*):

> It is important to remember that this legal dilemma did not occur by mistake. US whistleblower reform laws were passed as recently as 2012, with the US Whistleblower Protection Enhancement Act, but they specifically chose to exclude intelligence agencies from being covered by the statute. President Obama also reformed a key executive whistleblower regulation with his 2012 Presidential Policy Directive 19, but it exempted intelligence community contractors such as myself. The result was that individuals like me were left with no proper channels.

Lack of proper channels left Snowden with no course of action that the government would find acceptable if he chose to leak information, and no legal protection if he did so. This significant exception in the revised Whistleblower Protection Act has made it impossible for any intelligence officer to bring to light constitutional violations or other serious injustices, without putting his or her own careers at risk. *The Washington Post*, where Snowden was quoted on the matters, called this a "gray area" in the law.

In early March 2014, the US Supreme Court expanded the scope of whistleblower protections. Following the collapse of Enron Corporation, Congress enacted the Sarbanes–Oxley Act of 2002, which protected employees of public companies against retaliation from whistleblowing. In the case of *Lawson v. FMR LLC*, two former employees filed suits for wrongful termination against FMR, claiming the company had retaliated against them for whistleblowing. The plaintiffs argued that protection was granted to them through the Sarbanes-Oxley Act. FMR argued that the plaintiff's lawsuits be dismissed, and that the claim of protection through the Sarbanes–Oxley Act did not hold because the act only protected employees of public companies, not private ones. On March 4, 2014, in a 6–3 decision the Supreme Court ruled in favor of the plaintiffs and clarified the intent of the Sarbanes–Oxley Act of 2002. The Court's decision extended the act's whistleblower protections to include the employees of a public company's private contractors and subcontractors.

NBC News aired their interview with Snowden on May 28, 2014, during prime time. He spoke of his duties while working for the NSA and why he felt it was important that the information he leaked be made public. He currently has a legal team that will begin negotiations with the US government to see what resolution can be reached. Controversy continued to swirl around the players and the issues. Glenn Greenwald, the journalist who brought forward Snowden's findings, also appeared on the program to discuss his reaction to having access to Snowden and his information. Greenwald's recent book, *No Place to Hide: Edward Snowden, the NSA, and the US Surveillance State*, details his journey with Snowden. Journalist Michael Kinsley (a liberal columnist), in a review of Greenwald's book in the *New York Review of Books*, attacked him personally (and others like him), ultimately stating that when it comes to deciding what can be published by the press, "that decision must ultimately be made by the government." Barry Eisler, writing for the Freedom of the Press Foundation, disagreed, noting that many establishment journalists piled on Greenwald and Snowden in agreement with Kinsley, further evidence that the media was more interested in personalities and attacks than substantive discourse and protecting a free press.

The primetime NBC interview was loaded with media spin and

hype. NBC encouraged viewers to tweet their own responses on whether Snowden was a "patriot" or a "traitor." Upon return from each commercial break, NBC's host, Brian Williams, offered clearly slanted perspective and commentary on Snowden's remarks. A panel discussion on NBC's *Meet the Press* framed the Snowden debate in even more negative terms, questioning whether he was a traitor or a criminal. Given the framing and propaganda of the corporate media, in the case of Edward Snowden, more coverage has not necessarily been a good thing. It has been mostly bread and circuses.[13]

Although some do call for prosecution of reporters, many civil liberties organizations continue to recognize the significance of the Snowden reports. In June 2014, the Electronic Privacy Information Center (EPIC) awarded the *Guardian*—the publication in which Greenwald broke the story—the Champions of Freedom Award for their coverage of the issue. As this volume went to press, Greenwald, who is a cofounder of a new online publication called the *Intercept*, stated that he will soon be making public more information from the Snowden files, including a list of whom the NSA targeted inside the US.[14]

As *Censored 2015* was on its way to the publishers, several developments were afoot regarding whistleblowing—some good, some not. Over the past year, Congress has considered several calls for shield laws for journalists. One example, championed by senators Charles Schumer (D-NY) and Diane Feinstein (D-CA) and titled the Free Flow of Information Act, actually attempted to define *who* a journalist was rather than what journalism itself was, a move that clearly challenged the notion of a free press by restricting who was protected as an official journalist. Another example reported by Andrew Taylor at the Associated Press (AP), of an amendment proposed in the House by Representative Alan Grayson (D-FL), "would block the Justice Department from compelling journalists from testifying about confidential information or sources." The House version was broader in its protections than the Senate version, though at time of this publication, no final vote had occurred on a reconciled version. While Congress debated the matter, new organizations formed around whistleblowing and protection of sources like the Freedom of the Press Foundation and ExposeFacts, which is supported by legendary whistleblower

Daniel Ellsberg, who exposed the Pentagon Papers by having them read into the public record. Additionally, Freedom of the Press Foundation worked to maintain late activist Aaron Swartz's creation SecureDrop, which was adopted by the *Guardian* newspaper, among other organizations and publications like the *New Yorker* and ProPublica, as a means by which to protect sources in sensitive stories.

As noted, some of these developments may bode well for protecting whistleblowers, journalists, and their sources of critical information on controversial matters. However, other developments may not. In 2013, it was reported that the Obama administration had spied on numerous AP reporters and James Rosen at Fox News, and a year later, the Supreme Court ruled against the right of journalists to protect their sources in the case of *New York Times* journalist James Risen (not to be confused with Rosen). Regarding the ruling in the case, which involved former CIA officer Jeffrey Sterling as a source of classified information for Risen's 2006 book *State of War: The Secret History of the C.I.A. and the Bush Administration*, Trevor Timm of Freedom of the Press Foundation wrote,

Make no mistake, this case is a direct attack on the press. . . . While the fight for reporter's privilege will certainly continue, and is by no means dead in much of the country, this case is another reminder that reporters can no longer rely on the legal process to protect their sources. Surveillance has become the government's go-to tool for rooting out a record number of sources and chilling all kinds of investigative journalism. Out of the eight source prosecutions under the Obama administration, the Sterling case is the only one where a reporter was called to testify. As an unnamed national security official reportedly once said a year ago, "the Risen subpoena is one of the last you'll see. We don't need to ask who you're talking to. We know."

Those last passages are quite chilling, indeed. The US government is going so far as to liken journalists who claim privilege to protect confidential sources to criminals receiving drugs. But, in the cases of these journalists, the "drugs" they are receiving are often facts showing government corruption and wrongdoing, which would otherwise remain undiscovered. That's a real problem in terms of holding those in power accountable for their actions.

SOURCES:

Glenn Greenwald and Spencer Ackerman, "NSA Collected US Email Records in Bulk for More than Two Years Under Obama," *Guardian*, June 27, 2013, http://www.theguardian.com/world/2013/jun/27/nsa-data-mining-authorised-obama.

"NSA Inspector General Report on Email and Internet Data Collection Under Stellar Wind—Full Document," *Guardian*, June 27, 2013, http://www.theguardian.com/world/interactive/2013/jun/27/nsa-inspector-general-report-document-data-collection.

Glenn Greenwald and Ewen MacAskill, "NSA Prism Program Taps in to User Data of Apple, Google and Others," *Guardian*, June 6, 2013, http://www.theguardian.com/world/2013/jun/06/us-tech-giants-nsa-data.

Paul Harris, "US Data Whistleblower: 'It's a Violation of Everybody's Constitutional Rights,'" *Guardian*, September 12, 2012, http://www.theguardian.com/technology/2012/sep/15/data-whistleblower-constitutional-rights.

Charlie Savage, Alicia Parlapiano, and Sarah Wheaton, "Electronic Surveillance Under Bush and Obama," *New York Times*, June 7, 2013, http://www.nytimes.com/interactive/2013/06/07/us/07nsa-timeline.html.

Eric Lichtblau, "The People We Pay to Look Over Our Shoulders," *New York Times*, February 22, 2010, http://www.nytimes.com/2010/02/23/books/23watchers.html.

Dana Liebelson, "Why is Obama Bashing a Whistleblower Law He Already Signed?," *Mother Jones*, January 10, 2013, http://www.motherjones.com/politics/2013/01/obama-whistleblower-protections-signing-statement.

Glenn Greenwald, "Kiriakou and Stuxnet: The Danger of the Still-Escalating Obama Whistleblower War," *Guardian*, January 27, 2013, http://www.guardian.co.uk/commentisfree/2013/jan/27/obama-war-on-whistleblowers-purpose?INTCMP=SRCH.

Paul Harris, "Barack Obama's 'Extreme' Anti-Terror Tactics Face Liberal Backlash," *Guardian*, February 9, 2013, http://www.guardian.co.uk/world/2013/feb/09/barack-obama-extreme-anti-terror-tactics-liberal-backlash?INTCMP=SRCH.

Ed Pilkington, "Bradley Manning Prosecution to Call Full Witness List Despite Guilty Plea," *Guardian*, March 1, 2013, http://www.guardian.co.uk/world/2013/mar/01/bradley-manning-prosecution-guilty-plea.

Andrea Peterson, "Snowden: I Raised NSA Concerns Internally Over 10 Times Before Going Rogue," *Washington Post*, March 7, 2014, http://www.washingtonpost.com/blogs/the-switch/wp/2014/03/07/snowden-i-raised-nsa-concerns-internally-over-10-times-before-going-rogue.

Glenn Kessler, "Edward Snowden's Claim that He Had 'No Proper Channels' for Protection as a Whistleblower," March 12, 2014, *Washington Post*, http://www.washingtonpost.com/blogs/fact-checker/wp/2014/03/12/edward-snowdens-claim-that-as-a-contractor-he-had-no-proper-channels-for-protection-as-a-whistleblower.

"NBC News Exclusive with Brian Williams: Inside the Mind of Edward Snowden," NBC News, May 28, 2014, http://www.nbcnews.com/feature/edward-snowden-interview/watch-prime-time-special-inside-mind-edward-snowden-n117126.

Glenn Greenwald, *No Place to Hide: Edward Snowden, the NSA, and the US Surveillance State* (New York: Metropolitian Books, 2014).

Michael Kinsley, "Eyes Everywhere: 'No Place to Hide,' by Glenn Greenwald," *New York Review of Books*, May 22, 2014 (online version), http://www.nytimes.com/2014/06/08/books/review/no-place-to-hide-by-glenn-greenwald.html.

Barry Eisler, "Prioritizing Personalities Over a Free Press," Freedom of the Press Foundation, May 27, 2014, https://pressfreedomfoundation.org/blog/2014/05/prioritizing-personalities-over-free-press.

Andrew Taylor, "Reporter Shield Law Backers Sense Momentum after Surprise House Vote," Associated Press, June 3, 2014, http://www.usnews.com/news/politics/articles/2014/06/03/shield-law-backers-sense-momentum-after-house-vote.

Tisha Todd, "Controlling the Flow: Thoughts on the Free Flow of Information Act," *Huffington Post*, September 14, 2013, http://www.huffingtonpost.com/tricia-todd/dismantling-the-first-ame_b_3918368.html.

Ann E. Marimow, "A Rare Peek into a Justice Department Leak Probe," *Washington Post*, May 19, 2013, http://www.washingtonpost.com/local/a-rare-peek-into-a-justice-department-leak-probe/2013/05/19/0bc473de-be5e-11e2-97d4-a479289a31f9_story.html.

James Ball, "*Guardian* Launches SecureDrop System for Whistleblowers to Share Files," *Guardian*, June 5, 2014, http://www.theguardian.com/technology/2014/jun/05/guardian-launches-securedrop-whistleblowers-documents?CMP=twt_gu. For more on SecureDrop, see https://pressfreedomfoundation.org/securedrop.

Trevor Timm, "Supreme Court Rejects Reporter's Privilege Case, as *NYT* Reporter Faces Jail for Protecting his Source," Freedom of the Press Foundation, June 2, 2014, https://pressfreedomfoundation.org/blog/2014/06/supreme-court-rejects-reporters-privilege-case-nyt-reporter-faces-jail-protecting-his.

Censored 2014 #3

Trans-Pacific Partnership Threatens a Regime of Corporate Global Governance

SUMMARY: The Trans-Pacific Partnership (TPP) is a multinational trade agreement involving at least eleven Pacific Rim nations and over 600 corporations worldwide. If passed, it would be the largest trade agreement in history, and it would account for nearly 40 percent of the world's gross domestic product (GDP). Leaked text from the thirty-chapter agreement has revealed that negotiators have already agreed to many radical terms, granting expansive new rights and privileges for foreign investors and their enforcement through extrajudicial "investor-state" tribunals. There is almost no progressive movement or campaign whose goals are not threatened, as vast swaths of public-interest policy achieved through decades of struggle are targeted. Not only would this agreement govern global law on trade between nations, it would also place regulation of issues such as workers' rights, freedom of speech, and financial regulation in the hands of corporate interests. Equally concerning is the fact that all of the TPP negotiations have taken place behind closed doors, without the knowledge of the American public or their elected representatives.

UPDATE: In November 2013, WikiLeaks published the secret negotiated draft text of an entire TPP chapter on intellectual property rights. WikiLeaks' Julian Assange wrote, "If instituted, the TPP's IP [intellectual property] regime would trample over individual rights and free expression, as well as ride roughshod over the intellectual and creative commons. If you read, write, publish, think, listen, dance, sing or invent; if you farm or consume food; if you're ill now or might one day be ill, the TPP has you in its crosshairs." The exposure of this crucial segment of the TPP galvanized public attention on the TPP.

The intellectual property rights chapter showed that the TPP would have significant negative effects on public health for all the nations involved in the treaty. By allowing big pharmaceutical companies to increase drug prices, the TPP would make it even more difficult for people in developing countries to get necessary medicines. For example, by allowing pharmaceutical firms that produce HIV/AIDS drugs to dictate prices and to determine what medicines are available for government health care systems, the TPP would grant multinational corporations the power to supply only the most profitable, proprietary versions of those drugs while barring competitors from marketing inexpensive generic versions of them.

The agreement would also allow corporations to sue a country's government for profits lost due to restrictions on business required by a nation's laws. This includes the right to sue governments for imposing environmental standards that might limit corporate profits.

In June 2012, *Sojourners'* Elizabeth Palmberg released the list of 605 corporations that had official advisors participating in the TPP negotiations. From A to Z, the list read like a directory to the world's largest corporations. Of course, each corporation seeks to influence the representatives involved in negotiating the TPP to include provisions that favor its interests.

Although much of this lobbying is taking place "under the table," the Pharmaceutical Research and Manufacturers of America (PhRMa) and Pfizer are among the leaders in lobbying efforts, with more than forty reports mentioning the TPP. Other disclosures revealed that CitiGroup and Bank of America have sought to bribe the Obama administration's TPP trade negotiators with multimillion-dollar bonuses.

President Obama has recently nominated Robert Hollyman, a former lobbyist for the Stop Online Piracy Act (SOPA), as a TPP lobbyist in hopes of moving the deal forward. As Fang Lee reported, this move is significant because leaked TPP documents "reveal that the US is seeking to resurrect portions of the SOPA bill through the TPP." Lee quoted Susan Sell, a professor of political science at George Washington University, on how the United States seeks to advance intellectual property rules that "could not [be] achieved through an open democratic process."

At the same time, it hardly seems a coincidence that the United States' chief agriculture negotiator on the TPP is a former Monsanto lobbyist, Islam Siddiqui. Monsanto is the leading producer of genetically engineered seeds. The trade documents do not have a separate agriculture section but, as Barbara Chicherio and others have reported, rules affecting food are woven throughout the text. If this trade deal proves successful, countries with genetically modified organism (GMO)–labeling laws such as Australia, New Zealand, and Japan could no longer require that GM foods be labeled as such. Peru, which recently enacted a ten-year moratorium on all GMO plants and foods in order to protect local agriculture and ecological diversity, would arguably be the nation most affected by these proposed restrictions.

As impactful as the Trans-Pacific Partnership would be on the lives of millions of people around the world, it has received almost no coverage in the corporate media. For example, the nonprofit progressive research and information center Media Matters for America undertook a content analysis of weekday evening news programs broadcast from 5:00 P.M. to 11:00 P.M. on CNN, Fox News, MSNBC, ABC, CBS, NBC, and PBS from August 1, 2013, through January 31, 2014. Their research concluded that the three largest cable networks—CNN, MSNBC, and Fox News—had only covered the ongoing negotiations thirty-three times during that time period. Of those thirty-three mentions, thirty-two occurred on just one program, MSNBC's *The Ed Show.* Network broadcasts completely ignored the TPP, while *PBS NewsHour* mentioned it just once. Overall, corporate media have failed to cover the developments of this story.

Meanwhile, the Obama administration and Democrats in Congress have attempted to fast track the TPP, going so far as to change how they refer to it, once the American public began to understand its far-reaching impacts. As Pete Dolack reported for *CounterPunch,*

> The Democratic Party has responded to the resistance against ramming through new trade agreements by giving the process a new name. "Fast track" has been rebranded as "smart-track" and, voilà, new packaging is supposed to make us forget the rotten hulk underneath the thin veneer.

In January 2014, Senate Majority Leader Harry Reid (D-NV) publicly stated his opposition to fast-tracking the TPP. If Reid in the Senate decides not to introduce the bill, then the TPP is virtually dead in the water. However, this would not stop future presidents from pursuing the deal.

For more on the TPP, see *Censored 2015* story #3, "WikiLeaks Revelations on Trans-Pacific Partnership Ignored by Corporate Media," in this volume.

SOURCES:

"Secret Trans-Pacific Partnership Agreement (TPP) - IP Chapter," WikiLeaks, November 13, 2013, https://wikileaks.org/tpp/pressrelease.html.

"How the Trans-Pacific Partnership Would Impact You," Expose the TPP (undated), http://www.exposethetpp.org/TPPImpactsYou.html.

Elizabeth Palmberg, "The Insider List," *Sojourners,* June 29, 2012, http://sojo.net/blogs/2012/06/29/insider-list.

Lee Fang, "Obama Admin's TPP Trade Officials Received Hefty Bonuses from Big Banks," Republic Report, February, 17, 2014, http://www.republicreport.org/2014/big-banks-tpp.

Lee Fang, "Obama Nominates SOPA Lobbyist for TPP Trade Post," Republic Report, February 27, 2014, http://www.republicreport.org/2014/bsa-tpp.

Lee Drutman, "How Big Pharma (and Others) Began Lobbying on the Trans-Pacific Partnership before You Ever Heard of It," Sunlight Foundation, March 13, 2014, http://sunlightfoundation.com/blog/2014/03/13/tpp-lobby.

Eric Zuesse, "Harry Reid Effectively Kills Obama's TPP and TTIP International Trade Deals," OpEdNews, January 30, 2014, http://www.opednews.com/articles/Harry-Reid-Effectively-Kil-by-Eric-Zuesse-Corporate-Accountability_Corporate-Corruption-Crime_International-Trade-Agreements_President-Barack-Obama-POTUS-140130-857.html.

Craig Harrington and Brian Powell, "Study: Media Leave Viewers in the Dark about Trans-Pacific Partnership," Media Matters for America, February 5, 2014, http://mediamatters.org/research/2014/02/05/study-media-leave-viewers-in-the-dark-abouttra/197932.

Barbara Chicherio, "Trans-Pacific Partnership and Monsanto," Nation of Change, June 24, 2013, http://www.nationofchange.org/trans-pacific-partnership-and-monsanto-1372074730.

Pete Dolack, "How the Democrats Re-Branded Fast-Track," CounterPunch, April 25–27, 2014, http://www.counterpunch.org/2014/04/25/how-the-democrats-re-branded-fast-track.

Censored 2014 #14

Wireless Technology a Looming Health Crisis

SUMMARY: As a multitude of hazardous wireless technologies are deployed in homes, schools, and workplaces, government officials and industry representatives continue to insist on their safety despite growing evidence to the contrary. Extensive deployment of "smart grid" technology hastens this looming health crisis.

By now, many residences in the United States and Canada are installed with smart meters—which transfer detailed information on residents' electrical usage back to the utility every few minutes. Each meter has an electronic cellular transmitter that uses powerful bursts of electromagnetic radio frequency (RF) radiation to communicate with nearby meters, which together form an interlocking network. Such information can easily be used to determine individual patterns of behavior based on power consumption.

Utilities sell smart grid technology to the public as a way to "empower" individual energy consumers, allowing them to access information on their energy usage so that they may eventually save money by programming "smart" (i.e., wireless-enabled) home appliances and equipment to run when electrical rates are lowest. In other words, a broader plan behind smart grid technology involves a tiered rate system for electricity consumption that will be set by the utility, to which customers will have no choice but to conform.

UPDATE: Since the publication of "Wireless Technology a Looming Health Crisis" in *Censored 2014*, there have been new reports and studies further supporting the link between wireless technology and health hazards, especially cancers. Highlights of this research are reviewed in *Censored 2015* story #14, "Accumulating Evidence of Ongoing Wireless Technology Health Hazards," in this volume.

Dr. Martin Blank discussed electromagnetic frequencies (or EMFs) and the dangers they pose in his new book published by Seven Stories Press, *Overpowered: What Science Tells Us about the Dangers of Cell Phones and Other WiFi-Age Devices*. For example, *Overpowered* reviews the findings of a study conducted by Dr. Henry Lai and Dr. Narendra Singh. They wanted to know if non-ionizing radiation damages DNA, and specifically whether levels of EMF radiation considered "safe" by government standards had any such effects. Although there were conflicting interpretations of their study's findings, Lai believes there is a cause for concern and that precautionary action is necessary. On EMF damage of DNA, Blank summarized, "The levels of radiation at which Lai and Singh demonstrate this damage are well below the limits set by the current safety standards for technologies like cell phones, WiFi networks, and microwave ovens." In fact, earlier this year the French National Assembly banned WiFi technologies in preschools in their country and they are taking steps to further implement precautionary principles regarding wireless technology, including banning advertisements for WiFi devices that target children.

With many new and exciting applications of wireless technology, companies see opportunities for expansion and profit, while customers are promised *Jetsons*-like conveniences. In January 2014, for example, Google purchased Nest, a "smart home" company, for $3.2 billion. Privacy advocates questioned whether Nest intended to share customer data with Google. Google responded by assuring the public that its existing privacy policy "clearly limits" use of customer information to "providing and improving Nest's products and services."

But, as Jeromy Johnson and Regina Meredith alerted us, convenience comes at a steep price: the loss of privacy. "If you are concerned about privacy and surveillance now," they wrote in a January 2014 article, "wait until everything you own and most of your activities are connected wirelessly to the Internet." As Johnson and Meredith reported, wireless "smart" electrical meters have served as the gateway for allowing EMFs—and companies—into our homes. However, as they also reported, "to the surprise of the utility companies, a global resistance has developed against smart meters." In addition to privacy concerns, this movement also questions smart meters' health effects and whether they will produce the customer savings and environmental benefits that their advocates tout.

For example, in British Columbia, BC Hydro has begun to install smart meters for all of its customers. BC Hydro claims that, after "decades of research," there are no correlations between low-level radio frequency signals and health or environmental risks. According to BC Hydro, its customers should have no concerns about smart meters. BC Hydro consumers are not so sure. For instance, in a letter to the editor of the *Maple Ridge–Pitt Meadows Times*, reader Ron McNutt wrote, "BC Hydro, a government-established electrical monopoly, has without our knowledge or agreement made a material change in the way our electrical usage is monitored and controlled. A previously safe and CSA-approved analog meter is being replaced with the forced imposition of a wireless smart meter of dubious safety, with built-in privacy information and time-of-use billing capabilities."

Customers in both Canada and the United States who have been subjected to the required installation of smart meters have begun to demand the right to opt out. However, many companies force customers who opt out to pay additional charges to do so. In California, for example, Pacific Gas and Electric (PG&E) has begun its conversion to smart meters. PG&E has installed nine million smart meters in northern California, part of a $2.2 billion program. Customers of PG&E have an option to reinstall an analog meter, as the *San Jose Mercury News* reported in 2012, but in order to do so they must pay a one-time $75 fee and an additional charge of $10 per month, on top of the bill for their actual energy use. In August 2013, the PBS *NewsHour* featured a story on opposition to PG&E's smart meters, focused on the community of Fairfax in Marin County. Although PG&E considered the meters noncontroversial "tools of the trade," critics reacted otherwise. The *NewsHour* featured comments from Fairfax residents opposed to PG&E's smart meters, including Mary Beth Brangan, who told PBS, "A lot of people consider it extortion to have to pay to not have something on your house that can harm you." Activists in Fairfax, California, and other communities continue to call for a moratorium on the installation and use of smart meters.

For more on health hazards associated with wireless technology, see *Censored 2015* story #14, "Accumulating Evidence of Ongoing Wireless Technology Health Hazards," in this volume.

SOURCES:

Martin Blank, *Overpowered: What Science Tells Us about the Dangers of Cell Phones and Other WiFi-Age Devices* (New York: Seven Stories Press, 2014).

"France: The Law on Electromagnetic Waves in 5 Questions," Towards Better Health, January 25, 2014, http://mieuxprevenir.blogspot.ch/2014/01/france-law-on-electromagnetic-waves-in.html; this blog links to the original French press article at http://tempsreel.nouvelobs.com/societe/20140123.AFP8260/ondes-electromagnetiques-et-pesticides-en-debat-a-l-assemblee.html.

Marcus Wohlson, "What Google Really Gets Out of Buying Nest for $3.2 Billion," *Wired*, January 14, 2014, http://www.wired.com/2014/01/googles-3-billion-nest-buy-finally-make-internet-things-real-us.

Jeromy Johnson and Regina Meredith, "Smart Meters, The Opposite of Green," *Common Ground*, April 2014, 38–42; available online at http://www.emfanalysis.com/uploads/1/0/7/8/10781272/common_ground_article_april_2014.pdf.

BC Hydro, "Radio Frequency and Smart Meters," (undated), http://www.bchydro.com/energy-in-bc/projects/smart_metering_infrastructure_program/faqs/radio_frequency.html?WT.mc_id=rd_smartmeters_safety.

Ron McNutt, "Letter: Smart Meter Hold-outs Have Their Reasons," *Maple Ridge–Pitt Meadows Times*, letter to the editor, April 2, 2014, http://www.mrtimes.com/opinion/letters/letter-smart-meter-hold-outs-have-their-reasons-1.940882.

Dana Hull, "PG&E Customers Can Opt Out of SmartMeters—for $75, Plus $10 a Month," *San Jose Mercury News*, January 2, 2012, http://www.mercurynews.com/breaking-news/ci_19869073.

"California Activists Want Smart Meters Banned, Claim They're Bad for Health," *PBS NewsHour*, August 27, 2013, http://www.pbs.org/newshour/bb/science-july-dec13-meters_08-27.

Censored 2014 #25

Israel Gave Birth Control to Ethiopian Immigrants Without Their Consent

SUMMARY: In January 2013, after previously denying the allegations, Israel admitted that medical authorities had been giving Ethiopian immigrant women birth control injections without their knowledge or consent. The Israeli Health Ministry's director general, Roni Gamzu, ordered all gynecologists to stop administering the drugs that month. Israeli medical authorities had been injecting the Ethiopian women with Depo-Provera, a highly effective and long-lasting

form of contraception. Ali Abunimah, a writer for the Electronic Intifada, made the case that "this practice may fit the legal definition of genocide." Racism in Israel has made it extremely hard for Ethiopian immigrants to find peace and acceptance in the community. Controversy began in May 2012 when Israeli Prime Minister Benjamin Netanyahu warned that illegal immigrants from Africa "threaten our existence as a Jewish and democratic state."

UPDATE: In March 2014, Israel's Health Ministry director general Roni Gamzu announced that he would resign in June of this year. Israeli news organizations, including the *Jerusalem Post* and *Haaretz*, covered Gamzu's announcement and linked his resignation to a crisis in the management of the Hadassah hospital, but did not mention his role in the forced birth control scandal.

Perhaps because it would raise questions about the practice of forced birth control in the US, American corporate media have not addressed the Israeli case. As the Center for Investigative Reporting documented in July 2013, from 1997 to 2010, at least 148 female prisoners in California were subject to unwanted tubal ligations, a permanent form of birth control. Corey G. Johnson reported that, according to a database of contracted medical services for state prisoners, the state of California paid doctors a total of $147,460 to perform the procedures.

Although it appears that Ethiopian immigrants to Israel are no longer subject to birth control without their knowledge or consent, immigrants from Ethiopia and other African nations continue to endure racist policies intended to maintain Israel as a Jewish state. In December 2013, the Knesset, Israel's legislature, passed a new policy meant to curb illegal migration from Africa. The Entry into Israel Law makes it legal for state authorities to detain immigrants in prison for up to one year; in open facilities, immigrants could be detained even longer.

As David Sheen reported, to protest the new law and their treatment, on December 15, 2013, hundreds of non-Jewish African asylum-seekers left a detention center and refused to return from their twice-daily furloughs. The protesting asylum seekers walked through the desert during a winter storm to reach Jerusalem, where they protested against indefinite incarceration without trial. On December 24, an Israeli court indicted the first group of Sudanese refugees, who had peacefully protested in Jerusalem, in absentia. "In a chilling sign of government-sanctioned dehumanization," Sheen wrote, "the indictment against the accused listed them by number rather than name." Nevertheless, Sheen reported that, "Years from now, historians may look upon the final weeks of 2013 as the beginning of Israel's black civil rights movement."

Hostility toward immigrants is not exclusively the domain of the Israeli government. As shown in David Sheen and Max Blumenthal's short documentary film, *Israel's New Racism: The Persecution of African Migrants in the Holy Land*, many Israelis attack African immigrants, verbally and physically. Defending their actions against charges of racism, Israelis claim that they act to "protect Israel," and if that is considered racist, then they are "proud" to be called that.

SOURCES:

Corey G. Johnson, "Female Inmates Sterilized in California Prisons Without Approval," Center for Investigative Reporting, July 7, 2013, http://cironline.org/reports/female-inmates-sterilized-california-prisons-without-approval-4917.

"Defective Thinking," *America (National Catholic Review)*, March 24, 2014, http://americamagazine.org/issue/defective-thinking.

Lahav Harkov, "Anti-Migration Bill Passes Final Vote in Knesset," *Jerusalem Post*, December 10, 2013, http://www.jpost.com/National-News/Anti-migration-bill-passes-final-vote-in-Knesset-334511.

David Sheen, "Africans Demand Their Freedom in Israel," *Muftah*, December 26, 2013, http://muftah.org/africans-demand-their-freedom-in-israel.

Ami Kaufman, "Photo: In Official Document, Israeli Authorities Refer to Asylum Seekers as Numbers," +972, December 25, 2013, http://972mag.com/nstt_feeditem/photo-in-official-document-israeli-authorities-refer-to-asylum-seekers-as-numbers.

David Sheen and Max Blumenthal, "Israel's New Racism: The Persecution of African Migrants in the Holy Land," *Nation*, October 21, 2013, http://www.thenation.com/video/176762/israels-new-racism-persecution-african-migrants-holy-land.

Censored 2013 #3

Fukushima Disaster Worse than Anticipated
Update by Brian Covert

SUMMARY: Developing evidence from a number of independent sources suggests that the negative consequences of the 2011 Fukushima Daiichi nuclear disaster are far greater than first acknowledged or understood. The Environmental Protection Agency's radiation-detection network (RadNet) has serious drawbacks, including a lack of maintenance and equipment that is often improperly calibrated.

Censored 2013 also featured a chapter, "On the Road to Fukushima: The Unreported Story behind Japan's Nuclear-Media-Industrial Complex" by the author of this summary and update, that looked into the broader historical context of the Fukushima disaster. In that chapter, I showed how Japanese news media played a key role in promoting and advancing nuclear power in the post–World War II era. The chapter spotlighted Matsutaro Shoriki, Japan's first atomic energy commissioner and most influential owner of media companies, and his ties to the US government's Central Intelligence Agency, as well as how the *kisha club* (reporters' club) system, an institutionalized system of press self-censorship in Japan, helps to keep the truth about such crises as the Fukushima nuclear disaster from being fully and accurately reported.

UPDATE: Since last being covered in *Censored 2013*, the crisis at Fukushima has continued to drag on as the government of Japan and the nuclear power plant's operator, the Tokyo Electric Power Company (TEPCO), sought to gain some semblance of control over both the physical decommissioning of the crippled plant and the flow of information to the public about the crisis.

A series of mechanical and human error problems plagued the Fukushima plant in 2013, not the least of which was 400 tons of highly radioactive groundwater leaking daily from the plant and into the nearby Pacific Ocean. In a mantra of sorts that would regularly emanate from the authorities—to be dutifully repeated by Japan's compliant corporate media—such leakage of radioactivity from the Fukushima plant was not officially expected to harm human beings or nature in any way.

In September 2013, Tokyo was chosen to be the site of the 2020 Summer Olympic Games. Seemingly lost in all the celebratory press reporting in Japan was the fact that the Olympic site would be located only about 240 kilometers (150 miles) from the ongoing nuclear crisis at Fukushima.

A couple of months later in November, TEPCO began an unprecedented, highly dangerous operation of transferring about 1,500 fuel rods one-by-one from a Fukushima reactor to a separate storage pool. The operation was expected to take about a year, and if the slightest thing—human error, mechanical failure, forces of nature—went wrong within that year, potentially catastrophic levels of radiation could be released.

It can thus be considered no mere coincidence that right around this same time, the government of Japan also proceeded to ram a vaguely worded "state secrets bill" through its parliament that would, upon becoming law, make whistleblowing a crime of state that could result in a prison term of up to ten years. Any journalist who reported such a state secret could spend up to five years in prison.

The bill was passed into law a month later in December, with the blessing of the administration of US President Barack Obama and despite strong public opposition at home in Japan, as a necessary measure for protecting national security. Technically speaking, if the government of Japan wanted to prosecute a whistleblower or journalist for publicly exposing the sensitive operations at Fukushima, it now had the legal tools to do so.

As the third anniversary of the Fukushima disaster approached in March 2014, the authorities took media matters into their own hands.

TEPCO treated foreign and domestic news reporters alike to tightly controlled press tours of the crippled plant in an attempt to spin news coverage.

Three years after the Fukushima nuclear crisis began, the decommissioning process had barely gotten off the ground, tens of thousands of Japanese evacuees remained stranded in temporary housing, and both the government and TEPCO were moving to cut off compensation payments to victims of the accident. Some evacuees were being officially encouraged to return to their hometowns, despite serious concerns over lingering radiation there.[15]

From the local level in Japan to the international level, institutions were indeed anxious to move on, to put Fukushima behind them, and to regain the appearance of things returning to normal.

Both the International Atomic Energy Agency (IAEA) and the United Nations issued reports in early 2014 on the Fukushima crisis. In its report, the IAEA—headed by Japanese career diplomat Yukiya Amano—praised the quote-unquote "good progress" that it felt Japan had made in getting Fukushima under control, while overlooking much evidence to the contrary.[16] The UN's controversial report downplayed the possible links between the Fukushima accident and future cancer levels, standing in stark contrast to documented cases of rising thyroid cancer rates among children from the Fukushima area.[17]

Citizens in Japan have filed several lawsuits against TEPCO, Japanese government officials, and the manufacturers of the Fukushima nuclear reactors. United States naval personnel filed their own lawsuit against TEPCO in 2012 (and again in 2014). The sailors say they have been suffering extreme health problems ever since the aircraft carrier on which they were serving duty, the USS Ronald Reagan, was exposed to high radioactivity while on a mission offshore from Fukushima in 2011 to help Japanese victims of the earthquake and tsunami.

As of this writing (April 2014), TEPCO is seeking to get the "wholly implausible" lawsuit thrown out of court. The US Navy, for its part, has dismissed the connection between the Fukushima radiation and the health issues of the nearly eighty US service members who have joined the class-action lawsuit—this despite evidence that has recently surfaced showing that some higher-ups in the navy apparently knew at the time that the ship was getting hit by high radiation levels from Fukushima.[18]

This explosive story has been picked by Project Censored and reported by both independent and corporate media in the US and elsewhere. Yet in-depth news coverage of the US sailors' ongoing lawsuit against TEPCO remains largely missing from Japan's corporate-dominated press reporting.

Meanwhile, some persons working in the fields of media, academia, and scientific research in Japan claim to have been pressured by their organizations not to speak or write critically of nuclear power in general and/or Fukushima in particular.[19] In another case, a nuclear industry front group in Japan has reportedly filed a criminal complaint against an independent Japanese journalist/blogger in an attempt to silence her critical writings on Fukushima.[20]

The censoring of school textbooks in Japan has long been a contentious political issue, due to Japanese military atrocities committed during World War II being officially wiped clean from the pages of history books. Now, it seems, Fukushima is facing a similar fate: only one government-approved science textbook scheduled to be used in Japanese primary schools nationwide starting in 2015 includes any reference to the Fukushima nuclear disaster and its aftermath.[21]

For more on Fukushima, see *Censored 2015* story #13, "Lawsuit Challenges Nuclear Power Industry Immunity from Liability in Nuclear Accidents," in this volume.

SOURCES:

Kyle Cleveland, "Mobilizing Nuclear Bias: The Fukushima Nuclear Crisis and the Politics of Uncertainty," *Asia-Pacific Journal* 12, issue 7, no. 4 (February 17, 2014), http://japanfocus.org/-Kyle-Cleveland/4075.

Brian Covert, "Fukushima: An Update from Japan," Project Censored, December 15, 2013, http://www.projectcensored.org/fukushima-update-japan.

"Fukushima Fallout: Ailing US Sailors Sue TEPCO after Exposure to Radiation 30x Higher than Normal," *Democracy Now!*, March 19, 2014, http://www.democracynow.org/2014/3/19/fukushima_fallout_ailing_us_sailors_sue.

David Lochbaum, Edwin Lyman, Susan Q. Stranahan, and the Union of Concerned Scientists, *Fukushima: The Story of a Nuclear Disaster* (New York: New Press, 2014).

Project Censored, "The Project Censored Show on the Morning Mix," KPFA, March 7, 2014, http://www.kpfa.org/archive/id/100729. (Coverage of third anniversary of Fukushima nuclear accident.)

"Nuclear Lobby Still Gagging Independent Coverage Three Years after Disaster," Reporters Without Borders, March 11, 2014, https://en.rsf.org/japan-nuclear-lobby-still-gagging-11-03-2014,45980.html.

Teri Sforza, "Lawsuit: Fukushima Disaster Poisoned US Sailors," *Orange County Register*, April 6, 2014, http://www.ocregister.com/articles/radiation-608614-tepco-navy.html.

SUSAN RAHMAN, MA, is a behavioral sciences instructor at the College of Marin. She is currently researching Palestinian women who resist Israeli occupation. She teaches many courses that focus on differing forms of activism with a goal of social change. She lives in Sebastopol with her partner Carlos, daughter Jordan, and dog Rosie.

BRIAN COVERT is an independent journalist and author based in western Japan. He has worked for United Press International news service in Japan, as a staff reporter and editor for English-language daily newspapers in Japan, and as a contributor to Japanese and overseas newspapers and magazines. He is currently a lecturer in the Department of Media, Journalism, and Communications at Doshisha University in Kyoto.

Notes

1. See *Censored 2014: Fearless Speech in Fateful Times*, eds. Mickey Huff and Andy Lee Roth (New York: Seven Stories Press, 2013), 155–56.

2. For more on media spin, see Stuart Ewen's classic study, *PR!: A Social History of Spin* (New York: Basic Books, 1996). For an overview of the ways that establishment media distort news coverage, see Michael Parenti, "Monopoly Media Manipulation," May 2001, http://www.michaelparenti.org/MonopolyMedia.html.

3. "NBC News Exclusive with Brian Williams: Inside the Mind of Edward Snowden," May 28, 2014, http://www.nbcnews.com/feature/edward-snowden-interview/watch-primetime-special-inside-mind-edward-snowden-n117126; and Peter Hart, "Meet the Press Snowden Debate: Traitor or Criminal?" Fairness and Accuracy in Reporting, June 2, 2014, http://www.fair.org/blog/2014/06/02/meet-the-presss-snowden-debate-traitor-or-criminal/?utm_source=rss&utm_medium=rss&utm_campaign=meet-the-presss-snowden-debate-traitor-or-criminal.

4. See, for example, Glenn Greenwald, "Kiriakou and Stuxnet: The Danger of the Still-Escalating Obama Whistleblower War," *Guardian*, January 27, 2013, http://www.guardian.co.uk/commentisfree/2013/jan/27/obama-war-on-whistleblowers-purpose?INTCMP=SRCH.

5. See, for example, Zoe Carpenter, "A Grim Report on Press Freedoms Under Obama," *Nation*, October 10, 2013, http://www.thenation.com/blog/176586/grim-report-press-freedoms-under-obama; and Leonard Downie Jr. and Sara Rafsky, "The Obama Administration and the Press: Leak Investigations and Surveillance in Post-9/11 America," Committee to Protect Journalists, October 10, 2013, http://www.cpj.org/reports/us2013-english.pdf. See also Brian Covert, "Whistleblowers and Gag Laws," *Censored 2014*, 65–84.

6. "Glenn Greenwald's Partner Detained at Heathrow Airport for Nine Hours," *Guardian*, August 18, 2013, http://www.theguardian.com/world/2013/aug/18/glenn-greenwald-guardian-partner-detained-heathrow.

7. Michael Calderone, "Glenn Greenwald: 'Meet The Press' Interview Validates 'Incestuous' Washington Media Critique," *Huffington Post*, June 24, 2013, http://www.huffingtonpost.com/2013/06/24/glenn-greenwald-meet-the-press_n_3491290.html.

8. Katherine Fung, "Glenn Greenwald Reacts To Pulitzer Prize," *Huffington Post*, April 20, 2014, http://www.huffingtonpost.com/2014/04/20/glenn-greenwald-pulitzer-reliable-sources_n_5182297.html.

9. In fact, the United Nations Universal Declaration of Human Rights affirms freedom of the press as a *trans*-national right: "Everyone has the right to freedom of opinion and expression;

this right includes freedom to hold opinions without interference and to seek, receive and impart information and ideas through any media and regardless of frontiers." See Article 19, 1948, http://www.un.org/en/documents/udhr/index.shtml#a19.

10. For coverage of additional organizations engaged in these efforts, see chapter 4 of this volume. See also the Freedom of the Press Foundation, pressfreedomfoundation.org; and the new whistleblowing organization, ExposeFacts, exposefacts.org.

11. When *Censored 2014* went to press, Manning had not yet publicly stated the wish to be known as Chelsea. Thus, although *Censored 2014* refers to Bradley Manning, following her wishes, we use Chelsea Manning here.

12. WikiLeaks, "Collateral Murder," April 5, 2010, https://wikileaks.org/wiki/Collateral_Murder,_5_Apr_2010; see also CollateralMurder.com, http://www.collateralmurder.com.

13. By contrast, over the past year, daily news broadcasts by Abby Martin of Russia Today's *Breaking the Set* and Amy Goodman of *Democracy Now!* provided some of the best independent coverage regarding the ongoing war on whistleblowers and journalists.

14. There are additional controversies surrounding Glenn Greenwald's work, the creation of the *Intercept*, and his financial backer, Pierre Omidyar of eBay. Omidyar's financial ties to establishment types and the Democratic Party, as well as his involvement in the Ukraine and his interests in various political issues, have some people questioning how the *Intercept* may differ from other private media outlets. Some whistleblowers like Sibel Edmonds and Kevin Ryan question the motives and how they affect Greenwald's delay of the release of more Snowden files, while others question whether or not Snowden was a government operative on a disinformation campaign. When this volume went to press, questions about First Look Media and the *Intercept*, Greenwald's funders, and Snowden's intentions, while important to note and ask, were based on circumstantial and speculative claims. Time will tell what influence Omidyar has over what is published at the *Intercept*, and we should all remain vigilant when examining sources of information, even (perhaps especially) if we are inclined to trust and agree with them.

15. "Withholding of Radiation Readings Exposes Gov't Push for Evacuees' Return," *Mainichi*, March 27, 2014, http://mainichi.jp/english/english/perspectives/news/20140327p2a00m0na009000c.html.

16. Greg Webb, "IAEA Delivers Final Report on Decommissioning Efforts at Fukushima Daiichi," International Atomic Energy Agency, February 13, 2014, http://www.iaea.org/newscenter/news/2014/decommissioning.html. The full IAEA report can be viewed and downloaded from this page.

17. "The Fukushima-Daiichi Nuclear Power Plant Accident: UNSCEAR's Assessment of Levels and Effects of Radiation Exposure Due to the Nuclear Accident after the 2011 Great East-Japan Earthquake and Tsunami," United Nations Scientific Committee on the Effects of Atomic Radiation, April 2, 2014, http://www.unscear.org/unscear/en/fukushima.html. The full UN report can be viewed and downloaded from this page. See also Teruhiko Nose and Yuri Oiwa, "Thyroid Cancer Cases Increase Among Young People in Fukushima," *Asahi Shimbun*, February 8, 2014, http://ajw.asahi.com/article/0311disaster/fukushima/AJ201402080047.

18. See Kyle Cleveland, "Mobilizing Nuclear Bias: the Fukushima Nuclear Crisis and the Politics of Uncertainty," *Asia-Pacific Journal*, February 17, 2014, http://japanfocus.org/-Kyle-Cleveland/4075. For the US Department of Defense's official radiation registry on this issue, see "Operation Tomodachi Registry," https://registry.csd.disa.mil/registryWeb/Registry/OperationTomodachi/DisplayAbout.do.

19. Tomoko Otake, "Barakan Says Broadcasters Told Him to Avoid Nuclear Issues Till after Poll," *Japan Times*, January 22, 2014, http://www.japantimes.co.jp/news/2014/01/22/national/barakan-says-broadcasters-told-him-to-avoid-nuclear-issues-till-after-poll/-.UozR5yi3Q0U; and Tomoko Otake, "Scholar Quits NHK over Nuclear Power Hush-up," *Japan Times*, January 30, 2014, http://www.japantimes.co.jp/news/2014/01/30/national/scholar-quits-nhk-over-nuclear-power-hush-up/-.UozRaCi3Q0U. See also David McNeill, "Concerns Over Measurement of Fukushima Fallout," *New York Times*, March 16, 2014, http://www.nytimes.com/2014/03/17/world/asia/concerns-over-measurement-of-fukushima-fallout.html?_r=0.

20. "Nuclear Lobby Still Gagging Independent Coverage Three Years after Disaster," Reporters Without Borders, March 11, 2014, https://en.rsf.org/japan-nuclear-lobby-still-gagging-11-03-2014,45980.html.

21. "Fukushima Accident Mentioned in Only 1 Elementary School Science Textbook," *Asahi Shimbun*, April 20, 2014, http://ajw.asahi.com/article/behind_news/social_affairs/AJ201404100036.

CHAPTER 3

Mea Culpa, Mi Amore

Sorry for all the Junk Food News and News Abuse . . . Now Here's Some More

Nolan Higdon and Mickey Huff, with contributions by Lauren Freeman, Alexandra Blair, Bryan Reid, Sam Park, Crystal Bedford, Emilee Mann, Daniel Mizzi, Jess Lopez, Josie Ensley, Jessica Sander, and Darian Keeps

The myth of the "information society" is that we're drowning in knowledge . . . but it's easier to propagate ignorance.

—Robert N. Proctor, *Agnotology: The Making and Unmaking of Ignorance*[1]

INTRODUCTION: FORGET CELEBRITY APOLOGIES AND THE MALAYSIAN AIRLINER, WHERE'S THE NEWS?

For years, news industry people would tell Project Censored founder Dr. Carl Jensen that his criticisms were unfair and that the news was not censored. They argued that there was only a limited amount of space, of column inches in print, and that television news had a limited amount of the precious commodity of time. So, Jensen decided to start looking more at what the corporate media *did* spend their precious time and space on, and thus discovered a lot of what he called "Junk Food News"—Twinkies for the brain—or, the irrelevant, trivial stories corporate media cover at the expense of good journalism.

Fifteen years later, the second Project Censored director, Dr. Peter Phillips, noticed that some stories started out as legitimate news stories, but the way in which they were covered took away from the significance of the topics. This category was known as News Abuse—the framing or distortion of information for propagandistic purposes. Both Junk Food News and News Abuse have become commonplace in televised news media and the print press. In fact, new terms have emerged over the years to describe the shifting phenomena away from hard news reporting. The blurring of the lines between news and entertainment is referred to as "infotainment," while the increase in opinion-based reporting, designed to spin information and influence audiences, has been referred to as "Spinfluence."[2]

After the dawn of 24/7 cable news coverage in the 1980s, one could not really ask for more time or space. Jensen then described an emerging problem of news inflation. The more time there was for news, the less it was worth, and the content providers for news programming seemed to provide just that—less in terms of quality in content. For decades, the corporate news media have wasted that time reporting on many things unimportant to the American citizenry (e.g., Brittany Spears's exploits, Brangelina, keeping up with the Kardashians, faux controversies involving Muppets, and on and on). This past year, CNN demonstrated masterfully how to waste precious airtime. If they weren't too busy following Miley Cyrus's jostling posterior (and Katy Perry dissing her tongue), or reporting on the latest antics of Justin "bad boy" Bieber, they clearly became addicted to coverage of a Malaysian Airliner that went missing with its passengers in March 2014. While the missing airliner was tragic news at that moment, when compared to celebrity claptrap, it was hardly breaking news months later as CNN provided endless coverage of the affair. At one point, CNN even interrupted their program *Reliable Sources*, which had already addressed the missing plane, for a Breaking News segment about debris found in the Indian Ocean. Soon, CNN learned there *was* debris in the ocean, but not from a plane: it was simply trash (fishing gear and some dead jellyfish, among other things). Instead of covering the issue of pollution in the seas, or gyres, or its overall impact on the food chain, CNN simply concluded, Oh, it's just junk, now back to our regularly scheduled program of Junk Food/News Abuse, *Reliable Sources*, which had already been discussing the missing plane.[3] How's that for reliable? While CNN continued to ask 'round the clock, "Where's the plane?" many Americans were left to ask, "Where's the news?"

STATE OF THE SNOOZE

According to several studies, the state of where the news is, and where it appears to be heading, is troublesome. On March 12, 2014, CNN spent 256 of its 271 minutes of broadcast time with computer models and children's educational television personality Bill Nye the Science Guy to locate the missing plane, live, on air.[4] The whereabouts of that plane, as this volume went to press, were still not known. Meanwhile, as Nye fielded questions about the plane, independent journalists covered a) how the European Union voted to protect the Arctic by protecting the area around the North Pole, b) a report that found that, in 2013, Wall Street executives took home as much money as 1,085,000 Americans who work full time, and c) that the federal government views its ability to hack the computers of all United States citizens as progress.[5] As for those media critics who claimed to Carl Jensen that they did not censor, but, rather, employed news judgment: if that's the case, this is some pretty bad judgment.

That said, in its quest to cover all things irrelevant, CNN sadly did not stand alone. Their coverage of the missing airliner was only seventeen minutes fewer than MSNBC's coverage of the bridge scandal that saw New Jersey Governor Chris Christie allegedly closing the heavily trafficked George Washington Bridge to punish a New York politician's lack of support for Christie's reelection campaign (with a repeated dash of Christie's history of bullying people in public just for good measure).[6] Similarly, Fox News covered the GOP-created "Benghazi Scandal" for more than sixteen hours, running at least 225 segments on it over a two-week period.[7] In each of these cases, no conclusions were found, nothing emerged, other than the fact that the stories would be rehashed, retold, and recycled while other news went unreported.

However, this did not seem to go unnoticed in the viewing public. The corporate news fad of ad nauseam coverage of the irrelevant appears to be having a negative effect on the industry. A study by the Pew Research Center's Journalism Project, the Project for Excellence in Journalism, found that the Millennials (18–31 years old) are half as likely to watch television news as the Silent generation (67–84 years old).[8] The numbers continue to drop. All the cable news outlets show that the majority of their viewers are 62–68 years of age, with CNN boasting the "youngest," Fox the oldest.

According to the Pew Research Center's State of the Media 2014 report, "A year ago, the State of the News Media report struck a somber note, citing evidence of continued declines in the mainstream media that were impacting both content and audience satisfaction . . . many of these issues still exist, some have deepened and new ones have emerged."[9] The Pew study continues to note that their "first-ever accounting found roughly 5,000 full-time professional jobs at nearly 500 digital news outlets, most of which were created in the past half dozen years. The vast majority of bodies producing original reporting still come from the newspaper industry. But those newspaper jobs are far from secure. Full-time professional newsroom employment declined another 6.4% in 2012 with more losses expected for 2013."[10] Conglomeration and consolidation also grew at the local level, including in television, which likely contributed further to this trend.

The study also showed a decline for cable television, with TV still being the most go-to medium for news in the US: "The combined median prime-time viewership of the three major news channels—CNN, Fox News, and MSNBC—dropped 11% to about 3 million, the smallest it has been since 2007."[11] As Americans have continued to tune out on cable, network news showed some increase in viewers, though among NBC, CBS, and ABC, only a collective twenty-two million of Americans tuned in—a paltry sum in a nation of three hundred million people.[12] For instance, during CNN's nonstop coverage of the Malaysian plane, it had the lowest ratings for its 9:00 P.M. slot in its entire history.

Another notable issue with all network and cable news is not only that they are corporate owned (90 percent of media in the US is owned by six corporations), but that they all parrot establishment party views, particularly on economic and foreign policy matters. Fox is to the Republicans as MSNBC is to Democrats, and CNN keeps trying to catch up in what appears to be a race to the journalistic bottom. This is clearly a propaganda contest, not actual journalism.

Speaking of journalism, according to previous Pew polls, last year Americans saw PBS as the most "fair" and the most trusted of any major news network. However, is PBS really that much different than the other private networks? Perhaps not. Earlier this year, the Corporation for Public Broadcasting (CPB) asked that PBS reveal that they are not exactly "funded by viewers like you." In fact, about half of PBS's revenue comes from the private sector and is referred to as "underwriting," a clear euphemism for "advertising" if ever there was one.

According to David Sirota, the major program *PBS NewsHour* is actually mostly privately owned and produced by Liberty Media, and has been for twenty years. It is worth noting that the CEO of Liberty is a very politically active, right-wing billionaire. Perhaps that explains the two studies done by Fairness and Accuracy in Reporting from 2006 and 2010, which found the ratio of Republican/conservative to Democratic/liberal guests on *NewsHour* at 2–1 and 3–2 respectively, with only 4 percent of guests representing the public interests. Earlier this year, Liberty stated they would be "giving" the *NewsHour* over to PBS, but it is still unclear how many millions of public dollars went to the for-profit Liberty Media and their conservative CEO, under the auspices of supporting "public" broadcasting, despite calls from the CPB demanding transparency in such affairs. So much for PBS being the most "trusted" or "fair" source.[13] The real problem is that so many Americans still seem to believe such propaganda, which contributes to an overall intellectual decline in the populace, particularly regarding civic affairs.

It wouldn't be an update on the status of the news media without mentioning the late night jesters on Comedy Central, who are neither journalists nor newscasters. This doesn't stop America from tuning in to Jon Stewart and Stephen Colbert for more infotainment. According to a recent survey by the Brookings Institution and the Public Religion Research Institute, Jon Stewart's show is considered more trustworthy than MSNBC overall. In another study by the Annenberg Public Policy Center at the University of Pennsylvania, researchers found that in the last presidential election, Americans learned more about issues like campaign finance reform from Stephen Colbert than from MSNBC, CNN, Fox News, or broadcast evening news. Another study from 2012 showed that Americans that watched *The*

Colbert Report were more knowledgeable about facts regarding public affairs than those that watched Fox News. It says something about the poor state of journalism and news when Americans trust comedians over professional reporters at the major networks. And in the end, the joke is on us, while the corporate media owners laugh all the way to the bank.[14]

On a positive note, nonprofit media, such as ProPublica, showed the most gains. And, others are waiting to see what happens with other private ventures like First Look Media's the *Intercept*, which includes muckraker-styled journalists like Glenn Greenwald and Jeremy Scahill, though concerns persist regarding the interests and political ties of their funder, Pierre Omidyar of eBay. Time will tell, but one thing is for certain—Americans are turning away from corporate news (under which PBS is, increasingly, more appropriately categorized), and so the time is ripe for the growth and expansion of truly independent free press alternatives.

DUMB AND DUMBER, TOO, A REAL BUMMER

Nonsense is nonsense, but the history of nonsense is scholarship.

—Robert N. Proctor, *Agnotology*

At Project Censored, an ongoing concern that has emerged in past versions of this chapter is how the rise of Junk Food News and News Abuse may be connected to anti-intellectualism and a decline in overall public knowledge concerning world affairs and basic facts. The old axiom "garbage in, garbage out" can portend tragic trajectories for purportedly self-governing societies. Many scholars have addressed these issues over the years, and Project Censored has referred to many of their works, from Daniel Boorstin's *The Image* (1962) to Neil Postman's *Amusing Ourselves to Death* (1985), from Chris Hedges's *Empire of Illusion* (2009) to Morris Berman's *Why America Failed* (2011). And from Susan Jacoby's *The Age of American Unreason* (2008) to Robert Proctor's *Agnotology* (2008), the cultural production of ignorance, or nonsense, as Proctor claimed in the quote above, is a serious problem that requires serious scholarship and open discussion if we are to reverse the tide. Here is how C. J. Werleman of AlterNet described a sampling from a recent Gallop Poll on American ignorance and nonsense in action: 42 percent of Americans still believe God created human beings in their present form less than 10,000 years ago; the Carsey Institute at the University of New Hampshire published a study showing that only 28 percent of Tea Party Republicans trust scientists; and more than two-thirds of Americans, according to surveys conducted for the National Science Foundation, are unable to identify DNA as the key to heredity. Further, nine out of ten don't understand radiation and what it can do the human body, while one in five adult Americans believe the sun revolves around the Earth. A 2008 University of Texas study found that 25 percent of public school biology teachers believe that humans and dinosaurs inhabited the earth simultaneously. "This level of scientific illiteracy provides fertile soil for political appeals based on sheer ignorance," wrote Susan Jacoby in *The Age of American Unreason*.[15]

The expansion of Junk Food News and News Abuse presents a new dynamic to the problems facing educators of media literacy, which entails the competency to analyze and evaluate media stories and outlets. Faux news is a part of this cultural production of ignorance that a republic can scarcely afford, and it attacks the foundation of critical thinking that is integral to rational self-governance. Not only is the public uninformed as a result of watching Junk Food News, but it is also misinformed due to ubiquitous News Abuse stories, which further produce an ignorant populace.

Project Censored continues to collect these Junk and Abuse stories every year in order to draw awareness to the negative effects on viewers who consume it. This year's collection of stories demonstrates why turning off the corporate media and paying close attention to independent, transparently sourced journalism is crucial to those who want to be informed.

Project Censored is sorry to present its yearly report on the Junk Food News and News Abuse, though we continue to do so in order to document the continued problems with corporate news, and to draw attention to the independent journalists unearthing relevant stories that could and should be widely reported instead.

JUNK FOOD NEWS FROM 2013–14

Junk is the ideal product . . . the ultimate merchandise. No sales talk necessary. The client will crawl through a sewer and beg to buy.[16]
—William S. Burroughs in *Naked Lunch*

Almost thirty years after Carl Jensen coined the term Junk Food News,
Project Censored juxtaposes the corporate media fodder with the
more relevant stories covered by the independent press. The result is
a document of how the endless coverage of Justin Bieber's drunken
escapades, the location and victims of a twerking Miley Cyrus, or John
Travolta's inability to read a prompter at the Oscars distracted viewers
from relevant stories such as Amazon's $600 million contract with
the Central Intelligence Agency (CIA) to provide cloud computing
services and masses of personal data, or the true funding and politics
behind the Veterans Affairs Bill. What follows is merely a sampling
and analysis of some of the lowlights of Junk Food News of the past
year. If we were to try to cover it all, it would take the remainder of the
pages of this book. By chapter's end, we think our point will be clear
enough.

We begin with corporate media's fixation on the endless parade of
celebrity apologies for ignorant bigotry. The corporate media oft make
out on the ratings charts when exploiting the idiocy and misfortune
of others, and the endless stream of celebrity ignorance and public
relations–fueled apologies provided a field day to would-be journalists. Most celebs turned these politically incorrect infractions (a.k.a.
hate-laden, bile-spewing incidents) into PR stunts for their own individual careers (how enlightening being a bigot can be), while corporate media went on a feeding frenzy from one inane racial slur or
homophobic slight to the next. The media rarely stopped long enough
for the apologies to drip out of the offensive mouths that espoused
them before hungrily seeking the next fool in Hollywood's epithet
drivel parade.

Can a simple mea culpa erase the history behind such ignorance,
or the pain and injustice created? Or might it normalize this kind of
thoughtless behavior? Hey, these celebs apologized in the corporate
media, the very same media that also highlighted (even sought) their

indiscretions, thus creating a mutually beneficial cycle for some at the expense of many. Bigger questions not asked—is this really news? Should it be hyped or ignored? Is it Junk or News Abuse? Regardless, it has been a rising trend over the past decades, and we offer a sampling of the bigot's platter and more from this year's Junk Food News buffet. Corporate media unapologetically love a good mea culpa story for celebrity bad behavior. And for that, we're sorry.

All Apologies Tour: Celebrity Mea Culpas for Bigotry Big News

This past year, multiple celebrities quickly added the art of public apology to their acting repertoires in hopes their abounding verbal gaffes and indiscretions—which were actually racist and homophobic quips and slurs—would be quickly forgotten, or better, show that they were all contrite, upstanding, understanding, empathetic folks taking one for the cause, likely the one they just denigrated with their foul performances. Before long, the PR teams and lawyers swooped in to counsel the guilty figures in question by suggesting public apology as the route to go after being overheard making vile, hateful, and insulting statements. Of course, this apologetic PR blitz technique has been employed by many celebrity actors including Mel Gibson and Michael Richards, as well as former bicycling medalist Lance Armstrong, pro golfer Tiger Woods, rapper Kanye West, and government officials from President Bill Clinton and Secretary of Defense Robert McNamara, to former New York governor Elliot Spitzer and Newt Gingrich, and a gaggle of others that truly make a sorry lot.

This past year brought us news media with a fetish for catching a fresh batch of famous individuals saying politically incorrect things, then waiting for the requisite public apology, with ample room for discussion, debate, derision, and deconstruction about what it means for people's careers in between. It turns out that it means little, but for media coverage and celebrity PR, it's a gold mine. It is the news cycle story that keeps on giving. The corporate media and their contracted paparazzi bottom feeders hunted down soon-to-be regrettable offenders and then cover the ensuing apologies. The apologies are more a reflexive reaction by celebrity figures, after which they oft get

off with a finger wagging for their bad behavior, while some even generated their own social media bigotry pity parties. This corporate coverage of apology-ridden celebrities comes at the expense of covering more relevant news, and acts as a distraction from the root cause of such remarks in the first place, namely ignorance.

Going back to June 2013: celebrity apologies, and their distant cousin "clarification," stole the spotlight from other, more important stories. Starting with an appetizer that runs through to the dessert of celebrity apologies, the television personality and kitchen recipe guru Paula Deen found herself sued by former employees who alleged she had made racist statements at work.[17] Deen confirmed she had made the statements, but said she did not "hate" African Americans.[18] However, she admitted that she had used "the N-word" in past jokes.[19] The comment left many thinking that Paula Dean's apology was: Sorry, I'm a junk food eating racist, and more of this Junk Food News is what's on the menu.

As a result of the lawsuit, the corporate media covered how Deen's corporate backers were ending their relationship with her. The companies included Food Network, Smithfield Foods, Walmart, Target, QVC, Caesars Entertainment, Home Depot, J.C. Penney, Sears, Kmart, her publisher Ballantine Books, and the diabetes drug company Novo Nordisk—which depends on her down home fattening cooking to keep the diabetes illness expanding.[20] Deen's apology tour was covered endlessly by the corporate press, which included her February 2014 "comeback" at the South Beach Wine and Food Festival. There, Deen offered the ultimate meta mea culpa when she said, "If anybody did not hear me apologize, I would like to apologize to those who did not hear me."[21]

A few months later, actor Michael Douglas was a victim of giving too much oral sex to his wife, Catherine Zeta-Jones. "Without wanting to get too specific, this particular cancer is caused by HPV, which actually comes about from cunnilingus."[22] The corporate media went ablaze covering the comments by Douglas. While Dr. Marc Siegel argued that Douglas's comments had some validity, Douglas offered a clarification:[23] "I think we would all love to know where our cancer comes from. I simply, to a reporter, tried to give a little PSA announcement about HPV . . ."[24] This public service announcement just happened to sound like the tall tales emanating from a junior high school locker room, and the corporate press ate it up, but for public health purposes, no pun is intended.

The corporate coverage of Deen and Douglas came at the expense of stories more relevant to the viewing public. In the same month as Douglas's PSA, Edward Snowden's historic leaks, the CIA's reaction to cover up the leaks, and the military's effort to block their personnel from reading the files was not covered widely as the corporate media were busy on the celebrity apology tour.[25] Also at the same time that home-cooked Southern racial slurs and murmurs of carcinogenic cunnilingus filled the American airwaves and citizens minds, the US was quietly deploying troops to Egypt.[26]

In November 2013, Alec Baldwin was suspended from his MSNBC show for homophobic slurs directed toward a photographer. Baldwin allegedly yelled an extremely offensive homophobic command for fellatio from a gay man, as an insult and attack. Baldwin did not go for the direct apology: he first claimed that he had not uttered the anti-gay slur, that he'd said "fathead." He later conceded, "Words are important. I understand that, and will choose mine with great care going forward. Behavior like this undermines hard-fought rights that I vigorously support."[27] Behavior like this, indeed.

Just prior to the Baldwin episode, the corporate media focused on exposing the relationship fallout from the MTV Video Music Awards (VMA) performances, but the cause of this would be one of growing fascination for corporate media for months to come. Pop star Miley Cyrus and her boyfriend broke up in part due to the VMA twerking performance. The corporate media happily covered the handwritten apology from Cyrus to her boyfriend.[28] However, Cyrus was not the only one involved in the twerking scene who performed an apology. By May 2014, pop star Robin Thicke, Cyrus's twerkee at the VMA, performed a begathon in response to being separated from his wife Paula Patton. Thicke's apology included a song dedicated to getting her back titled "Lost Without U."[29] During the Baldwin and Cyrus coverage, corporate media could have covered the fifty million people whose access to food in the US was endangered by federal budget cuts, or could have explained that the resumption of US drone strikes in Pakistan killed not only a Taliban chief, but the hopes of halting the drone program amid cries that such strikes often kill many innocents.[30]

In December 2013, when former South African President Nelson Mandela died, US President Barack Obama attended the funeral. He took the opportunity to take a selfie—a photo taken by one of the people in the photo—at the funeral with other world leaders. The corporate media, sensing an Obama apology for said media-highlighted gaffe, waited for him to repent. The *New York Post* demanded Obama apologize.[31] However, Obama did not apologize. In fact, the only apology came from the photographer who took the photo of the leaders taking a selfie. He stated, "I took these photos totally spontaneously, without thinking about what impact they might have."[32] Indeed, the public witnessed a meta-apology from a nonthinking photographer in place of a thoughtful explanation from world leaders regarding actions that resembled those of disrespectful, adolescent fools. Better yet, it would have been nice for Obama to apologize for the CIA and US involvement in the arrest of a young Mandela in 1962 in the first place.

Before any undue fretting, the reader will be pleased to know the corporate media did fulfill its apology coverage quota the same month that Obama didn't apologize, when *Duck Dynasty* star Phil Robertson was suspended from his A&E program *Duck Dynasty*.[33] The corporate media quickly uncovered the reason for his suspension—his description of what was sinful during a *GQ* interview: "Start with homosexual behavior and just morph out from there. Bestiality, sleeping around with this woman and that woman and that woman and those men."[34] Then to clarify his comment he added homosexuals with a seemingly random assortment of others arguing, "We just love 'em, give 'em the good news about Jesus—whether they're homosexuals, drunks, terrorists. We let God sort 'em out later, you see what I'm saying?"[35] The corporate media was on hand for his response, which stated, "However, I would never treat anyone with disrespect just because they are different from me. We are all created by the Almighty and like Him, I love all of humanity. We would all be better off if we loved God and loved each other."[36] It sounds like there is some incongruity in Robertson's remarks. Perhaps God can help sort 'em out.

Instead of focusing on Robertson, who was possibly using the incident to generate publicity for his show and a possible Republican office run (he was spouting his nonsense in *GQ*, after all, where it would clearly be seen), the corporate media could have focused more on the hundred-city tour for a livable wage by workers.[37] They also could have covered how fifty-two-year-old Guantánamo Bay detainee Ibrahim Idris testified about the systematic torture in the facility, or they could have covered how the 2010 Gulf of Mexico oil spill has been linked to dolphin death and disease.[38] Instead, the corporate media were more interested in giving Robertson a sensationalist boost, keeping all their Ducks and Dynasties in a row, and a predictable one at that.

The start of 2014 showed that it would be another mea culpa New Year as the corporate media would continue to cover apologies at the expense of relevant news. In January 2014, New Jersey Governor Chris Christie was said to have knowingly allowed staffers to close down the George Washington Bridge in September 2013. The closure was political payback to Democratic mayor of Fort Lee Mark Sokolich, who had endorsed Christie's gubernatorial opponent the year prior.[39] Christie's "apology" focused on shifting the blame from himself—"I am outraged and deeply saddened to learn that not only was I misled by a member of my staff, but this completely inappropriate and unsanctioned conduct was made without my knowledge"—as he removed the staffers said to be involved.[40] Republican-leaning Fox News basically ignored the scandal—because it negatively affected a Republican—while Democrat leaning MSNBC supplied near 'round-the-clock coverage of the scandal—because it negatively affected a Republican.[41] By March 2014, Christie said apologies were off the table because his lawyers told him he had been cleared.[42] But for the corporate media, the topic of apologies was all that was on the table, whether they were forthcoming or not, promised, or even unnecessary.

While the Christie fodder poured from the corporate press like digital diarrhea, more relevant stories went uncovered. During Christiegate, important new studies showed that nearly half of Americans live paycheck to paycheck, and we learned that more crude oil spilled from train wrecks in 2013 than the previous four decades combined.[43] Corporate media could also have covered how Congress vigorously passed a bill to hide US drone strikes from the public.[44] We can only assume they are sorry for not doing so. The only way the corporate media might notice their own shortcomings is if they covered their own apology tour.

In April 2014, the corporate media hit the gold mine of apology opportunites as then owner of the National Basketball Association team the Los Angeles Clippers, octogenarian Donald Sterling, was recorded on the phone telling his thirty-one-year-old girlfriend, "It bothers me a lot that you want to broadcast that you're associating with black people . . . you don't have to have yourself with, walking with black people."[45] Sterling was allowed the same opportunity as many other celebrities to apologize, which was still a distraction from relevant news, as with previous offenders. However, when Sterling appeared on CNN's *Anderson Cooper 360*, his apology included the statement, "Jews, when they get successful, they will help their people—and some of the African Americans, maybe I'll get in trouble again and they don't want to help anybody."[46]

To those listening, it may have *seemed* like Sterling said: "Sorry, I was alive when racism was acceptable, so, I don't know what else to say." Instead of covering Sterling's Archie Bunker–like perspective and non-apology apology, which is only newsworthy to a point, the corporate media could have covered how the chairman of the Federal Communications Commission (FCC), former telecom lobbyist Tom Wheeler, was working to kill net neutrality by supporting the dismantling of equal access to the Internet, allowing so-called "fast lanes," so that companies can pay more money to get faster service at the expense of those who cannot afford it.[47] If that wasn't enough, media viewers would have learned a lot more if corporate media told them that, twice in two days, the US authorized drone strikes in Yemen, killing forty people. Or that US drone strikes have killed over 2,400 people in the past five years, including upward of 950 innocent civilians, close to 200 of whom were children.[48] There will likely be no apologies regarding these latter matters, unless they involve a celebrity gaffe, or a twerking pop star.

In June 2014, the corporate media treated audiences to the apology of actor Jonah Hill. He sought forgiveness on Jimmy Fallon's *The Tonight Show* for a video TMZ picked up, which showed Hill strongly suggest to a paparazzi photographer, in quite vulgar terms, that he perform fellatio on him, addressing him with a derogatory term for a gay man.[49] Fallon praised Hill for his bravery to apologize on air only to mock him the following night to laughter. Also in June 2014, corporate media put pressure on already beleaguered pop star Justin Bieber to apologize for a 2009 video that showed him making racists comments and joking about being in the Ku Klux Klan.[50] *Mea culpa.* Now that's infotainment.

And Now in Other Junk Food News: Twerking across the Red Line

In August 2013, headlines covered the anger, shock, and disgust of Americans. What could it be? The widening income gap? Sluggish economic recovery? Climate change? New drone strikes in several countries killing civilians? NO! It was Miley Cyrus's performance at the MTV Video Music Awards. Cyrus's dance routine, known as twerking, with fellow performer Robin Thicke singing his hit "Blurred Lines," was seen as provocative and caused quite a stir.[51] Corporate media followed the outrage head to tail, literally, but not just because of ensuing apologies as previously noted. *The New York Times* called it "trickster-esque" and claimed, "apparently nobody has said 'no' for the last 6 months or so [to Cyrus]."[52] CNN reported that MTV gave Cyrus airtime to respond to all the "hate" she received for her indiscretion while twerking in public on a married man.[53] *The Washington Post* asked, "But what exactly is so disturbing about Miley Cyrus?"[54]

While Cyrus's twerking dominated the headlines, Robin Thicke's father reminded the world, "[By the way,] they're killing people with chemical weapons in Syria."[55] The statement has some truth considering that while the corporate media fought for a scoop on Cyrus's posterior, they ignored that the Obama administration had overstated its certainty that the Syrian government had crossed "a red line" and used chemical weapons on its citizens.[56] The Syrian story was released shortly after *Foreign Policy* wrote about CIA documents that proved the US had helped Iraq use chemical weapons in the Iraq–Iran War of the 1980s.[57] While Cyrus's bottom worked its way to the top of the corporate news, these same outlets missed an opportunity not only to cover the history of US hypocrisy on chemical weapons, but also the empowering story of Vermont activists who shut down a nuclear power plant in response to its environmental and health impacts on the local populace.[58] However, instead of reporting more on these stories, the corporate media were all about twerking. We rhetorically ask, who is the ass?

Bad Boy Bieber: Delivering Headlines Only the NSA Could Love

Despite the enormity of the government spying issue related to Edward Snowden and the National Security Administration (NSA)—which undermines the Constitution through a complex set of programs that have yet to be widely covered in the corporate media—these same outlets still found time to cover pop star Justin Bieber's antics. From racing up and down his street and annoying neighbors to having obnoxious parties, bad boy Bieber grabbed headlines with his too cool to care demeanor.

During an interview about the NSA in spring 2014 with former US Congresswoman Jane Harman (D-CA), MSNBC cut away for "breaking news." The "news" was that Justin Bieber would be appearing before a judge for a charge of driving under the influence (DUI).[59]

Fox News had followed suit earlier in the month, declaring a "Fox News Alert" when Bieber turned himself into the police for an assault charge.[60] Breaking news? The momentous questions regarding privacy and spying in the digital age, issues of national security, and the war on terror were placed on hold for what Americans really needed to know—Bieber's in trouble! There was even a petition that received over 100,000 signatures (and major media coverage) to deport Bieber back to his native land—Canada. Meanwhile, more in-depth discussion about civil rights and NSA spying got lost in the dust of Bieber's yellow Lamborghini joyride.

CIA Barbie: An Unapologetic Campaign

In February 2014, Mattel, the creators of Barbie, released a picture of the famed doll in a black and white one-piece swimsuit with "unapologetic" scribbled underneath the plastic icon.[61] The picture made the cover of *Sports Illustrated*'s fiftieth-anniversary swimsuit edition.[62] Both Fox and ABC News covered this less than historic moment in human history with feature spots.[63] The image was a response to the long-standing controversies surrounding Barbie as Mattel has found itself fighting off criticism from feminist groups who claim that the doll distorts young girls' views of themselves (it surely has been proven to be anatomically distorted, but Mattel doesn't seem to bother with that).[64] To combat the accusations, Mattel came out with a line of over 150 career Barbies that do everything from architecture to veterinary work. According to Fox, Mattel has had enough of trying to placate everyone, so it has started what is being called the Unapologetic Campaign.[65]

While that debate raged in the corporate media about whether or not Barbie—a plastic doll, an inanimate object—should join the previously noted celebrity apology tour, the same corporate media ignored the collusion between big business and government that resulted in widespread wanton spying on the American people. They ignored an independent news story that had a headline (during the Barbie coverage), "Amazon Poised to Help Obama Assassinate US Citizen?" The story explained that Amazon—the online sales giant owned by Jeff Bezos, who recently bought the *Washington Post*—has a $600 million contract with the CIA to provide cloud computing services and masses of personal data.[66] Maybe it was a job for CIA Barbie—at least that way the corporate media could work the with the Amazon story. Similarly, in late February 2014, Common Dreams reported, "With a program codenamed 'Optic Nerve,' the documents reveal how the [National Security] agency hacked into the camera feeds of those using Yahoo! webchats, capturing both snapshots of conversations and metadata associated with the communication."[67] However, Americans who debated Barbie via Skype while shopping on Amazon remained ignorant of who was watching and collecting their data, what they might do with it, and how that was more important than the Unapologetic PR Campaign for a toy.

Republicans Let it Go: Travoltafying Veteran Affairs

In March 2014, the 86th Academy Awards, an event held once a year to celebrate the stars of the Hollywood film industry and award them for their artistic excellence, were held in Los Angeles, California. The corporate media lay in wait to cover both the evening's red carpet rides and also the possible celebrity gaffes. John Travolta delivered big with his epic mispronunciation of Broadway and *Glee* actress Idina Menzel's name, calling her the wickedly talented "Adele Dazeem" as he introduced her to millions before she performed her song "Let it Go," from the hit movie *Frozen*. Indeed, while Menzel was wickedly talented, Travolta was wickedly embarrassing as a professional actor who can't read a prompter and didn't care enough to bother to read her name in advance. Is this really newsworthy? No. But that didn't stop the corporate media as they ridiculed Travolta with headlines such as "John Travolta's Flub on Idina Menzel's Name," while online sites sprouted like wild to "Travoltify" one's name.[68] In response to public pressure, Travolta publicly apologized and sent a bouquet of flowers to Menzel.[69] The apology was a must-see media event for many Americans. We are still waiting for the media to send those flowers to the public, however, as an apology for such epic failures in news judgment. Perhaps we should simply Let it Go.

While the corporate media entertained viewers with Hollywood elites, US Military Veterans continued to lose benefits. During the Travolta coverage, corporate media ignored that Senate Republicans blocked the passage of the Veterans Affairs Bill, which grants veterans quality health care and education opportunities.[70] The Republicans offered to consider its passage in exchange for tougher sanctions on Iran; thus, veterans' health and educational benefits were seen as an opportunity to gain Republican political points.[71] However, a potential discussion about the importance of funding veterans was sidelined while the media worked to embarrass Travolta . . . who has been embarrassing himself since the disco days of *Saturday Night Fever*.

If only Travolta would mangle the Syrian leader Bashar al-Assad's name while Miley twerks on him in the driver's seat of Bieber's yellow Lamborghini while on an apology tour for Barbie . . . maybe then the corporate media would pay attention to serious world affairs, US involvement and complicity in them, and how they affect the rest of us.

NEWS ABUSE AS PROPAGANDA

When a well-packaged web of lies has been sold gradually to the masses over generations, the truth will seem utterly preposterous and its speaker a raving lunatic.

—Dresden James, British novelist

Project Censored continues to track News Abuse stories reported in the corporate media, as they have become more plentiful over the years. They represent the ongoing propaganda efforts of corporate media owners and government elites. This past year, there were many such stories that revolved around old themes from the Cold War that resembled an "us vs. them" mode of thinking. From US and North Atlantic Treaty Organization (NATO) policy regarding Syria, Ukraine, Russian resistance, double standards on civil liberties, and so-called free trade, it was a year ripe with News Abuse propaganda.

In 2013–14, the corporate media in the US resurrected a Cold War frame of reporting while examining stories about spying, free speech, and the invasion of sovereign nations—all involving foreign policy, the Middle East, Russia, and US/NATO interests. Corporate media rehashed and rekindled old stereotypical fears and distracted Americans from the hypocrisy and problems with US policy by focusing on "the other," by demonizing foreign leaders, and by attempting to blatantly rewrite history and selectively apply international law. There was a lot to report in terms of News Abuse, and what follows is merely a sampling, a best of the worst of the ongoing propaganda campaigns that masquerade as journalism. It would make an interesting movie—spies vs. spies, shooting the messenger, Cold War intrigues and propaganda volleys, international trade secrets, and conspiracies for global power. If only it were actually fiction.

Shooting the Messenger: The Tale of Edward Snowden

In 2013, Edward Snowden, a former analyst for the CIA and the NSA, released documents detailing the extent of covert surveillance operations and data collection both in the United States and abroad. The documents revealed that the NSA was spying on American citizens and those of both enemy and ally countries, buying user data from private companies with US tax dollars, and developing an increasingly important role in US targeted drone killings overseas.[72] These leaks revealed that Director of National Intelligence James Clapper lied when he had testified to Congress that the US did not collect data on its citizens "wittingly." Similarly, they showed that NSA Director General Keith Alexander lied when he assured journalists: "No one has willfully or knowingly disobeyed the law or tried to invade your civil liberties or privacy."[73]

The documents further revealed a myriad of violations of constitutionally protected rights, especially against free speech protected under the First Amendment and privacy granted under the Fourth Amendment.[74] The documents revealed various ways in which government agencies could evaluate individuals who speak out against the system. Current tactics include using social media to launch online "reputation-destruction campaigns," targeting individuals seeking access to agency-flagged websites including WikiLeaks and the anonymous web browsing service TOR, and posing as fake Facebook servers to inject malware capable of covertly taking over microphones and webcams on personal computers.[75]

Rather than investigate and expose the government officials and the complicit politicians, the corporate media attacked Snowden for exposing the crimes. Bob Schieffer has worked with CBS since 1969 and now hosts their Sunday morning talk show *Face the Nation*. In June 2013, Schieffer said Snowden "Is No Hero."[76] On his August 11, 2013, broadcast, Schieffer welcomed former NSA Director Michael Hayden, Republican congressman Peter King, and Democrat Dutch Ruppersberger as guests to discuss Snowden. All three opposed Snowden's leak.[77] Since the panel included both a Republican and a Democrat, Scheiffer's charade was meant to carry the illusion of fairness (false balancing), yet both party representatives have been outspoken in favor of government surveillance. And it is difficult to imagine a larger conflict of interest than Hayden's position as former NSA director and his current partnership in the Chertoff Group—a corporation that profits from government surveillance contracts.[78]

The corporate media have fed into the government's bogus claim of Snowden being a traitor with headlines such as "Traitor or Hero?"[79] Article III in the US Constitution notes, "Treason against the United States, shall consist only in levying war against them, or in adhering to their enemies, giving them aid and comfort. No person shall be convicted of treason unless on the testimony of two witnesses to the same overt act, or on confession in open court."[80] Despite the fact Snowden has committed nothing resembling the Constitution's version of treason, the corporate media made it sound like a crime with *Meet the Press* host David Gregory declaring Snowden guilty and suggesting that journalist Glenn Greenwald, who reported on the leaked materials, "aided and abetted" Snowden, a treasonous enemy. Gregory asked Greenwald, "Why shouldn't you be charged with a crime?"[81] Gregory later contended that to classify Greenwald's work as journalism was somehow debatable.[82] Gregory's questions set an insidious precedent for so-called mainstream outlets by reframing NSA spying into a discussion of Greenwald's bona fides as a journalist. Gregory was doing what the corporate media seem to do best—shooting the messenger.

While the media debated Snowden's legal status, the implications of the government's crimes were repackaged as nonexistent by the corporate press. CBS's *60 Minutes* ran a piece on the NSA, hosted by John Miller, whose opening statement necessitated full disclosure:[83] Miller was previously a Federal Bureau of Investigation (FBI) spokesman and a high-ranking official in the Office of the Director of National Intelligence. The piece allowed NSA Director Keith Alexander to suggest the agency's activities were minimal. Alexander redundantly refuted claims that the NSA was collecting Americans' email and phone records, a blatant lie that escaped Miller's crippled scrutiny.[84] News outlets virtually ignored the criminality of colorful death threats Snowden received from various public officials.[85]

Debate about the legality behind Snowden's actions effectively silenced all else in order to justify US spying. For example, there was a media blackout of Snowden's candid live interview from Germany.[86] The interview featured a poised Snowden eloquently discussing the scope and implications of the documents he shared with Greenwald. Though independent journalists have made attempts to link to the video, many hosts have been forced to take it down and were targeted with distributed denial of service (DDoS) attacks.[87] When it comes to the Snowden leaks in the US, shooting the messenger involves firing rounds layers deep.

Chemical Imbalance: Obama's Red Line in Syria

The end of August 2013 had all major media sources playing the same headlines: chemical weapons had been used in Syria. After years of an ongoing civil war in Syria, on August 21, sarin gas was used in a town on the outskirts of Damascus.[88] According to the Organisation for the Prohibition of Chemical Weapons, the last time chemical weapons were used on the similar scale was in Iraq in 1988, which led to the international ban of all chemical weapons.[89] The question in Syria was, who used the weapons? Was it President Bashar al-Assad's military attacking its own civilians? Or was it rebels trying to draw international attention to Syria's civil war?

The United States targeted President Assad's regime for culpability. US Secretary of State John Kerry claimed that Assad's regime had caused the deaths of 1,429 people, including over 400 children.[90] Many members of Congress began to doubt the total, claiming that the death toll was inflated.[91] The Associated Press stated that an organization that monitors deaths in Syria had confirmed 502 deaths,

barely a third of what US officials stated.[92] Regardless of the death toll, Obama's administration was certain that it was Assad's regime that had used chemical weapons, even though there was no definite evidence.

As the corporate media braced itself for war coverage in Syria, President Obama mused about a missile strike on Syria without congressional approval.[93] Meanwhile, the corporate media beat the war drums. In an interview on *Fox News Sunday*, the *Weekly Standard* editor and conservative pundit William Kristol stated that America has to go to war because Syria has crossed Obama's red line.[94] *The Washington Post* stated that if chemical weapons were used, then there needed to be "direct US retaliation against the Syrian military forces responsible."[95] The national media watchdog group Fairness and Accuracy in Reporting (FAIR) surveyed all of the major broadcasting channels between August 21 and September 10. Results of the survey showed that there was nearly a two-to-one ratio of pro-war broadcasting.[96]

Congress failed to muster the support for an invasion, and many antiwar protestors spoke out against proposed attacks on Syria. Meanwhile Russian President Vladimir Putin stepped up to propose a diplomatic response to the affair. Even with US invasion off the table, the media continued to have guests pushing US opinion in support of an invasion. After initially calling for Obama to seek congressional support before an attack, Fox News host Sean Hannity bashed Obama for turning to Congress.[97] Former Secretary of Defense Donald Rumsfeld spoke out to many different media sources, criticizing "the so-called commander-in-chief" for not invading.[98] Somewhere, lost in the fog of war propaganda, were the emerging facts as reported by Seymour Hersh (and others) that Assad was not responsible for the gas attacks after all. British intelligence proved this after sampling the sarin gas, which they determined could not be from Assad, and the US joint chiefs helped persuade Obama to hold off on strikes.[99] Of course, the corporate media did not report on this matter, and Obama did not admit this to the public. The only red lines crossed were those of irrationality. Fortunately, in this case, critical thinking prevailed and the pro-war propaganda of the corporate media failed.

Olympic Medals for Hypocrisy: Spying vs. Spying

The twenty-first century government spying by the United States and Russia offered corporate media an opportunity to seriously address the issue and its public implications. Instead, in a stark example of News Abuse, the corporate media railed against Russian surveillance at the Sochi Olympics while justifying broad spying programs in the US. They also ignored or downplayed the revelations of former National Security Agency contractor Edward Snowden and the *Guardian*'s Glenn Greenwald who reported on the matter (discussed previously in this chapter).[100] At the same time, corporate media reported without question establishment attacks on Snowden.

President Obama claimed, "I don't think Mr. Snowden was a patriot."[101] A defense department strategy memo for destroying whistleblowers explained, "Hammer this fact home. . . . Leaking is tantamount to aiding the enemies of the United States."[102] Former CIA director James Woolsey advocated that Snowden be hanged if found guilty.[103] Former US ambassador to the UN John Bolton took a similar position arguing that Snowden "[o]ught to swing from a tall oak tree."[104]

The corporate media relentlessly reiterated the government's message. The editorial board of the *Washington Post* published an op-ed suggesting Snowden surrender himself.[105] *Gawker's* Hamilton Nolan facetiously stated, "Take note, potential leakers and whistleblowers inside the US government: the official stance of the *Washington Post's* editorial board is that you should shut up and go to jail."[106] Greenwald accused MSNBC talk show hosts of bias and said they were "desperate to distract attention away from [the NSA] disclosures."[107]

While spying was denied or defended in the US, and those who reported on it were attacked, the same standards were not extended overseas. Russia, host of the 2014 Winter Olympics in the city of Sochi, implemented extensive security measures purportedly to ensure the safety of every individual attending the events. This was particularly in response to two suicide bombings that had taken place in Volgograd one month before the opening ceremonies, incidents that sparked a panic regarding the safety and security of the town.[108] In response to comments made regarding unfit Sochi hotel accommodations, Dmitry Kozak admitted to having obtained surveillance of hotel occupants turning on their showers and allowing them to run all day.[109]

Instead of defending Russia's need for surveillance the same way they had done for the US, the same corporate media lambasted the Russian government for spying. The conservative news and opinion website the *Daily Caller* reported that in Sochi, Russia was "using spy cameras installed in hotel bathrooms and showers."[110] ABC News titled an article "The Other Sochi Threat: Russian Spies, Mobsters Hacking Your Smartphones."[111] Professor Ron Deibert stated, "The scope and scale of Russian surveillance are similar to the disclosures about the US programme but there are subtle differences to the regulations."[112] Owen Matthews of *Newsweek* claimed, "The 2014 Sochi Olympics have become a giant testing ground for some of the most intensive, extensive and intrusive electronic surveillance operations ever mounted."[113] NBC made up a story, later proven false if not impossible, that claimed visitors would be hacked the moment they landed in Russia.[114]

The media blitz against Russian spying during the Olympics was especially hypocritical considering that both the *Wall Street Journal* and the United States Computer Emergency Readiness Team (US-CERT), a division of the Department of Homeland Security, admitted that the US had spied on people attending the 2002 Olympics in Salt Lake City, Utah.[115] The Olympic coverage served to make Americans feel good about their government, and their "freedom," by criticizing Russia for doing what corporate media refused to cover about the US government—earning a Gold Medal performance for maintaining Olympic double standards.

Do as We Say, Not as We Do: Parroting the Establishment on Ukraine

The corporate media further abused its power in 2013–14 by acting as a microphone rather than a critic of US relations with Ukraine. In 2013, protests in the sovereign nation of Ukraine by citizens against the ruling class became visible.[116] The corporate media lauded the underdog story of the Ukrainian people rising up to overcome what was increasingly referred to as a corrupt and extravagant regime under ousted president Viktor Yanukovych.[117] Corporate media parroted the official narrative, failing to ask important questions regarding US involvement in Ukraine and further polarizing tensions with Russia.

The first sign of US involvement in the Ukraine protests came from a BBC report that found an audio recording of US Assistant Secretary of State Victoria Nuland and US Ambassador to the Ukraine Geoffrey Pyatt discussing a new government in Ukraine, on which a voice, which appears to be Nuland, says to Pyatt, "Fuck the EU."[118] She was expressing her impatience with lack of European Union action regarding Ukrainian resistance to the current pro-Russian president. Although US officials have neither confirmed nor denied the legitimacy of the tape, Nuland held a press conference apologizing for the remarks.[119] Rather than focusing on the implications of US involvement in the Ukraine protests, the *New York Times* referred to the recordings as part of an "increasingly Cold War-style contest."[120]

Corporate media continued to parrot US politicians after Russia began its 2014 incursion into Eastern Ukraine in what was a rapidly developing and complex affair. Kerry appeared on NBC's *Meet the Press* in response to Russia's move and stated that "this is an act of aggression that is completely trumped up in terms of its pretext. It's really nineteenth-century behavior in the twenty-first century."[121] MSNBC host David Gregory allowed these remarks to stand unchallenged rather than drawing the obvious parallels between Russian military actions in Ukraine and the United States invasions of Iraq, Afghanistan, Libya, and Syria, among others, in the twenty-first century. Silence on this hypocrisy is a form of support by the corporate media for US/NATO involvement in Ukraine (like the silence of the corporate media of the illegality under international law of the coup in Kiev).

Most corporate news outlets in the US have also ignored incriminating evidence suggesting that some members of the new Ukrainian government had neo-Nazi ties, and instead sensationalized and reframed the conflict to pit the US against Russia.[122] Like the original Cold War—which, it seems, may never have ended—the war is not "cold" for the Ukrainian people. While Russia's actions are routinely scrutinized and their president demonized for "invading a sovereign nation," the corporate press ignore that the US has admittedly pumped more than $5 billion into the Ukraine to make sure the outcome is favorable to US interests.[123] In fact, the post-coup Ukrainian interim leader, Arseniy Yatsenyuk (whom Nuland affectionately referred to as "Yats"), was handpicked by Nuland and the State Department, and the president elected after the coup, Petro Poroshenko, was referred to as "our insider" by the US State Department, WikiLeaks documents revealed. He was seen as a vehicle to work Ukraine into NATO at the behest of then Secretary of State Hillary Clinton. This is probably why the US dumped billions of dollars into the Ukraine in recent years, for a favorable outcome, which seems to have paid off for US and Western powers at the expense of the people of Ukraine.[124]

The News Abuse was so bad in the Ukraine coverage that US media actually had the audacity to condemn the Russian media coverage of the invasion of a sovereign nation. This led to a propaganda war on the airwaves. The Russian government funds the news network Russia Today (RT), which has been called the propaganda arm of Russia in the US.[125] RT has many shows, but one stood out—a daily program on what media in the US doesn't cover called *Breaking the Set*. Host Abby Martin[126] was hailed by the US corporate media shortly after Russia's 2014 incursion into Ukraine for saying on her show, "I can't stress enough how strongly I am against any state intervention in a sovereign nation's affairs. What Russia did was wrong. . . ."[127]

RT reporter Liz Wahl went further and quit RT on the air to protest Russian policy (perhaps a coy move to attract future employers as a PR stunt).[128] Fox, CNN, and NBC lauded the anchors for challenging Russia.[129] However, the praise was short-lived once Martin criticized US media for not responding to the Iraq invasion the way she responded to Ukraine. Martin noted that in "the lead-up to the Iraq War, [US media was] parroting exactly what the establishment said."[130] Martin's claim is widely supporting. The media watchdog group Fairness and Accuracy in Reporting found that, in the weeks leading up to the US–Iraq War, "viewers were more than six times as likely to see a pro-war source as one who was anti-war" which resulted in 68 percent of US citizens supported the war under false pretenses.[131]

While many in US corporate media trashed RT for being propaganda, they scarcely noted complicity in their own and the problem of self-censorship. Martin also noted, "The corporate media [have] fired multiple anchors for simply speaking out against the Iraq War." This is corroborated by the removal of Bill Maher's long-running show *Politically Incorrect* from ABC after 9/11, and the canceling of MSNBC's *Jesse Ventura's America* and *The Phil Donahue Show* prior to the Iraq War, and numerous others cases, like the firing of Peter Arnett from both NBC and CNN.[132] Entire books have been written and documentary films made on the matter. Martin's comments about the US were a rare case of having the corporate media's News Abuse called out on its own turf. In terms of US TV news, Martin was truly breaking the set.[133]

TPP is MIA

The Trans-Pacific Partnership (TPP), which made it into the top five of the twenty-five most censored stories in *Censored 2014*, has smoothly transitioned into News Abuse. The TPP is a proposed trade agreement between the US and several other countries resulting in the largest one of its kind in history. Meant to act as an economic counterweight to China, the TPP evolved into something that includes China in the future. The negotiations have lacked public participation though some 600 corporations are involved. As a result of corporate negotiations and inspiration from previous trade agreements such as NAFTA, the TPP would increase corporate-controlled courts that would enable corporations to challenge environmental, health, and worker safety laws, among other things.[134]

The coverage of TPP by the corporate press has been sparse and incomplete. A Media Matters study of nightly network and cable news found that the TPP was covered only thirty-four times in the six-month period, thirty-two of the instances were on MSNBC's *The Ed Show*, making it the only show to offer routine coverage of the matter, while CNN and the PBS *News Hour* each covered the TPP once.[135] Print outlets such as the *New York Times* gave TPP scant coverage.[136] Some attention came when ABC reported on a letter, signed by several celebrities, urging trade negotiators to ban the hunting of dolphins in Japan in the TPP.[137] However, the implications and reality of the TPP were not expressed clearly. The next day, Common Dreams reported that more than 550 organizations have petitioned in opposition to the presidential fast-track authority to pass the TPP without congressional approval, while another fifty groups want to end the TPP negotiations altogether.[138] In 2014, *Huffington Post* reported that the deal would include calls for more fracking and off-shore drilling.[139]

While corporate media ignored or obfuscated the TPP negotiations, other journalists uncovered major elements of corruption. *Republic Report* found that the current US trade representative for TPP, Michael Forman, and Under Secretary for International Trade nominee Stefan Selig have received multimillion-dollar bonuses for quitting their jobs at investment banking firms to join the negotiations.[140]

The Cato Institute, a libertarian organization that is for free trade, has repeatedly reported on the areas of sovereignty that will be lost if the TPP is passed, including matters surrounding net neutrality.[141] The World Socialist Web Site found that the agreement is aimed in part to limit China's access to supplies from Malaysia, should a war break out with the US.[142] All in all, the TPP sounds like another too big to fail, too big to jail development that shifts democratic governance, national sovereignty, and the interests of the global public far below the interests of the transnational corporate/capitalist class, and should be reported upon and scrutinized far more than it has been to date.

CONCLUSION

There is opportunity to expose these things [misinformation and disinfor-
mation] through good journalism, good pedagogy, good scholarship. You
need an educated populace.[143]

—Robert N. Proctor

It's been thirty years since Project Censored founder Carl Jensen started chronicling and analyzing Junk Food News, nearly half that time since Peter Phillips broadened the study with News Abuse, and we continue in that tradition. Given the near ubiquity of these issues, and their troublesome historical trajectory, it is almost impossible to ignore them. In 1995, Carl Jensen wrote,

> [S]ince we will all benefit from a more responsible media, we all really should help bring it about. To do this, the corporate media owners should start to earn their unique First Amendment privileges. Editors should rethink their news judgment. Journalists should persevere in going after the hard stories. Journalism professors should emphasize ethics and critical analysis and turn out more muckrakers and fewer buckrakers. The judicial system should defend the freedom-of-the-press provision of the First Amendment with far more vigor. And the public should show the media it is more concerned with the high crimes and misdemeanors of its political and corporate leaders than it is with the crimes and gossip of celebrities. The effort will be well worth it.[144]

Twenty years later, we couldn't agree more. While we are sorry to have to continue writing about such affairs, we do so knowing that, as Carl Jensen put it, "we will all benefit from a more responsible media." We have high hopes that the many independent journalists and civic organizations that continue in this common struggle to create a better and more informed global society will achieve increased success with each passing year. We at Project Censored would have no apologies if one day our efforts were no longer needed in that struggle. Until then, we march on, together.

NOLAN HIGDON is an adjunct professor of history at numerous colleges in the San Francisco Bay Area. He was previously a student intern with the Project, and is now a faculty advisor for Project Censored.

MICKEY HUFF is the director of Project Censored; professor of social science and history at Diablo Valley College where he cochairs the history area; and is co-host with Dr. Peter Phillips of *The Project Censored Show*, which is syndicated and airs on Pacifica Radio.

LAUREN FREEMAN, ALEXANDRA BLAIR, BRYAN REID, SAM PARK, CRYSTAL BEDFORD, EMILEE MANN, DANIEL MIZZI, JESS LOPEZ, JOSIE ENSLEY, JESSICA SANDER, and DARIAN KEEPS are student interns with Project Censored.

Special thanks to Nolan Higdon's Diablo Valley College, San Ramon Campus, "Critical Reasoning in History" class, Spring 2014; and to Mickey Huff's Diablo Valley College "Critical Reasoning in History" classes from Fall 2013 and Spring 2014.

Notes

1. Robert N. Proctor and Londa Schiebinger, eds., *Agnotology: The Making and Unmaking of Ignorance* (Stanford: Stanford University Press, 2008), ch. 1; see also Michael Hiltzik, "Cultural Production of Ignorance Provides Rich Field for Study," *Los Angeles Times*, March 9, 2014, http://articles.latimes.com/2014/mar/09/business/la-fi-hiltzik-20140307. Thanks to Dr. Rob Williams for the source.

2. For a recounting of the development of Junk Food News, please see Carl Jensen, *Censored: The News That Didn't Make the News—and Why* (Chapel Hill NC: Shelburne Press, 1993), 89–96. See also Carl Jensen and Project Censored, *Censored 1994* (New York: Four Walls Eight Windows, 1994), 142–43; Jensen added to this sentiment in "Junk Food News 1877–2000," as chapter 5 in *Censored 2001*, ed. Peter Philips (New York: Seven Stories Press, 2001), 251–64; Since *Censored 2010*, the Junk Food News and News Abuse chapter has been chapter 3 of each volume: in *Censored 2010: The Top 25 Censored Stories of 2008–09*, eds. Peter Phillips and Mickey Huff (New York: Seven Stories Press, 2009); Mickey Huff and Frances A. Capell, "Infotainment Society: Junk Food News and News Abuse for 2008/2009" in *Censored 2011*, eds. Mickey Huff and Peter Phillips (New York: Seven Stories Press, 2010); "Manufacturing Distraction" in *Censored 2012: Sourcebook for the Media Revolution*, ed. Mickey Huff (New York: Seven Stories Press, 2011); "Framing the Messengers" in *Censored 2013: Dispatches from the Media Revolution*, eds. Mickey Huff and Andy Lee Roth (New York: Seven Stories Press, 2012); "American Idle: Junk Food News and News Abuse and the Voice of Freedumb" in *Censored 2014: Fearless Speech in Fateful Times*, eds. Mickey Huff and Andy Lee Roth (New York: Seven Stories Press, 2013); "U Can't Touch This: Junk Food News and News Abuse Is off the Infotainment Charts!" For more on "Spinfluence," see Nick McFarlane, *Spinfluence: The Hardcore Propaganda Manual for Controlling the Masses* (Great Britain: Carpet Bombing Culture, 2013).

3. Catherine Taibi, "CNN Interrupts Its Own Show to Report that Objects Found in Ocean Might Just Be Trash," *Huffington Post*, March 30, 2014, http://www.huffingtonpost.com/2014/03/30/cnn-missing-plane-coverage_n_5059203.html?ncid=fcbklnkushpmg00000018.

4. Dorsey Shaw, "CNN Spent an Insane Amount of Time Covering Missing Flight 370 Wednesday Night," BuzzFeed, March 13, 2014, http://www.buzzfeed.com/dorsey/cnn-spent-an-insane-amount-of-time-covering-missing-flight-3.

5. Jacob Chamberlain, "EU Votes to Save the Arctic," Common Dreams, March 12, 2014, http://www.commondreams.org/headline/2014/03/12-7; Sarah Anderson, "Wall Street Bonuses and the Minimum Wage," Institute for Policy Studies, March 12, 2014, http://www.ips-dc.org/reports/wall_steet_bonuses_and_the_minimum_wage; Ryan Gallagher and Glenn Greenwald, "How the NSA Plans to Infect 'Millions' of Computers with Malware," *Intercept*, March 12, 2014, https://firstlook.org/theintercept/article/2014/03/12/nsa-plans-infect-millions-computers-malware.

6. Dorsey Shaw, "Breaking Down Minute-By-Minute Cable News' Coverage of the Chris Christie Bridge Scandal," BuzzFeed, January 9, 2014, http://www.buzzfeed.com/dorsey/breaking-down-minute-by-minute-cable-news-coverage-of-the-ch.

7. Emily Arrowood, "REPORT: Fox's Nonstop Benghazi Coverage Is a $124 Million Boon for the GOP," Media Matters, June 3, 2014, http://mediamatters.org/blog/2014/06/03/report-foxs-nonstop-benghazi-coverage-is-a-124/199547.

8. Andrew Khohut, "Pew Research Surveys of Audience Habits Suggest Perilous Future for News," PEW Research Center, October 4, 2013, http://www.pewresearch.org/fact-tank/2013/10/04/pew-surveys-of-audience-habits-suggest-perilous-future-for-news.

9. Pew Research Journalism Project, "State of the News Media 2014," Pew Research Center, March 26, 2014, http://www.journalism.org/2014/03/26/state-of-the-news-media-2014-overview.

10. Ibid.

11. Pew Research Journalism Project, "Key Indicators in Media and News," Pew Research Center, March 26, 2014, http://www.journalism.org/2014/03/26/state-of-the-news-media-2014-key-indicators-in-media-and-news/.

12. Joshua Krause, "Death Throes: The Mainstream Media Is Hanging on by a Thread," The Daily Sheeple, June 2, 2014, http://www.thedailysheeple.com/death-throes-the-mainstream-media-is-hanging-by-a-thread_062014; Hadas Gold, "May Cable News Ratings Spare No One," *Politico*, May 29, 2014, http://www.politico.com/blogs/media/2014/05/may-cable-news-ratings-spare-no-one-189393.html; David Swanson, "Limits of MSNBC," *War is a Crime*, May 25, 2014, http://warisacrime.org/content/limits-msnbc.

13. David Sirota, "After Pledging Transparency, PBS Hides Details of New Deal with Billionaire Owner of NewsHour," *Pando*, March 7, 2014, http://pando.com/2014/03/07/after-pledging-transparency-pbs-hides-details-of-new-deal-with-billionaire-owner-of-newshour.

14. Jack Mirkinson, "Jon Stewart Is A More Trusted News Source than MSNBC, Study Says," *Huffington Post*, June 10, 2014, http://www.huffingtonpost.com/2014/06/10/jon-stewart-more-trusted-msnbc-poll_n_5479859.html; Katherine Fung, "We're Learning More from Stephen Colbert Than the Actual News, Study Says," *Huffington Post*, June 6, 2014, http://www.huffingtonpost.com/2014/06/02/colbert-news-study-campaign-financing_n_5431713.html.

15. C. J. Werleman, "The Results Are In: America Is Dumb and on the Road to Getting Dumber," *AlterNet*, June 4, 2014, http://www.alternet.org/education/results-are-america-dumb-and-road-getting-dumber; Frank Newport, "In US, 42% Believe Creationist View of Human Origins," *Gallup*, June 2, 2014, http://www.gallup.com/poll/170822/believe-creationist-view-human-origins.aspx?ref=image.

16. William S. Burroughs, *Naked Lunch*, 50th ann. ed. (New York: Grove Press, 1959, 2009), 201.

17. Jessica Anderson, "Paula Deen Racism Claim 'Lacks Standing,' Because Plaintiff Is White, Georgia Lawyer Says: Do You Agree?" *Huffington Post*, June 25, 2013, http://www.huffingtonpost.com/2013/06/25/paula-deen-racism-claim-lacks-standing-georgia-lawyer-says-tell-us_n_3496183.html.

18. Today staff and news writers, "Paula Deen Said She Used Slur but Doesn't Tolerate Hate," *Today*, June 20, 2013, http://www.today.com/food/paula-deen-said-she-used-slur-doesnt-tolerate-hate-6C10388323.

19. Scott Collins, "Report: Paula Deen Admits Using N-word, telling Racist Jokes," *Los Angeles Times*, June 19, 2013, http://www.latimes.com/entertainment/tv/showtracker/la-et-st-report-paula-deen-admits-using-nword-making-racist-jokes-20130619-story.html.

20. Rene Lynch, "Paula Deen Fired by Food Network over Use of Racial Epithet," *Los Angeles Times*, June 21, 2013, http://articles.latimes.com/2013/jun/21/news/la-dd-paula-deen-fired-by-food-network-over-use-of-the-nword-20130621; Associated Press, "Paula Deen Dropped as Smithfield Foods Spokeswoman," *National Post*, June 25, 2013, http://arts.nationalpost.com/2013/06/25/paula-deen-dropped-by-smithfield-foods-amid-n-word-controversy-home-shopping-network-qvc-also-reviewing-business-relationship-with-celebrity-cook; Anne d'Innocenzio, "Wal-Mart Ends Relationship with Paula Deen," Yahoo! News, June 26, 2013, http://news.yahoo.com/wal-mart-ends-relationship-paula-193152834.html; Hollie McKay, "Target, QVC Latest Companies to Drop Paula Deen Products," Fox News, June 28, 2013, www.foxnews.com/entertainment/2013/06/25/target-drops-paula-deen; Rachel Tepper, "Paula Deen Dropped by Caesars Entertainment, Loses Four Casino Buffets," *Huffington Post*, June 26, 2013, http://www.huffingtonpost.com/2013/06/26/paula-deen-caesars-entertainment_n_3503411.html; Clare O'Connor, "Paula Deen Dumped by Home Depot and Diabetes Drug Company Novo Nordisk as Target, Sears, QVC Mull Next Move," *Forbes*, June 27, 2013, http://www.forbes.com/sites/clareoconnor/2013/06/27/paula-deen-dumped-by-home-depot-and-diabetes-drug-company-novo-nordisk-as-target-sears-qvc-mull-next-move; Maria Halkias, "J. C. Penney Is the Latest Retailer to End its Relationship with Paula Deen," *Dallas Morning News*, Biz Beat blog, June 28, 2013, http://bizbeatblog.dallasnews.com/2013/06/j-c-penney-is-the-latest-retailer-to-end-its-relationship-with-paula-deen.html; Hollie McKay, "Sears, KMart Latest Retailers to Drop Paula Deen Products," Fox News, June 28, 2013, http://www.foxnews.com/entertainment/2013/06/28/sears-drops-paula-deen/#ixzz2XXot9V7d; Hillel Italie, "Paula Deen Cookbook Dropped by Publisher," Associated Press, June 28, 2013, https://tv.yahoo.com/news/paula-deen-cookbook-dropped-publisher-201528415.html.

21. Paula Forbes, "South Beach Wine & Food Festival 2014: Paula Deen, Burger Bash, and More," *Eater*, February 24, 2014, http://eater.com/archives/2014/02/24/south-beach-wine-food-festival-2014-paula-deen-burger-bash-and-more.php.

22. David Li, "Michael Douglas Oral Sex Gave Me Cancer," *New York Post*, June 3, 2013, http://nypost.com/2013/06/03/michael-douglas-oral-sex-gave-me-cancer.

23. Healthy Day Reporter, "Michael Douglas Blames His Cancer on Oral Sex: Experts Say the Claim Is Probably Correct, Because Tumors Caused by HPV Virus Much More Responsive to Treatment," Web MD, June 3, 2013, http://www.webmd.com/sexual-conditions/news/20130603/michael-douglas-blames-his-throat-cancer-on-oral-sex.

24. "Michael Douglas Clarifies Comment about Oral Sex and Cancer," CNN, June 4, 2013, http://marquee.blogs.cnn.com/2013/06/04/michael-douglas-clarifies-comment-about-oral-sex-and-cancer.

25. Andrea Germanos, "CIA's Plan to Crush Leaks Gets Leaked," Common Dreams, June 27, 2013, http://www.commondreams.org/headline/2013/06/27-1; Sarah Lazare, "Military Blackout: Army Blocks Access to NSA News Reports 'The Army Is Scared of its Own Soldiers,'" Common Dreams, June 28, 2013, http://www.commondreams.org/headline/2013/06/28-1.

26. Sarah Lazare, "US Military Quietly Deploying Hundreds of Soldiers to Egypt," Common Dreams, June 24, 2013, http://www.commondreams.org/headline/2013/06/24-6.

27. TMZ Staff, "Alec Baldwin—Suspended by MSNBC, Issues Apology for Homophobic Rant," TMZ, November 15, 2013, http://www.tmz.com/2013/11/15/alec-baldwin-suspended-msnbc-apology.

28. "Did Miley Write an Apology Letter to Liam?," *Extra*, November 5, 2013, http://www.extratv.com/2013/11/05/miley-cyrus-wrote-apology-letter-to-liam-hemsworth-after-twerking-with-robin-thicke.

29. TMZ Staff, "Robin Thicke Gushes on Stage . . . I'm Lost Without Paula," TMZ, February 27, 2014, http://www.tmz.com/2014/02/27/robin-thicke-concert-paula-patton-dedicates-song-lost-without-u-fairfax.

30. Ramy Srour, "Less Food for More Hungry," Inter Press Service, November 5, 2013, http://www.ipsnews.net/2013/11/less-food-for-more-hungry; Ashfaq Yusufzai, "Drone Attack Kills More Than Taliban Chief," Inter Press Service, November 2, 2013, http://www.ipsnews.net/2013/11/drone-attack-kills-more-than-taliban-chief.

31. Andrew Kirell, "Seriously?! NY Post Columnist Demands Obama Apologize for 'Selfie' Story," Media-Ite, December 12, 2013, http://www.mediaite.com/print/seriously-ny-post-columnist-demands-obama-apologize-for-selfie-story.

32. Roberto Schmidt, "The Story behind 'That Selfie,'" Agence France Presse, December 11, 2013, http://sweetness-light.com/archive/photog-apologizes-for-catching-obamas-selfie#.U5FPGC-glv2M.

33. Drew Magary, "What the Duck?," GQ, January 2014, http://www.gq.com/entertainment/television/201401/duck-dynasty-phil-robertson.

34. Dana Ford, "'Duck Dynasty' Star Suspended for Anti-Gay Remarks," CNN, December 12, 2013, http://www.cnn.com/2013/12/18/showbiz/duck-dynasty-suspension.

35. "What Duck Dynasty's Phil Robertson Actually Said in GQ Interview," Americans for Truth about Homosexuality, December 23, 2013, http://americansfortruth.com/2013/12/23/what-duck-dynastys-phil-robertson-actually-said-in-gq-interview.

36. "GLAAD Slams Duck Dynasty Star, Phil Robertson Backtracks on Anti-Gay Remarks," Gossip Cop, December 18, 2013, http://www.gossipcop.com/phil-robertson-apology-gay-homophobic-apologizes-homosexuality-sin-glaad-response-reaction.

37. Lauren McCauley, "Workers Demand Livable Wage in Hundred-City Strike Fast Food Employees Will Walk off the Job Thursday in Movement's Largest Demonstration Yet," Common Dreams, December 18, 2013, http://www.commondreams.org/headline/2013/12/04-9.

38. Sarah Lazare, "Freed Gitmo Detainee: 'We Were Subjected to Meticulous, Daily Torture,'" Common Dreams, December 20, 2013, http://www.commondreams.org/headline/2013/12/20-5; Jacob Chamberlain, "Study Shows Gulf Oil Spill Linked to Dolphin Disease and Death," Common Dreams, December 19, 2013, http://www.commondreams.org/headline/2013/12/19-2..

39. Abby D. Phillip and Shushannah Walshe, "Chris Christie Fires Top Aide, Apologizes for Bridge Scandal," ABC News, January 9, 2014, http://abcnews.go.com/Politics/chris-christie-fires-top-aide-apologizes-bridge-scandal/story?id=21474242.

40. Molly Redden and Andy Kroll, "Chris Christie's Bridge Scandal, Explained," Mother Jones, January 8, 2014, http://www.motherjones.com/politics/2014/01/chris-christie-bridge-traffic-jam-emails.

41. Ben Dimiero et al., "REPORT: Fox News Buries Christie Bridge Scandal with Less than 15 Minutes of Coverage," Media Matters, January 9, 2014, http://mediamatters.org/research/2014/01/09/report-fox-news-buries-christie-bridge-scandal/197505; Mea Mark, "FOX News Doesn't Seem to Be Aware that Chris Christie is Involved in Multiple Scandals," Freak Out Nation, January 19, 2014, http://freakoutnation.com/2014/01/19/fox-news-doesnt-seem-to-be-aware-that-chris-christie-is-involved-in-multiple-scandals; Dorsey Shaw, "Breaking Down Minute-By-Minute Cable News' Coverage of the Chris Christie Bridge Scandal," BuzzFeed, January 9, 2014, http://www.buzzfeed.com/dorsey/breaking-down-minute-by-minute-cable-news-coverage-of-the-ch.

42. Michael Barbaro, "Inquiry Is Said to Clear Christie, but that's His Lawyers' Verdict," New York Times, March 23, 2014, http://www.nytimes.com/2014/03/24/nyregion/inquiry-is-said-to-clear-christie-but-thats-his-lawyers-verdict.html?_r=0.

43. Sarah Lazare, "Nearly Half of Americans Living Paycheck to Paycheck," Common Dreams, January 31, 2014, http://www.commondreams.org/headline/2014/01/31-7; Curtis Tate, "More Oil Spilled from Trains in 2013 than in Previous 4 Decades, Federal Data Show," McClatchy, January 20, 2014, http://www.mcclatchydc.com/2014/01/20/215143/more-oil-spilled-from-trains-in.html.

44. Sarah Lazare, "Congress Secretly Moves to Keep Drone Program Under CIA Control," Common Dreams, January 16, 2014, http://www.commondreams.org/headline/2014/01/16-9.

45. "L.A. Clippers Owner to GF: Don't Bring Black People to My Games . . . Including Magic Johnson," TMZ, April 25, 2014, http://www.tmz.com/2014/04/26/donald-sterling-clippers-owner-black-people-racist-audio-magic-johnson.

46. "PR Disaster: Donald Sterling's Apology for Racist Comments Only Makes Things Worse," CBS News, May 14, 2014, http://www.cbsnews.com/news/pr-disasters-donald-sterlings-apology-for-racist-comments-only-makes-things-worse.

47. Jon Queally, "FCC Chairman Tom Wheeler Defends Rules that Will Destroy Internet as We Know It," Common Dreams, April 30, 2014, http://www.commondreams.org/headline/2014/04/30-6.

48. Jon Queally, "US Drones Bomb Yemen for Second Time in Two Days," Common Dreams, April 20, 2014, http://www.commondreams.org/headline/2014/04/20-4; Jack Searle, "Drone Warfare," Bureau of Investigative Journalism, January 23, 2014, http://www.thebureauinvestigates.com/2014/01/23/more-than-2400-dead-as-obamas-drone-campaign-marks-five-years.

49. Steve Almasy, "Actor Jonah Hill Apologizes for Using Homophobic Slur," CNN, June 5, 2014, http://www.cnn.com/2014/06/03/showbiz/jonah-hill-homophobic-slur.

50. Antoinette Bueno, "Justin Bieber Apologizes for Second Racist Video," *Entertainment Tonight*, June 5, 2014, http://www.etonline.com/news/147111_justin_bieber_uses_the_n_word_and_jokes_about_joining_the_ku_klux_klan.

51. Justin Harp, "Robin Thicke Dad Defends Miley Cyrus amid MTV VMA's Scandal," *Hearst Magazine*, August 28, 2013, http://www.digitalspy.com/music/news/a510508/robin-thicke-dad-defends-miley-cyrus-amid-mtv-vmas-scandal.html.

52. Jon Caramanica, "Stubborn Persistence of Pop," *New York Times*, August 28, 2013, http://www.nytimes.com/2013/08/27/arts/music/mtv-video-music-awards-review.html?_r=3&adxnnl=1&adxnnlx=1395961419-ETj5gamp7vYys89hj7zg/A.

53. Lisa Respers France, "Miley Cyrus Responds: I Wanted to Make History,'" CNN, September 4, 2013, http://www.cnn.com/2013/09/03/showbiz/celebrity-news-gossip/miley-cyrus-vma-response.

54. Clinton Yates, "Miley Cyrus and the Issues of Slut-Shaming and Racial Condensation," *Washington Post*, August 26, 2013, http://www.washingtonpost.com/entertainment/music/miley-cyrus-and-the-issues-of-slut-shaming-and-racial-condescension/2013/08/26/f3aee436-0e68-11e3-bdf6-e4fc677d94a1_story.html.

55. Justin Harp, "Robin Thicke Dad Defends Miley Cyrus amid MTV VMA's Scandal."

56. Jim Naureckas, "UN Report Provides Information, Not 'Intelligence,'" Fairness and Accuracy in Reporting, September 17, 2013, http://www.fair.org/blog/2013/09/17/un-report-provides-information-not-intelligence.

57. Shane Harris and Mathew Aid, "Exclusive: CIA Files Prove America Helped Saddam as He Gassed Iran," *Foreign Policy*, August 23, 2013, http://www.foreignpolicy.com/articles/2013/08/25/secret_cia_files_prove_america_helped_saddam_as_he_gassed_iran.

58. Sarah Lazare, "Nuke Plant to Shut Doors: Environmental Victory But Vital Work Still Ahead," August 27, 2013, http://www.commondreams.org/headline/2013/08/27-4.

59. "Justin Bieber- MSNBC Knows What the People Want," *Guardian*, January 24, 2014, http://www.theguardian.com/media/mediamonkeyblog+ustelevision.

60. "Justin Bieber Surrenders to Police for Assault Charge: As seen on 'On the Record with Greta Van Susteren,'" Fox News, January 29, 2014, http://foxnewsinsider.com/2014/01/29/justin-bieber-surrenders-police-assault-charge.

61. Associated Press, "You Want Controversy? Just Put Barbie on SI Cover," Fox Sports, February 12, 2014, http://msn.foxsports.com/buzzer/story/barbie-sports-illustrated-swimsuit-issue-cover-unapologetic-ignites-controversy-50th-anniversary-021214.

62. Ibid.

63. "Barbie Cover Sparks Controversy," ABC News, February 14, 2014, http://abcnews.go.com/GMA/video/barbie-sports-illustrated-swimsuit-edition-22514149; "Barbie Stirs Controversy on the Cover of Sports Illustrated," *Fox News Insider* (as seen on Fox and Friends Weekend),

February 15, 2014, http://foxnewsinsider.com/2014/02/15/barbie-stirs-controversy-cover-sports-illustrated-swimsuit-edition.

64. Ibid.

65. Associated Press, "You Want Controversy? Just Put Barbie on SI Cover."

66. Sorca Jordan, "Amazon Poised to Help Obama Assassinate U.S. Citizen," Project Censored, February 12, 2014, http://www.projectcensored.org/amazon-poised-help-obama-assassinate-u-s-citizen.

67. John Queally, "'Truly Shocking': Govt Spies Hacked into Live Webcam Chats of Millions," Common Dreams, February 27, 2014, http://www.commondreams.org/headline/2014/02/27-2.

68. Joe Dziemianowicz, "Oscars 2014: John Travolta's Flub of Idina Menzel's Name at the Academy Awards Has Raised Her Profile," New York Daily News, March 4, 2014, http://www.ny-dailynews.com/entertainment/oscars/travolta-oscar-flub-equals-higher-profile-idina-menzel-article-1.1709421; Chris Kirk and Jim Festante, "The Adele Dazeem Name Generator," Slate, March 3, 2014, http://www.slate.com/articles/arts/low_concept/2014/03/john_travolta_called_idina_menzel_adele_dazeem_what_s_your_travolta_name.html.

69. Alyssa Toomey, "John Travolta Apologized to Idina Menzel After Adele Dazeem Screw Up—Find Out What He Sent Her!" E! Entertainment, March 19, 2014, http://www.eonline.com/news/522882/john-travolta-apologized-to-idina-menzel-after-adele-dazeem-screw-up-find-out-what-he-sent-her.

70. Bryant Jordan, "Senate Fails to Pass Veteran Benefits Bill," Military.com, February 27, 2014, http://www.military.com/daily-news/2014/02/27/senate-fails-to-pass-veteran-benefits-bill.html; Jason Easley, "Senate Republicans Betray U.S. Vets by Blocking Veterans Benefits Bill," PoliticusUSA, February 27, 2014, http://www.politicususa.com/2014/02/27/senate-republicans-betray-u-s-vets-blocking-veterans-benefits-bill.html.

71. Ben Armbruster, "Senate GOP Blocks Vets' Benefits Bill over Diplomacy-Killing Iran Sanctions," Think Progress, February 27, 2014, http://thinkprogress.org/world/2014/02/27/3343681/gop-kills-vets-iran-sanctions.

72. Stephen Braun et al., "The Big Story: Secret to Prism Program: Even Bigger Data Seizure," Associated Press, June 15, 2013, http://bigstory.ap.org/article/secret-prism-success-even-bigger-data-seizure; Timothy Jones, "Germany and EU Targets for US Espionage, Spiegel Reports," DW.DE, November 8, 2013, http://www.dw.de/germany-and-eu-targets-for-us-espionage-spiegel-reports/a-17011863; Barton Gellman and Laura Poitras, "U.S., British intelligence Mining Data from Nine U.S. Internet Companies in Broad Secret Program," Washington Post, June 7, 2013, http://www.washingtonpost.com/investigations/us-intelligence-mining-data-from-nine-us-internet-companies-in-broad-secret-program/2013/06/06/3a0c0da8-cebf-11e2-8845-d970ccb04497_story.html; "Millions in US Tax Dollars Go to Big Data for Wiretap Capabilities," Russia Today, June 6, 2013, http://rt.com/usa/govt-pays-verizon-att-surveillance-922; Jeremy Scahill and Glenn Greenwald, "The NSA's Secret Role in the U.S. Assassination Program," Intercept, February 10, 2014, https://firstlook.org/theintercept/article/2014/02/10/the-nsas-secret-role; Christian Stöcker,"Friedrichs Wunschliste: Der Innenminister und das NSA-Prinzip," Der Spiegel, June 11, 2013, http://www.spiegel.de/netzwelt/netzpolitik/friedrichs-wunschliste-der-innenminister-und-das-nsa-prinzip-a-932147.html.

73. Brian Fung, "Darrell Issa: James Clapper Lied to Congress about NSA and Should Be Fired," Washington Post, The Switch blog, January 27, 2014, http://www.washingtonpost.com/blogs/the-switch/wp/2014/01/27/darrell-issa-james-clapper-lied-to-congress-about-nsa-and-should-be-fired; Jennifer Pelt, "3 Top US Officials Discuss Cybersecurity in NYC," Big Story, August 8, 2013, http://bigstory.ap.org/article/3-top-us-officials-discuss-cybersecurity-nyc.

74. Spencer Ackerman and Dan Roberts, "NSA Phone Surveillance Program Likely Unconstitutional, Federal Judge Rules," Guardian, December 16, 2013, http://www.theguardian.com/world/2013/dec/16/nsa-phone-surveillance-likely-unconstitutional-judge; Marjorie Cohn, "NSA Metadata Collection: Fourth Amendment Violation," Huffington Post, January 16, 2014, http://www.huffingtonpost.com/marjorie-cohn/nsa-metadata-collection-f_b_4611211.html; Michael Calderone, "U.S. Accused of Spying on McClatchy Journalist from New Zealand; Investigation Underway," Huffington Post, August 1, 2013, http://www.huffingtonpost.

com/2013/08/01/spying-mcclatchy-journalist-new-zealand_n_3689820.html; "NSA Spied on Al Jazeera Communications: Snowden Document," *Der Spiegel*, August 31, 2013, http://www.spiegel.de/international/world/nsa-spied-on-al-jazeera-communications-snowden-document-a-919681.html; Josh Gerstein, "Judge: NSA Phone Program Likely Unconstitutional," *Politico*, December 2013, http://www.politico.com/story/2013/12/national-security-agency-phones-judge-101203.html; Karen McVeigh, "NSA Surveillance Program Violates the Constitution, ACLU Says," *Guardian*, August 27, 2013, http://www.theguardian.com/world/2013/aug/27/nsa-surveillance-program-illegal-aclu-lawsuit.

75. Glenn Greenwald, "How Covert Agents Infiltrate the Internet to Manipulate, Deceive, and Destroy Reputations," *Intercept*, February 24, 2014, https://firstlook.org/theintercept/2014/02/24/jtrig-manipulation; Ryan Gallagher and Glenn Greenwald, "How the NSA Plans to Infect 'Millions' of Computers with Malware," *Intercept*, March 12, 2014, https://firstlook.org/theintercept/article/2014/03/12/nsa-plans-infect-millions-computers-malware.

76. "Bob Schieffer: Edward Snowden 'Is No Hero' (Video)," *Huffington Post*, June 16, 2013, http://www.huffingtonpost.com/2013/06/16/bob-schieffer-edward-snowden_n_3450490.html.

77. Lindsey Boerma, "NSA Debate: Will Reforms Ease Public Concern or Compromise Safety," CBS News, August 11, 2013, http://www.cbsnews.com/8301-3460_162-57598015/nsa-debate-will-reforms-ease-public-concern-or-compromise-safety.

78. Glenn Greenwald, "Michael Hayden, Bob Schieffer and the Media's Reverence of National Security Officials," *Guardian*, August 12, 2013, http://www.theguardian.com/commentisfree/2013/aug/12/michael-hayden-nsa-media-reverence.

79. Adam Edelman, "Edward Snowden, Hero or Traitor? NSA Leaker Divides Political World in Sometimes-Unpredictable Ways," *New York Daily News*, June 11, 2013, http://www.nydailynews.com/news/politics/edward-snowden-hero-traitor-nsa-leaker-divides-political-world-sometimes-unpredictable-ways-article-1.1369586; Ashley Fantz, "NSA Leaker Ignites Global Debate: Hero or Traitor?," CNN, June 10, 2013, http://www.cnn.com/2013/06/10/us/snowden-leaker-reaction; Lee Ferran, "In Their Own Words: Alleged NSA Leaker a Hero or a Traitor?," ABC News, June 11, 2013, http://abcnews.go.com/blogs/headlines/2013/06/in-their-own-words-alleged-nsa-leaker-a-hero-or-a-traitor; "Edward Snowden: Hero or Traitor?," Fox News, June 10, 2013, http://video.foxnews.com/v/2469910653001/edward-snowden-hero-or-traitor/#sp=show-clips; "Do You Think Snowden Is a Traitor or a Hero?" MSNBC, March 10, 2014, http://www.msnbc.com/ronan-farrow/watch/do-you-think-snowden-is-a-traitor-or-a-hero-190264387807; Dylan Stableford, "Is Edward Snowden a Hero or a Traitor?," Yahoo! News, June 11, 2013, https://news.yahoo.com/blogs/lookout/snowden-hero-traitor-190447620.html.

80. United States Constitution, http://www.archives.gov/exhibits/charters/constitution_transcript.html.

81. Andrew Beaujon, "Journalists react to controversial questions David Gregory asked Glenn Greenwald," *Poynter*, June 24, 2013, http://www.poynter.org/latest-news/mediawire/216685/journalists-react-to-controversial-question-david-gregory-asked-glenn-greenwald/; "Frank Rich Eviscerates David Gregory," *Daily Kos*, June 26, 2013, http://www.dailykos.com/story/2013/06/26/1219287/-Frank-Rich-Eviserates-David-Gregory; and Jack Mirkinson, "David Gregory to Glenn Greenwald: 'Why Shouldn't You be Charged With a Crime?' (Video)," *Huffington Post*, June 23, 2013, http://www.huffingtonpost.com/2013/06/23/david-gregory-glenn-greenwald-crime_n_3486654.html.

82. Ibid.

83. Kevin Poulsen, "60 Minutes Puff Piece Claims NSA Saved U.S. From Cyberterrorism," *Wired*, December 2013, http://www.wired.com/threatlevel/2013/12/60-minutes. See also Jack Mirkinson, "'60 Minutes' Trashed for NSA Piece," *Huffington Post*, December 16, 2013, http://www.huffingtonpost.com/2013/12/16/60-minutes-nsa_n_4452568.html.

84. Spencer Ackerman, "NSA Goes on 60 Minutes: The Definitive Facts behind CBS's Flawed Report," *Guardian*, December 2013, http://www.theguardian.com/world/2013/dec/16/nsa-surveillance-60-minutes-cbs-facts; David Folkenflik; "60 Minutes' Criticized for NSA Report,"

NPR, December 18, 2013, http://www.npr.org/2013/12/18/255185849/60-minutes-criticized-for-nsa-report.

85. Glenn Greenwald, "Inside the Mind of James Clapper," *Intercept*, February 24, 2014, https://firstlook.org/theintercept/2014/02/24/inside-mind-james-clapper; Benny Johnson, "America's Spies Want Edward Snowden Dead," BuzzFeed, January 16, 2014, http://www.buzzfeed.com/bennyjohnson/americas-spies-want-edward-snowden-dead; "Snowden to Ask Russian Police for Protection after US Threats—Lawyer," RT News, January 21, 2014, http://rt.com/news/snowden-russian-police-help-967.

86. Msmolly, "Over Easy: The New Snowden Interview Blackout," *Firedoglake*, February 7, 2014, http://my.firedoglake.com/msmolly/2014/02/07/over-easy-the-new-snowden-interview-blackout.

87. Alex Gauthier, "American Media Ignores Edward Snowden Interview on German News Network," *IVNus*, January 31, 2014, http://ivn.us/2014/01/31/german-news-network-broadcasts-edward-snowden-interview; Jay Syrmopoulos, "Media Blacks Out New Snowden Interview the Government Doesn't Want You to See," *Ben Swann Truth In Media*, January 31, 2014, http://benswann.com/media-blacks-out-new-snowden-interview-the-government-doesnt-want-you-to-see.

88. "'Clear and Convincing' Evidence of Chemical Weapons Used in Syria, UN Team Reports," United Nations News Centre, September 16, 2013, http://www.un.org/apps/news/story.asp?NewsID=45856#.Uxy8yIWh5fs.

89. "Brief History of Chemical Weapons Use," Organisation for the Prohibition of Chemical Weapons, https://www.opcw.org/about-chemical-weapons/history-of-cw-use.

90. John Kerry, "Full Text of John Kerry's Statement on Syria," *USA Today*, August 31, 2013, http://www.usatoday.com/story/news/politics/2013/08/30/text-john-kerry-syria-statement/2749051.

91. Mark Hosenball, "Syria Chemical Weapons Death Toll Cited by Obama Administration May Be Inflated," *Huffington Post*, September 12, 2013, http://www.huffingtonpost.com/2013/09/12/syria-chemical-weapons-deaths_n_3917025.html.

92. Jim Kuhnhenn, "Difference Aside, Iraq War Haunts Obama on Syria," Associated Press, August 31, 2013, http://bigstory.ap.org/article/difference-aside-iraq-war-haunts-obama-syria.

93. Tracy Connor, "Obama on Fence about Syria Strike Without Congress' Approval," NBC News, September 9, 2013, http://www.nbcnews.com/news/us-news/obama-fence-about-syria-strike-without-congress-approval-v20407499.

94. Simon Maloy, "Fox News Sunday Beats Syria War Drums," Media Matters, April 28, 2013, http://mediamatters.org/blog/2013/04/28/fox-news-sunday-beats-syria-war-drums/193809.

95. Washington Post Editorial Board, "The U.S. Should Examine Allegations of a Chemical Attack in Syria," *Washington Post*, August 21, 2013, http://www.washingtonpost.com/opinions/syrian-attack-should-prompt-us-investigation-into-chemical-weapons/2013/08/21/92d263f4-0a7b-11e3-8974-f97ab3b3c677_story.html.

96. Peter Hart, "The Illusion of Debate Over Striking Syria," Fairness and Accuracy in Reporting, November 1, 2013, http://fair.org/extra-online-articles/the-illusion-of-debate-over-striking-syria.

97. Thomas Bishop, "After Calling for Obama to Get Congressional Approval on Syria, Hannity Attacks Him for Doing It," Media Matters, September 4, 2013, http://mediamatters.org/blog/2013/09/04/after-calling-for-obama-to-get-congressional-ap/195711.

98. Jennifer Skalka Tulumello, "Donald Rumsfeld Lambasts Obama on Syria: 'Take Responsibility,'" *Christian Science Monitor*, September 5, 2013, http://www.csmonitor.com/USA/DC-Decoder/2013/0905/Donald-Rumsfeld-lambastes-Obama-on-Syria-Take-responsibility-video.

99. D. S. Wright, "Seymour Hersh: Tests Revealed Sarin Attack in Syria Not from Assad," *Firedoglake*, April 7, 2014, http://news.firedoglake.com/2014/04/07/seymour-hersh-tests-revealed-sarin-attack-in-syria-not-from-assad.

100. Nolan Higdon, "Millennial Media Revolution—Part 4," Project Censored, February 2014, http://www.projectcensored.org/millennial-media-revolution-part-iv-response-tells-working.

101. Paige Lavender, "Obama: 'I Don't Think Mr. Snowden Was a Patriot' (VIDEO)," *Huffington Post*, August 9, 2013, http://www.huffingtonpost.com/2013/08/09/obama-edward-snowden_n_3733560.html.

102. Marisa Taylor and Jonathan S. Landay, "Obama's Crackdown Views Leaks as Aiding Enemies of U.S.," *McClatchy Washington Bureau*, June 20, 2013, http://www.mcclatchydc.com/2013/06/20/194513/obamas-crackdown-views-leaks-as.html#storylink=cpy.

103. Lucas Tomlinson, "Ex-CIA Director: Snowden Should Be 'Hanged' if Convicted for Treason," Fox News, December 17, 2013, http://www.foxnews.com/politics/2013/12/17/ex-cia-director-snowden-should-be-hanged-if-convicted-for-treason.

104. Mollie Reilly, "John Bolton: Edward Snowden 'Ought to Swing from a Tall Oak Tree,'" *Huffington Post*, December 17, 2013, http://www.huffingtonpost.com/2013/12/17/john-bolton-edward-snowden_n_4461196.html.

105. Washington Post Editorial Board, "How to Keep Edward Snowden from Leaking More NSA Secrets," *Washington Post*, July 1, 2013, http://www.washingtonpost.com/opinions/how-to-keep-edward-snowden-from-leaking-more-nsa-secrets/2013/07/01/4e8bbe28-e278-11e2-a11e-c2ea876a8f30_story.html?hpid=z4.

106. Jack Mirkinson, "Washington Post's Edward Snowden Editorial Draws Incredulous Reaction," *Huffington Post*, July 2, 2013, http://www.huffingtonpost.com/2013/07/02/washington-post-edward-snowden-editorial_n_3535146.html?icid=hp_front_top_art.

107. Michelangelo Signorile, "Glenn Greenwald, Guardian Reporter, Blasts Media, MSNBC Over Edward Snowden Stories," *Huffington Post*, July 16, 2013, http://www.huffingtonpost.com/2013/07/16/glen-greenwald-media-edward-snowden-stories_n_3600016.html.

108. Steven Lee Myers, "Determined to Miss Nothing, Russia Trains All Eyes on Sochi," *New York Times*, January 18, 2014, http://www.nytimes.com/2014/01/19/world/europe/intensive-security-for-winter-olympics.html.

109. Paul Sonne, Gregory L. White, and Joshua Robinson, "Russian Officials Fire Back at Olympic Critics," *Wall Street Journal*, February 6, 2014, http://online.wsj.com/news/articles/SB10001424052702304680904579366712107461956

110. Josh Voorhees, "Russian Official Lets It Slip that There Are Cameras in the Olympic Hotel Bathrooms," *Slate*, February 6, 2014, http://www.slate.com/blogs/the_slatest/2014/02/06/russia_olympic_shower_cams_hosts_dismiss_hotel_complaints_by_citing_video.html.

111. James Gordon Meek, "The Other Sochi Threat: Russian Spies, Mobsters Hacking Your Smartphones," ABC News, February 5, 2014, http://abcnews.go.com/Blotter/sochi-threat-russian-spies-mobsters-hacking-smartphones/story?id=22361222.

112. Shaun Walker, "Russia to Monitor 'All Communications' at Winter Olympics in Sochi," *Guardian*, October 7, 2013, http://www.theguardian.com/world/2013/oct/06/russia-monitor-communications-sochi-winter-olympics.

113. Owen Mathews, "Russia Tests 'Total Surveillance' at the Sochi Olympics," *Newsweek*, February 2, 2014, http://mag.newsweek.com/2014/02/14/russia-tests-total-surveillance-sochi-olympics.html.

114. "Hacked Within Minutes: Sochi Visitors Face Internet Minefield," NBC News, February 5, 2014, http://www.nbcnews.com/video/nightly-news/54273832/#54273832; Phil Nickinson, "NBC News and the Bullshit 'ZOMG Sochi Olympics Android Hack' Story," *Android Central*, February 6, 2014, http://www.androidcentral.com/nbc-news-and-bullshit-zomg-sochi-olympics-android-hack-story.

115. Andrew Wittenburg and Kimberly Dozier, "Report: NSA Was Spying on Salt Lake City during Olympics," *Desert News*, August 21, 2013, http://www.deseretnews.com/article/865585064/Report-NSA-was-spying-on-Salt-Lake-City-during-Olympics.html?pg=all; "Security Tip (ST14-001) Sochi 2014 Olympic Games," United States Computer Emergency Readiness Team, February 4, 2014, https://www.us-cert.gov/ncas/tips/ST14-001.

116. "Why Is Ukraine in Turmoil?," BBC, February 22, 2014, http://www.bbc.com/news/world-europe-25182823.

117. Phil Black, Nick Paton Walsh, and Michael Pearson, "Diplomatic Talks in Ukraine Last Until Dawn, a Day after 100 May Have Died," CNN, February 21, 2014, http://www.cnn.

com/2014/02/20/world/europe/ukraine-protests; "Kiev," CBS News, January 23, 2014, http://www.cbsnews.com/pictures/ukrainian-protests-grow-more-violent;

Will Englund, "In Violent Turn, Ukraine Fighting Kills at Least 25," *Washington Post*, February 19, 2014, http://www.washingtonpost.com/world/ukraine-protests-once-more-turn-violent-four-reported-dead/2014/02/18/ba9173f4-98af-11e3-80ac-63a8ba7f7942_story.html;

Kathy Lally, "Ukraine Blames Yanukovych-Directed Police Units in Sniper Killings," *Washington Post*, April 3, 2014, http://www.washingtonpost.com/world/ukraine-accuses-former-president-yanukovychs-of-involvement-in-sniper-deaths/2014/04/03/fb63ffcc-0710-4ab5-9acc-1bcd5a715eaa_story.html; Sergei Loiko, "Snipers Kill 20 Protesters in Ukraine; Allies Turn against Yanukovich," *Los Angeles Times*, February 20, 2014, http://articles.latimes.com/2014/feb/20/world/la-fg-ukraine-snipers-20140221; Olga Rudenko, "Ukraine: Yanukovych Used Paid Killers with Russian Help," *USA Today*, April 3, 2014, http://www.usatoday.com/story/news/world/2014/04/03/ukraine-yanukovych-russian-arrests/7248293; Alice Speri, "Ukraine's Disgraced President Might Have Smuggled a Boatload of Cash to Russia," Vice News, April 29, 2014, https://news.vice.com/article/ukraines-disgraced-president-might-have-smuggled-a-boatload-of-cash-to-russia.

118. Jonathan Marcus, "Transcript of Leaked US Ukraine Call," BBC News, February 7, 2014, http://www.bbc.com/news/world-europe-26079957; "'F**k the EU': Snr US State Dept. Official Caught in Alleged Phone Chat on Ukraine," Russia Today, February 6, 2014, http://rt.com/news/nuland-phone-chat-ukraine-927.

119. Ed Pilkington, "US Official Apologizes to EU Counterparts for Undiplomatic Language," *Guardian*, February 6, 2014, http://www.theguardian.com/world/2014/feb/06/us-ukraine-russia-eu-victoria-nuland.

120. Andrew Higgins and Peter Baker, "Russia Claims U.S. Is Meddling Over Ukraine," *New York Times*, February 7, 2014, http://www.nytimes.com/2014/02/07/world/europe/ukraine.html. Also see Peter Baker, "U.S. Points to Russia as Diplomats' Private Call Is Posted on Web," *New York Times*, February 7, 2014, http://www.nytimes.com/2014/02/07/world/europe/us-points-to-russia-as-diplomats-private-call-is-posted-on-web.html; and P. J. Crowley, "Calls Show Diplomacy a Contact Sport," BBC News, February 7, 2014, http://www.bbc.com/news/world-us-canada-26085432.

121. "Meet the Press Transcript: March 2, 2014," NBC News, March 2, 2014, http://www.nbcnews.com/meet-the-press/meet-press-transcript-march-2-2014-n42471.

122. Michael Hughes, "The Neo-Nazi Question in Ukraine," *Huffington Post*, March 11, 2014, http://www.huffingtonpost.com/michael-hughes/the-neo-nazi-question-in_b_4938747.html.

123. Doyle McManus, "The Dawn of Cold War II," *Los Angeles Times*, March 5, 2014, http://articles.latimes.com/2014/mar/05/opinion/la-oe-mcmanus-column-ukraine-cold-war-20140305; John Schindler, "How to Win Cold War 2.0.," *Politico*, March 2014, http://www.politico.com/magazine/story/2014/03/new-cold-war-russia-104954.html#.Uz3a3a1dWSM; Global Research News, "American Conquest by Subversion: Victoria Nuland's Admits Washington Has Spent $5 Billion to 'Subvert Ukraine," Centre for Research on Globalization, February 7, 2014, http://www.politico.com/magazine/story/2014/03/new-cold-war-russia-104954.html#.Uz3a3a1dWSM.

124. Michael Collins, "Ukraine President Once Agent for US State Department," Information Clearing House, June 10, 2014, http://www.informationclearinghouse.info/article38760.htm; Eric Draitser, "High-Motor Propaganda: Ukraine, Intervention, and America's Doublethink," *CounterPunch*, March 3, 2014, http://www.counterpunch.org/2014/03/03/ukraine-intervention-and-americas-doublethink. See also the book edited by Stephen Lendman, *Flashpoint in Ukraine: How the US Drive For Hegemony Risks WWIII* (Atlanta: Clarity Press, 2014).

125. "Is RT State-Run?," RT, June 16 2011, http://rt.com/usa/rt-government-broadcasting-radio.

126. Disclaimer: Abby Martin is on the board of directors of the Media Freedom Foundation, which is the nonprofit that oversees Project Censored, and Martin has worked with Project Censored in the past.

127. John Aravosis, "Russia Censors RT News Host's Blistering Critique of Ukraine Invasion (Video)," *America Blog*, March 4, 2014, http://americablog.com/2014/03/russian-state-media-host-blasts-russian-invasion-ukraine-video.html.

128. Josh Feldman, "RT Anchor Resigns On-Air: I Can't Be Part of Network 'That Whitewashes the Actions of Putin,'" *Mediaite*, March 5, 2014, http://www.mediaite.com/tv/rt-anchor-resigns-on-air-i-can%E2%80%99t-be-part-of-network-that-whitewashes-the-actions-of-putin.

129. "Russia Today Anchor Who Quit on Air Says It Was Not a Political Stunt," Fox News, March 6, 2014, http://foxnewsinsider.com/2014/03/06/russia-today-anchor-who-quit-air-says-it-was-not-political-stunt; Henry Austin, "Russia TV Anchor Refuses Crimea Job After Slamming Invasion," NBC News, March 4, 2014, http://www.nbcnews.com/storyline/ukraine-crisis/russia-tv-anchor-refuses-crimea-job-after-slamming-invasion-n43746; "European Leaders Meet in Brussels; Explosive Interview with Pope Francis; RT Anchor Resigns On Air; Mom Drives Kids Into Ocean," CNN, March 6, 2014, http://edition.cnn.com/TRANSCRIPTS/1403/06/nday.02.html; Greg Botelho, "Anchor Quits: I Can't Be Part of Network 'That Whitewashes' Putin's Actions," CNN, March 6, 2014, http://www.cnn.com/2014/03/05/world/europe/russia-news-anchor-resigns; and Catherine Taibi, "Russia Today Anchor Speaks Out Against Invasion of Ukraine: 'What Russia Did Is Wrong,'" *Huffington Post*, March 4, 2014, http://www.huffingtonpost.com/2014/03/04/russia-today-anchor-abby-martin-putin-ukraine-rt_n_4895679.html.

130. Jeff Mirkinson, "RT Anchor Abby Martin Rips American Media, Spars With Piers Morgan," *Huffington Post*, March 6, 2014, http://www.huffingtonpost.com/2014/03/06/abby-martin-piers-morgan-russia-today_n_4910744.html.

131. Steve Rendall and Tara Broughel, "Amplifying Officials, Squelching Dissent," Fairness and Accuracy in Reporting, May 1, 2003, http://fair.org/extra-online-articles/amplifying-officials-squelching-dissent; Steven Kull, Clay Ramsay, and Evan Lewis, "Misperceptions, the Media, and the Iraq War," *Academy of Political Science*, December 1, 2013, http://www.abdn.ac.uk/sociology/notes06/Level4/SO4530/Assigned-Readings/Seminar%2011.2.pdf; and Sheldon Rampton and John Stauber, *Weapons of Mass Deception: The Uses of Propaganda in Bush's War on Iraq* (New York: Penguin, 2003).

132. Josh Feldman, "RT's Abby Martin Goes Off on 'Corporate Media' Propaganda During Piers Morgan Interview," *Mediaite*, March 5, 2014, http://www.mediaite.com/tv/rt%E2%80%99s-abby-martin-goes-off-on-%E2%80%98corporate-media%E2%80%99-propaganda-during-piers-morgan-interview; Andrew Kirell, "If Bill Maher Made the Same Controversial 9/11 Comments Today, Would He Have Lost His Show?," *Mediaite*, October 9, 2012, http://www.mediaite.com/tv/if-bill-maher-made-the-same-controversial-911-comments-today-would-he-have-lost-his-show; Dennis J. Bernstein, "Silencing Donahue and Anti-War Voices," *Consortium News*, January 15, 2012, http://consortiumnews.com/2012/01/15/silencing-donahue-and-anti-war-voices; James Poniewozik, "In the Obama Era, Will the Media Change Too?" *Time*, January 15, 2009, http://content.time.com/time/magazine/article/0,9171,1871916,00.html; Eric Roper, "Ventura Says MSNBC Nixed His Show for Not Supporting Iraq War," *Star Tribune*, November 30, 2009, http://www.startribune.com/politics/blogs/78150302.html; Shindu Parameswaran, "War, Devastation, and Who's Cashing in on Them," *Arbitrage Magazine*, April 2013, http://www.arbitragemagazine.com/features/profiting-vs-profiteering.

133. For more on works showing censorship in the US press, see Kristina Borjesson, *Into the Buzzsaw: Leading Journalists Expose the Myth of the Free Press* (New York: Prometheus Books, 2002); and *Feet to the Fire: The Media After 9/11, Top Journalists Speak Out* (New York: Prometheus, 2005). See also John Pilger's film *The War You Don't See*, 2010, http://johnpilger.com/videos/the-war-you-dont-see.

134. James F. Tracy. "Plutocracy, Poverty, and Prosperity," in *Censored 2014: Fearless Speech in Fateful Times*, eds. Mickey Huff, Andy Lee Roth (New York: Seven Stories Press, 2013), 91–93.

135. Craig Harrington and Brian Powell, "Study: Media Leaves Viewers in the Dark about Trans-Pacific Partnership," Media Matters, February 5, 2014, http://mediamatters.org/research/2014/02/05/study-media-leave-viewers-in-the-dark-about-tra/197932.

136. Thomas B. Edsall, "Free Trade Disagreement," *New York Times*, February 4, 2014, http://www.nytimes.com/2014/02/05/opinion/edsall-free-trade-disagreement.html.

137. "Celebrities Want to Tie Trade Pact to Dolphin Hunt," ABC News, February 5, 2014, http://abcnews.go.com/Entertainment/wireStory/celebrities-tie-trade-pact-dolphin-hunt-22385320.

138. Jon Queally, "As TPP Opposition Soars, Corporate Media Blackout Deafening," Common Dreams, February 6, 2014, http://www.commondreams.org/headline/2014/02/06.

139. Zach Carter and Kate Sheppard, "Read the Secret Trade Memo Calling for More Fracking and Offshore Drilling," *Huffington Post*, May 19, 2014, http://www.huffingtonpost.com/2014/05/19/trade-fracking_n_5340420.html.

140. Lee Fang, "Obama Admin's TPP Trade Officials Received Hefty Bonuses from Big Banks." *Republic Report*, February 17, 2014, http://www.republicreport.org/2014/big-banks-tpp.

141. Margot Kaminski et al., "Intellectual Property in the Trans-Pacific Partnership: National Interest or Corporate Handout?," Cato Institute, March 5, 2014, http://www.cato.org/multimedia/events/intellectual-property-trans-pacific-partnership-national-interest-or-corporate.

142. John Roberts, "Malaysian Court Overturns Acquittal of Opposition Leader Anwar," World Socialist Web Site, March 11, 2014, http://www.wsws.org/en/articles/2014/03/11/mala-m11.html.

143. Hiltzik.

144. Carl Jensen, *Censored: The News that Didn't Make the News and Why—The 1995 Project Censored Yearbook* (New York: Four Walls Eight Windows, 1995), 175.

CHAPTER 4

Media Democracy in Action
Inspiring We the People

Compiled by Andy Lee Roth and Mickey Huff, with contributions by Patrice McDermott, OpenTheGovernment.org; Davey D, Hard Knock Radio; Shahid Buttar, the Bill of Rights Defense Committee; Rob Williams and Julie Frechette, the Action Coalition for Media Education; David Cobb, Move to Amend; and Dave Maass, Electronic Frontier Foundation

Participation. That's what's going to save the human race.

—Pete Seeger (May 3, 1919–January 27, 2014)[1]

In March 2014, the *Los Angeles Times* ran a story on Robert Proctor, a professor of the history of science at Stanford University. According to the article, Proctor is "one of the world's leading experts in agnotology," the study of "the cultural production of ignorance."[2] By examining misinformation campaigns ranging from Nazi science to Big Tobacco and the sugar industry, these studies show how misinformation is both hard to uproot once established and also harmful to the creation of constructive public policy. The antidote, Proctor has contended, is to expose misinformation for what it is "through good journalism, good pedagogy, good scholarship. You need an educated populace."[3]

The individuals and organizations featured in this chapter have dedicated themselves not only to fostering a more informed public, but also to promoting direct participation in political decision-making, whether through local, state, or national government, or via nongovernmental channels in our communities. The contributors to this year's Media Democracy in Action chapter—including OpenTheGovernment.org, Hard Knock Radio, the Bill of Rights Defense Committee, the Action Coalition for Media Education, Move to Amend, and Electronic Frontier Foundation——exemplify what Project Censored means when we say that an informed public is essential to robust democracy.

"Doubt is our product," was the message in an internal Brown & Williamson memo from 1969.[4] The memo advocated targeting the "mass public" as "consumers" who could be distracted by "controversy" from the mounting scientific evidence that linked smoking and disease. Today's merchants of doubt, considering issues from climate change to genetically modified organisms (GMO foods), also seek a mass public, preoccupied by distractions and taught to think of itself first and foremost as consumers, not only of products, but of ideologies. Fortunately, however, as Project Censored has highlighted since its inception in 1976, when the public is armed with the skills of critical thinking and media literacy, as well as informed by a truly independent press, We the People become much more than a bewildered herd ready to buy whatever those in power pitch to us. That danger remains as real and consequential today as in 1969. But owing to the organizations and individuals like those featured here, the opportunities to become informed and, on that basis, inspired to participate have never been greater.

AMERICANS FOR LESS SECRECY, MORE DEMOCRACY: OPENTHEGOVERNMENT.ORG

Patrice McDermott

Ten years after OpenTheGovernment.org's official launch, open government is having a "moment." Talk of transparency is hard to avoid these days for reasons both good and bad. On one hand, on his first day in office, President Barack Obama pledged to create "an unprecedented level of openness in government." The president has indeed launched a number of initiatives that are, as their name implies, focused on openness: the Open Government Initiative, the Open Government Directive, the Open Government Partnership, etc. On the other hand, disclosures made by Edward Snowden and the fight over the Senate Select Committee on Intelligence's torture report have made it clear that there is not nearly enough openness in government, and that national security secrecy continues to contribute to the government overstepping its authority.

OpenTheGovernment.org (OTG) is a coalition of more than eighty groups fighting the good fight for accountable government, an informed public, safer environments, protection of civil liberties, and more. Our small staff acts as a watchman and an organizer, alerting and organizing the community to push back against encroaching secrecy where necessary and pushing for meaningful open government policy reforms where possible.

OpenTheGovernment.org exists because open government policy matters. Journalists and the public need easier access to government documents. Voters require information about their representatives—what they are doing and who is influencing them—and about legislation that affects them. Families living near factory farms, for example, need to know about those operations' environmental impacts.

In our work, we recognize that the smallest policy decision can undercut the public's right to know. Last summer, OTG staff and several of our partners were made aware of troubling provisions tucked away in two versions of the massive Farm Bill. Together, we successfully stripped the Senate's bill of language that would have that would have prohibited the Environmental Protection Agency (EPA) from releasing basic information about any owner, operator, or employee of a livestock operation. The House's bill, however, entered conference with even more expansive and dangerous language that would have cut off access to information about agricultural operations as well as livestock operations. The language was so broad it would have extended the Freedom of Information Act's (FOIA) privacy protections to corporate farms. The coalition and our allies presented a united front and pushed back. The language was dropped.

We also recognize that government initiatives that seem positive on their face require the input and expertise of outsiders to be meaningfully implemented. OTG took advantage of US involvement in the creation of the Open Government Partnership (OGP)—an international platform that requires countries to create concrete, open government action plans in collaboration with civil society—to focus the Obama administration's attention on a number of the community's high priority issues. In addition to pushing for the initial US plan to address these issues, we created an evaluation process intended to keep the plan from turning into a "check the box" exercise. In preparation for the second US plan, which was scheduled to be released in December 2013, we reached out to our partners and beyond to create our own plan to present to the administration. Ultimately, the second US plan was diverse and ambitious, and largely reflective of civil society's input. It addressed many of the same issues highlighted by our organizations. Long-standing priorities included modernizing the administration of FOIA, such as bringing records management into the digital age and overclassification, and also emerging topics like surveillance transparency and making it easier for the public to understand who truly owns a company. Although the commitments vary in terms of level of detail, the number of substantive commitments and the possibility that some of them will lead to real and lasting improvements in openness are both notable. The proof of the plan's value will be in its execution. We are continuing to work with our partners and allies to make sure the promises of this plan are carried out in a meaningful way.

We believe there's a need for open government at the heart of every issue. But not every organization has the resources necessary to have any of their staff devote time and attention to open government issues. That's why we're here. Thanks to initiatives like the Open Government Partnership, the president's Open Government Directive, and the dedication of staff in the White House and Congress, the opportunities to advance government transparency are many. But the consequences of excessive secrecy are still great, as the public is still shut out from understanding all of what its government is doing in its name. The stakes are high and the opportunities are great. Together, we're prepared to push for less secrecy and more democracy.

To learn more about OpenTheGovernment.org and the coalition's work, see www.openthegovernment.org.

PATRICE MCDERMOTT, PHD, MLN, is executive director of OpenTheGovernment.org and author of *Who Needs to Know?: The State of Public Access to Federal Government Information.* In 2011, she received the James Madison Award from the American Library Association in recognition of her work to champion, protect, and promote public access to government information and the public's right to know. She was inducted into the National Freedom of Information Act Hall of Fame in 2001. A frequent speaker on public access and open government issues, she holds a doctorate in political science from the University of Arizona and an MLn in library and information management from Emory University.

FROM DR. KING TO HARD KNOCK RADIO: THE ARC OF MEDIA JUSTICE

Davey D

For many, August 11, 1967, is probably an insignificant date, especially as it pertains to the civil rights movement. There was no special legislation being signed. There were no major marches, demonstrations, civil unrest, or social upheavals. It was a Friday, and Dr. Martin Luther King had just arrived in Atlanta from San Francisco to address the National Association of Radio Announcers at their annual convention.

Some who are up on history know this speech as one that was titled "Transforming a Neighborhood into a Brotherhood," where King focused on addressing economic injustices and the War in Vietnam. However, it's the first part of this speech that is truly remarkable and sadly overlooked. Here, Dr. King spoke about the power of the media—and, in particular, black radio—and the important role that the many announcers and disc jockeys in attendance played in furthering the civil rights struggle. King asserted:

> I value this opportunity to address you this evening, because in my years of struggle both North and South, I have come to appreciate the role the radio announcer plays in the life of our people. For better or for worse, you are opinion makers in the community, and it's important that you remain aware of the power that is potential in your vocation.[5]

King went on to add that the masses of Black folks were totally dependent upon radio, while television—which was emerging and attractive to many—spoke to the needs and values of the white middle class. Thus, Black radio represented the heart and soul of Black folks.

King noted that some Black radio jocks like Magnificent Montague, who were shut down by the police, were being unfairly blamed for the civil unrest that was taking place in many cities around the country because folks used the DJs' slogans and on-air sayings during riots. King noted that was an attempt to obscure the many and significant contributions that Black radio jocks had made on behalf of the movement.

He then name checked announcers like Pervis Spann, Too Tall Paul White, and Georgie Woods, among others, and noted the roles they played in Freedom Summers in Mississippi, demonstrations in Birmingham and fundraising for the work being done. King asserted that, via their on-air banter and soul music, members of the National Association of Radio Announcers helped create important cultural bridges between Blacks and Whites, which made the process of integration easier.

He concluded that their ability to impact and transform the masses was something that even Alexander the Great could not do. It's an incredible speech that has been lost in history, even though the speech was actually pressed and released as a now hard-to-find record.

A year later, the association's convention was marred by violence: organized crime figures descended upon the convention to disrupt plans by the group to open a broadcasting school and to consolidate their power by purchasing more radio stations.

The National Association of Radio Announcers also came under attack from Black militants who felt they needed to move away from integration and adopt a more revolutionary tone. After that 1968 convention, Black radio underwent significant changes; many of the most outspoken personalities were being silenced by consolidation or strict format changes pushed forth by white owners who stressed "More Music, Less Talk"—a concept that was heralded as groundbreaking at the time. Black radio stations dropped the name "Black" and substituted the term "urban" to make white advertisers and listeners feel more comfortable.

In August 1979, almost twelve years to the day after Dr. King's speech, at the Jack the Rapper Convention organized by renowned Black radio announcer Jack Gibson in Atlanta, Minister Louis Farrakhan addressed a body of Black radio disc jockeys. Unlike King, the minister's remarks were scathing. He addressed the co-opting of Black radio and how many in the room had been hired specifically to exploit and mislead the masses in a one-sided conversation that prioritized un-politicized foolery.

Farrakhan noted that they were willing tools for an industry that was in the business of mind control, and he cited examples of how their listeners emulated these deejays and embraced the ideology and products that they touted. He warned the deejays that the airwaves were sacred and that, if they continued dumbing down and silencing the community, they would be held accountable and their heads would one day roll when folks rose up and pushed back.

Excerpts from Farrakhan's 1979 speech would later be sampled by a number of rap artists pushing for change throughout the years, including the iconic group Public Enemy, who may have been the first to do it.

This brief rundown of history is important because it underscores a decades-old battle that has existed in the Black community over media and the roles that those of us who are able to speak to the community should be playing. This history takes on even more importance in the wake of massive media consolidation, which reached an apex in 1996 under the Telecommunications Act and has not slowed down since. Indeed, we currently find ourselves in battles to save net neutrality, to keep full access to the new technological media landscape.

Our daily syndicated show, Hard Knock Radio, which has just celebrated its twelfth year, is predicated on our mission to build important cultural bridges—not so much between Black and white, but among marginalized communities that have also found their voices exploited and excluded, to use the airwaves as a tool for transformation: essentially, to give voice to the voiceless. That voiceless community includes independent artists and cultural workers; political prisoners; overworked and underappreciated frontline educators who oppose the school-to-prison pipeline; citizens fighting mass privatization; and activists dealing with all manner of issues like immigration, police, and corporate terrorism. With Hard Knock Radio currently based in a region that is home to Silicon Valley, where great technological advancements and billions are being made daily, we aim to remind all of us of our collective humanity and to lay out what that means. We build on King's title, "Transforming a Neighborhood into a Brotherhood"; today, we would add "Sisterhood," and any other title that denotes inclusivity.

In his 1967 speech, Dr. King took time to address the role of technology and the vast, "dazzling" advances made by "modern man" in what at that time was called the "Jet Age." King astutely pointed out that while man had invented remarkable machines that could think for us, and vessels that could travel faster than sound or pierce the skies to reach outer space, these examples of great technological prowess were marred by a "poverty of the spirit." He asserted that the dilemma facing America was such that if we couldn't bring an end to racial strife and economic inequality, or learn to deal with each other as neighbors, we would one day perish as fools, in spite of our modern feats. Each day, when we crack the mics on Hard Knock Radio, we strive not to perish.

DAVEY D is a longtime journalist, an adjunct professor at San Francisco State University, and a media justice advocate. Along with Anita Johnson, Weyland Southon, and Tsadae Neway, he is a cofounder of the award-winning, daily syndicated show *Hard Knock Radio*, which originates out of KPFA 94.1FM on Pacifica. His website is www. daveyd.com.

FIGHTING THE SURVEILLANCE STATE ONE CITY AT A TIME: THE BILL OF RIGHTS DEFENSE COMMITTEE (BORDC)

Shahid Buttar

A President's Prescient Warning

Sixty years ago, a president and war hero warned the American people that the industries supplying our military were poised to one day threaten democracy in the United States. He said, in seemingly prophetic terms:

> In the councils of government, we must guard against the acquisition of unwarranted influence, whether sought or unsought, by the military-industrial complex. The potential for

the disastrous rise of misplaced power exists and will persist. We must never let the weight of this combination endanger our liberties or democratic processes. We should take nothing for granted. Only an alert and knowledgeable citizenry can compel the proper meshing of the huge industrial and military machinery of defense with our peaceful methods and goals, so that security and liberty may prosper together.[6]

President Dwight D. Eisenhower's warning was neither radical nor misguided. He precisely predicted the course of future events, and his concerns were quintessentially patriotic. These were central themes in the final speech of a Republican president, the last to reach our nation's highest office having also ascended the ranks of the military.

Half a century later, when the George W. Bush administration took advantage of 9/11 to mount an assault on basic constitutional principles like the separation of powers, much of the country was caught off-guard. A combination of compliant legislatures, sycophantic mass media, cultural hysteria, and deferential courts combined to enable overbearing policing and intelligence practices that dramatically eroded rights to speech, assembly, due process, and equal protection under the laws.

Even as the cast of characters in Washington changed, the war on the Constitution continued. The rise of remote robotic assassination, the revelation of mass secret surveillance, and the resignation of accountability for government torture have all happened under the Obama administration. In the long arc of history, America has spent this millennium's first decade-and-a-half sliding in a demonstrably authoritarian direction.

We the People Respond

But We the People have not resigned our rights without a fight. And while we may be down, we are far from out.

Inspired by the Bush administration's excesses, but equally concerned about the Obama administration's continuation of its disturbing legacy, a transpartisan, multiethnic grassroots network working to restore fundamental constitutional rights continues to grow today. Around the country, that movement finds support in resources, training, analysis, and coordination from the Bill of Rights Defense Committee (BORDC).

After the Bush administration introduced the USA PATRIOT Act,[7] grassroots activists from all corners of the country banded together to raise their voices to defend fundamental constitutional values threatened by government surveillance.

By early 2002, local committees formed in several cities around the country and came together to establish a national organization to coordinate their local organizing efforts. BORDC was founded to cultivate grassroots activism defending democracy in America from mass surveillance, with two guiding implementation principles: first, Americans of diverse ethnicities with wide-ranging points of view and political persuasions share interests in constitutional rights; and, second, in the face of mounting executive fiat and popular fear blinding the eyes of legislators, only together—by taking action at the local level—can those communities build sufficient power to overcome the entrenched opposition of the military-industrial complex.

Stoking a National Controversy

Resolutions affirming the Bill of Rights, and particularly repudiating the PATRIOT Act, spread like wildfire across the United States. Under the Bush administration, over four hundred cities took official action to dissent from federal surveillance policy, alongside eight states as politically diverse as California and Idaho.

When the PATRIOT Act's dangerous surveillance powers were reauthorized in 2005, the one senator who voted against it in 2001 escalated his resistance, leading a filibuster by reading into the congressional record hundreds of local resolutions that had passed at that point. Congress did eventually submit to reauthorization, but, driven by dissent from around the country, at least insisted upon placing sunset provisions to invite recurring debate going forward.

As the PATRIOT Act was reauthorized several times under the Obama administration, Congress and the courts—driven and enabled by a litany of duplicate executive "intelligence" agencies—went on to enable even more dramatic assaults on constitutional rights.

In 2008, Congress enacted amendments to the Foreign Intelligence Surveillance Act (FISA), essentially legalizing the unconstitutional mass surveillance regime revealed by Edward Snowden five years later. Undeterred by the shameful history of the Japanese–American internment, Congress in 2011—three years into the Obama administration—gave the military the power to detain Americans indefinitely without trial in its National Defense Authorization Act (NDAA) beginning in 2012.

The People Strike Back

The 2013 Snowden revelations firmly documented that government crimes committed in secret for over a decade remained ongoing. The daily experiences of communities of color around the US—especially in low-income areas, where profiling according to either race, religion, or point of view has long subjected residents to arbitrary stops, searches, and police violence—affirm that equally atrocious abuses happen every day in plain sight.

Only by uniting the voices of all Americans who share an interest in constitutional rights can We the People overcome the military-industrial juggernaut that President Eisenhower warned us of sixty years ago. The way BORDC works to unite those disparate communities is to focus the attentions of local, grassroots coalitions on policies and practices of law enforcement and intelligence agencies, like local police departments, that abuse their rights in common.

In 2013, successful campaigns on opposite ends of the country illustrated how this strategy can transform the policy debate.

In California, we worked with a novel coalition of libertarians, peace and justice activists, and Japanese–American advocates to challenge the NDAA's domestic detention provisions.[8] A grassroots coalition mounted a statewide public education campaign, securing a bill signed by the governor that pledged the state to respect the right to trial. They're back at it in 2014, with another campaign to challenge the ability of the National Security Agency (NSA) to recruit students in California and undermine the integrity of its criminal justice system.[9]

Mere weeks after the victory in Sacramento, a coalition in Asheville, North Carolina, culminated several years of grassroots organizing with their city's adoption of the nation's most wide-ranging and expansive municipal civil liberties policy,[10] even in the face of active opposition from law enforcement agencies and police unions.[11] Like a similar measure in New York City,[12] it offered something for everyone by addressing profiling alongside surveillance.

Our nation's founders were not scared of the many security threats they confronted. They intelligently reserved greater fear of our own government growing tyrannical. The specter of security undermining individual liberty is precisely why they wrote the Constitution as an elaborate design to restrain potential government excesses. President Eisenhower warned us that our "councils of government" would be increasingly vulnerable to co-optation. That's what inspires BORDC to mobilize diverse Americans at the local level, where We the People still have a voice.

BORDC works with grassroots activists from all walks of life and political persuasions by providing materials, campaign platforms, training, guidance, micro-grants, and introductions to diverse local allies to amplify their respective voices. To learn more about the Bill of Rights Defense Committee, or to deploy these resources in your own community, please visit www.BORDC.org.

SHAHID BUTTAR leads the Bill of Rights Defense Committee. He frequently writes and speaks about surveillance, detention, torture, as well as the constitutional rights and checks and balances they each offend. Shahid's work at BORDC also includes guiding grassroots coalitions in a dozen cities mounting resistance to abusive policies and local police practices. He graduated from Stanford Law School in 2003. In his individual capacity, he organizes artist collectives, and performs around the country as an electronica DJ and MC.

ACTION COALITION FOR MEDIA EDUCATION (ACME): SMART MEDIA EDUCATION FOR THE TWENTY-FIRST CENTURY

Rob Williams and Julie Frechette

Welcome to the twenty-first century.

A century in which we need Smart Media Education, funded and operated independently of state and corporate interests, #morethanever.

Big picture? We not only live in the most mediated society in world history, but the world's most "connected." "The Machine Is Us"—and

"The Machine Is Us/ing Us," as Kansas State University digital anthropology professor Michael Wesch explains in his much-watched YouTube video.[13] New digital media's double-edged sword helps sharpen our minds as we confront the great Media Paradox of our time.

To wit: as we blithely email, Facebook, Tweet, Instagram, and Pinterest our way into our "LinkedIn" twenty-first century, publishing personal stories of meaning and power built on our digital demographic data, the Lords of the Cloud are busy surveilling, sorting, sifting, aggregating, and sharing our personal information with the world's most powerful corporations and government entities, often without our informed consent (#readthefineprint).

A decade ago, we media educators were working in the midst of a media-saturated world of 3,000 commercial messages daily, a world in which 90 percent of our media content was ultimately owned by six transnational media corporations with "nothing to tell but everything to sell," as George Gerbner, dean of the University of Pennsylvania's Annenberg School for Communication, famously observed.[14] Instead of promoting health, wealth, and wisdom, powerful corporations designed their media stories to put profit and the interests of global for-profit media networks above all else, promoting disease, debt, and distraction. "We live in the most media-saturated society in world history," explained veteran author, activist, and media critic Jean Kilbourne. "ACME's approach to media education is critical for us all, giving us the tools to make sense of our media culture and to engage in changing it. This is vital for our students, our schools, our communities, and ultimately, for our democracy."[15]

In the twenty-first century, the stakes are even higher. Our media stories are now "shared" through an ever-growing network of social media channels. The world's most powerful for-profit new digital media corporations—Google, Facebook, Amazon, Apple—built and manage these proprietary digital networks to aggregate our personal data, surveil our social networks, and condition us to be better buyers.

How do we challenge the Lords of the Cloud and Big Media interests, who care more about building brand loyalty, mining our data, and separating us from our cash than they do about our children, our classrooms, our communities, and our commons? It begins with the kind of media education ACME has been organizing and practicing since 2002. "The problem we face with a hyper-commercial, profit-obsessed media system is that it does a lousy job of producing citizens in a democracy," noted media scholar and author Robert McChesney. "A solution is real media literacy education that doesn't just make people more informed consumers of commercial fare, but makes them understand how and why the media system works so they may be critics, citizens, and active participants. This is the type of media education ACME is committed to doing."[16]

Independently funded media literacy education plays a crucial role in challenging Big Media's monopoly over our culture, helping to move our world toward a more just, democratic, and sustainable future. Free of any funding from Big Media, ACME is part of the emerging Smart Media Education network, a global coalition run by and for media educators that champions a three-part mission:

1. Teaching media education knowledge and skills—through keynotes, trainings, and conferences—in classrooms and communities to foster more critical media consumption and more active participation in our democracy.
2. Supporting media reform. No matter what one's cause, media reform is crucial for the success of that cause, and since only those who are media-educated support media reform, media education must be a top priority for all citizens and activists.
3. Democratizing our media system through education and activism.

"As the online media environment becomes more 'personalized,' commercial interests literally choose the news, information, opinion, and products we have access to. ACME's approach to media education helps us understand that these choices are being made for us in the name of profit—not democracy," concluded community cable TV maven Lauren-Glenn Davitian. "Armed with this knowledge, we can insist on public access to all kinds of information, media production, and distribution. Otherwise our hands are tied and our communities are doomed."[17]

Given the urgent need for viable media literacy initiatives as part of a pluralized digital pedagogy, ACME unites us in our cause for smart media education grounded in democratic principles and advocacy. Ultimately, by collaborating with other media literacy educators and activists, we can improve the lives of young people and our global citizenry by providing resources and support to those who champion the goals of media reform by diversifying media production, media narratives, and audience engagement.

Learn more about ACME at www.smartmediaeducation.net.

ROB WILLIAMS, PHD, is the board copresident of the Action Coalition for Media Education (ACME). A musician, historian, journalist, and professor of communications/media studies, he lives and works in the once and future Vermont republic.

JULIE FRECHETTE, PHD, is professor of communication at Worcester State University in Massachusetts, where she teaches courses on media studies, critical cultural studies, media education, and gender representation. She recently coauthored the textbook *Media In Society*, published in 2014, and, in 2002, her book, *Developing Media Literacy in Cyberspace: Pedagogy and Critical Learning for the Twenty-First-Century Classroom*, was among the first to explore the new "multiple literacies" approach for the digital age. She is the author of numerous articles and book chapters on media literacy, critical cultural studies, and gender and media, and serves as a board member of the Action Coalition of Media Educators. She earned her PhD at the University of Massachusetts–Amherst.

MOVE TO AMEND: THE FASTEST GROWING MOVEMENT YOU'VE PROBABLY NEVER HEARD OF

David Cobb

Corporations are not merely exercising political power today—they have become de facto ruling institutions. Über wealthy individuals and unelected, unaccountable corporate CEOs make the fundamental public policy decisions in this country. They decide the levels of toxins and poisons that will be in our air and water, what work we do and how much we get paid to do it, what kind of health care we get, and what our country's energy policy will be. "We the People" get to decide between Coke or Pepsi and paper or plastic at the grocery store. Citizens are treated as consumers or workers but rarely as sovereign human beings with the right to decide how our society will be organized.

Indeed, a peer-reviewed scientific study conducted by Princeton University professor Martin Gilens and Northwestern University professor Benjamin Page concluded that the United States operates more like an oligarchy than a democratic republic. "The central point that emerges from our research is that economic elites and organized groups representing business interests have substantial independent impacts on US government policy, while mass-based interest groups and average citizens have little or no independent influence."[18]

Two lynchpins for understanding how this happened are a pair of illegitimate, court-created legal doctrines. The first is corporate personhood and the second is that money equals political speech.

Corporate personhood is shorthand for the notion that a corporation must be treated as if it were a person with inherent unalienable rights. This means that corporate lawyers can argue to overturn any law that attempts to control corporate harm and abuse on the basis that the law somehow violates a corporation's "constitutional rights." That means laws designed to protect the environment, worker safety, public health, and welfare, or to regulate campaign finance—literally any democratically enacted law—can be challenged. And many have been. To see the depressingly long list, check out the amazing timeline created by Jan Edwards of the Women's International League for Peace and Freedom.[19]

That money equals political speech is the equally odious court-created doctrine that holds that making a political contribution or spending money to influence an election is a form of speech protected by the First Amendment. This doctrine has been used to gut even the flimsiest campaign finance laws and has allowed the wealthy to control the electoral process of this country.

The egregious 2010 Supreme Court decision in *Citizens United v. Federal Election Commission* combined these two doctrines. In essence, the Supreme Court has allowed a ruling elite to steal our sacred right to self-government and fundamentally perverted the notion that the United States can be a democratic Republic. Even worse, they have used the legal system to legitimize the theft.

Happily, there is a growing grassroots movement in this country that says loudly and clearly "*Ya basta!* Enough already!"

Move to Amend is a coalition of groups and individuals that has exploded on the political landscape calling for a constitutional amendment to abolish both of these doctrines.

Despite being virtually ignored by corporate media, during its short existence, Move to Amend has:

- Grown to over 340,000 supporters,
- Assisted in passing over 500 city or county resolutions in support of the amendment,
- Helped 16 state legislatures pass resolutions in support of the amendment,
- Created 150 local affiliates working locally on passing the amendment, and
- Passed referendums in support of the amendment at the ballot box in over 200 jurisdictions, many of which are politically conservative.

Of particular note, the leadership of Move to Amend looks a lot like the United States. The National Leadership Team is gender balanced and has strong representation across racial and ethnic lines. The members are also spread out across every region of this country, with folks in urban, rural, and suburban communities.

The leadership has studied successful movements of the past—abolitionists, women's suffrage, trade unionists, and civil rights. Like many readers of Project Censored, they have come to the conclusion that real movements are not birthed—or even led by—politicians or leaders of nonprofits but by committed individuals.

The leadership of Move to Amend understands that it will require a social movement to amend the Constitution to make the US the democratic republic that the creation myth of this country promises. They are absolutely committed to building a movement that is broad and deep, based in local communities, multiracial, multiethnic, and intergenerational.

MOVE TO AMEND'S PROPOSED 28TH AMENDMENT TO THE US CONSTITUTION[20]

House Joint Resolution 29 introduced February 14, 2013

SECTION 1. [*Artificial Entities Such as Corporations Do Not Have Constitutional Rights*]

The rights protected by the Constitution of the United States are the rights of natural persons only.

Artificial entities established by the laws of any State, the United

States, or any foreign state shall have no rights under this Constitution and are subject to regulation by the People, through Federal, State, or local law.

The privileges of artificial entities shall be determined by the People, through Federal, State, or local law, and shall not be construed to be inherent or inalienable.

SECTION 2. *[Money is Not Free Speech]*

Federal, State, and local government shall regulate, limit, or prohibit contributions and expenditures, including a candidate's own contributions and expenditures, to ensure that all citizens, regardless of their economic status, have access to the political process, and that no person gains, as a result of their money, substantially more access or ability to influence in any way the election of any candidate for public office or any ballot measure.

Federal, State, and local government shall require that any permissible contributions and expenditures be publicly disclosed.

The judiciary shall not construe the spending of money to influence elections to be speech under the First Amendment.

To join the effort, go to www.MoveToAmend.org and sign the petition, or call (707) 269-0984.

DAVID COBB is a principal with the Program on Corporations, Law, and Democracy (POCLAD). He has sued corporate polluters, lobbied elected officials, run for political office himself, and has been arrested for nonviolent civil disobedience. In 2004, he ran for president of the United States on the Green Party ticket and was responsible for demanding a recount in Ohio. He serves on the National Leadership Team of Move to Amend.

ELECTRONIC FRONTIER FOUNDATION: BEFORE, AFTER, AND NOW—HOW THE SNOWDEN LEAKS REVITALIZED MEDIA COVERAGE OF DIGITAL PRIVACY

Dave Maass

If Edward Snowden hadn't escaped the country with a massive cache of secret intelligence agency documents and leaked them to the press, then June 5, 2013, would only have been notable to me as the day that

Wall Street Journal investigative reporter Jennifer Valentino-DeVries met my dogs.

Instead, that was the day that the media fully rebooted the global debate over electronic privacy.

Valentino-DeVries was visiting EFF's new offices on the outskirts of San Francisco's Tenderloin district to talk to our attorneys about National security letters (NSLs). These are secret orders that the Federal Bureau of Investigation (FBI) issues to telecommunications companies, without judicial review, to demand user data. Even though I'm EFF's media relations coordinator, I tend to leave these interviews to our legal team since it's so difficult to know what we can and can't say about our cases challenging NSLs. We can't even name our clients, and as much as they would like to talk about the issue, our clients remain gagged by the NSLs. What we can say is, in March 2013, a judge agreed with our argument that NSLs are unconstitutional, although the ruling is on hold while the government appeals. Valentino-DeVries, who was among the small group of reporters covering our slowly progressing cases, stopped by my office on the way out; all I had to add was an introduction to my office-loafing terriers, Marlowe and Buster.

It's funny to imagine how that encounter would've gone if it had only happened a couple hours later.

The first leak, reported by Glenn Greenwald in the *Guardian*, was an order from the Foreign Intelligence Surveillance Court confirming what we have alleged for years: the National Security Agency has been gathering call-records data on millions of innocent Americans. The phone lines blew up with calls from reporters who wanted EFF's expert analysis. The next day, Laura Poitras and the *Washington Post*'s Barton Gellman came out with a report on PRISM, the NSA program that obtains user communications and stored data from Internet corporations such as Google and Facebook. It was like the media had launched a DDoS attack[21] on our phone lines, with as many thirty interview requests coming in per hour. By Friday, we had to bring in pizza and chain people to their desks to handle the reporter requests. Then, on Sunday, the *Guardian* revealed Snowden's identity, complete with a picture of his laptop with an EFF sticker. We were in the middle of the storm and we weren't sure how long it would last.

As I write this almost a year later, the debate over electronic surveillance refuses to go away, remaining as a major policy issue on the local, national, and international levels. Much of this is due to a sea change in how the press views the newsworthiness of digital privacy.

A prime example is in the coverage of the Foreign Intelligence Surveillance Court (often referred to as the FISA court), the secret judicial panel tasked with overseeing and approving the government's electronic surveillance programs. For years, we have been suing under the Freedom of Information Act (FOIA) to obtain opinions issued by the FISA court, but before the "Summer of Snowden," the lawsuits were a hard sell to reporters. The story was just too procedural to make for sexy headlines. Now, however, reporters are interested in every motion we file in these cases—particularly as nearly every document the government has posted to its official ICOnTheRecord Tumblr page on NSA spying has been in response to FOIA litigation. The records we wrenched free include opinions showing that NSA mass surveillance violated the Fourth Amendment and that the NSA had made substantial misrepresentations to the court.

The new media attention has extended beyond the NSA. Reporters are now zeroing in on local law enforcement surveillance as well, such as the use of automatic license plate readers, drones, and Stingrays (a kind of fake cell tower that gathers data indiscriminately). We've also noted increased interest in our intellectual property work as it applies to Internet freedom, including our copyright and patent reform efforts and our opposition to the intellectual property clauses in the Trans-Pacific Partnership agreement (which made story #3 in *Censored 2014* and, thanks to WikiLeaks, appears again in this year's *Censored 2015* Top 25 list).

We are a seeing a renaissance in digital rights reporting, with privacy and Internet freedom again becoming an actual beat for many reporters after dropping off in the mid-2000s. Digital security specialists—such as Bruce Schneier, Jacob Appelbaum, and Ashkan Soltani—are sharing bylines on stories in national media outlets. Retired NSA chief Keith Alexander was the first guest to be skewered, grilled, and served by John Oliver on his new HBO show, "Last Week Tonight," while the *Washington Post* and *Guardian* shared the Pulitzer for public service journalism. EFF's press call traffic has eased a little, I believe, in part because reporters don't need as many pundits to spell out how the technology works or why the NSA's programs are dangerous. These journalists have become the experts, advocates, and activists themselves.

To learn more about the Electronic Frontier Foundation's work and how to get involved in the defense of civil liberties in the digital world, go to www.eff.org.

DAVE MAASS advocates for transparency and free expression through media relations and investigative research at the Electronic Frontier Foundation. Prior to joining EFF, he worked as an investigative journalist in every state along the US–Mexico border, covering issues including law enforcement, campaign finance, and technology. He is also a columnist for *San Diego CityBeat* and a contributor to Blastr.com.

Notes

1. *Pete Seeger: The Power of Song*, dir. Jim Brown, Concert Productions International, 2007; quoted in Doug Pibel, "In Review: Peter Seeger: The Power of Song," *YES! Magazine*, November 7, 2007, http://www.yesmagazine.org/issues/liberate-your-space/in-review-pete-seeger-the-power-of-song.
2. Michael Hiltzik, "Cultural Production of Ignorance Provides a Rich Field for Study," *Los Angeles Times*, March 9, 2014, http://articles.latimes.com/2014/mar/09/business/la-fi-hiltzik-20140307. For a book-length treatment on the topic of agnotology, see Robert Proctor and Londa Shienbinger, eds., *Agnotology: The Making and Unmaking of Ignorance*, (Stanford: Stanford University Press, 2008). See also Naomi Oreskes and Erik M. Conway, *Merchants of Doubt: How a Handful of Scientists Obscured the Truth on Issues from Tobacco Smoke to Global Warming* (New York: Bloomsbury Press, 2010). We thank Rob Williams for bringing the aforementioned *Los Angeles Times* article to our attention.
3. Hiltzik, "Cultural Production of Ignorance."
4. "Smoking and Health Proposal," Brown & Williamson, 1969; available through the University of California, San Francisco's Legacy Tobacco Documents Library, http://legacy.library.ucsf.edu/tid/rgy93foo;jsessionid=F708AEFC13F8722B9878057E6E89D78E.tobacco03. Brown & Williamson marketed the Kool, Raleigh, and Viceroy brands of cigarettes.
5. "MLK Addresses the National Association of Radio Broadcasters," (August 11, 1967), King Center Archive, http://www.thekingcenter.org/archive/document/mlk-addresses-national-association-radio-announcers.
6. Farewell address by President Dwight D. Eisenhower, January 17, 1961; Final TV Talk 1/17/61 (1), Box 38, Speech Series, Papers of Dwight D. Eisenhower as President, 1953–61, Eisenhower Library; National Archives and Records Administration, http://www.ourdocuments.gov/doc.php?flash=true&doc=90.
7. USA PATRIOT was an acronym for "Uniting and Strengthening America by Providing Appropriate Tools Required to Intercept and Obstruct Terrorism." The 2001 act is commonly referred to as the PATRIOT Act.
8. Adwoa Masozi, "California Outlaws Indefinite Detention," People's Campaign for the Constitution (Bill of Rights Defense Committee), October 3, 2013, http://www.constitutioncampaign.org/blog/?p=15024; and Nadia Kayyali, "California Assembly Bill 351 Passed Nearly Unani-

mously out of the State Assembly," People's Campaign for the Constitution (Bill of Rights Defense Committee), May 31, 2013, http://www.constitutioncampaign.org/blog/?p=13547.

9. Matthew Kellegrew, "California Senate Challenges NSA Spying," People's Campaign for the Constitution (Bill of Rights Defense Committee), May 20, 2104, http://www.constitutioncampaign.org/blog/?p=17058.

10. WLOS News, "Asheville Civil Liberties Resolution," November 16, 2013, https://www.myworldnews.com/Channel/162-wlos/Story/269110-asheville-civil-liberties-resolution;   and "Asheville City Council Unanimously Passes A Civil Liberties Resolution," *Down with Tyranny* (blog), October 25, 2013, http://downwithtyranny.blogspot.com/2013/10/asheville-city-council-unanimously.html#sthash.VnMB7Ip6.dpuf.

11. Roger McCredie, "Police Benevolent Association: 'Civil Liberties Resolution' Could Spell Trouble for Asheville," *Tribune*, November 12, 2013, http://www.thetribunepapers.com/2013/11/12/pba-civil-liberties-resolution-could-spell-trouble-for-asheville.

12. Michael Figura, "NYC Passes Policing Reforms over Mayor's Veto," People's Campaign for the Constitution (Bill of Rights Defense Committee), August 26, 2013, http://www.constitutioncampaign.org/blog/?p=14641.

13. Michael Wesch, "Web 2.0 . . . The Machine is Us/ing Us," no date, http://youtu.be/6gmP4nkoEOE.

14. See, for example, George Gerbner, "Reclaiming Our Cultural Mythology," *Ecology of Justice* 38 (Spring 1994), 40. Also accessible at: http://www.context.org/iclib/ic38/gerbner.

15. "Testimonials," Smart Media Education for the 21st Century, http://smartmediaeducation.net/our-testimonials.

16. Ibid.

17. Ibid.

18. Martin Gilens and Benjamin I. Page, "Testing Theories of American Politics: Elites, Interest Groups and Average Citizens," *Perspectives on Politics*, forthcoming (Fall 2014). As *Censored 2015* went to press, a draft copy could be found at http://www.princeton.edu/~mgilens/Gilens homepage materials/Gilens and Page/Gilens and Page 2014-Testing Theories 3-7-14.pdf.

19. Jan Edwards, "Timeline of Personhood Rights and Powers," Move to Amend, www.movetoamend.org/sites/default/files/timeline_hmprint.pdf.

20. For the full text of the amendment, with clear explanations of its technical terms (including, for example, the difference between "natural" and "artificial" persons), see https://movetoamend.org/wethepeopleamendment.

21. According to DigialAttackMap.com, "A Distributed Denial of Service (DDoS) attack is an attempt to make an online service unavailable by overwhelming it with traffic from multiple sources. They [the attackers] target a wide variety of important resources, from banks to news websites, and present a major challenge to making sure people can publish and access important information." See http://www.digitalattackmap.com/understanding-ddos.

CHAPTER 5

Service Learning
The SUNY–Buffalo State and Project Censored Partnership

Michael I. Niman

Recent exposés have documented the exploitation of college student interns: some internships, during which unpaid students essentially take the place of paid employees—performing mundane tasks rather than engaging in pedagogically fruitful and intellectually challenging activities and thus gaining nothing of value—are a legally dubious form of exploitation. Other internships have unprepared (and often unsupervised) students arrive at workplaces as if they were going to a class, or acquiring skills while supervisors train them, but ultimately fail to have the students provide anything in return to their host institutions. The ideal internship experience is symbiotic, where a student's skills and intellectual horizons both grow, while the host organization benefits from an ongoing dynamic relationship with a university or college.

In recent years, this relationship often manifests not just as internships, where individual students venture out onto job sites, but as service learning courses, where entire classes, including their professors, are wed to host organizations, integrating a collaborative work enterprise into the day-to-day classroom experience. The State University of New York (SUNY) Faculty Senate differentiates service learning from both simple volunteerism and complex internships. Volunteerism, they point out, like service learning, requires a commitment to help others. Service learning, however, like a good internship, is also "focused on specific educational outcomes for those who do such service." As such, the experience is symbiotic for both the host and the students.

Unlike an internship experience, service learning is tightly integrated within a specific course environment, involving not just students, but the seasoned expertise of a professor as well. In this way, service learning projects also promote "public scholarship," answering the call for professors to move beyond the academy and engage with communities so that public service projects benefit directly from their expertise. This is especially important for public institutions, most of which have public service as a central tenet of their mission statements.

SUNY–Buffalo State, as SUNY's largest comprehensive college and the only one centrally situated in an urban environment, has emerged as a leader in service learning. Our mission to serve our community, our location adjacent to a dynamic, culturally rich neighborhood that currently is home to a large population of refugees and migrants—from Africa, Asia, the Middle East, and Latin America—and our location in a large border city adjacent to a rich agricultural area, have all provided us with many opportunities for service learning collaborations with not-for-profit community advocacy organizations.

Buffalo State also houses SUNY's largest journalism program. While our community is rich with service learning opportunities, there is nothing on the ground here—or anywhere for that matter—quite like Project Censored. Though Project Censored is physically situated, legally chartered, and academically hosted in California, the reality is that the breadth and depth of Project Censored's reach is global: on the web, and in bookstores both nationally and internationally. Though I've traveled to California to attend a Project Censored Awards Ceremony, as well as to attend a Project Censored conference, I've never seen or been to a Project Censored office, though I have it on good authority that such a thing exists. There is no iconic Project Censored building or campus, just like there's no Free Speech Valley in California. I've met with Project Censored folks not only in California, but also at conferences and meetings scattered around the continent. Project Censored, like the censorship that it exposes, is everywhere, while being nowhere specific. So, I thought, why couldn't it be in my city, on my campus, and in my classroom, mingling with my students, just as I've mingled with Project Censored activists around the continent and online?

Traditionally, Service Learning is intertwined with notions of community—of connecting academic communities with physical communities, creating a mutually beneficial relationship. That's the history, but it's also a short history, as the concept of course-integrated service learning has barely been around for two decades. During this time, both the Internet as a whole and social media specifically have challenged our commonly accepted concepts of community, with anthropologists and sociologists doing ethnographic fieldwork in digital spaces. Of course, the concept of community has long transgressed physical space, with diasporas and ideological communities as old as human migration. Investigative reporters and members of the alternative press, with our unique struggles and sometimes-shared experiences of oppression, are clearly a community. And the Internet has allowed me to bring this community into my classroom as a dynamic presence.

This is the argument I constructed when, as a SUNY Service Learning Fellow, I petitioned to make my Alternative Media course at SUNY–Buffalo State a service learning course with Project Censored as my partner. I was surprised to learn that nobody else had previously proposed this and that, as with other new service learning partnerships, we'd be in uncharted territory. The idea, it turned out, made perfect sense to both the Project Censored staff and to the Buffalo State Office of Volunteer and Service Learning. So off we sailed, testing the water with what Project Censored and I termed a "pilot project."

Another major difference between an internship and service learning in the SUNY system is that, as the SUNY Faculty Senate puts it, "internships are structured experiences in a discipline" that "require a sequence of prior courses and a knowledge base for student success." By comparison, "service learning does not assume a ladder of prior courses or developed skills; students at any level can engage in this pedagogy." The theory is that the tightly integrated participation of a professor would make up for the lack of experience on the part of the students, allowing students to engage in real-world professional experiences at an earlier stage in their academic tracks. As a result, students who participate successfully in these classes gain self-esteem and intellectual maturity, are less likely to drop out or transfer, and are more likely to become engaged in other community or campus activities. Service learning course veterans also tend to take subsequent courses more seriously, maintaining higher grade point averages, better positioning themselves for grad school or professional employment.

With most censored stories now originating in the alternative press, my theory was that, in searching for censored stories to validate, my students would become familiar with another world of media. Hence, this seemed like an ideal match for an alternative media course. What I didn't expect, going into this project, was that only two out of twenty-three students would have had any exposure to what we would term "alternative media." Some seemed to have little, if any, exposure to news media of any sort. This situation did, however, fit the bill for a service learning course, open to students at any level.

What shocked me more than the students' lack of experience with alternative media was what quick studies they were. Events in the world kept catching them off-guard. The stories they were hearing and seeing seemed incomplete. They had a hunger to find the missing pieces—the censored stories.

I began the semester by constructing a web page (http://mediastudy.com/picks.html) that linked to a wide array of alternative news sources. The semester started out with discussions of various forms of censorship and self-censorship, followed by tips on finding a censored story. I organized the students into five groups—with the first task to name their groups. We got "Team WTF," "Team Liger" ("like a cross between a Lion and a Tiger"), and of course "Team No Name," and so on. The course met for nearly three hours once a week. Students brought food. Every week, students would engage course readings on the alternative press, scour the links I provided, and come into class and give reports on different alternative media outlets they'd encountered. We'd discuss whether or not we thought they were alternative media (sorry, *Huffington Post*), and why. By the third week, we started discussing group nominations for censored stories, working with research tools such as LexisNexis to determine if the stories fit the criteria of censored news. By the fourth week, students started cross-referencing and evaluating sources to determine the credibility, and hence, the validity, of the stories. By mid-semester, we had our first Validated News Stories, and the monumental task of editing them down to two hundred or so words.

I don't want to make this seem like it was easy. It wasn't. There were many false leads, leads that didn't pan out, and write-ups of stories that just didn't make any sense. But I don't recall another class in which students seemed to blossom intellectually at such a fast rate. Once they discovered the world of alternative media, they couldn't let go of it. Web-addicted as students are, many became obsessed with this new online neighborhood—to the point of neglecting social media to instead surf this new terrain, weaving their new and old Internet lives together by posting their newfound world on their old social media networks. The class took over a large portion of their lives and mine, with excited student emails coming in around the clock. Students took on new stories to explore both as teams and as individuals, going beyond course expectations—an exhausting process for all involved.

By the end of the semester, students in this class had validated and published over a dozen censored stories, including one that was ranked by Project Censored judges as the #4 top censored story of the year[1]—written by a team with no prior alternative media experience. However, success in validating stories was always secondary to learning. Not every team or student succeeded in validating a censored story, but every effort to validate a story was rewarded with a story of its own. Students would work on a story for a few weeks only to have a major media outlet pick it up, making it no longer censored. Though the students sometimes felt like they'd just been passed in a race, or worse yet, thrown out of the game, I explained that while it might not be good for their aspirations to discover the next big censored story, overall it was a good thing that the corporate media was doing their job, reminding them why we expose censored stories, and why ideally, there wouldn't be any censored stories to expose. Hence, it's important that grading formulas take into account not the final product, but the effort, strategies, and experiences involved with getting there, no matter where there might be. It was important to always encourage students, especially when they thought they were failing.

At the end of every semester, students anonymously evaluate their courses. The numerical feedback for this course could not be any higher—literally. I understood that this really wasn't about me. I was coordinating this course more than I was teaching it, mostly pointing students in the direction of suspected censored stories, then guiding them through the validation process. And, as the students wrote, their first-hand encounter with the reality of corporate media censorship combined with their experience of the personal agency developed in thwarting that censorship was transformative. The Project Censored service learning partnership not only gave my students a rich academic experience and a new set of skills, it didn't just give some of them publications for their resumes or CVs—it transformed them into media makers and activists.

For instructors and students interested in learning more about how to include Project Censored curriculum in your school, visit the "Project Censored in the Classroom" webpage at http://www.project-censored.org/project-censoreds-commitment-to-independent-news-in-the-classroom.

MICHAEL I. NIMAN,PHD, is a professor of journalism and media studies at SUNY–Buffalo State in New York. An archive of his writings is available at mediastudy.com. He is currently planning on developing his investigative reporting class into a Project Censored service learning course as well.

Note

1. "Obama's War on Whistleblowers," in *Censored 2014: Fearless Speech in Fateful Times*, eds. Mickey Huff and Andy Lee Roth (New York: Seven Stories Press, 2013), 72–75; see also chapter 2 in this volume for an update on this story.

CHAPTER 6

Rewriting Apartheid

News Media Whitewashing of South Africa and the Legacy of Nelson Mandela

Brian Covert

Apartheid in South Africa was a legalized and institutionalized system of racial segregation and economic "separate development," imposed by a European minority population on an African majority. From 1948 to 1994, this system robbed millions of South African citizens of basic human rights, destroyed countless individual lives, broke up families and uprooted entire communities, and sent thousands of its people beyond its borders into exile.

South African apartheid also divided the international community of nations, and pitted the citizens of a number of countries against their own governments in demanding an end to political and economic support of the apartheid system. For years on end, hardly a day went by without news about apartheid and South Africa being carried by some news organization or another, somewhere on the planet.

The passing of former South African president Nelson Rolihlahla Mandela in 2013 at age ninety-five, and his extraordinary life over those nine decades as arguably the greatest statesman of modern times, gave the press worldwide a golden opportunity to go back and dig deeply into the history of apartheid, the long and often bloody road that Mandela and his people had taken to freedom, and the roles that various other countries had played in that process.

Yet the corporate press in the United States and elsewhere passed by—if not avoided—this opportunity, and, in consequence, important news stories about apartheid South Africa and Mandela's legacy went underreported, misreported, or not reported at all. The crime of apartheid—an "indelible blight on human history," as Mandela himself aptly called it[1]—was all but rewritten out of history and media memory in the wake of Mandela's passing.

This report, using a diversity of available sources (print and audio-visual, database and web-based, corporate and independent media), attempts to correct that rewritten record by covering some of the more important issues surrounding Mandela, South Africa, and apartheid that corporate media either distorted or deleted altogether.

A SANITIZED STRUGGLE

When African-American journalists who have reported on the South African scene for some of the biggest American news outlets reviewed the US corporate media's performance in reporting Nelson Mandela's death, prominent among their criticism was the sanitizing from most coverage of one key element of the Mandela story: the armed struggle.[2]

An informal survey of corporate media coverage of Mandela's passing shows that criticism to be well-founded.

"Mandela is often mentioned in the same breath as Mahatma Gandhi and Martin Luther King Jr., who also changed nations through nonviolence. Yet Gandhi and King were killed before their dreams were realized," reported the Associated Press shortly after Mandela's passing.[3] CNN labeled the late Mandela a "pacifist" as well as someone who was "greatly inspired by Gandhi, by the nonviolent struggle."[4]

It is true that Mandela did follow the policy of nonviolent resistance espoused by his political organization, the African National Congress (ANC), up until the early 1960s. But it is also a fact that increasingly brutal crackdowns and the South African government's outlawing of the ANC and other grassroots organizations pushing for peaceful change led Mandela and others to create in 1961 a new armed wing of the ANC called "Umkhonto we Sizwe" (Spear of the Nation), or "MK" for short. Mandela served as the guerrilla army's first commander in chief.

In Mandela's first-ever television interview, conducted with a British reporter in May 1961 during the year or so that Mandela was an underground fugitive in South Africa, he made his position clear:

There are many people who feel that it is useless and futile for us to continue talking peace and nonviolence against a government whose reply is only savage attacks on an unarmed and defenseless people. And I think the time has come for us to consider, in the light of our experiences in this stay at home [protest campaign], whether the [nonviolent] methods which we have applied so far are adequate.[5]

A month after this interview, Mandela launched Umkhonto we Sizwe; six months later in December 1961, MK conducted its first acts of sabotage by setting off bombs at electric power stations and government offices around South Africa. The ANC's armed struggle had begun.

Media Faces of Mandela

Even against that historical background, however, some in the US news media could not resist the temptation of tacking on a few other inaccurate faces as well to the Gandhi/King face of Mandela.

NBC aired interviews from South Africa in the wake of Mandela's passing with former US presidents Bill Clinton and Jimmy Carter, both of whom compared Mandela to Gandhi and King. Carter went one better, adding a comparison of Mandela to Mother Teresa, the late Albanian nun who had been made a saint by the Catholic Church.[6]

To some in the US black community, this kind of reportage smacked of a media whitewashing of Mandela's true face: that of an African patriot who had helped bring the apartheid regime down to its knees by taking up arms and fighting back.

"In whitewashing the image of Mr. Mandela, the corporate media's plan is to do to Mandela what was done to Dr. Martin Luther King, namely, to make him a one-dimensional peacemaker who had no other agenda than to appease his enemies," wrote a columnist for the *Final Call*, the newspaper of the US-based Nation of Islam, once the spiritual home of the late African-American leader Malcolm X.[7]

Reverend Jesse Jackson, a former aide to King, expressed similar sentiments. "There is an attempt to do in his [Mandela's] death what they could not do in life—take away his story," Jackson said while in

South Africa for Mandela's memorial services. "He did not go to jail as some out-of-control youth who needed to be matured. He went in as a freedom fighter and came out as a freedom fighter."[8]

And in an audio report from prison in the US, African-American journalist/activist Mumia Abu-Jamal commented: "At his passing, American media has painted [Mandela] as a kind of African 'civil rights' leader, perhaps Martin Luther King the Fifth, with a halo of white hair." Abu-Jamal added, "In fact, it is dangerously misleading to make of Mandela a King or a Malcolm [X]. He was neither. He was himself: an African lawyer who used every tool available to him— legal when he could, illegal when he must—to resist a system that crushed African lives like peanut shells. He was a revolutionary, an armed guerrilla, and commander of a guerrilla army. . . ."[9]

But if the US corporate media were quick to sanitize Mandela's legacy, there were also some prominent African Americans who did their share to help out.

In an interview broadcasted on the NBC *Today* show, former US secretary of state Colin Powell said of Mandela: "He went for love. He said, 'Let's reach out and show love and reconciliation.' He kind of reminds me of the experience of the United States. He's [like] our [George] Washington, and our [Abraham] Lincoln, and our Martin Luther King all rolled in one."[10]

That same line was followed by US President Barack Obama during his public tribute to Mandela at a soccer stadium in the South African black township of Soweto. Obama compared Mandela to Gandhi, to King, to "America's founding fathers," and to Lincoln: "Emerging from prison, without the force of arms, [Mandela] would—like Abraham Lincoln—hold his country together when it threatened to break apart."[11] (Contrary to Obama's claim, in fact, MK, the "force of arms" that Mandela had organized and led before he went to prison, was still waging guerrilla war and was still a potent political tool against the apartheid regime when Mandela came out of prison twenty-seven years later.)[12]

All absurd likening aside of Mandela to US presidents Washington and Lincoln and to Mother Teresa, what did Mandela himself make of such comparisons between his struggle and nonviolent movements led by renowned figures like Gandhi and King?

In a 1999 special edition of *Time* magazine devoted mostly to Albert Einstein as "person of the century," Mandela penned a two-page tribute to Gandhi that laid it all out:

> Gandhi remained committed to nonviolence; I followed the Gandhian strategy for as long as I could, but then there came a point in our struggle when the brute force of the oppressor could no longer be countered through passive resistance alone. We founded Umkhonto we Sizwe and added a military dimension to our struggle.
>
> Gandhi himself never ruled out violence absolutely and unreservedly. He conceded the necessity of arms in certain situations. He said, "Where choice is set between cowardice and violence, I would advise violence. . . . I prefer to use arms in defense of honor rather than remain the vile witness of dishonor. . . ."
>
> Violence and nonviolence are not mutually exclusive; it is the predominance of the one or the other that labels a struggle.[13]

One US independent cable television outlet posed the question after the ex–South African leader's death: was Mandela a terrorist or a pacifist?[14] The correct answer is that he was neither one. Until the US media get this basic question straight, it is doubtful that the true legacy of Mandela as a revolutionary figure in his own right will be reported to and understood by the wider public.

USA: THE CIA CONNECTION

For years following Nelson Mandela's arrest by South African police in 1962, rumors swirled that the US government's Central Intelligence Agency (CIA) had somehow been involved. Yet despite the importance of this issue to the apartheid saga, the American media's reporting of it over time has ranged from sporadic, erratic coverage at best to no coverage at all.

In 1986, while Mandela was serving his second decade of a life sentence in prison, the long-rumored CIA connection finally broke the surface of the news barrier. Three South African newspapers, including the *Star* daily paper of Johannesburg, reported that a US government diplomat in South Africa (who reportedly had a little too much to drink at a farewell party) admitted that two decades earlier he had been working for the CIA and had been the one who passed on the tip to South African authorities of Mandela's underground whereabouts.[15]

An independent US television producer, John Kelly, had been looking into those same rumors stateside as well: "I initially obtained a 1962 secret CIA report about the penetration and surveillance of the ANC, and this led me to begin an investigation. And right at that time, CBS News contacted me because a story had broken in the Johannesburg *Star* about the general incident, about the original arrest of Mandela."[16]

And so it was that on August 5, 1986—twenty-four years to the very day after the arrest of Mandela—the American public first heard of the CIA connection when anchor Dan Rather announced it during prime time on the *CBS Evening News*.[17]

The two-minute-long segment, though framed within the narrow context of Cold War hostilities between the US and the Soviet Union, nevertheless expanded on the *Star*'s story and gave a name and a visible face to the loose-tongued US diplomat: Donald Rickard, a former consular officer based in South Africa. The CBS report quoted "US intelligence sources" as saying that Rickard had been working in South Africa at the time of Mandela's arrest under diplomatic cover for the CIA.[18]

The long-held rumors had finally been backed with hard facts and were now out there waiting to be investigated further by the esteemed American Fourth Estate.

And then . . . silence. No major US media picked up the explosive story from there—not the big papers of record such as the *New York Times* and *Washington Post* or any other of the US television networks.[19] US-based British journalist Andrew Cockburn did manage to cleverly slip the news about the CIA and Mandela into an article he contributed to the *Times*, but Cockburn's story appeared on an op-ed page, not on the news pages.[20]

There the CIA connection to Mandela stayed, buried at the bottom of the dead-news pile and unreported to the public for another four years.

Liberating the Story

One week after the February 11, 1990, release of Mandela from prison, *Newsweek* magazine touched on the CIA connection: "[B]etrayed by informers—some accused the CIA, though no one ever proved it—he went out one day disguised as a chauffeur, ran into a roadblock and lost his freedom for the next 27 years."[21]

But just as they had done a few years before with CBS, the US media on the whole took a pass on following up that information.[22]

Then, a few months later, with Mandela in Europe and planning to visit North America next, the CIA connection was dug up again and put back into the headlines and airwaves in a big, unexpected way.

Joseph Albright and Marcia Kunstel, two reporters from the Washington DC bureau of Cox News Service—through the company's flagship newspaper, the regional *Atlanta Journal-Constitution*—published details of the US government's "increasingly embarrassing secret" of the 1962 CIA tip leading to Mandela's arrest.[23]

In the Cox News report, an anonymous "former US official" quoted another South Africa–based US CIA operative, Paul Eckel, as saying within hours of Mandela's capture: "We have turned Mandela over to the South African security branch. We gave them every detail, what he would be wearing, the time of day, just where he would be. They have picked him up. It is one of our greatest coups."[24]

The front-page *Journal-Constitution* story also quoted Gerard Ludi, a former South African intelligence operative, as saying that the CIA had a "deep cover" South African agent working in the inner circle of the ANC branch in Durban back in 1962, and that the deep-cover agent reported to the top US officer working for the CIA in South Africa at the time, Millard Shirley. "Millard was very proud of that operation," Ludi was quoted as saying.

Caught with their proverbial pants down, the Big Media Feeds in the US that for so long had gone out of their way to avoid investigating the CIA connection to Mandela—the *Washington Post* and *New York Times* in particular—were now forced to report the story, and did so: they mostly repeated the *Journal-Constitution* story while adding no original reporting of their own to it, aside from contacting the CIA to ask for a comment.[25]

But the CIA was not commenting; neither was the White House.[26] Then–US president George H. W. Bush, a former CIA director, was publicly evasive about the new CIA-Mandela revelations—even though it was Bush himself, as vice president under prior US president Ronald Reagan, who had approved the inclusion of Mandela and the ANC in an international "Terrorist Group Profiles" index that had been compiled just two years before in 1988.[27]

African-American leaders demanded a full disclosure of the CIA's role in Mandela's original arrest and a US government apology to him.[28] But during Mandela's first whirlwind tour of US cities soon afterward in summer 1990, neither a full disclosure nor an official apology to Mandela ever came—not from Bush or any other US president after him, including Barack Obama.

The Struggle Continues

When Mandela died, the CIA role in his arrest was revived among some independent and alternative media. But most of the US establishment press once again showed no sign of wanting to go back and revisit the story.[29]

Though the details have remained officially unconfirmed, it is generally known today that both US and British government spy agencies had the activities of a number of South African antiapartheid activists like Mandela under close surveillance for decades, both within South Africa and overseas, and were sharing that information with their South African intelligence counterparts.[30]

In early 2014, a month after Mandela's death, the online *Huffington Post* reported that Ryan Shapiro, an activist and PhD student at the Massachusetts Institute of Technology (MIT), had filed a federal lawsuit against the CIA, seeking information on the agency's connection to the late Mandela's arrest.[31] The lawsuit seeks for the CIA to disclose its connections to South African intelligence agencies, plus any other information that it may have on past investigations of the late Mandela and of antiapartheid movements in both the US and South Africa.[32]

In March, *Democracy Now!* broke the story that Shapiro had also filed lawsuits against the Federal Bureau of Investigation (FBI), National Security Agency (NSA), and Defense Intelligence Agency (DIA), seeking information on what they too have in their files on the arrest and activities of the late Mandela.[33]

The CIA connection to Mandela is, by any standard of news, a story worth investigating and reporting. Yet the facts of that connection remain mostly hidden to this day behind a Great Wall of official obscurity and a US corporate media whiteout. It has been a real struggle for more than fifty years for the whole truth of this important story to come out in the media and, to borrow a phrase from the international antiapartheid movement of the time, the struggle for that truth continues.

JAPAN: "HONORARY WHITE"

Following Nelson Mandela's passing, an article in the *Japan Times* daily newspaper in Tokyo typified much of the generally respectful coverage in the Japanese vernacular and English-language press on the former South African president.

The Times reported on Mandela's three visits to Japan in his lifetime, the last one being in 1995, a year into his presidency: "During the five-day official visit, he expressed appreciation for Japan's support during South Africa's struggle to end racial segregation and achieve democracy."[34]

But as an alert reader of the story correctly pointed out, such news coverage in Japan gave a greatly distorted view of the true relationship that had existed back then between Japan Inc. and apartheid South Africa.

In fact, at the time Japan was playing both sides of South Africa's racial divide, giving lip service to "support" for Mandela and the black antiapartheid struggle while also remaining fully engaged in trade with the country's white-ruled apartheid regime.

Missing from this and other news reporting in Japan following Mandela's death was the one controversial factor that defined the Japan–South Africa relationship throughout the Cold War era: the preferential status known in Japanese as *meiyo hakujin* ("honorary white"), which was officially bestowed on the Japanese people by the South African government and accepted as such by Japan's government and business community.

The honorary white status for Japan had first been set by South Africa back in 1930—even before formal diplomatic ties between the two nations were established in 1937, and long before South Africa's official apartheid policies of "separate development" of the country's races became the law of the land starting in 1948.

The idea of the South African government back in those early days was to grease the wheels of trade with Japan by issuing a special, short-term exemption for Japanese tourists, students, and wholesale merchants and buyers of South African products to reside in South Africa.[35] The honorary white designation was seen from the beginning by the Japanese government as a positive step for "our mutual commerce and amicable relations."[36]

What that meant in daily life was that any Japanese visitor to South Africa granted an honorary white exemption—unlike most South Africans of color—would be allowed to live in whites-only residential areas, to frequent whites-only facilities such as restaurants and public swimming pools, and to use whites-only public transportation such as buses. (As time went on, however, even those honorary white Japanese found themselves being discriminated against and unaccepted by white South African society.)

Japan came under increasing pressure by the international community, especially African nations, from the 1960s onward to take a stronger stand against apartheid. Yet while other Western countries had been forced by domestic and international pressures over the years to reduce trade with South Africa, Japan was steadily holding the course and in some areas even increasing its ties.

Thus in 1986, for the first time ever, Japan had the dubious "honor" of becoming the world's number-one trading partner with apartheid South Africa. That honor was repeated again the following year in 1987.[37]

Condemnation of Japan–South Africa relations now seemed to come from all corners, domestic and foreign.

In December 1988, the United Nations passed a resolution expressing grave concern at the growing repression in South Africa and calling for more severe international measures to further isolate Pretoria. To Tokyo's horror, the UN General Assembly singled out Japan by name in its resolution, calling upon "those States which have increased their trade with South Africa and, particularly, Japan, which recently emerged as the most important trading partner of South Africa, to sever trade relations with South Africa."[38] The government of Japan ignored that urgent UN recommendation.

Mandela in Japan

Erased too from Japanese news coverage following Mandela's death was the controversy that surrounded his first two visits to Japan in the early 1990s.

The first visit was in October 1990, eight months after his release from prison in South Africa. Mandela, then ANC deputy president, was invited by the Japanese government on an official state visit to Japan during a fundraising swing that he and an ANC delegation were making through Asian nations and Australia.

Upon his arrival in Japan, Mandela received a warm welcome from the public as he addressed a stadium crowd of about 20,000 Japanese and foreign-resident supporters in the city of Osaka.[39] But in the days that followed in Tokyo during Mandela's meetings with government and business leaders, then–prime minister Toshiki Kaifu of Japan personally turned down Mandela's request for $25 million, saying Japanese laws did not permit such financial funding of overseas political organizations.[40]

The financial shunning from Japan—apartheid South Africa's second-largest trading partner at the time—was a major one, and the only such rejection that Mandela and the ANC received from any of the other countries on that first Asian tour.

That snub was followed up by another one a half-year later in April 1991, when the International Press Institute (IPI), a press advocacy organization based in Austria, invited Mandela to be the keynote speaker at that year's IPI annual conference in the Japanese city of Kyoto.

Word was out from the ANC's office in Tokyo that the Japanese government had put one condition on Mandela's upcoming visit: no politically oriented speeches while he was in Japan as a private citizen. That would mean that unlike all the other countries Mandela had been visiting, no big ANC fundraising events could be held in Japan, and consequently no large sums of money would be going back home with Mandela to South Africa for the antiapartheid struggle.

And that is exactly how it played out during his second visit to Japan. Mandela gave his address on the importance of press freedoms to the international gathering of journalists in Kyoto, then quietly departed Japan before most of the Japanese media and public knew he was even in the country.[41]

Diplomatic Moves

The reason behind such an embargo on public appearances by Mandela became clear enough just a few months later when Japan, like other countries anxious to get trade back on track, lifted many of its already weak sanctions against South Africa.

Some months after that in early 1992, despite vehement protests from the ANC at that stage, Japan and South Africa resumed full diplomatic ties, opening embassies in each other's nations for the first time.[42]

"It was a great setback for Japan's diplomacy in the post–Cold War [period], ruining all that we've tried to build through the years," Jerry Matsila, the ANC's representative in Tokyo, said of the premature moves. "The image that I've tried to build among black Africans is that Japan is morally conscious and should be given a chance. They've destroyed all of that."[43]

A few months later in June 1992, white South African President F. W. de Klerk paid an official visit to Japan as the first head of state from South Africa ever to set foot on Japanese soil.[44]

As things turned out, it was Mandela who was elected president two years later in 1994 in South Africa's first democratic elections. A year into his presidency in 1995, Mandela returned to Japan for his third and last visit to the country, this time as head of state of a free South Africa.

Following Mandela's death in 2013, prominent government officials of the current ultra-right-wing administration of Japan were quick to dispense with accolades for the late South African leader, in the process giving history a good, old-fashioned rewriting. The Japanese ambassador to the United Nations, for one, fondly remembered Mandela's supposed "strong connection with Japan."[45]

Likewise, unreported in most Japanese media coverage of Mandela's death was any sign at all that South Africa's discriminatory "honorary white" status had ever existed—a status that Japan Inc., in its pursuit of ever more profits, had embraced right up to the end of apartheid, even at the cost of being internationally ostracized.

CENSORED TRUTHS

Well-known media personalities in the US took the opportunity of Nelson Mandela's passing to swap old war stories of their past coverage of South Africa and to generally pat themselves on the back for a job well done.[46]

"[T]his broadcast made a commitment to cover [Mandela's] struggle when few others were," one ABC News anchor presumptuously announced. "*Nightline* has been there every step of the way on his long walk to freedom."[47]

But if those in the US corporate media had bothered to check the historical record, they would have found a much different story to report: one of the more shameful periods in US press history in which the American media submitted to outside censorship and even censored themselves and others when it came to coverage of apartheid in South Africa.

Removing the Images

In 1985 and again the following year, South African President P. W. Botha declared a state of emergency in the country.

In an attempt to remove brutal images of police and military repression from the news reports of the world, the South African government began expelling from the country foreign news correspondents whose coverage was deemed anything less than flattering of apartheid. Foreign media outlets remaining in South Africa toned down their reports.

The desired result was soon achieved: the "bad news" about South Africa disappeared almost overnight from corporate media coverage and from public view.

Richard M. Cohen, a CBS News senior producer, was among the

outspoken few within the US journalistic community at the time who called for US media companies based in South Africa to pull out of the country rather than continue to censor their own news coverage under the apartheid regime's draconian laws.

Cohen blasted his profession's performance in a *New York Times* opinion article: "We play an insidious game of video appeasement with the [South African] government. Walk up to the line. Don't cross it. Show as much as you think you can get away with, never more."[48]

But some elites in the US media establishment preferred to play that game. Following Cohen's article appearing in the *Times*, his boss, CBS News president Howard Stringer, personally wrote a letter to South African government information officials, reassuring them that CBS intended to play by the rules as long as it remained in the country.[49]

Not even the highly respected anchor Walter Cronkite, America's favorite avuncular figure of TV news, was beyond the reach of US media self-censorship. Following a trip by Cronkite to South Africa, where he and a CBS News crew had filmed partly in secret for a planned documentary called *Children of Apartheid*, executives at CBS took the highly unusual step of having a South African lawyer sign off on the TV program before it could be aired to viewers in the United States. "I've never been involved in one where that's been done," Cronkite responded. "I found that whole process quite strange."[50]

In 1988, the government of Canada commissioned a study of the effects of South African censorship of the media. The study found that news coverage about South Africa by the leading US commercial television networks—CBS, NBC, and ABC—dropped dramatically in the wake of South African government press restrictions. "Pretoria has been largely successful in removing scenes of poverty, violence, and human rights violations from the television newscasts of the western world," the report found.[51]

Incident at Capitol Hill

Following up on the Canadian government study, a US congressional hearing was arranged in Washington DC over two days in March 1988 before the House Committee on Foreign Affairs' subcommittee on Africa to investigate the extent of South African government censorship on the US public.[52]

It was on the second day of the subcommittee hearing that some heavy hitters in the American media industry were scheduled to testify on censorship in South Africa and tell it "the way it was": Cronkite of CBS News; John McChesney, a senior editor with National Public Radio (NPR); former *Boston Globe* editor Tom Winship, representing the Washington DC–based Center for Foreign Journalists; political commentator Hodding Carter III, who worked in the US Department of State under past president Jimmy Carter; and Richard Manning, former Johannesburg bureau chief for *Newsweek*.[53]

When the time came for them to testify before Congress that day, however, not one of those influential media persons even bothered to show up—not even Uncle Walter of CBS News.

A seemingly stunned Howard Wolpe (D-MI), the subcommittee's chairman, said that a fear by American journalists of putting themselves or their US news companies "at serious risk of retaliation by the South African government" was the real reason behind most of the no-shows that day, and the reason that other unnamed journalists had declined earlier invitations to testify to the subcommittee as well.[54]

"These events are truly alarming," Wolpe said, opening the second day's hearing. "They suggest that South Africa's manipulation of the United States press penetrates well beyond South Africa's borders. It extends right into Capitol Hill."[55]

CBS News later denied any such fear of retaliation by South Africa, saying only that it was "not appropriate" for Cronkite to appear "before a House committee under circumstances in which the editorial process, protected by the First Amendment, could come under scrutiny."[56]

With most of the subcommittee's star witnesses now suddenly absent, the final day of the congressional hearing turned into a searing indictment of US media cooperation with apartheid.

The only journalist to show up that day was Kenneth Walker, a former ABC News correspondent then working for *USA Today* television. He testified how, as an African-American reporter, he had lobbied ABC News management for years to send a correspondent to South Africa to regularly cover the volatile situation there. When ABC had finally relented and broadcasted a special edition of its *Nightline* program live from South Africa in 1985, he said, it "subsequently became the most honored program in the history of broadcast news."[57] (A far cry from ABC having "been there every step of the way," as a *Nightline* anchor would boast two decades later.)

The real issue, Walker emphasized, was not that the US press, with all its resources, could not fully report on the crisis facing the majority black population of South Africa due to censorship, but rather that the American press would not take the risk. "I think once again the basic problem in South Africa really has less to do with restrictions than it does with the will and nerve of the management of US news organizations," he testified.[58]

In the end, Walker's damning statements that day about his own profession, like the rest of the congressional hearing's two days of testimony, disappeared into a media vacuum. Not a single US national newspaper or TV network reported on the congressional hearing on South African censorship.[59] The proceedings appeared only on the C-SPAN cable television network in a live broadcast.

By the time of Mandela's death twenty-five years later, US television media could not devote enough air time to South Africa. News personalities gushed with praise and personal anecdotes of Mandela as a much-loved and respected international figure. Take, for example, ABC News correspondent Ron Claiborne, on why it was "always difficult for me personally" to be professionally detached when reporting on Mandela: "Something kept getting in the way—the fact that I admired the man deeply."[60]

But if the US media, especially broadcast media, had gone beyond all the sentimental small talk and been more honest about their own past coverage of South Africa, they could have reported on how the US press had been no stranger to issues of censorship and self-censorship over the years. For media companies busy rewriting apartheid and priding themselves on "being there every step of the way," however, that was one news story that would go unreported following Mandela's demise.

THE NEXT MANDELA

No sooner had Mandela passed away than some in the media started scurrying around in search of a worthy replacement.

"[W]hile Nelson Mandela's work is sadly done, his dream is unfinished. The search for 'the next Mandela' is on," a Canadian children's rights activist declared in the *Globe and Mail* newspaper of Toronto.[61]

"The next Nelson Mandela of the world is rotting in a jail cell tonight, just like Mandela nearly withered for 27 years on Robben Island," surmised one senior writer for the *Philadelphia Daily News*. "Or he is on someone's terrorist watch list, or she is segregated and searched every time she travels through an international airport."[62]

"Where is the [next] British Mandela prepared to fight—really fight—for equal opportunities? To rail against the same injustices that galvanized Mandela: poverty and lack of human dignity?" a former British Broadcasting Corporation (BBC) announcer pleadingly asked.[63]

One right-wing media personality in the USA found the answer there among his own listeners: "I tell you, *you* are the next Nelson Mandela. You are the next Martin Luther King. You are the next Gandhi. You are the next Abraham Lincoln. You are the next George Washington."[64]

And on an NPR program titled "Who is the Next Mandela?," a *New York Times* columnist found it "kind of frustrating, frankly, that so much of the analysis has been backward-looking at the mistakes that the US made when Mandela was in prison years ago," preferring instead to move on and "stand up for people in various parts of the world who are now in prison and now need our help."[65]

Mandela, while he was alive, seemed to be an irresistible media choice when it came to reporting news related to South Africa. But by focusing on some vague notion of who might occupy Mandela's high pedestal on the global stage now that he is gone, those in the media are overlooking some bigger, more critical questions that need to be asked and reported about the country today.

This year marks exactly twenty years since the end of apartheid in 1994 and the birth of a democratic South Africa. A new generation, the so-called "born-frees"—those born into a free, post-apartheid nation—has now come of age. In May of this year they became the first of their generation to be eligible to vote in South Africa's parliamentary elections, the first national elections held after Mandela's death.

But as South African writer T. O. Molefe has noted, South Africa today is a country with huge economic, social, and educational disparities that threaten to undo the reconciliation of the "rainbow nation" that Mandela worked to bring together in his lifetime.[66]

At the time of Mandela's death, *Mandela: Long Walk to Freedom*, a South African–produced epic motion picture based on his autobiography, was showing at big movie theaters in cities around the world to great media acclaim.[67]

Showing in various countries around the same time to smaller audiences and with much less US media attention was a documentary film, *Dear Mandela*, also South African–produced, that raises some very uncomfortable but pressing issues. The film shows how masses of poor black residents of the country's sprawling shantytowns (officially called "informal settlements") continue to be forcibly evicted as a matter of local government policies, and how the ANC, the party of Mandela, is viewed as both condoning excessive police violence and being behind mob actions against those so-called shack dwellers who dare to protest their living conditions.[68]

There are many within and outside of South Africa who see the race-based apartheid system of the past as essentially having been replaced by a class-based apartheid system over the past two decades. The born-frees of today's South Africa have inherited from apartheid extremely high levels of poverty, joblessness, and homelessness, with most of the nation's arable land remaining in wealthy white minority hands instead of in poor majority black hands. Molefe expressed what is surely on the minds of many other young South Africans when he said: "Today, an economic revolution is what is needed most if South Africa is to continue on the path to reconciliation."[69]

Who will be the next Mandela to finish the revolution, indeed?

Whoever it is, let us hope that by the time the corporate media do find their elusive next Nelson Mandela, some of the more substantive news stories concerning the legacy of the original Mandela and South African apartheid—the armed struggle, the CIA, honorary white, and media censorship and self-censorship, among them—will have been duly looked into and accurately reported by the press once and for all.

BRIAN COVERT is an independent journalist and author based in western Japan. He has worked for United Press International news service in Japan, as staff reporter and editor for English-language daily newspapers in Japan, and as contributor to Japanese and overseas newspapers and magazines. He is currently a lecturer in the Department of Media, Journalism, and Communications at Doshisha University in Kyoto.

Notes

1. Quoted in "Statement by Nelson Mandela, Deputy President of the African National Congress," United Nations Special Committee against Apartheid, June 22, 1990, http://www. un.org/en/events/mandeladay/statement_SCAA_1990.shtml.
2. Richard Prince, "Praise, Disgust for S. Africa Coverage—Reporters Who've Covered Mandela Critique Their Peers," Maynard Institute, December 11, 2013, http://mije.org/richardprince/ praise-disgust-s-africa-coverage.
3. Jesse Washington, "Few Heirs Apparent to Mandela's Symbol of Freedom," Associated Press, December 7, 2013, http://bigstory.ap.org/article/few-heirs-apparent-mandelas-symbol-freedom.
4. Faith Karimi and Saeed Ahmed, "Nelson Mandela: 10 Surprising Facts You Probably Didn't Know," CNN, December 6, 2013, http://edition.cnn.com/2013/12/06/world/africa/nelson-mandela-surprising-facts. See also the CNN quote in Peter Hart, "Nelson Mandela and Nonviolent Resistance," Fairness and Accuracy in Reporting (FAIR), December 6, 2013, http:// www.fair.org/blog/2013/12/06/nelson-mandela-and-nonviolent-resistance.
5. Jeremy Barnes, "Nelson Mandela's First TV Interview in 1961," Independent Television News (ITN), July 2, 2013, http://www.itn.co.uk/World/79701/nelson-mandelas-first-tv-interview-in-1961.
6. Carrie Dann, "Clinton: Mandela's Example 'Went Way Beyond Political Leadership,'" NBC News, December 7, 2013, http://www.nbcnews.com/politics/politics-news/clinton-mandelas-example-went-way-beyond-political-leadership-v21794273. See also Erin McClam, "Carter: Mandela Belongs Next to MLK, Gandhi and Mother Teresa," NBC News, December 9, 2013, http://www.mediaandlife.com/2013/12/09/carter-mandela-belongs-next-to-mlk-gandhi-and-mother-teresa.
7. Jackie Muhammad, "'Sanitizing' Mandela," Final Call, January 6, 2014, http://www.finalcall. com/artman/publish/Perspectives_1/article_101108.shtml.
8. George E. Curry, "Claiming Nelson Mandela's Legacy: South Africans Struggle to Define Former President's Image," Charlotte Post, January 5, 2014, http://www.thecharlottepost.com/ news/2014/01/05/state-national/preserving-nelson-mandela-s-legacy.
9. Mumia Abu-Jamal, "Mandela Sanitized," Prison Radio, December 8, 2013, http://www.prisonradio. org/media/audio/mumia/mandela-sanitized-437-b-mumia-abu-jamal#.
10. Quoted in "Remembering Nelson Mandela," Today, TheGrio.com/MSNBC, December 6, 2013, http://thegrio.com/2013/12/06/why-we-have-to-celebrate-nelson-mandelas-revolutionary-past.
11. "President Obama Speaks at a Memorial Service for Nelson Mandela," White House, December 10, 2013, http://www.whitehouse.gov/photos-and-video/video/2013/12/10/president-obama-speaks-memorial-service-nelson-mandela.
12. For an informative short history of MK by a South African academic and activist, see Janet Cherry, Spear of the Nation: Umkhonto we Sizwe—South Africa's Liberation Army, 1960s-1990s (Athens: Ohio University Press, 2011). For an insiders' account by two former South African MK fighters, see Thula Bopela and Daluxolo Luthuli, Umkhonto we Sizwe: Fighting for a Divided People (Alberton, South Africa: Galago Books, 2005).
13. Nelson Mandela, "The Sacred Warrior," Time, December 31, 1999, 124.
14. WHDT-TV, "Mandela: Terrorist or Pacifist?," Next News Network, December 13, 2013, http:// www.youtube.com/watch?v=SyEbxx1pnCY. For a related story, see also Diana Cariboni, "Mandela, Pacifist or Rebel?," Inter Press Service, December 6, 2013, http://www.ipsnews. net/2013/12/mandela-pacifist-rebel.
15. David James Smith, Young Mandela (London: Weidenfeld & Nicolson, 2010), 274.

16. Quoted in an interview with the syndicated news program *South Africa Now*, as broadcasted on WNYC-TV in New York in June 1990 during Mandela's first US visit (from a VHS copy in the author's possession).

17. Reported by Allen Pizzey, *CBS Evening News*, August 5, 1986. The video clip can be viewed at http://www.youtube.com/watch?v=VzFdAe_rXLw.

18. Ibid. See also William Blum, *Rogue State* (Monroe, Maine: Common Courage Press, 2005), 288–90.

19. Reported by Eric Nadler, *South Africa Now*, broadcasted on WNYC-TV, June 1990.

20. Andrew Cockburn, "A Loophole in US Sanctions Against Pretoria," *New York Times*, October 13, 1986, http://www.nytimes.com/1986/10/13/opinion/a-loophole-in-us-sanctions-against-pretoria.html?smid=tw-share.

21. Tom Mathews, "Nelson Mandela: the Leader No One Knows," *Newsweek*, February 19, 1990, http://www.newsweek.com/nelson-mandela-leader-no-one-knows-207004.

22. "CIA Role in Mandela's Capture?," Fairness and Accuracy in Reporting (FAIR), March 1, 1990, http://fair.org/extra-online-articles/cia-role-in-mandelas-capture.

23. Joseph Albright and Marcia Kunstel, "CIA Tip Led to '62 Arrest of Mandela," *Atlanta Journal-Constitution*, June 10, 1990, A1. A shorter version of the story as it was carried in the *Chicago Tribune* can be viewed online at http://articles.chicagotribune.com/1990-06-10/news/9002170271_1_anti-apartheid-activities-gerard-ludi-cia-spokesman-mark-mansfield.

24. Ibid.

25. See George Lardner Jr. and David B. Ottaway, "CIA Linked to Mandela's 1962 Arrest," *Washington Post*, June 11, 1990, A18. See also David Johnston, "CIA Tie Reported in Mandela Arrest," *New York Times*, June 10, 1990, http://www.nytimes.com/1990/06/10/world/cia-tie-reported-in-mandela-arrest.html.

26. Associated Press, "Bush Quiet on Mandela-CIA Report," *Philadelphia Inquirer*, June 13, 1990, A9.

27. Robert Windrem, "US Government Considered Nelson Mandela a Terrorist until 2008," NBC News, December 7, 2013, http://www.nbcnews.com/news/investigations/us-government-considered-nelson-mandela-terrorist-until-2008-v21794290. Mandela would stay on that terrorism watch list for another twenty years, until Bush's son, US President George W. Bush, had Mandela removed from that list in 2008, just a few years before Mandela died. The original 1988 US government report on terrorism can be viewed at http://upload.wikimedia.org/wikipedia/commons/b/bb/Terrorist_Group_Profiles.pdf.

28. Ben Smith III, "Apology Urged for Mandela," *Atlanta Journal-Constitution*, June 11, 1990, D1. See also Michael Clements, "Disclosure Urged of CIA Role in Mandela's Capture in 1962," *USA Today*, June 13, 1990.

29. "'One of Our Greatest Coups': the CIA & the Capture of Nelson Mandela," *Democracy Now!*, December 13, 2013, http://www.democracynow.org/2013/12/13/one_of_our_greatest_coups_the. See also "CIA and Mandela: Can the Story Be Told Now?," Fairness and Accuracy in Reporting (FAIR), December 10, 2013, http://fair.org/home/cia-and-mandela-can-the-story-be-told-now.

30. See Jeff Stein, "The Day Mandela was Arrested, with a Little Help from the CIA," *Newsweek*, December 5, 2013, http://www.newsweek.com/day-mandela-was-arrested-little-help-cia-223935?piano_t=1. See also Aislinn Laing, "British Intelligence 'Birdwatchers Spied on Nelson Mandela's Hideout,'" *Telegraph*, July 9, 2013, http://www.telegraph.co.uk/news/worldnews/nelson-mandela/10169630/British-intelligence-birdwatchers-spied-on-Nelson-Mandelas-hideout.html.

31. Matt Sledge, "CIA Sued to Solve Decades-Old Nelson Mandela Mystery," *Huffington Post*, January 8, 2014, http://www.huffingtonpost.com/2014/01/08/cia-nelson-mandela_n_4559058.html. See also Adam Klasfeld, "Was CIA Involved in Mandela's Arrest?," *Courthouse News Service*, January 9, 2014, http://www.courthousenews.com/2014/01/09/64371.htm.

32. A copy of the original lawsuit documents filed by Shapiro can be viewed at http://www.sparrowmedia.net/2014/01/nelson-mandela-cia-foia-lawsuit.

33. "Exclusive: NSA, FBI, DIA Sued over Refusal to Disclose US Role in Imprisonment of Nelson Mandela," *Democracy Now!*, March 25, 2014, http://www.democracynow.org/2014/3/25/exclusive_nsa_fbi_dia_sued_over.

34. Masaaki Kameda, "Japan Offers Tributes to Human Rights Giant," *Japan Times*, December 6, 2013, 1, http://www.japantimes.co.jp/news/2013/12/06/national/japan-offers-tributes-to-human-rights-giant.

35. Masako Osada, *Sanctions and Honorary Whites: Diplomatic Policies and Economic Realities in Relations Between Japan and South Africa* (Westport, Connecticut: Greenwood Press, 2002), 39.

36. Quoted in Jun Morikawa, *Japan and Africa: Big Business and Diplomacy* (London: Hurst & Company, 1997), 37. For a Japanese-language account by the same author covering much of the same territory, see also Jun Morikawa, *Minami Afurika to Nihon* [South Africa and Japan] (Tokyo: Dobunsha, 1988).

37. Osada, *Sanctions and Honorary Whites*, 76–77. See also Masako Osada, "Japanese-South African Relations During the Apartheid Era," in *Japan and South Africa in a Globalising World*, eds. Chris Alden and Katsumi Hirano (Hampshire, UK: Ashgate Publishing Limited, 2003), 53–56.

38. Resolution 43/50, "Policies of Apartheid of the Government of South Africa," United Nations General Assembly, December 5, 1988, http://www.un.org/documents/ga/res/43/a43r050.htm.

39. "More than 20,000 Welcome Mandela in Western Japan," Associated Press, October 28, 1990, http://www.apnewsarchive.com/1990/More-Than-20-000-Welcome-Mandela-in-Western-Japan/id-7d978f6175082f484bdeb7fd406f7405.

40. Ronald E. Yates, "Mandela Takes Plea for Aid to Japanese," *Chicago Tribune*, October 31, 1990, http://articles.chicagotribune.com/1990-10-31/news/9003310201_1_nelson-mandela-anti-apartheid-movement-south-africans.

41. From the author's personal recollections and experience of actual events in April 1991.

42. "Tokyo and Pretoria Re-establish Full Ties," *Japan Times*, January 14, 1992, 1.

43. Wayne Lionel Aponte, "Warming to Pretoria Decried," *Japan Times*, February 18, 1992, 3.

44. Emiko Ohki, "De Klerk Trip Lauded," *Japan Times*, June 2, 1992, 3.

45. Quoted in "Statement by H. E. Ambassador Kazuyoshi Umemoto at the Special Meeting to Commemorate Mr. Nelson Mandela," Permanent Mission of Japan to the United Nations, December 19, 2013, http://www.un.emb-japan.go.jp/statements/umemoto121913.html.

46. See interview with former anchor Ted Koppel in ABC News, "'Nightline's' Historic Nelson Mandela Interview," YouTube.com, December 6, 2013, http://www.youtube.com/watch?v=3rn6QC27czo. See also ABC News, "'This Week': Remembering Nelson Mandela," YouTube.com, December 8, 2013, http://www.youtube.com/watch?v=JSy4pXgWrqw.

47. Anchor Juju Chang, quoted in ABC News, "'Nightline's' Historic Nelson Mandela Interview."

48. Richard M. Cohen, "To Reporters: Quit South Africa," *New York Times*, August 31, 1987, http://www.nytimes.com/1987/08/31/opinion/to-reporters-quit-south-africa.html.

49. Peter J. Boyer, "CBS Asks Advice on Cronkite Show on Apartheid," *New York Times*, November 5, 1987, http://www.nytimes.com/1987/11/05/movies/cbs-asks-advice-on-cronkite-show-on-apartheid.html.

50. Ibid.

51. Quoted in the film *Mandela—Free at Last*, produced by Globalvision, 1990 (VHS edition). For the original study, see *A Report on South African Censorship and Information Management*, Department of External Affairs, Government of Canada, January 22, 1988.

52. "Media Restrictions in South Africa," C-SPAN, March 15, 1988, http://www.c-span.org/video/?1637-1/media-restrictions-south-africa.

53. For a moving account of the late Manning's reporting experiences in and expulsion from South Africa, see Richard Manning, *'They Cannot Kill Us All': An Eyewitness Account of South Africa Today* (Boston: Houghton Mifflin Company, 1987).

54. *Media Restrictions in South Africa: Hearings before the Subcommittee on Africa of the Committee on Foreign Affairs, House of Representatives, One Hundredth Congress, Second Session, March 15 and 16, 1988* (Ann Arbor: University of Michigan Library, 1988), 167.

55. *Media Restrictions in South Africa*, 168.
56. "Journalists Skip Hill Hearing," *Broadcasting* magazine, March 1, 1988, http://americanradiohistory. com/Archive-BC/BC-1988/BC-1988-03-21.pdf.
57. *Media Restrictions in South Africa*, 183.
58. *Media Restrictions in South Africa*, 186.
59. Danny Schechter, "South Africa: Where Did the Story Go?," Fairness and Accuracy in Reporting (FAIR), March 1, 1988, http://fair.org/extra-online-articles/south-africa-where-did-the-story-go.
60. Quoted in "Nelson Mandela Remembered for His Charismatic Leadership," ABC News, December 7, 2013, http://abcnews.go.com/GMA/video/nelson-mandela-remembered-charismatic-leadership-21133484.
61. Craig Kielburger, "A Nation of Next Mandelas," *Globe and Mail*, December 13, 2013, http://www.theglobeandmail.com/globe-debate/a-nation-of-next-mandelas/article15968390.
62. Will Bunch, "The World's Next Mandela is Rotting in Jail Somewhere," Philly.com, December 8, 2013, http://www.philly.com/philly/blogs/attytood/The-worlds-next-Mandela-is-rotting-in-a-jail-somewhere.html.
63. Robin Lustig, "Where is the Next Nelson Mandela?," *Huffington Post*, December 9, 2013, http://www.huffingtonpost.co.uk/robin-lustig/nelson-mandela_b_4409728.html. See also Tom Geoghegan, "Mandela Death: Who Next as the World's Elder Statesman?," BBC, December 17, 2013, http://www.bbc.com/news/magazine-22389954.
64. Glenn Beck, quoted in "Beck Tells His Audience They are 'the Next Nelson Mandela,'" Right Wing Watch, December 10, 2010, http://www.rightwingwatch.org/content/beck-tells-his-audience-you-are-next-nelson-mandela.
65. Nicholas Kristof of the *New York Times*, quoted in "Who is the Next Mandela?," National Public Radio, December 11, 2013, http://www.npr.org/templates/story/story.php?storyId=250204535.
66. T. O. Molefe, "South Africa's Failing Grade," *New York Times*, January 15, 2014, http://www.nytimes.com/2014/01/16/opinion/molefe-south-africas-failing-grade.html. See also T. O. Molefe, "Mandela's Unfinished Revolution," *New York Times*, December 13, 2013, http://www.nytimes.com/2013/12/14/opinion/molefe-mandelas-unfinished-revolution.html.
67. *Mandela: Long Walk to Freedom* official website, http://mandelafilm.com.
68. *Dear Mandela* official website, http://www.dearmandela.com.
69. Molefe, "Mandela's Unfinished Revolution."

CHAPTER 7

"We Can Live without Gold, but We Can't Live without Water"

Contesting Big Mining in the Americas

Dorothy Kidd

INTRODUCTION

In early November 2013, a coalition from South and North America went to Washington to demand that "home countries" take responsibility for human rights violations perpetrated abroad by their national mining corporations. They called for lawmakers in the United States and the Inter-American Commission on Human Rights (IACHR) of the Organization of American States (OAS) to support new legal remedies for indigenous and rural communities affected by an "increased level of conflict, protest and social disruption" due to mining. They linked the problems in part to neoliberal free trade agreements that give inordinate power to mining corporations and investors and all but remove any legal mechanisms for redress by affected communities, citizens and mine workers. As Pedro Landa of the Honduran Centre for Collective Development said, "In countries like Honduras . . . it's easy to pass laws that facilitate the extractive industries, especially mining. . . . These companies are more powerful than governments, and can simply buy off officials."[1]

Several watchdog organizations have reported on the troubling pattern of violence in more than 300 Latin American communities affected by mining. In 2010, the Center for International Environmental Law reported numerous instances of private property destruction, forced displacement, death threats, arbitrary detention, kidnapping and assassination related to mining conflicts in Central America.[2] Global Witness documented forty-six extra-judicial killings at mining sites in Peru, between 2002 and 2013;[3] and Reporters without Borders stated that nine journalists who covered mining stories were murdered in Honduras between 2009 and 2013, with another eighteen deaths likely due to their reporting about mining.[4] And, in 2011, James Anaya, the United Nations Special Rapporteur on the Rights of Indigenous Peoples reported so much harm from extractive industry activity around the globe that he dedicated his remaining term in office to the issue.[5]

The rapid increase in mining and resource exploitation is among the less-reported consequences of the rise of neoliberal capitalism in the 1980s. Since then more than ninety countries have introduced new laws that give additional rights to corporate mining interests and favor them with reduced taxes, and environmental, labor, and human rights regulations. As a result of the ensuing rush of mining exploration and extraction, host communities, many of them indigenous, are engaged in what are, with no exaggeration, bitter struggles over life and death, including rape, assaults and murders, environmental degradation, loss of control over local governance, violence towards women and long-standing ways of life.

If you were to depend on commercial news, you would know little about this. In the last decade, the *New York Times* has run only eight articles, with only two reporting on mining-affected communities.[6] You could get more information by scouring the business press, such as Reuters, Bloomberg News, or *Business News America*. Mining conflicts affect their investor readership and they run stories from time to time; but they very seldom provide anything more than a snapshot of the problems. However, the good news about this story is that, if you have access to the Internet, there is a lot of information available. Although previous generations of social movements depended on the dominant media to get their story out, that is no longer entirely the case. The mining-affected communities themselves, national coalitions and mining watchdog groups, and indigenous, alternative, environmental, and human rights media networks are making these stories available in many different forms (and I include some of the better websites and documentary videos in the Additional Resources section at the end of this chapter).

Part of the drive behind this new rush for gold and other minerals is the rise of China. Nonetheless, the most notorious flag is that of Canada, which hosts approximately 60 percent of the foreign mining companies in Latin America, and has been involved in four times as many human rights violations as those from other countries.[7] In this chapter, I focus primarily on Canadian mining in the Americas. I begin with an examination of the "Washington consensus," the neoliberal policies of the US government and supranational organizations such as the World Bank, International Monetary Fund (IMF) and World Trade Organization (WTO) which have empowered transnational capitalist enterprise. I then move north to look at what's been called the "Toronto consensus," the historical and contemporary political and economic conditions which led to the new Canadian rush for gold, silver and other minerals within Canada, and throughout Latin America. Then, complicating the narrative, I examine some of the tensions that have arisen as the so-called "pink wave" of more left-wing Latin American governments has adopted the resource extraction model to jumpstart their economies and fulfill their social and political mandates.

In the second section, I examine the parallel story of resistance. Eduardo Galeano encapsulated the colonial record in his magisterial *Open Veins of Latin America: Five Centuries of the Pillage of a Continent*.[8] The record of mining in Canada can similarly be summed up as the enclosure of the commons of indigenous peoples, an "appropriation of local resources, a risk to community health, and a threat to the contact-traditional economy of hunting and trapping."[9] On both continents, mining has led to serious toxic effects for the water and soil, and major social disintegration, especially as the introduction of a higher wage economy has increased inequality, alcohol and drug abuse, and violence against women.[10]

This new rush for gold and other minerals has some new characteristics. Although the Americas still contain significant mineral deposits, much of the easily mined high-grade ore is gone, necessitating exploration further and further afield. While the miners and mining unions played a very important role in the culture and politics of several countries, such as Bolivia, Chile, Mexico, the US, and Canada, today's key protagonists are indigenous communities who are mobilizing locally and trans-locally via intertwined networks of mining-affected communities and indigenous peoples. Their goals are about much more than "just saying *no*." Drawing on the legacy of Latin American social movements, most communities are attempting to widen the scope of participatory democracy through the use of local assemblies, plebiscites, and other inventive forms of community organizing. Confronting a new set of neoliberal rules, they are allying with environmental and human rights organizations to change the rules of the game in all available legal forums, as exemplified by the coalition in Washington. Finally, they are creatively using media and trans-local communications networks to record the story and circulate it themselves, circumventing the dominant corporate media.

NEOLIBERALISM, NEO-EXTRACTIONISM: THE BACK STORY

During the 1980s, the national governments of the US and other rich countries, and global financial institutions such as the International Monetary Fund and the World Bank, promoted renewed foreign investment and development of mining in countries of the global south. Governments were encouraged to open up their lands, economies, and decision-making to foreign mining companies, as part of structural adjustment programs (SAPs) and free trade agreements. The argument was that the potential profits could provide employment, tax revenues, and spill-on effects for local economies, as well as substantial new infrastructure, such as roads, transport and communications, schools, and health clinics. The governments of more than seventy countries signed on, privatizing national production and distribution bodies, and introducing regulations favoring multinational corporations through reduced foreign ownership restrictions and corporate taxes, or softened environmental, labor, and human rights regulations.[11]

This push to big mining by the IMF and the World Bank was stepped up in the 1990s: between 1994 and 1999, the highest amount of credit was allocated to mining.[12] The subsequent bilateral and multilateral trade and investment agreements gave corporations the right to sue states, among other new rights; instead of state regulation, social and environmental concerns were to be addressed through voluntary codes and corporate social responsibility (CSR) programs favored by the Canadian and other governments.[13]

THE TORONTO CONSENSUS

Currently, the Toronto Stock Exchange is the global center for mining capital, and home to 56 percent of the world's public mining companies with investments in one hundred countries; the Vancouver Stock Exchange primarily raises venture capital. Mining in Canada is part of the legacy of colonial history; in the twentieth century it was one of the primary vectors for the Canadian state to advance a "modernization" agenda, especially among aboriginal communities;[14] and operated with a strong base of financial investment, skilled engineers, technicians and miners, and endorsement in government planning at all levels.

Today the Canadian mining sector is highly concentrated with the largest seventy companies accounting for 90 percent of the assets.[15] Ready access to capital, strong domestic state support, and corporate-friendly laws have provided a climate in which Canadian companies make up three-quarters of mining operations abroad, and a third of the conflicts concerning local communities, environmental degradation and unethical behavior, according to a leaked report from the Prospectors and Developers Association of Canada.[16] Not without resistance from the opposition parties and civil society, as we see below, the Conservative government has strongly endorsed mining. During their term, they have provided export credits and risk insurance for Canadian companies, lobbied hard with Latin American governments to implement pro-mining policy reforms, and intervened on behalf of mining companies at the expense of local and indigenous communities.[17]

The high rate of conflicts is also due to the changing character of global mining and the shifting balance of power between mining corporations and communities. The global financial crisis has accelerated the demand and the price for gold, silver, and other precious metals, as a safe haven from the dollar and other currencies. Most

Canadian companies, with the exception of Barrick Gold and Gold-corp, are "juniors" or small, risky start-ups staffed by geologists and mining engineers. With much of the high-grade ores gone, they use toxic chemicals in open-pit mines to extract the low-grade ores, often leveling and contaminating land and watersheds. Welcomed by most national governments, mining companies operate with the idea that they are protected by investment treaties. Exploring for new sites, they encounter indigenous peoples who often lack formal title to the land, and sub-surface rights to the minerals, and have far less political and cultural capital. In this neocolonial nexus, mining companies seldom conduct adequate environmental studies or get prior consent from local communities—and almost never consider that economic development should be directed by local citizens.

Canadian companies are not the only players in mining. Many of the new governments of the "pink wave"—in Bolivia, Venezuela, Brazil, and Ecuador—came to power on the strength of promises about reclaiming national sovereignty of their resources. Indeed, many national governments have changed the operating rules with the mining and other resource corporations, at least at the top: they have won tax and other concessions as part of strategies to drive economic growth, have been able to pay off some of their debts to international finance institutions, increase much-needed spending on social needs, and send a message to the rich countries of renewed regional economic strength.[18] However, the pink turn to the extractionist model has not reduced the concerns of indigenous and rural communities that are continuing to resist the encroachment of mining because of its serious impact on the health and welfare of local communities, and contribution to conflict. The Observatory of Mining Conflicts in Latin America has documented almost 200 conflicts as a result of 207 mining projects that affect close to 300 communities, most of them indigenous.

AFTER RECOGNITION

Indigenous peoples face the harshest of conditions of poverty, social and economic exclusion, and exploitation and depletion of their wealth by governments and corporations. In Canada, the political mobilization of First Nations peoples from the 1960s onward led to a degree of sovereignty over their territories—a Supreme Court decision that mandated consultation and accommodation by companies and governments and more equal treatment of traditional ecological knowledge with scientific data and impact assessments.[19] In Latin America, indigenous groups drew on the organizational and political mobilizations of previous decades, and, in the 1980s and '90s, developed networks that gained strength in the international arena. Paradoxically, some of the constitutional reforms that gave symbolic recognition to indigenous peoples (Colombia 1991, Guatemala 1993, Mexico 1993, and Peru 1993) partly resulted from neoliberal development programs; with more substantive constitutional reforms in Ecuador (2008) and Bolivia (2009) due to political mobilization.[20]

The importance of indigenous struggles in countering neoliberal regimes came to world attention when the Zapatistas, an organization of indigenous people in the highly resource-rich state of Chiapas, challenged the North American Free Trade Agreement (NAFTA) in 1994. This renewed cycle of capitalist accumulation centered on resource extraction has sparked a new round of indigenous mobilization across South and North America. Indigenous activists have moved beyond requests for recognition and inclusion to challenge the claims that nation states and corporations exert over their territories and the larger visions of neoliberal development.

ACTING "AS IF": COMMUNITY CONSULTATIONS

Most indigenous groups already have a developed set of procedural rules for natural resource management, called Aboriginal or Traditional Law, and are aware of their standing in international law. A striking pattern of their practice of mining justice is that they operate "as if" they should be consulted and treated fairly, whether their rights are formally recognized in nonindigenous state and corporate forums, or not. One of the most common examples are the consultas or community referendums on mining that have taken place in over seventy communities throughout the Americas, and which draw their legitimacy from Convention 169, the Indigenous and Tribal Peoples Convention of the International Labour Organization.

This convention calls for mandatory consultation, participation, and prior consent to natural resource development. Twenty-two countries, including Spain, Denmark, and the Netherlands in Europe, and most Latin American countries, have ratified the convention; the US, Canada, Australia, and New Zealand have not.[21] While the majority of the referenda have taken place among indigenous communities, non-indigenous communities have also asserted this right to protect their water supplies, agricultural activities, and ways of life, and to develop their land for alternative uses from big mining.

The first consulta took place in 2002 in Tambogrande, Peru. Long the backbone of the national economy, President Alberto Fujimori had privatized and deregulated mining in the 1990s. When the Vancouver-based Manhattan Minerals got the concession for an open cast gold and copper mine in 1999, local mango and lime farmers became concerned about the impact on their water supply and rich agricultural lands, and the potential displacement of nearly half the town's 8,000 inhabitants. After a demonstration left a number of townspeople and police injured, and the subsequent murder of community leader Godofredo García Baca, residents formed a Defense Front with the support of the Catholic Church and nongovernmental organizations (NGOs). They joined a national network of mining-focused citizens' organizations, which provided advice and technical support, and links to international NGOs. They then organized a nonbinding referendum in which 98 percent voted against the mine (including 73 percent of eligible voters). Under intense national and international pressure, the Peruvian government canceled the project in 2003.[22] Since then, the people of Tambogrande have continued to mobilize in support of other mining-affected communities.

The success of Tambogrande was due to their local organizing, their strategic use of communications, and their connections with national and transnational solidarity networks. Rather than just saying "no" to a foreign mining concern, they framed their campaign as support for sustainable agriculture, and for the active participation of local people in deciding their own future and determining their own economic development.[23] Using different kinds of messaging in Peru, other Latin American countries, and North America, the story of the successful Tambogrande campaign has inspired communities across Latin America and Canada.[24] In North America, Oxfam and Earthworks incorporated the strategic lessons of Tambogrande in their "No Dirty Gold" campaign; and Tambogrande activists—including, notably, Ulises Garcia, son of the murdered community leader Godofredo Garcia, toured across Canada. The documentary video about the campaign, *Mangos, Murder, and Mining,* screened in film festivals and other events around the world, and was circulated via the web.

News coverage of the Tambogrande campaign provides a good case study of the news patterns of mining conflicts. LexisNexis Academic lists twenty-two stories about Tambogrande between 2001 and 2007, with fourteen from the three Toronto commercial daily newspapers, three from US commercial news sources, and the rest from the United Kingdom. The majority (fourteen) targeted business or mining industry readers, including four stock market reports, and four were reports on the film. In fact, the only *New York Times* story about Tambogrande was a posting about the documentary. In addition to aggregating many of the commercial news stories on their website, UK watchdog organization Mines and Communities posted a further thirty-five articles and reports from independent news agencies and websites; mining NGOs in Peru; and transnational mining watchdog, and environmental and indigenous groups.

HOLDING MINING COMPANIES TO ACCOUNT IN GUATEMALA

In 1997, the Guatemalan government passed a neoliberal mining law that declared all Guatemalan subsoil property of the state, and guaranteed equal legal protections for foreign and national companies.[25] Communities in Guatemala have fought back against this law in a number of different ways; plebiscites have been especially common, with an estimated 700,000 voting against metal mining. One of the most active campaigns has taken place in the indigenous communities of Sipakapa in the northwestern highlands of Guatemala in protest of the Marlin gold mine, a project that was partly funded by the World Bank. Residents were particularly concerned with water and soil contamination, the destabilizing effects of controlled explosions on housing, and the social disintegration, inequality, and violence toward women brought on by the introduction of 2,000 local and migrant workers.[26] For forty days starting in late 2004, they blockaded a section of the Pan American highway that provided mine access before police and soldiers violently intervened, and one protestor was killed.[27] Thousands then protested in the streets. Later, in 2005, the communities held a local referendum to halt the mine. In response, Glamis, now called Goldcorp, cited their investment rights and sued in court. In 2007, the high court in Guatemala ruled that the people's referendum was legal but nonbinding.

The communities have continued to mobilize. Well aware of events in other Latin American mining-affected communities, they have linked with local and national organizations such as MadreSelva, Oilwatch, the Catholic church, and the Municipal Development Councils (los Consejos Municipales de Desarrollo [COMUDE]),[28] as well as with NGOs, mining watchdog organizations, environmental, and indigenous movements in Canada and northern Europe.[29] They not only rejected the mine, but also articulated a different cultural and economic model of development. They began to renew older Mayan self-governance structures and values of collective solidarity, communitarian access to land and to natural resources, and ecologically sustainable development practices.[30]

The campaign escalated in scope and scale. They solicited independent reports and a number of different studies from UN agencies, university-based research centers, and human rights and environmental NGOs, all of which cited social and health problems and human rights violations.[31] In 2007, eighteen of the communities asked the IACHR for precautionary measures from the Guatemalan state, and in 2010, the IACHR and the ILO Committee of Experts made recommendations to the Guatemalan government to suspend the mine. The government agreed, but never took any steps to do so.

In 2012, the communities, operating through the Council of Western Peoples (CPO), challenged the constitutionality of the country's mining law for its lack of respect for indigenous peoples, and their right to free, informed, and prior consent. Soon after, two very different international delegations arrived in Guatemala. Goldcorp brought a group of Canadian politicians on a company-paid trip to lobby the government; and Guatemalan and Canadian civil society organizations convened a People's International Health Tribunal on the impact of Goldcorp in Guatemala, Honduras, and Mexico on July 4, 2012.[32] In March 2013, the Guatemala high court upheld the mining law. CPO's response was to take the suit to the IACHR.[33] Meanwhile Goldcorp announced changes to its corporate practices, saying it would respect the rights of indigenous communities as set out in the ILO protocol.

Then, in May 2013, while international media focused on the trial of former Guatemalan dictator Efraín Ríos Montt, another conflict erupted into violence with almost no international press coverage, involving a mine owned 40 percent by Goldcorp. Eight communities in southeastern Guatemala were attempting to stop the proposed mine of Vancouver-based Tahoe Resources. An overwhelming majority of residents of all eight communities rejected the mine. Then, when several residents were killed in a couple of different incidents, the national government declared a state of siege.[34]

The same month, allies in Canada, organized through the Mining Injustice Solidarity Network, protested outside and inside the annual shareholder meeting of Goldcorp in Toronto, demonstrating a new level of transnational solidarity. A network of Canadian citizens' organizations have recognized the damage of Canadian mining companies to mining-affected communities, as well as national political and economic systems, in Latin America and Canada alike. The WikiLeaks revelations of Canadian government complicity in abuse and repression, and the recognition of the unduly tight connection between Canadian pension plans and the mining industry,[35] has angered and motivated many Canadian citizens, who are new to global notoriety. The growing Canadian mining justice network is beginning to harness its greater access to the Internet and North American media, lobby politicians, contract legal services, question pension plan managers who invest in abusive enterprises, engage in shareholder activism, raise financial resources to assist communities in publicizing harms and abuses, and obtain political support to reform legislation.[36]

Recognizing that many countries where mining is taking place, such as Guatemala, have weak court systems, a group of mining activists, advocates, and legal specialists have brought a handful of cases before the Ontario and Quebec courts.[37] Until recently unsuccessful, a set of three civil cases brought by the Guatemalan community of Lote Ocho against HudBay has led to two legal victories. Unsuccessful in their pursuit of a criminal case in Guatemala, the Mayan communities claimed that the security staff of a subsidiary company was responsible for gang rapes, injuries, and a death in Guatemala. In a historic ruling, one of the cases was allowed to go ahead by the Ontario Superior Court of Justice. In another related legal victory, HudBay agreed to have another of the cases heard in Canada.

"WE CAN LIVE WITHOUT GOLD BUT WE CAN'T LIVE WITHOUT WATER"

Across the border, in El Salvador, a national campaign led to a presidential suspension of metal mining licenses in 2009, in order to protect freshwater supplies. The global precedent was the result of two principal campaigns that culminated in the formation of La Mesa, the National Roundtable against Mining. The first, in the river basin of the country's largest river, the Lempa, in the north-central district of Cabañas, focused on the Vancouver-based gold company Pacific Rim. One of their slogans was, "We can live without gold but we can't live without water."[38]

Pacific Rim offered jobs and tax revenues, but the Roundtable considered that few local residents had the requisite technical skills and that the 3 percent profits over the project's projected six-year operation were not enough to compensate for the negative impact of the cyanide ore process on rural farming and fishing economies and on water supplies.[39] In the other major conflict, involving a gold mine that had been operated by the Milwaukee-based Commerce Group, testing by the Salvadoran environment and natural resources ministry had found "nine times the accepted levels of cyanide and 1,000 times the accepted levels of iron."[40]

However, the two companies fought back, citing their investment rights under the Dominican Republic–Central American Free Trade Agreement. They are suing the Salvadoran government for more than $400 million through the International Centre for Settlement of Investment Disputes, whose mandate is to protect investment rights.

Civil society organizations fear that the legal challenge will have a chilling effect. If the tribunal forces El Salvador to pay the companies, it will make goals such as universal access to clean water very difficult. With a decision due in Washington in the spring of 2014, more than three hundred civil society groups from Latin America, the US, Canada, and Australia are calling on the World Bank for a review of the lawsuit.[41]

MINING-AFFECTED COMMUNITIES IN CANADA

Indigenous communities are sharing their tactics across the hemisphere. First Nations communities in Canada have adapted the community referenda, the use of communications media, and other organizing strategies, such as the collection of both indigenous and Western scientific knowledge about historical uses of resources. One example is the Oji-Cree community of Kitchenuhmaykoosib Inninuwug (KI), once known as Big Trout Lake. KI lies south of James Bay, in Nishnawbe Aski Nation of northwestern Ontario, a region rich in gold, platinum, uranium, base metals, and nickel. Even though three Canadian Supreme Court decisions have stipulated that aboriginal people must be consulted with regards to their treaty rights and interests, several junior Canadian mining companies began prospecting in their territories without prior consultation.[42] In response, in 2005, five of the communities declared a mining exploration moratorium. Soon after, in 2006, Toronto-based platinum mining company Platinex set up a drilling camp on the traditional lands of KI.

For eleven years, KI battled Platinex, holding a referendum, developing community studies, occupying the proposed mine site, and circulating their struggle via their own grassroots media and allied networks. At one point, Platinex sued KI for $10 billion, invoking their neoliberal investment rights. The resulting protest led to a jail sentence for six community leaders, after which traditional elders led an 850-mile walk to Toronto, with protests outside the jail site and in front of the provincial legislature, before the provincial government finally agreed to buy out Platinex in late 2009.[43] Then, with Platinex gone, KI was forced to battle a second mine project of the De Beers diamond corporation, then a third from God's Lake Resources, which they protested outside the annual convention of the Prospectors and Developers Association Conference at the Toronto Convention Centre. Finally, in 2012, the Ontario provincial government paid $3.5 million to buy out the company's controversial gold mining claims.[44]

The Kitchenuhmaykoosib Inninuwug community effectively combined on-the-ground organizing with protests in Toronto, the site of the provincial legislature and of global mining's financial center. They told their own story through a creative use of communications and media resources, producing their own reports, circulated on YouTube, and supporting the making of two documentary films. They also arranged for regular reports from the regional media hub, Wawatay Native News, as well as circulating news stories on the national aboriginal website Defenders of the Land, and the international Indigenous Environmental Network.

DIGITAL NETWORKS OF CONTENTION

The commercial news media have all but ignored the stories of mining-related conflicts. The fact that we know about them at all, and from the perspective of affected communities, is because of the sophisticated use of media by the transnational solidarity campaign. For if mining and other capitalist enterprises have advanced via information and communication networks, indigenous and other social justice movements have adapted some of those same information and communications networks to promote a very different model of development. Activists and their advocates are creating their own local communications media in multiple forms: from face to face forums, referenda, and occupations; to traditional dance, song and theater, community radio and video, and web-based media.

The mining justice network (listed in Additional Resources at the end of this essay) functions as a set of informative and mobilizing hubs for organizations active with local, national, and transnational scopes. They provide de facto a transnational answer to the damage caused by transnational corporations. They reach out to their readership from a wide variety of angles and with different styles of address that vary from the primarily informative, including press releases and articles that do not make it to the commercial media, the storytelling of video clips, and the more practically oriented "Action" pages. They address mining exploitation from multiple angles with the purpose of tying together numerous different arenas of struggle, from indigenous and community rights, labor, environmental, and human rights; governmental regulation; and corporate planning.

CONNECTING THE COMMONS

The conflicts over Canadian mining in the Americas are only one part of a growing global story. It is emblematic of a business model that operates with support at the highest corporate and state levels, with profit-making goals that have little regard for the destruction to people, lands, and systems of governance in both the mining-affected and host countries, or to the planetary problems of global warming. However, just as neo-extractionism is global, so too is the resistance to it, as we can see in the courageous and creative action of more than three hundred mining-affected communities. Unlike earlier struggles of commoners against the appropriation and exploitation of their resources, and of indigenous communities during the colonial period, mining-affected communities are now less isolated from one another. They have stopped a few Canadian mining companies, such as Manhattan Minerals in Tambogrande in Peru, Copper Mesa in the Intag valley in Ecuador, and Meridian Gold from Esquel in Argentina.

Their ever-evolving chain of support links campaigns across several different vectors of action—from protests, consultas, documentary videos, legal suits, and political mobilization—to the different communities of common interest (indigenous, environmental, counter-globalization, labor, human rights), thus increasing the effectiveness of each campaign and of the overall effort. Although the lack of commercial news coverage in the US—the dominant hub of global news—remains a major hurdle to getting the story out, there is no shortage of news. I encourage readers to watch the available videos and become familiar with the available resources, some of which are listed below, as, unfortunately, big mining is coming to a town near you all too soon.

ADDITIONAL RESOURCES

Mining Justice Networks

Communities in Peaceful Resistance to Escobal Mine (Guatemala), www.resistencapacificaelescobal.blogspot.ca

Defenders of the Land, www.defendersoftheland.org

Goldcorp out of Guatemala (*Coalición Internacional Contra la Minería Injusta en Guatemala (CAMIGUA)* / International Coalition Against Unjust Mining in Guatemala), www.goldcorpoutofguatemala.com

First Nations Women Advocating Responsible Mining, www.fnwarm.com

Idle No More, www.idlenomore.ca

KAIROS Canada-Resource Extraction campaign, www.kairoscanada. org/sustainability/resource-extraction

Mines and Communities, www.minesandcommunities.org

Mining Injustice Network, www.solidarityresponse.net

Mining Justice Alliance, www.miningjusticealliance.wordpress.com

Mines, Minerals and People, www.mmpindia.in

MiningWatch Canada, www.miningwatch.ca

Latin America Observatory of Mining Conflicts, www.conflictosmineros.net

Protest Barrick, www.protestbarrick.net

Teztan Biny / Fish Lake, Tsilhqot'in Nation, www.teztanbiny.ca

Documentary Films

Bajo Suelos Ricos (*Under Rich Earth*), dir. Malcom Rogge, 2008, 92 min. Documents farm community resistance to Copper Mesa, a Canadian company in the Intag Valley of Ecuador. www.underrichearth. ryecinema.com

Blue Gold: The Tsilhqot'in Fight for Teztan Biny, dir. Susan Smitten, 2010, 41 min. Blue Gold documents the Tsilhqotin peoples' unanimous rejection of Taseko Mines Ltd.'s proposal to drain Teztan Biny (Fish Lake) in order to stockpile mining waste. www.vimeo.com/9679174

The Business of Gold in Guatemala: Chronicle of a Conflict Foretold, dir. Colectif Guatemala 2011, 54 min. Examines resistance to Goldcorp's Marlin mine in both Guatemala and Canada.

Choropampa: The Price of Gold, dirs. Ernest Cabellos and Stephanie Boyd, 2002, 65 min. Residents of Choropampa, Ecuador, seek redress from the Newmont Mining Corporation and the Ecuadorian government in the aftermath of a major mercury spill in their community. www.guarango.org/choropampa/en

Colombia's Gold Rush Al Jazeera English, "Fault Lines," seas. 3, ep. 4 [June 4, 2011], 25 min. "Nowhere is the gold fever sweeping South America more lethal than in Colombia, where the gold rush has become 'a new axle' in Colombia's civil war." www.aljazeera.com/ programmes/faultlines/2011/07/2011757127575176.html *Note: May not be accessible in the United States.*

Late Night Sunrise, dirs. Michael Watts and David McNulty, 2009, 32 min. In the town of Cabañas, El Salvador, resistance to the El Dorado mine of Vancouver-based mining company Pacific Rim comes at a high cost.

Locked Out 2010, dir. Joan Sekler, 2010, 59 min. Shows the struggle between mineworkers in Boron, California, and the global mining company Rio Tinto. www.lockedoutmovie.org & www.youtube.com/ watch?v=okgfgxGgw6Q

Marmato, dir. Mark Grieco, 2011, 87 min. Spanish with English sub-titles. Depicts conflict with Colombia Gold Fields, a Canadian mining company.

Open Sky, dir. Ines Compan, 2009, 52 min. In rural northwest Argentina, the indigenous Kolla's land and quality of life is threatened after the government permits a Canadian company, Standard Silver to construct an open-sky silver mine in Mina Pirquitas. www.icarusfilms.com/new2010/os.html

El Oro o la Vida (Gold or Life): *Recolonization and Resistance in Central America*, dir. Álvaro Revenga, 2011 57 min. Examines transnational mining expansion in Central America: recolonization and resistance.

Silence is Gold, dir. Julien Fréchette, 2012, 78 min. Depicts the judicial proceedings pitting Canadian mining companies Barrick Gold and Banro against the writers of Noir Canada, which investigated Canadian mining company practices in Africa. www.nfb.ca/film/silence_is_gold

Sipakapa NO se vende: the Mayan Peoples' Resistance to Gold Mining, dir. Álvaro Revenga, 2005, 55 min. Spanish with English subtitles. Follows the popular plebiscite organized in the municipality of Sipakapa, Guatemala—where the majority rejected the Goldcorp mine.

Tambogrande: Mangos, Murder, Mining, dirs. Ernesto Cabellos and Stephanie Boyd, 2007, 94 min. The story of the campaign for health care and justice after a mercury spill by the world's largest gold corporation. www.guarango.org/tambogrande/en/index.html

They Come for the Gold, They Come for it All, dirs. Pablo D'Alo Abba and Cristián Harbaruk, 2009, 81 min. How the citizens of Esquel in the Patagonia Andes organized to defeat a mining project near their town. www.vienenporeloro.com.ar

Trou Story / The Hole Story, dirs. Richard Desjardins and Robert Monderie, National Film Board of Canada, 2011, 79 min. A humorous social commentary about the history of mining in Canada.

DOROTHY KIDD, PHD, first encountered the Canadian mining boom in the 1980s in a series of very different communications jobs. Working for a commercial printer, she printed the stock certificates for Vancouver's junior exploration companies, researched the labor structure of British Columbia's mining companies for a government project, and witnessed the exploration companies arriving while working for aboriginal communications organizations in northern Ontario and northern Labrador. A longtime alternative media producer and researcher, she currently teaches and chairs the department of media studies at the University of San Francisco.

Notes

1. Carey L. Biron, "South of the Border, Mining is King," Inter Press Service, November 1, 2013, Center for International Environmental Law, *Environmental Defenders in Danger: The situation in Mexico and Central America in the Context of the Mining Industry.* (Washington, D.C.: Center for International Environmental Law, October 2010). Prepared for the Hearing of the Inter-American Commission on Human Rights on the Situation of Environmentalists in Mesoamerica.

3. *Deadly Environment: The Dramatic Rise in Killings of Environmental and Land Defenders,* Global Witness, report (2014), http://www.globalwitness.org/deadlyenvironment.

4. Reporters without Borders, "Another Journalist Murdered A Month Before General Elections" October 25, 2013, http://en.rsf.org/honduras-another-journalist-murdered-a-25-10-2013,45384.html.

5. James Anaya, "Statement of Special Rapporteur to UN General Assembly, 2011," October 17, 2011, http://unsr.jamesanaya.org/statements/statement-of-special-rapporteur-to-un-general-assembly-2011.

6. Only two articles report on the resistant role of local communities: Leslie Moore, "Business: A Town's Protests Threaten Argentina's Mining Future," New York Times, April 20, 2003; and Randal Archibold, "First a Gold Rush, Then the Lawyers," New York Times, June 25, 2011. Simon Romero published three articles: "In Colombia, New Gold Rush Fuels Old Conflict," New York Times, March 3, 2011; "Tensions Over Chinese Mining Venture In Peru," New York Times, August 14, 2010; and "In Bolivia, Untapped Bounty Meets Nationalism," New York Times, February 2, 2009. Three stories comment more generally about the role of mining in Latin America: Alexei Barrionuevo, "In South America, a Mine of Riches and an Economic Sinkhole," New York Times, September 11, 2010; William Neuman, "As a Boom Slows, Peru Grows Uneasy," August 19, 2013; and Enrique Krauze, "Latin America Leans Forward," New York Times, December 29, 2013.

7. "Canadian Government Abdicates Responsibility to Ensure Respect for Human Rights," MiningWatch Canada, May 16, 2011, http://www.miningwatch.ca/news/canadian-government-abdicates-responsibility-ensure-respect-human-rights.

8. Eduardo H. Galeano, *Open Veins of Latin America: Five Centuries of the Pillage of a Continent* (New York: Monthly Review Press, 1997[1973]),

9. Arn Keeling and John Sandlos, "Environmental Justice Goes Underground? Historical Notes from Canada's Northern Mining Frontier," *Environmental Justice* 2, no. 3 (2009): 117–25, 120.

10. Ibid.

11. Turkey has been a major site of renewed mining activities and resistance. See Sükrü Özen and Hayriye Özen, "Peasants Against MNCs and the State: The Role of the Bergama Struggle in the Institutional Construction of the Gold-Mining Field in Turkey," *Organization* 16, no. 4 (July 2009): 547–73.

12. Jeannette Graulau, "'Is Mining Good for Development?': The Intellectual History of an Unsettled Question," *Progress in Development Studies* 8, no. 2 (April 2008): 129–62.

13. Liisa North and Laura Young, "Generating Rights for Communities Harmed by Mining: Legal and Other Action," *Canadian Journal of Development Studies / Revue canadienne d'études du développement* 34, no. 1 (2013): 96–110.

14. Keeling and Sandlos, ibid.

15. Paul Bocking, "Canadian Mining and Labor Struggles in Mexico: The Challenges of Union Organizing," *Working USA: The Journal of Labor & Society* 16, no. 3 (September 2013): 331–50.

16. Paul Weinberg, "Canada's Parliament Buckles under Weight of Mining Industry," Inter Press Service, November 8, 2010, http://www.ipsnews.net/2010/11/canadas-parliament-buckles-under-weight-of-mining-industry.

17. "Backgrounder: A Dozen Examples of Canadian Mining Diplomacy," MiningWatch Canada, October 8, 2013, http://www.miningwatch.ca/article/backgrounder-dozen-examples-canadian-mining-diplomacy.

18. Barbara Hogenboom. "Depoliticized and Repoliticized Minerals in Latin America," *Journal of Developing Societies* 28, no. 2 (June 2012): 133–58. See especially the accounts of activists in the chapters on Central America, Peru, Bolivia, and Argentina in Clifton Ross and Marcy Rein, eds., *Until the Rulers Obey: Voices from Latin American Social Movements* (Oakland: PM Press: 2014).

19. Gail Whiteman, "All My Relations: Understanding Perceptions of Justice and Conflict between Companies and Indigenous Peoples," *Organization Studies* 30, no. 1 (January 2009): 101–20, 112.

20. North American Congress on Latin America (NACLA), "Introduction. After Recognition: Indigenous Peoples Confront Capitalism," *NACLA Report on the Americas* 43, no. 5 (September/October 2010), 11–12.

21. "Ratifications of C169—Indigenous and Tribal Peoples Convention, 1989 (No. 169)." NORMLEX (International Labor Organization), http://www.ilo.org/dyn/normlex/en/f?p=NORMLEXPUB:11300:0::NO::P11300_INSTRUMENT_ID:312314.

22. Kaitlyn Duthie, "Local Votes and Mining in the Americas," MiningWatch Canada, May 14, 2012, http://www.miningwatch.ca/es/node/6950.

23. Håvard Haarstad and Arnt Fløysand, "Globalization and the Power of Rescaled Narratives: A Case of Opposition to Mining in Tambogrande, Peru," *Political Geography* 26 (2007), 300.

24. Tambogrande is cited on the Mines and Communities website as an important precedent in at least fifteen reports from NGOs and mining groups in Peru, Argentina, and Guatemala.

25. Beth Geglia, "Guatemala Highest Court to Hear Landmark Challenge against Mining Law," Mines and Communities, August 1, 2012.

26. North and Young, 102.

27. William N. Holden and R. Daniel Jacobson. "Civil Society Opposition to Nonferrous Metals Mining in Guatemala." *Voluntas: International Journal of Voluntary & Nonprofit Organizations.* (2008) 19:325–350 December 1, 2008: 340-341.

28. Leire Urkidi, "The Defence of Community in the Anti-Mining Movement of Guatemala," *Journal of Agrarian Change* 11, no. 4, (October 2011): 556–80, 565.

29. William N. Holden and R. Daniel Jacobson, "Civil Society Opposition to Nonferrous Metals Mining in Guatemala," *Voluntas: International Journal of Voluntary & Nonprofit Organizations* 19, no. 4 (December 2008):325–350, 338.

30. Urkidi.

31. North and Young, 102.

32. Peoples' International Health Tribunal, "Peoples' Tribunal: Goldcorp Guilty of Damaging Environment and Indigenous Communities," *Rabble,* July 16, 2012.

33. Center for International Environmental Law (CIEL), Western People's Council (CPO) and MiningWatch Canada, "Guatemala's Highest Court Denies Justice to Indigenous Peoples Affected by Mining," Mines and Communities, March 19, 2013, http://www.miningwatch.ca/es/node/7091.

34. Sandra Cuffe, "State of Siege: Mining Conflict Escalates in Guatemala," Upside Down World, May 2, 2013, http://upsidedownworld.org/main/guatemala-archives-33/4270-state-of-siege-mining-conflict-escalates-in-guatemala.

35. North and Young, 105

36. North and Young, 104.

37. North and Young, 97.

38. Ross and Rein, 93.
39. Emily Achtenberg, "A Mining Ban in El Salvador?," *NACLA Report on the Americas* (September/October 2011): 3–4, https://nacla.org/article/mining-ban-el-salvador.
40. Meera Karunananthan, "El Salvador Mining Ban Could Establish a Vital Water Security Precedent," *Guardian*, June 10, 2013.
41. Center for International Environmental Law, Council of Canadians, Institute for Policy Studies, MiningWatch Canada, Oxfam, SalvAide and Sister Cities, "International Coalition Supports El Salvador in Battle Against Canadian Mining Company," MiningWatch Canada, April 9, 2014.
42. David Peerla, *No Means No: The Kitchenuhmaykoosib Inninuwug and the Fight for Indigenous Resource Sovereignty* (Denton TX: Cognitariat Publishing, 2012), http://www.miningwatch.ca/sites/www.miningwatch.ca/files/No Means No.pdf.
43. Rick Garrick, "KI Says no to Debeers," *Wawatay News*, December 23, 2010, http://www.wawataynews.ca/archive/all/2010/12/23/ki-says-no-de-beers_20821.
44. Shawn Bell, "Ontario Pays Gold's Lake to End KI Conflict," *Wawatay News*, April 12, 2012, http://www.wawataynews.ca/archive/all/2012/4/12/ontario-pays-god-s-lake-end-ki-conflict_22643.

CHAPTER 8

Law Enforcement–Related Deaths in the US

"Justified Homicides" and Their Impacts on Victims' Families

Peter Phillips, Diana Grant, and Greg Sewell

For over a decade and a half, Project Censored researchers at Sonoma State University have been monitoring law enforcement–related deaths in the United States. In the most recent phase of this research, we interviewed members of fourteen families who had lost a loved one in a law enforcement incident. In this study, we let the families tell their stories in their own voices, and we report the commonalities in their trauma and mistreatment by law enforcement and the corporate media after the death of their loved ones.

Law enforcement agencies in the United States have been involved in excess of 600 deaths annually for at least the past fifteen years. In addition to the people dying on the street or in their homes through law enforcement–related activities, research shows that several hundred people a year die in local jails. In 2011, according to the Office of Justice Programs, 885 inmates died in the custody of local jails. Thirty-nine percent died within the first week of being jailed.[1] This number, combined with deaths on the outside, allows us to estimate that more than 1,500 people die annually in law enforcement–related circumstances, whether in custody or in the course of law enforcement actions in the victims' communities. It is reasonable to assume that some portion of these deaths is attributable to officer mistakes, overreactions, or deliberate acts that result in death.

But almost always, despite obviously questionable behavior by law enforcement personnel, no charges are filed. Investigations of law enforcement–related deaths, either internally within departments or by outside agencies, nearly always rule that homicides are justified and followed departmental procedures.

It is extremely rare for police departments to rule a death as unjustified, or to charge an officer with neglect, manslaughter, or murder. One of these rare cases was the 2009 New Year's shooting of Oscar Grant by Bay Area Rapid Transit (BART) police officer Johannes Mehserle. Mehserle was convicted of involuntary manslaughter and received two years in prison. In a civil trial, Grant's mother, Wanda Johnson, and Grant's young daughter, Tatiana, received financial settlements from BART totaling $2.8 million as a result of the shooting.

In 1998, Project Censored cosponsored a research study with the Stolen Lives Project, a group born out of the October 22nd Coalition.[2] Through funding from the San Francisco Foundation, Karen Saari, a legal researcher in Sonoma County, California, spent a good part of a year searching the newspaper databases LexisNexis and ProQuest at Sonoma State University for articles on law enforcement–related deaths. She was searching for police shootings and any situation reported in the newspapers where someone died in the presence of law enforcement officers. Besides gunshots, deaths included suicides, car accidents, shootings, drowning, and Taser use.

To our knowledge, this was the first time such a study had been attempted in the US. During the twelve-month period from October 1, 1997, to October 1, 1998, Saari found news stories on 694 deaths in the presence of law enforcement in the United States. Department of Justice figures at the time listed about 350 people killed by police in the previous year, so Saari's research showed a significantly larger rate of death among civilians in law enforcement incidents than was previously known at the time.

The newspaper deaths reported in 1997 show that eighty-one were related to excessive application of restraint techniques, and that ninety-one were reported to be suicides, although the ruling of suicide was questionable in a number of cases. Deaths occurred throughout the US, with California leading the nation.[3]

In 2011, Jim Fisher used Internet searches to identify 1,146 police shootings that year. Among these were news reports indicating that 607 people had died by police shooting. This was a slightly higher rate of shooting deaths than had been reported in 1997–98 but did not include Taser, restraint deaths, and suicides. Fisher found that the vast majority of the people shot had been between the ages of twenty-five and forty-nine, a result similar to Saari's report a decade earlier. In 2011, two victims of the police had been fifteen years of age, and one girl had been only sixteen. Fifty of the dead were armed with BB guns, pellet guns, or toy replica firearms.[4]

Project Censored sought to verify the numbers of law enforcement–related deaths in a more recent year. A team of Project Censored student researchers, including Greg Sewell, Rio Molina, Vanessa Pedro, and Jessica Clark, conducted a sample survey using Google, LexisNexis, and ProQuest for three months in 2013. They found fifty-two law enforcement–related deaths reported in US newspapers for May 2013, forty-nine deaths for August, and forty-seven for December. The total of 148 deaths in three months of 2013 suggests that as many as 600 civilians may have died in the hands of law enforcement officers over the course of 2013—numbers that are very similar to the 1997–98 and 2011 findings.

Prior research documents that the number of persons killed by local law enforcement officers in the United States that are reported in official sources does not match the number that are reported in the media. Determining the nature and reasons for this discrepancy requires putting together pieces of data from sources with divergent definitions and measurements of death by law enforcement.

Available statistics for the Federal Bureau of Investigation (FBI) track justifiable homicide by law enforcement, which the FBI defines as "the killing of a felon by a law enforcement officer in the line of duty." According to FBI data, justifiable homicides by law enforcement totaled 369, 367, and 393 deaths in 1997, 1998, and 2011, respectively.[5] The FBI data for 2007–12 shows that justifiable homicides by law enforcement averaged 396 deaths per year.[6] FBI data for 2013 is not yet available.

The Bureau of Justice Statistics (BJS) provides data for 2003–09 on Arrest Related Deaths (ARD), including "homicide by law enforcement." This is the most recent data published from the ARD data collection program, which uses a much more inclusive definition than the FBI's justifiable homicides data. The ARD data "includes homicides by law enforcement personnel as well as deaths attributed to suicide, intoxication, accidental injury, and natural causes."[7] Thus the ARD reports 4,813 total deaths for January 2003 to January 2009, of which 61.5 percent (2,931) were classified as homicide by law enforcement.[8] The homicide victims were classified as 42 percent White, non-Hispanic; 32 percent Black, non-Hispanic; 20 percent Hispanic; and 7 percent "other" or "unknown." Males accounted for 96 percent of homicides.[9] Related data also shows that from 1980 to 2008, most such homicides were intraracial, with Cooper and Smith noting that "two-thirds involved police officers and felons of the same race."[10]

WHAT DOES THE DATA TELL US?

There are several hundred people who die annually during encounters with local law enforcement (or shortly thereafter in hospitals, as measured in one database). Variations across years and jurisdictions may be attributable to a variety of factors, including increased use of Tasers, and increases in the proportion of justifiable homicides by law enforcement that involved victims deemed mentally ill.[11] For example, Loftin et al. found that Supplemental Homicide Report data for justifiable homicides by police in 1976–98 differed significantly from National Vital Statistics Data on deaths at both the national and statewide levels. The authors concluded that both databases underreport justifiable homicides by police.[12]

Bureau of Justice Statistics (BJS) analyses of FBI data on justifiable homicides show that such killings declined from 1980 to the early 1990s, then rose again in the mid-1990s, declined till 2000, then rose slightly again. Although the data trends described above apply to both justifiable homicides by law enforcement and private citizens, the BJS report notably stated, "The number of justifiable homicides committed by police exceeded the number committed by citizens."[13]

Unfortunately, there are notably different ways that law enforcement–related deaths are defined and measured, which makes comparisons across data sources, jurisdictions, and years problematic. In addition, there are missing data for some jurisdictions for some time periods.[14]

THE MILITARIZATION OF DOMESTIC LAW ENFORCEMENT

The social science literature has addressed these issues in a number of ways, especially by examining the process of militarization of law enforcement agencies in the United States. We see a transition from the deployment of police as individuals within a community-oriented process to an increase in the deployment of teams of Paramilitary Police Units (PPUs), most notably as SWAT (Special Weapons And Tactics) teams. This has been coupled with a transition to a more aggressive rather than community-oriented form of "cop culture," fueled by media representations that support a "show balls" attitude where street-level police are portrayed as getting things done, not mired down by procedure and bureaucracy.

Researchers distinguish between militarism and militarization. *Militarism* describes an ideology, while *militarization* refers to the implementation of that ideology. At the core of militarism as an ideology is the belief that the threat of force or its actual use is, in the words of one prominent scholar on the issue of police militarization, "the most appropriate and efficacious means to solve problems."[15] Militarization is a *process* that police agencies undergo.[16] This process began in the late 1970s and intensified during the 1980s, especially under the Reagan administration's "war on drugs."[17] In 1981, an amendment to the 1878 Posse Comitatus Act (PCA) and the Cooperation Act of 1981 authorized the transfer of military training and weaponry to federal, state, and local police agencies, escalating the national trend in law enforcement to adopt military objectives, methods, and equipment.[18] As Peter B. Kraska summarized, "[T]he normalization of PPUs into routine police work, the patrol function, and in so-called 'order enforcement campaigns,' points to an enduring internal militarization not likely to recede anytime in the near future."[19]

In 1992, under George H. W. Bush's administration, the "weed and seed" initiative was implemented. This project was intended to "weed" out criminals and to "seed" social programs in blighted urban neighborhoods.[20] President Bush insisted that the drug war was to be fought house-to-house, neighborhood-by-neighborhood, and community-by-community, which laid the foundation for the militarization of law enforcement.[21] The reality of this program was that it expanded the budget of law enforcement and spent very little on social programs.

Then, as Stephen Hill and Randall Beger summarized,

> Following the Oklahoma City bombing incident in 1995, President Bill Clinton proposed amending the PCA to allow the military to aid civilian authorities in investigations involving "weapons of mass destruction." In the aftermath of Hurricane Katrina, the Bush administration sought to gut the PCA to allow the military a wider role in disaster relief efforts. Stephen Muzzatti has also documented how, using "successful" drug task forces as a model, US law-enforcement agencies sought to create Joint Terrorism Task Forces (JTTFs) with the FBI throughout the 1990s. By the end of 2001, there were already close to 100 such units. Thus, in Muzzatti's opinion, rather than initiating the process of police militarization, the "War on Terrorism" has "normalized and accelerated" it.[22]

A survey of law enforcement agencies conducted in the 1990s about the creation of paramilitary-style units discovered that over 89 percent of the responding agencies with city populations over 50,000 citizens had at least one or more paramilitary police units. This same survey found that 70 percent of the responding agencies with city populations of fewer than 50,000 citizens also had at least one or more paramilitary police units.[23] In March 2014, the *Economist* reported that federal grants, made possible through the war on drugs and more recently the "war on terror," provided funds for the purchase of heavy weaponry used by paramilitary police units. "Between 2002 and 2011 the Department of Homeland Security disbursed $35 billion in grants to state and local police," the article revealed.[24] According to the Associated Press, the US Department of Defense provided military surplus equipment, including 165 mine-resistant ambush-protected vehicles (or MRAPs), to nearly 13,000 law enforcement agencies across the country that participate in what is known as the 1033 Program. This program permits the transfer of military surplus to law enforcement agencies. In fiscal year 2012, $546 million worth of property was transferred this way.[25]

Beyond funding and equipment for paramilitary police units, police academies emphasize weapons and training. According to Matthew J. Hickman's 2005 study of 626 state and local law enforcement academies that offer basic training, "the greatest amount of required instruction time was in firearms skills (median sixty hours)."[26] When combined with forty-four hours of self-defense training, along with twelve hours on nonlethal weapons training, officer weapons and self-defense training comprised around 16 percent of total academy training hours.[27]

Jennifer Hunt and Peter K. Manning observed that, within law enforcement circles, it was a much graver error for a street cop to use too little force and to begin developing a reputation among fellow officers as a shaky officer than to engage in excessive force and be told by colleagues to calm down. When officers do not use enough force they are subject to reprimand, gossip, and avoidance in the police subculture. Using excessive force may establish an officer's status as a street cop who does real police work rather than as an inside desk man.[28]

Research has documented that law enforcement officers typically hold shared beliefs about the importance of aggressiveness and selectivity in the conduct of their professional duties. Police culture research shows that officers hold positive attitudes toward aggressive stops of cars and "checking out people," as well as favorable attitudes toward selective enforcement of laws (e.g., assigning felonies a higher priority).[29]

The dangers associated with law enforcement work often prompt officers to distance themselves from citizens, whom many officers orient to as threats to their safety. The coercive authority that officers possess also separates them from the public. The cultural prescriptions of suspiciousness, and maintaining an edge over citizens by creating, displaying, and maintaining their authority, all serve to further divide police and the members of the communities they supposedly serve and protect.[30] Officers who are socially isolated from citizens, and who develop strong loyalties to the fellow officers on whom they rely for protection, often develop an "us vs. them" attitude toward citizens. The group culture among officers and the mechanisms used to cope with the strains of the occupation, are related to the use of coercion over citizens—that is, it is the culture for officers to "show balls"[31] on the street during encounters with citizens.[32]

JUSTIFYING USE OF FORCE

Legal justification for the use of force is most frequent when law enforcement officers deem suspects to be resistant, when citizen or officer safety is threatened, in cases of increased suspect culpability, and when making arrests.[33] "When the encounter is officer-initiated (i.e., proactive)," one scholar suggested, "officers may be quicker to assert their authority and to do it more forcefully, perhaps because police legitimacy is lower than when the officer is invited or called on."[34] A final factor helps explain variation across different agencies in the use of force: "Findings suggest that the use of force over citizens is a function of officers' varying commitments to the traditional culture of policing."[35]

Criminology researchers have found that newspaper articles employ various strategies of symbolic communication to construct images and mobilize meanings that legitimize police violence.[36] Daryl Meeks observed that "urban policing has been assisted by pejorative media representations of the urban underclass, which serve to increase the fear of urban crime while exacerbating the stereotyping and social labeling of the urban underclass as an undeserving, dysfunctional, and noncontributing group of the American social structure."[37]

John Thompson defined "expurgation of the other" as the symbolic construction of scapegoats who must be resisted or purged.[38] Along these lines, news articles typically portray deadly force victims or perpetrators as evil, strange, or threatening manifest expurgation.[39] Police officers and officials allegedly call upon such images when concocting "cover stories" for police homicides.[40] One specific type of expurgation—reference to prior criminal history—merits special designation because it is a core feature of "cop vigilante" narratives but marginal to self-defense justifications because police shooters are rarely aware of victims' criminal pasts.[41]

Research on police officers has noted the negative attitudes that police hold toward citizens,[42] and of officers' distrust of the citizens they police.[43] In addition, officers have historically not believed that those outside the policing profession would assist them in performing their duties, and even if "outsiders" did try to assist, they would not be of any real help.[44]

In sum, the traditional view of police culture posits that officers

should, almost uniformly, hold strongly unfavorable views of both citizens and supervisors, show disdain and resentment toward procedural guidelines, reject all roles except that which involves fighting crime, and value aggressive patrolling tactics and selectivity in performing their law enforcement duties.

Mainstream newspapers periodically document and problematize the inability or unwillingness of police and judicial agencies to hold police accountable for killing civilians.[45] Absent from these investigations is a discussion of how these same newspapers often normalize, obscure, and rationalize police violence. The victims of police homicide are generally not presented in the same sympathetic manner as are most murder victims.[46] The use of crime frames raises the specter of the predatory criminal, a vilified and racialized media icon.[47] Patterns of expurgation and reactive/passive and active constructions suggest that news stories generally present police killings as the logical consequences of victims' lawless or troubled behavior.[48]

In 2001, B. Keith Payne performed a set of two experiments showing how race affected respondents' perceptions of whether an object was a harmless tool or a dangerous weapon.[49] The experiments revealed that research subjects made reflex associations between black male faces and guns. The first experiment showed that, when time was unlimited, participants identified guns faster when primed with black faces compared with white faces. While the first experiment demonstrated a racial bias in reaction times, the second showed that the bias was replicated when participants were forced to respond rapidly: when primed with a black face, participants more frequently misidentified a harmless item—such as a nonthreatening hand tool—as a dangerous handgun.

GIVING VOICE TO VICTIMS' FAMILIES

Based on the hypothesis that changes in police behavior would likely reduce the number of law enforcement–related deaths in the United States, we decided to interview the families of people who had died in law enforcement–related incidents. Our research team interviewed fourteen individuals who were immediate family members of people who died in law enforcement–related incidents in northern California between 2000 and 2010. At least one year had passed between the date of the death of their loved one and the date of the interview. Interviews were recorded and transcribed for analysis and comparison. All the names of the interviewees and the victims are to remain anonymous to protect the families' privacies. Researchers used a standardized interview guide with thirty-four questions and were trained in sensitive interview techniques by a professional post-traumatic stress disorder (PTSD) counselor. The research methods for this study were approved by the Institutional Review Board for the Rights of Human Subjects at Sonoma State University.

What follows is a brief outline of the key facts, as reported by family members, for the fourteen cases, as well as the families' opinions on the death of their loved ones. In all fourteen cases, the investigating police departments ruled the deaths justifiable homicide. In case #9, a narcotics officer was indicted by the grand jury but was found innocent in a court trial. All the family members interviewed strongly believe that police overreacted and that their loved one should not have been killed under the circumstances.

CASE #1. *White male, age 29, San Anselmo, prior history of mental illness, in-home traumatic episode, victim charges police with small steak knife, shot to death.*

INTERVIEWEE #1: "I think [the police officer] acted hastily. . . . The cop that did it shouldn't have a gun. . . . He is the problem."

CASE #2. *Black male, age 19, high school senior, Hayward, shot in back of head while running away from Bay Area Rapid Transit (BART) police, no record of mental illness, no weapons present.*

INTERVIEWEE #2: "The police and the media just said . . . the officer felt threatened by my son and had to shoot him. Very few newspapers changed their story or apologized when they found out my son was shot in the back of the head."

CASE #3. *Black male, age 30, Rohnert Park, prior drug use, shot in back running from police after car chase, no record of mental illness, no weapons present.*

INTERVIEWEE #3: "He was running from the police. . . . They shot him in the back . . . murdered by the police."

CASE #4. *Black male, age 27, Oakland, prior drug use and sales, no history of mental illness, shot in back running from police, threw away handgun before being shot, financial settlement to family from civil trial.*

INTERVIEWEE #4: "He had to run because he had a pistol on him. The police chased him. He ran around the corner and threw away the gun. The cop saw him throw away the gun and I guess decided it was OK to go ahead and shoot. He was shot two or three times in the back."

CASE #5. *Black male, age 23, San Francisco, bipolar and depressed, confrontation in movie theater over smoking, shot forty-eight times by nine officers, no weapons, financial settlement to family from civil trial.*

INTERVIEWEE #5: "[The police] evacuated all the theater . . . and they got in and shot him forty-eight times. [The cops] posted stuff on my son's website. I checked the IP address and it came from the police station. [They wrote,] who cares about your dead baboon on welfare?"

CASE #6. *Black male, age 73, Ukiah, long history of mental illness, local psych unit asked police to pick him up so he could take his medications, runs to his apartment chased by police dog, dog attacks him and he responds with sharp object, shot several times in back and side by police.*

INTERVIEWEE #6: "In my opinion he was murdered."

CASE #7. *Black male, age 30, Rohnert Park, self-employed rapper, prior arrests for marijuana and passing counterfeit money, no recorded mental illness, ran from police after traffic stop, shot in back, no weapons present.*

INTERVIEWEE # 7: "He ran [from the car after a stop] and was shot immediately in the back. And then he was dead. He and the officer that shot him . . . had gone to school together and played basketball together."

CASE #8. *White male, age 39, Petaluma, prior depression and minor drug use, not taking his medications, traumatic episode called 911 himself, rampaging in his parents' home, Tasered by police three times and dies, no weapons present.*

INTERVIEWEE #8: "The police . . . are supposed to protect you and take care of you, and we were following the rules."

CASE #9. *Latino male, age 40, San Jose, prior felon, no history of mental illness, mistaken identity car chase by undercover narcotics officers, runs from car and shot in back by officer, bleeds to death after delayed medical care, no weapons present, financial settlement to family after civil suit.*

INTERVIEWEE #9: "My uncle happens to drive by a stakeout and he fits the description of a Mexican guy with a mustache . . . in a blue van. The undercover narcotic officers gave chase . . . my uncle didn't know who they were. . . . He ends up on a one-way street and stops his car, and starts to run away. My uncle jumps a fence and the officer shoots him in the middle of the back. They let him lay there for eleven minutes bleeding. . . . Finally they let the ambulance in and he dies on the way to the hospital."

CASE #10. *Black male, age 16, 127 lbs., Sebastopol, no prior criminal record, depressed, traumatic episode in van parked in family driveway with small carving knife, pepper sprayed and shot six times by county sheriff, financial settlement to family from civil trial.*

INTERVIEWEE #10: "The officer was highly reactive and he didn't assess the situation, he immediately jumped into plan of action and that escalated the situation rather than contain[ed] it. Both officers said they feared for their life, yet these officers were both more than twice the weight of my 127 lb. son."

CASE #11. *Latino male, age 34, San Jose, prior drug use, no history of mental illness, single officer confrontation 3:00 AM in front of his children's and ex-partner's home, Tasered by officer, physical struggle, shot four times, no weapons present.*

INTERVIEWEE # 11: "His autopsy report showed that he had been hit four times with bullets through his left side. He was unarmed. The police said they are trained to stop a threat. And I said, Well my god if this officer felt threatened what about a shot to the leg or something . . . and he responded, No we are trained to shoot center space in the body. You know if you can't shoot center space you won't be a police officer."

CASE #12. *White male, age 24, Santa Rosa, mentally ill ward of the state, schizophrenic, in and out of care facilities since age 14, stopped taking medication and had psychotic incident in his home shared by three men, picked up small kitchen knife and is Tasered and then shot by police four times, small financial settlement from civil suit.*

INTERVIEWEE #12: "There are probably a great many combat veterans in the police . . . you have been taught to kill. They could have stepped back. The first thing they could have done is not make him come out of his room. Anyone who knows anything about mental patients who are off their meds—just get them somewhere quiet and alone."

CASE #13. *White-Korean male, age 30, Santa Rosa, mental illness (bipolar and PTSD), fired gun because he was afraid of intruders in his attic, taken outside by police, ran at officers shot, no weapon in possession at time of shooting.*

INTERVIEWEE #13: "They kept shouting orders at him, I believe there were six officers, they approached in formation all of them with their guns aimed at him, and to someone in this mental state it was extremely threatening way to approach him. [They had him on the ground] and kept shouting confusing orders to him, turn your head to the right, turn your head to the left, then he jumped up . . . and they shot him with a rifle in the chest, right in the heart. None of this would have happened, all they had to do was say we are here to help, we understand you are hearing intruders, do you mind if we take a look?"

CASE #14. *Black male, double amputee in wheelchair, age 61, and his son, age 21, Oakland, police arrive seeking proof of vaccination for dog that was reported to have bitten someone in the home, father killed with one shot to heart, son killed with thirteen shots, officer dies (family says from friendly fire), police claim son had a shotgun, mother says no gun in the house, tape recording hidden by police for six years revealed cooperative son and no shotgun blast.*

INTERVIEWEE #14: "I think the reason officers do what they do is because they can. It is just like any human reaction that if there are not consequences, then you have a green light. . . . They don't pay lawsuits, the taxpayers do. They seldom get fired for wrongdoing. So basically what they do is with impunity because they know the odds of any negative impact coming back to them . . . is negligible."

We asked the families to tell us about their loved ones' backgrounds, education levels, favorite memories, and what they were like as a person. We thought this was important to give a human face to the deceased. Each person killed by the police had family and close relationships. Some had mental illness, but were under care and working to improve. Some had prior run-ins with the law. By asking these questions, we learned about aspects of the victims' personalities and humanity that were missing from the official police and news accounts of their deaths.

The deceased were described in the following terms: creative, artistic, loving, warm, compassionate, nice, trying to figure out where he belonged in the world, having a sense of humor, loved motorcycle riding, delightful, good hearted, happy, friendly, happy-go-lucky, helpful to a lot of people, reachable, fun, outgoing, passionate, kind, sweet, gentle, intelligent, spiritual, loved weightlifting, leader, good with people, popular, great smile, and very caring.

Some favorite memories were described as follows: fishing on the San Francisco Bay; he taught me how to drive a stick shift; he could impersonate anyone; we liked to walk together down Stage Street; he was wonderful on the stage, acting; we played basketball a lot as kids, he loved baseball but would only bat—never played outfield; he made my heart smile; he was very happy when he got a baby brother; bobbing up and down in the water free and happy; and my favorite memory is being hugged by him.

Most of the families complained that the police lied to them after the death of their family member and that the media backed up the police. In most cases, immediate family members were isolated from each other, as they were taken to the police station. Families were kept from knowing that their loved one was dead. Questioning by police was designed to build a negative case against the deceased.

INTERVIEWEE #1: "It is always the same, the police . . . just band together."

INTERVIEWEE #2: "There was a knock on the door, and a parent's worst nightmare came true to us. The media and the official report said he had been shot in the chest. When we got to the hospital we found out he had been shot in the back. The doctors told my wife and me that he had very little possibilities of survival, and [in] the case he did survive, it would most likely be in a vegetative state. After three agonizing days, we decided to disconnect him from life support."

INTERVIEWEE #3: "They didn't want to give me any information . . . when you get a phone call in the middle of the night that somebody's just died, you kind of want some information. Then the newspaper wrote like he was terrible, a gang member. He was murdered by the police."

INTERVIEWEE #4: "Well, from the beginning we felt the police were covering up something that happened. . . . They said they shot him because he pointed a gun at them—that never happened [he was shot in the back]. Channel 2 came out and my aunt asked me to do the interview . . . they needed to put a report on TV. They [just] want you to see the face of someone on TV in pain."

INTERVIEWEE #5: "When I got to the hospital, three officers came to me and [said], "You need to follow us to the homicide department. Your son died at the scene.' So they interrogated me for five hours. Then what I didn't know was his girlfriend was in the room next to mine. So, when they finally let me go—didn't offer me a ride cab or nothing. I call his girlfriend, and said, 'Your man is dead,' and I heard her screaming 'mother fuckers,' . . . all along she was asking (the police) 'How is he,' 'Tell me he is OK,' and they kept saying, 'He is just fine.' So they were interrogating both of us to see whatever kind of dirt they could find on him to discredit his case. They lied to her for five hours about his condition."

INTERVIEWEE #6: "I don't think [the media] focused on the police investigation. There was nothing on the fact that this was a criminal act by the police. It was there and then it was gone."

INTERVIEWEE #7: "I think it was in the paper for one day, and then it was gone. It just disappeared like it never happened."

INTERVIEWEE #8: "We witnessed what happened (about 10:00 PM) and we were put in a patrol car, no shoes, my husband was still in his pajamas. . . . It seemed like hours before they took him out of the house in an ambulance. They wouldn't tell us if he was alive or dead. We were taken into the police office and told not to speak to each other about the incident. At 3:00 AM, the Petaluma police came in and told us he had passed away."

INTERVIEWEE #9: "The [police chief] lied to us. One of the detectives said something negative about my cousin, and the chief said they should take the guy off the case, but that never happened. They interviewed both my cousins, separated them out. The newspaper called my grandma saying, 'We heard your son got shot,' my grandma calls my mom all hysterical. . . . First the media was trying to dehumanize him like they do . . . when someone gets shot by a cop. Later as the facts came out, the media kind of changed its mind on things, but a lot of the time they were just there for the story."

INTERVIEWEE #10: "I started towards the van (to see my son) and the police pushed me away towards the house. They detained us in this room, I looked out the window and his body was on the driveway with a blue sheet and a white sheet over it, his hand was sticking out (with handcuff on). I was really disturbed. I couldn't go to see (my son). They held us for an hour then took us to Santa Rosa Police Department. Our house was searched, our computers were seized, our home was photographed, wastebaskets searched, vitamins placed in a row on the counter and photographed. We were treated really unfairly. The police investigation was very biased. In our case, the Santa Rosa police conducted an investigation of the Sonoma County sheriffs (who shot our son), but the sheriff's office was investigating another case (at the same time) for the Santa Rosa police."

INTERVIEWEE #11: "[My mother, my cousin, and I] went down to the police station to find out what happened. We were immediately separated and not allowed to talk to anyone. We were put into little rooms and left for hours (3:00 AM to 10:00 AM). We kept asking, Is he OK? They responded he was in the hospital with shots in his arm. My sister was at home and they announced his death on the news. [The police] were withholding the fact that he had died because they needed us to talk to them. The officer came in and told me to get off the phone, and I exploded saying I am not getting off the fucking phone, you know that the father of my children had been shot and killed by you guys."

INTERVIEWEE #12 did not respond to this question.

INTERVIEWEE #13: "The police took my daughter-in-law and her kids to the police station and questioned them for hours, including my two-year-old and ten-year-old grandchildren. I didn't know any of this until the police came to my door the next day. They said, 'Are you aware your son had an altercation with the police last night?' He continued, 'Well, there is no easy way to say this, but your son was killed,' and they then just started asking me questions about our relatives' names, addresses, and phone numbers and any information they could get from me. . . . Some of the things the media wrote right, and some definitely were wrong. They didn't come to check with the family about the facts. So I wasn't happy with the news coverage."

INTERVIEWEE #14: "I drove home and there were 8 to 10 police cars around the house. They would not tell me what had happened. One said, 'I will take you downtown and you will be told there.' They put me in a room by myself for a half hour before anyone came in to tell me what happened. My youngest son was in the house and he was taken down to the police station and interrogated as well. They wouldn't let us back in the house until 2:00 to 3:00 AM the next day. It was all over the news, and the police lied about having to shoot our dog because it was running loose in the house. That dog was always chained.

"It was a media circus for a week. They could have cared less about my husband and son. The only reason the media was interested in this case at all was because it was the first time an officer had died in a really long time."

Certainly, the sudden death of a loved one is a very traumatic event for anyone. However, adding in isolation, interrogations, and lies will undoubtedly magnify the trauma. These families carry a deep-seated anger toward the police or other law enforcement officers, not only for killing their loved ones but also for what they see as gross mistreatment by authorities after the event. Not only do they understand that after a law enforcement–related death police immediately circle the wagons and go into protective mode, but they also see the media as complicit in accepting press releases from the police unquestioningly and conducting little in the way of investigative reporting.

Unfortunately, cases like Oscar Grant and our fourteen interviews continue to emerge in northern California, and the nation and the police seemingly always rule the death "justified homicide."

In March 2014, San Francisco police shot to death a twenty-eight-year-old black man in a security guard uniform wearing a Taser. Police claim he started to pull his Taser, and they shot him fourteen times. Family members and community question how police could have mistaken a Taser for a gun.[50]

In February 2014, an off-duty San Antonio Police Department officer shot twenty-three-year-old Marquis Jones in the back. The off-duty officer was working security at a local restaurant. After a minor accident involving the car in which Jones was a passenger, he turned and walked away from a confrontation between the officer and a friend. The officer pushed aside the friend and fatally shot Jones in the back, without warning. Jones's parents are now suing the city of San Antonio, the officer, and the owners of the restaurant.[51]

MEDIA COVERAGE OF THE ANDY LOPEZ CASE

In November 2013, investigative reporter Dennis Bernstein described the death of Andy Lopez at the hands of a Sonoma County sheriff:

On October 22, at 3:14 in the afternoon, 13-year-old Andy Lopez was walking to a friend's house on the outskirts of Santa Rosa,

California, to return the friend's toy rifle, when two Sonoma County sheriff deputies drove up behind him in a marked police car and say they mistook the replica AK-47 for a real gun. Sheriff's Deputy Erick Gelhaus, a training officer with 24 years' experience in the department, later told investigators that he shouted at the boy to drop his "gun" and that when Lopez turned, Gelhaus feared for his life and opened fire, riddling the eighth-grader with seven bullets from a 9 mm Smith & Wesson handgun. According to the other deputy, who was driving the car and who did not open fire, the shooting was over in just a few seconds, even before he had time to move from behind the wheel and take cover behind his door.[52]

Part of the tragic irony of this shooting was that it occurred on October 22nd, the very day that the national Coalition to Stop Police Brutality, Repression and the Criminalization of a Generation uses to encourage awareness of police homicides.

In a twenty-eight-minute independent "Groundswell for Peace" production, Elaine B. Holtz, host of the long-running program *Women's Spaces,* discussed the findings from an independent autopsy with Frank Sainz of the Justice Coalition for Andy Lopez (JCAL). The autopsy showed a pattern eight shots, with seven hitting Lopez, including a shot into his side through his heart. At no point did Lopez actually face the sheriff; he was shot in the side, wrist, and back. Frank Sainz went on to say that "incompetent deputy Sheriff Erick Gelhaus made a mistake. . . . He is [a] loose cannon, who is known to pull his weapon."[53]

The Andy Lopez shooting created a firestorm of protest, marches, demonstrations, and other arrests for several months in the Santa Rosa area. Many people could not understand how the sheriff did not determine that a thirteen-year-old boy in shorts was just a neighborhood kid out for a walk. The day after the shooting the Santa Rosa *Press Democrat* published a photo provided by the Sonoma County Sheriff's Department, comparing Lopez's plastic toy gun to a real AK-47. This comparison led many readers to immediately assume that the sheriff had good grounds to shoot Lopez. Letters to the editor went so far as to blame his parents for letting him play with a lookalike weapon. *The Press Democrat* did not publish images of a youthful

Andy Lopez depicting him as a smiling, thirteen-year old who bore no resemblance to an armed adult criminal.

A Sonoma State University (SSU) student research team in the Spring 2014 Investigative Sociology class examined the extent to which local media coverage of the Andy Lopez shooting influenced public opinion regarding the case. They also explored if the media's portrayal of the shooting was adequate, fair, or complete. The SSU students concluded in their report, "After reviewing a variety of media source depictions of the Andy Lopez shooting and speaking to community members about their perceptions of the case, we have concluded that the local media's coverage of the event has influenced the community to believe the shooting was justified."[54] On July 7, 2014, the Sonoma County District Attorney's Office announced at the end of their five-month investigation it would not file criminal charges against deputy Gelhaus for the Lopez shooting.[55]

EXTERNAL ACCOUNTABILITY AS ONE POTENTIAL SOLUTION

It is cases like Lopez's and others listed above that remind us that it is unlikely that all of these law enforcement–related deaths are justified. As interviewee #10 stated, "If there are one hundred police fatalities, statistics will tell you that (all) hundred wouldn't be justified. . . . If every single police fatality is justified, can justice prevail?" Interviewee #10 also questioned the validity of police agencies investigating each other, instead of an external community review process.

The question becomes what can be done to help families find justice in these tragic cases?

The Spring 2014 SSU Investigative Sociology research team also wrote about how the city of Davis, California, has a unique method to investigate police-related issues. Davis uses an independent police auditor and ombudsperson to review and investigate police behavior.

Bob Aaronson is the independent police auditor for the City of Davis, working directly for the mayor. Aaronson's responsibilities include taking and reviewing police department citizen complaints, as well as interacting with community members and organizations. In an interview, Aaronson explained that his work benefits both the police department and the community it serves. The different experiences of community members and police officers lead to misunderstandings. In his role as an independent auditor, Aronson is able to bridge this gap by explaining to officers how they are being perceived, and by helping the community to understand the duties of the police.

Aaronson also stated that his job provides external accountability, which he believes is a benefit to both the department and community. Aaronson suggested that establishing a civilian review board or other community oversight could benefit both the community and the police department. He believes that police departments want to do the best job that they can and that they appreciate community feedback that helps them do a better job. Aaronson also stated that if civilian oversight is properly administered, it has a tendency to reduce the number of lawsuits filed against police departments in law enforcement–related actions.

CONCLUSION

The best available evidence shows that more than 1,500 people die every year as a result of law enforcement engagements. At that rate, law enforcement related deaths are neither unusual nor trivial. They constitute a major social problem. However, the public is poorly informed about the scope of this social problem for two basic reasons. First, official investigations of law enforcement–related deaths nearly always determine that those deaths were justifiable homicides. Second, news accounts of law enforcement–related deaths typically emphasize official law enforcement perspectives, while they vilify the victims and marginalize the perspectives of the victims' families.

The national push toward militarized police with homeland security oversight is certainly not reducing this death rate. Long-term racism continues to show abuses affecting people of color to greater degrees than white people. The culture of policing tends to reward aggressive behavior and diminish efforts to mitigate shooting deaths. And families of law enforcement–related death victims are mistreated and abused by police departments and the corporate media.

The hiring of an independent police auditor by the City of Davis is one step in the right direction, but much more is needed. We propose that the widespread development of democratic citizen involvement in community policing is essential to addressing this problem. This means that local community members, politicians, and police departments need to seek real citizen oversight, with paid independent staff who can research and review police policies and behaviors. Community policing would help to minimize the circle-the-wagons syndrome that is characteristic in the aftermath of many law enforcement–related deaths.

We also recommend a comprehensive review of police training, which must put greater emphasis on the use of nonlethal interventions and non-aggressive practices, especially in mental heath cases. Given the testimony presented above, mental health and social service support for the families of victims of law enforcement–related deaths is an important social justice need for people already suffering serious trauma.

We propose that news organizations employ their own ombudsperson who can operate like university professors with tenure, to undertake in-depth investigations in cases such as Andy Lopez's, where the evidence calls into question any official judgment of justifiable homicide by law enforcement. In those instances, news organizations' ombudspersons should work in cooperation with community police review boards in order to assure full transparency in the review of law enforcement actions and policies, and to encourage that law enforcement departments make policy changes and take corrective actions to retrain, or to remove from service, officers found to be unjustifiably aggressive or violent.

In the long run, these proposals promise to save cities money by reducing lawsuits, and, more importantly, they promise to save lives by encouraging law enforcement officers and agencies to act in ways that protect community members, and that hold them accountable when they do not.

The authors wish to acknowledge research assistance by Sonoma State University students Rio Molina, Vanessa Pedro, Jessica Clark, Tara Kostan, Alejandro Agua, and Jesus Vasquez (2013–14), and Amelia Albertini, Reham Ariqat, Veronica Bowers, Sandra Campos, Samantha Burchard, Sabrina Clark, Angelica Contreras, Alora Fowler, Kristin Laney, Ryan Larkin, Adam Lesh, Chris McManus, Rebecca Newsome, Adrienne Mead, Angela Pak, Blanca Rios, Chris Riske, Joe Risko, Ronni Poole, Jameka Rothschild, Steven Rutherford, Ryan Stevens, Lindsey Tanner, Lesley Tiffany-Brown, Josh Travers, Garret West, Chelsea Wilson, and Aragon Wyatt (2009–10).

PETER PHILLIPS, PHD, is a professor of sociology at Sonoma State University, and president of Media Freedom Foundation/Project Censored.

DIANA GRANT, PHD, is a professor of criminology and criminal justice studies at Sonoma State University.

GREG SEWELL is a senior research assistant in sociology and a recent graduate of Sonoma State University.

Notes

1. Department of Justice's Bureau of Statistics, "Number Of Jail Deaths At Lowest Recorded Level During 2011," PR Newswire, August 13, 2013, http://www.prnewswire.com/news-releases/ number-of-jail-deaths-at-lowest-recorded-level-during-2011-219403261.html. See also, Michael Winerip and Micheal Schwirtz, "Rikers: Where Mental Illness Meets Brutality in Jail," *New York Times*, July 14, 2014, http://www.nytimes.com/2014/07/14/nyregion/rikers-study-finds-prisoners-injured-by-employees.html; and Andre Damon, "Torture and Death in America's Prisons," World Socialist Web Site, July 15, 2014, http://www.wsws.org/en/articles/2014/07/15/pers-j15. html.

2. For more about the Stolen Lives Project, please see http://www.stolenlives.org. Beginning in 1996, activists in New York organized a national protest day on October 22 each year. The October 22nd Coalition to Stop Police Brutality, Repression, and the Criminalization of a Generation says that they "bring forward a united, powerful, visual coalition of families victimized by police terrorism." For more information, please see http://www.october22.org.

3. Karen Saari, "What the Government Doesn't Want You to Know, How Many Do Cops Kill?," *CounterPunch*, December 1, 2000, http://www.unz.org/Pub/Counterpunch-2000dec01-00001.

4. Jim Fisher, "Police Involved Shooting Statistics: A National One-year Survey," *Jim Fisher True Crime*, December 25, 2013, http://jimfishertruecrime.blogspot.com/2012/01/police-involved-shootings-2011-annual.html.

5. See Alexia Cooper and Erica L. Smith, "Homicide Trends in the United States, 1980–2008," U.S. Department of Justice (November 2011), NCJ 236018, http://www.bjs.gov/content/pub/ pdf/htus8008.pdf; FBI, "Expanded Homicide Data Table 14," Crime in the United States, 2011, http://www.fbi.gov/about-us/cjis/ucr/crime-in-the.u.s/2011/crime-in-the-u.s.-2011/ tables/expanded-homicide-data-table-14.

6. Expanded Homicide Data Table 14, ibid.

7. Andrea M. Burch, "Arrest-Related Deaths, 2003-2009–Statistical Tables," Bureau of Justice Statistics (November 17, 2011), NCJ 235385, http://www.bjs.gov/index.cfm?ty=pbdetail&iid=2228.

8. Ibid., 1.

9. Ibid., 6, especially table 6.

10. Cooper and Smith, "Homicide Trends," 33.

11. E. Fuller Torrey et al., *Justifiable Homicides by Law Enforcement Officers: What is the Role of Mental Illness?*, joint report of Treatment Advocacy Center and National Sheriffs' Association, September 2013, http://tacreports.org/storage/documents/2013-justifiable-homicides.pdf.

12. Colin Loftin et al., "Underreporting of Justifiable Homicides Committed by Police Officers in the United States, 1976–1998," *American Journal of Public Health* 93, no. 7 (2003): 1117–21.

13. Cooper and Smith, "Homicide Trends," 32.

14. Burch, "Arrest Related Deaths," 7.

15. Peter B. Kraska, "Militarization and Policing—Its Relevance to 21st Century Police," *Policing* 1, issue 4 (2007): 1–13, http://cjmasters.eku.edu/sites/cjmasters.eku.edu/ files/21stmilitarization.pdf, quote at page 3.

16. Paul Chevigny, *The Edge of the Knife: Police Violence in the Americas* (New York: New Press, 1995).

17. Abigail R. Hall and Christopher J. Coyne, "The Militarization of US Domestic Policing," *Independent Review* 17, no. 4 (Spring 2013): 485–504; Stephen Hill and Randall Beger, "A Paramilitary Policing Juggernaut," *Social Justice* 36, no. 1 (2009): 25–40, accessible online at

http://www.thefreelibrary.com/A+paramilitary+policing+juggernaut.-a0214203822; and Daryl Meeks, "Police Militarization in Urban Areas: The Obscure War Against the Underclass," *Black Scholar* 35, no. 4 (2006): 33–41.

18. Hill and Beger, ibid., 29.

19. Kraska, "Militarization and Policing," 11.

20. Meeks.

21. Ibid., 35.

22. Hill and Beger, "Paramilitary Policing," 29; the following are sources referenced in Hill and Beger's quote, Matthew Carlton Hammond, "Note: The Posse Comitatus Act: A Principle in Need of Renewal," *Washington University Law Quarterly*, 1997, 75: 953–89; *Progressive*, "Comment: Preserve Posse Comitatus," 2005, http://progressive.org/november2005, also viewed online at http://www.thirdworldtraveler.com/Civil_Liberties/Preserve_Posse_Comitatus. html; Stephen L. Muzzatti, "The Police, the Public, and the Post-Liberal Politics of Fear: Paramilitary Policing Post-9/11," in *Public Policing in the 21st Century: Issues and Dilemmas in the U.S. and Canada*, eds. James F. Hodgson and Catherine Orban (New York: Criminal Justice Press, 2005).

23. Diane Cecilia Weber, "Warrior Cops: The Ominous Growth of Paramilitarism in American Police Departments," 1999, viewed online at http://.cato.org/pubs/briefs/bp50.pdf.

24. "Paramilitary Police, Cops or Soldiers? America's Police Have Become Too Militarized," *Economist*, March 22, 2014, http://www.economist.com/news/united-states/21599349-americas-police-have-become-too-militarised-cops-or-soldiers.

25. Michael Vertanin, "Spoils of War: Police Getting Leftover Iraq Trucks," Associated Press, November, 24, 2013, http://bigstory.ap.org/article/spoils-war-police-getting-leftover-iraq-trucks; Michael Kunzelman, "Little Restraint in Military Giveaways," Associated Press, July 31, 2013, http://bigstory.ap.org/article/ap-impact-little-restraint-military-giveaways.

26. Matthew J. Hickman, "State and Local Law Enforcement Training Academies," US Department of Justice, Bureau of Justice Statistics, January 2005, http://www.bjs.gov/content/pub/ pdf/slleta02.pdf.

27. Ibid. See also Gregory B. Morrison and Timothy K. Garner, "Latitude in Deadly Force Training: Progress or Problem?," *Police Practice and Research* 12, no. 4 (August 2011): 341–61.

28. Jennifer Hunt and Peter K. Manning, "The Social Context of Police Lying," *Symbolic Interaction* 14, no. 1 (Spring 1991): 51–70.

29. Michael K. Brown, *Working the Street: Police Discretion and the Dilemmas of Reform* (New York: Russel Sage Foundation, 1988).

30. Peter K. Manning, "The Police Occupational Culture in Anglo-American Societies," in *The Encyclopedia of Police Science*, ed. William G. Bailey (New York: Garland, 1995), 472–75.

31. Elizabeth Reuss-Ianni, *Two Cultures of Policing* (New Brunswick, N.J. Transaction, 1983).

32. William Terrill, Eugene A. Paoline III, and Peter K. Manning, "Police Culture and Coercion," *Criminology* 41, no. 4 (2003): 1003–34.

33. William Terrill and Stephen D. Mastrofski, "Situational and Officer Based Determinants of Police Coercion," *Justice Quarterly* 19, issue 2 (2002): 101–34.

34. Albert J. Reiss, *The Police and the Public* (New Haven: Yale University Press, 1972).

35. Terrill et al., "Police Culture," 1023, 1026.

36. See, for example, Paul J. Hirschfield and Daniella Simon, "Legitimating Police Violence: Newspaper Narratives of Deadly Force," *Theoretical Criminology* 14, no. 2 (2010): 155–82.

37. Meeks, "Police Militarization."

38. John Thompson, *Ideology and Modern Culture* (Cambridge, UK: Polity Press, 1990), 64–65.

39. Phil Scraton and Kathryn Chadwick, "Speaking Ill of the Dead: Institutionalized Responses to Deaths in Custody," *Journal of Law and Society* 13, no. 1 (1986): 93–115.

40. See, for example, Hunt and Manning, "Social Context of Police Lying"; William B. Waegel, "How Police Justify the Use of Deadly Force," *Social Problems* 32, no. 2 (1984): 144–55; and Chevigny, *Edge of the Knife*.

41. Hirschfield and Simon, "Legitimating Police Violence," 162.

42. Reuss-Ianni, *Two Cultures*, Jerome H. Skolnick, *Justice Without Trial: Law Enforcement in Democratic Society* (New York: Wiley, 1994.); and William A. Westley, *Violence and the Police: A Sociological Study of Law, Custom, and Morality* (Cambridge, MA: MIT Press, 1970).

43. Terrill et al., "Police Culture," 1006.

44. Malcolm K. Sparrow, Mark H. Moore, and David H. Kennedy, *Beyond 911: A New Era for Policing* (New York: Basic Books, 1990).

45. Regina Lawrence, *The Politics of Force: Media and the Construction of Police Brutality* (Berkeley, CA: University of California Press, 2000). For examples of news coverage addressing this issue, see David Jackson, "Holes in the Files: Investigations of Police Shootings Often Leave Questions Unanswered," *Washington Post*, November 17, 1998, A1; Anemona Hartocollis, "Fatal Shootings by Police: Hard to Investigate, Even Harder to Prosecute," *New York Times*, December 4, 2006, B1; Sam Roe, David Heinzmann, and Steve Mills, "The Rush to Clear Police in Shootings: Shielded from the Truth," *Chicago Tribune*, December 4, 2007, http://www.chicagotribune.com/news/local/chi-071205cops-htmlstory,0,2906787.htmlstory.

46. Moira Peelo, "Framing Homicide Narratives in Newspapers: Mediated Witness and the Construction of Virtual Victimhood," *Crime Media Culture* 2, no. 2 (2006): 159–75.

47. Stuart Hall et al., *Policing the Crisis: Mugging, the State, and Law and Order* (London: Macmillan, 1978); and Gregg Barak, "Between the Waves: Mass Mediated Themes of Crime and Justice," *Social Justice* 21, issue 3 (1994): 133–47.

48. Hirschfield and Simon, "Legitimating Police Violence," 175–76.

49. B. Keith Payne, "Prejudice and Perception: The Role of Automatic and Controlled Processes in Misperceiving a Weapon," *Journal of Personality and Social Psychology* 81, no. 2 (2001): 181–92, http://www.unc.edu/~bkpayne/publications/Payne_2001_Prejudice-And-Perception.pdf.

50. Joseph Mayton, "Police Killing Inflames San Francisco Community, Revealing Further Divides," Occupy.com, March 28, 2014, http://www.occupy.com/article/police-killing-inflames-san-francisco-community-revealing-further-divides.

51. David Lee, "Shot in the Back by San Antonio Police," Courthouse News, April 16, 2014, http://www.courthousenews.com/2014/04/16/67094.htm.

52. Dennis J. Bernstein, "Gunning Down a Boy with a Toy," Consortium News, November 6, 2013, http://consortiumnews.com/2013/11/06/gunning-down-a-boy-with-a-toy-gun.

53. Elaine Holtz, *Women's Spaces*, interview with Frank Sainz, May 17, 2014, http://www.youtube.com/watch?v=uJjGZVftgg4&feature=share&list=UUcY3Yh_DuEu10sQocKozL7Q.

54. Tara Kostan, Alejandro Agua, and Jesus Vasquez, "Andy Lopez Investigation," unpublished research paper completed for "Investigative Sociology," Sonoma State University, Spring 2014; available from the first author.

55. Julie Johnson, "Sonoma County D.A.: No Criminal Charges for Sheriff's Deputy in Andy Lopez Shooting," *Press Democrat*, July 7, 2014, http://www.pressdemocrat.com/article/20140707/articles/140709728. This breaking development occurred as this volume went to press.

CHAPTER 9

It is Easier to Imagine the Zombie Apocalypse than to Imagine the End of Capitalism

Zara Zimbardo

A democratic civilization will save itself only if it makes the language of the image into a stimulus for critical reflection—not an invitation for hypnosis.

—Umberto Eco[1]

The history of capitalism can be told as a monster story from beginning to end.

—Annalee Newitz[2]

INTRODUCTION: MONSTROUS SYSTEMS

In recent years, the specter of the zombie apocalypse has loomed large in the collective American imagination in film and television, YouTube videos and themed parties, novels[3] and blogs, costumed marches and marathons, shooting target companies and survivalist groups, video-games and counterterrorism training, zombie "splatstick" comedies and zom-rom-coms, and used in course curricula from elementary to college levels to teach topics from geography to public health to sociology. It is common to hear people complain, "I feel like a zombie" after hours spent staring at television or computer screens, or to comment on how groups of people absorbed in their digital devices resemble a zombie horde. *Pride and Prejudice and Zombies*, Seth Grahame-Smith's 2009 parody of Jane Austen's novel of manners, was a *New York Times* bestseller. AMC network's *The Walking Dead* is the most watched television drama in basic cable history. Tongue-in-cheek zombie preparedness trainings occur across the nation, imparting real emergency skills for a mock-pocalypse. Zombie productions across diverse modes appear with such accelerating frequency that it is not easy to catch up with their shifting meanings, which is strange perhaps because zombies are known as the slowest of monsters.

Hidden in plain sight, what untold stories do ubiquitous zombie hordes point to? The variations of the contemporary evolution of the zombie apocalypse are worth taking seriously as a dominant myth of our times.[4] What are we talking about when we talk about zombies? One view may be to see zombies as escapism—a pop culture trend that distracts attention from urgent issues. However, I argue that zombies and the apocalyptic scenarios that are now frequently associated with them provide a forum for speaking about the unspeakable. Zombies as threat and as comedy overlap as "monstrous placeholders"[5] that point to the gap of what we are not directly talking about—what is censored in our collective public discourse—including economic and ecological crises that are psychologically indigestible. Immersion in prolific undead fiction can steer us to nonfiction that is repressed or blocked from view. Indeed, it is easier to imagine disintegrating cannibalistic corpses covering the planet than to imagine a sustainable shift in our socioeconomic system.

Monster stories can always tell us something meaningful about the society they come from. They do valuable cultural work to embody the fears of a given age, revealing social repressions and cultural anxieties. "Monster" derives from the Latin *monere*, meaning a warning or omen. The undead omen that zombies shamble toward points us to past, present, and future conditions of living death, the frightening underbelly of modernity. In this view, "monster stories are one of the dominant allegorical narratives used to explore economic life in the United States."[6] Beyond macabre aesthetics, campy dramatizations, media spectacle and ironic brain-eating commentary, stories that ooze with zombies vividly "present the 'human face' of capitalist monstrosity."[7] This increasingly normalized pop culture obsession points our attention to the "nonhuman condition" in the flesh-eating systems of late-era capitalism. A collective recurring nightmare that mirrors our waking ones, pop culture monsters repeatedly return in what Fredric Jameson calls the "political unconscious" of a powerful and troubled country.[8] Seeing America through its monsters asks us to engage the roots of our country's monster obsessions as substantial, complex, and revealing, rather than as mere ephemera of popular culture.

The metaphorical breadth of the zombie embraces contradiction, as it is capable of representing vastly divergent threats, of natural and unnatural disaster, war and terrorist attacks. The zombie apocalypse, in its many (re)incarnations, operates to illustrate what we are collectively imagining and may describe what we are actually seeing. Zombies represent the end of the world as we know it, the total breakdown of human society, and the cannibalization of humanity.[9] The zombie apocalypse "speaks to some of the most puzzling elements of our sociohistorical moment, wherein many are trying to ascertain what lies in store for humanity after global capitalism—if anything."[10] What apocalyptic futures is our country rehearsing, and how do they signal both despair of, and hope for, fundamental change?

This chapter looks at what the zombie metaphor has signified over the past century, and questions why it continues to be so prevalent in our culture. Its millennial popularity has exploded off the screen and into real life, offering insight into how we process systemic economic, social, and environmental horror. I trace the evolution of this undead figure through broad stages of global capitalist expansion, from New World slavery in Haiti, to American consumerism and militarism, to the networked neoliberal era, in which plague anxieties, apocalyptic scenarios, and near-future dystopian fiction are defining genres of our historical moment. A recurrent monster in the history of capitalism, zombies reflect what is monstrous in an economic system "that seems designed to eat people whole."[11]

THE ZOMBIE LABORER AND IMPERIAL HAUNTING

Unlike canonical monsters with origins in European tradition, such as vampires and werewolves, or that were established in literature before appearing in film, zombies are a unique New World creation, which transitioned directly from folklore to the screen. The mythological origins of the zombie are rooted in Haitian *vodou* (known popularly as "voodoo") religion, which combined West African and Lower Congo beliefs in spirits, *nzambi* or *zombé*, that could become caught between worlds, trapped in a container, as liminal beings that were neither living nor dead. Zombification was understood to be a reversible state of *hypnosis*, under the control of a vodou practitioner who could work with spells or potions to make the living appear as dead, a form of mind control under direction by the zombie master.

During the era of the transatlantic slave trade, the image of the *nzambi* was adapted to the horrors that tore people from their communities, stripped them of their selves, reduced to laboring flesh for sale. Under the French occupation of Haiti, once the largest slave economy, the zombie image transmuted to emphasize a lack of personhood and endless plantation labor. French masters used the threat of zombification as a form of social control over slaves. Though suicide might otherwise have seemed an escape from enslavement on sugar plantations, masters taught their slaves that, rather than returning to Africa and freedom, slaves who killed themselves would become zombies. In "A Zombie Is a Slave Forever," Amy Wilentz recounted this history: "To become a zombie was the slave's worst nightmare: to be dead and still a slave, an eternal field hand."[12]

Salt was understood to be the cure to the zombified state.[13] Its taste had the power to restore a person's soul and willpower. With this knowledge, masters maintained control by keeping their zombies' food tasteless.

Zombie legends acquired their modern form during the US occupation of Haiti (1915–34), when US marines brutally deployed forced labor to build infrastructure, renewing the trope of the master who controls the animated dead. "This view of the living dead, which entered the American culture industry in the 1930s and 1940s, carried a critical charge: the notion that capitalist society *zombifies* workers, reducing them to interchangeable beasts of burden, mere bodies for the expenditure of labor-time."[14] William Seabrook's 1929 novel *The Magic Island* laid the template for the figure of the zombie to enter into American consciousness, describing *vodou* practices of Haitian culture, and eyewitness accounts of zombies as described in the chapter, "Dead Men Working in the Cane Fields." Vodou adherents could supposedly raise the dead for incessant toil. Zombie stories circulated as a key lens to make sense of the colonial relationship between the US and Haiti, self and other, using sensationalistic and racist tropes projected onto Haitian culture. As zombie legends took root in the US, they expressed imperialist anxieties associated with colonialism and slavery, fears of racial mixing and specters of white people becoming dominated through zombification. Entering the American culture industry with films such as Victor Halperin's *White Zombie* (1932) and Jacques Tourneur's *I Walked with a Zombie* (1943), the figure of the zombie may be understood in a postcolonial mode, as they revealed more about Western fears than about Caribbean traditions or *vodou* belief and practice. "By allowing native voodoo priests to enslave white heroines, these inherently racist movies terrified Western viewers with the thing they likely dreaded most at that time: slave uprisings and reverse colonization."[15]

In the nineteenth century, the figure of the cannibal had served as an ideological means of separating the colonial world into civilized and non-civilized. The zombie effectively continued this work in films of the 1930s to '60s.[16] Drawing on the insights of Wade Davis, who produced ethnographic accounts of zombiism in Haiti, Chris Vials described "the indissociable relationship between Haiti and B-grade horror in the popular imagination" as "a direct product of U.S. imperialism."[17] Early zombie fiction was shaped in part by fears of Haiti as an independent black republic and the imagined terror of white enslavement. Representations of voodoo were woven with tales of cannibalism to underscore Haitian primitivism. As Chera Kee posed, "what better way to justify the 'civilizing' presence of marines in Haiti than to project the phantasm of barbarism?"[18] Annalee Newitz summarized:

> Stories about the undead are best understood in the context of anxieties about many kinds of race relationships that develop in the wake of colonialism. The undead are liminal beings who exist between the worlds of life and death. They represent the sorts of identities that erupt into being when different racial groups collide violently with one another and produce horrifying new cultures of deprivation and oppression.[19]

A perfect monster for the age, the zombie's arrival in the US was linked both with the system of slavery and slave rebellion, as the Haitian Revolution of 1804 demonstrated a historic challenge to colonial power structures.[20]

While American audiences could watch zombie films that depicted the superstitious "other," the image of a zombified worker held up a monstrous mirror to the loss of autonomy and freedom at home, where workers found themselves employed as mass-mechanized laborers, reduced to pawns in larger productive systems that produced frightening, zombie-like conditions. As David Skal has written, "The shuffling spectacle in films like *White Zombie* (1932) was a nightmare vision of the breadline. . . . Millions already knew that they were no longer completely in control of their lives; the economic strings were being pulled by faceless, frightening forces."[21] Between the 1930s and 1960s, zombie fiction served to depict a range of different masters, from aliens, to communists and mad scientists, all of whom wielded zombifying control.

"THEY'RE US, THAT'S ALL"

Zombiism was first presented not as a disease but a reversible state, in which occult practices rendered hypnotized victims as soulless husks. George A. Romero is credited with single-handedly revolutionizing the depiction of zombies with his 1968 film, *Night of the Living Dead*. Romero's movie created the distinct subgenre of the cannibalistic horde that replicates itself through flesh-eating infection. Romero recast "them" as "us," eliminated the puppet master, and created a new type of zombie, found not in some other land or magical culture but at home. Cannibalism, once projected onto the colonized Other, turned inward. Romero also bestowed the viral zombies' with one weakness: a shot or stab to the head.

His 1978 follow-up, *Dawn of the Dead,* further shifted the stage from the private domesticity of a Pennsylvania farmhouse to public space, in the newly emerged structure of the shopping mall, replacing the voodoo zombie as a living dead laborer with the viral ghoulish consumer. Embodying the hungry gaze capitalism directs toward humans and commodities, the zombie consumer satirizes a mindless, manic consumer system collapsing under its own excess. This insatiable monster both consumes and produces more consumers.

In *Night of the Living Dead* (directed by George Romero, 1968), zombies surround a farmhouse, trapping survivors inside, where they watch televised reports of the escalating national catastrophe outside.

Apocalyptic narratives in which everyday people are irreversibly transformed into monsters allows for significant social critique. Kyle William Bishop, in *American Zombie Gothic*, noted, "By painfully illustrating the destruction of the social systems that have become so essential in the United States of the 1970s, Romero paints not a grim dystopian vision of how things *might* be but rather the way things already *are*."[22] As Aalya Ahmad observed, from the late 1960s on, zombie movies could be read as critiques of what Naomi Klein has termed "disaster capitalism"; we are repeatedly shown how, in Ahmed's words, "the zombie apocalypse stops the machine, but the machine's effects clearly linger on in the survivors."[23] As characters in Romero's *Dawn of the Dead* explain, zombies roaming the shopping mall act out of habit, reproducing the behaviors of their former, human selves. As the mall-trapped survivors gaze upon the moaning hordes scraping at display windows, one asks, "What the hell are they?" to which another responds matter of factly, "They're us, that's all."[24]

The emergent subgenre of the apocalyptic zombie invasion introduced by Romero's *Night of the Living Dead* took inspiration from

Richard Matheson's 1954 novel *I Am Legend,* which laid the template for the undead narrative of a human minority confronting the mutant majority, and confronting one's own mutated humanity in the process. Bishop pointed out that "the primary details in Romero's series of zombie films are in essence bland and ordinary, implying that such extraordinary events could happen to anyone, anywhere, at any time."[25] Normal everydayness is rendered terrifying, with once-secure sites becoming claustrophobic, barricaded fortresses susceptible to invasion. In today's popular zombie walks,[26] flash mobs, and public performances of recent years, participants dress up in specific roles and occupations, zombie grooms and brides, cheerleaders, doctors, just as Romero depicted in his series, wearing the costumes of one's former self, a reminder that "we are you." Catastrophe inhabits intimate familiarity, mere degrees away. Because they are not supernatural monsters, zombies terrify us through their uncanny resemblance to ourselves, rather than their otherness.

This juncture of the mindless worker and the mindless consumer lays bare the social and environmental violence of capitalist exploitation and accumulation. Forms of labor in megacorporations reproduce life-denying conditions for workers whose labor in turn makes hyper-consumption possible. Wilentz invokes contemporary sweatshop labor: "There are many reasons the zombie, sprung from the colonial slave economy, is returning now to haunt us. . . . The zombie is devoid of consciousness and therefore unable to critique the system that has entrapped him. He's labor without grievance. He works free and never goes on strike. You don't have to feed him much."[27] In *Catastrophism: The Apocalyptic Politics of Collapse and Rebirth,* David McNally has reminded us that, while zombies have morphed to signify and satirize American consumption, the critical image of the zombie laborer has risen in sub-Saharan Africa in the neoliberal structural adjustment era.[28] "Throughout the African subcontinent, the figure of the zombie-laborer has come to depict the dirty secret of late capitalism: that rather than a high-tech world of frictionless circuits of accumulation, capitalism continues to subsist on hidden sites of sweated labor."[29] Zombies stagger forward as embodiments of capital itself, insatiable and heartless.

George A. Romero's modern zombie cycle coincided with the Tet offensive in Vietnam, a time when images of death and violence were broadcasted regularly in what became known as the "living room war."[30] Looking back, various scholars have pointed out how the historical events of the last third of the twentieth century—including its wars, revolutions, and social movements—helped to prepare the ground for the resurrection of the undead in film and television. "The legacy of the Vietnam War," W. Scott Poole has written, "became a silent partner in the birth of modern horror."[31] Romero's makeup artist Tom Savini, known as the "Godfather of Gore," was a Vietnam veteran, who strove to create realistic images of death, dismemberment, and bodily dissolution. Reel zombies lunged on screen as Americans became accustomed to seeing real-life images of traumatized human bodies. *Night of the Living Dead* offered a vision of horror that could not be contained, one in which the society's official protective agencies and security mechanisms proved useless. When the Museum of Modern Art screened *Night of the Living Dead*—the first major American institution to do so—the text for an accompanying installation described the film as "a metaphor for societal anxiety" in the age of Vietnam and the assassinations of Martin Luther King Jr. and John F. Kennedy: "Americans identified with the film's most shocking suggestion: death is random and without purpose. No one dies for the greater good or to further the survival of others. Instead, people die to feed faceless, ordinary America."[32]

In zombie cinema from the time of Vietnam to the present, America is depicted as literally devouring itself. Analyzing Romero's *Night of the Living Dead* and Bob Clark's 1972 zombie film *Deathdream*, Karen Randell examined how "the fantastic specter of the zombie articulate[d] issues of loss and mourning for the American war dead and missing in a way that was not being addressed by the war films of the period."[33] Could zombies' exponential increase in our contemporary US mediascape be understood, similarly, as expressing loss and mourning for, in Judith Butler's words, the "ungrievable lives" of uncountable victims of US military aggression in Iraq, Afghanistan, and other sites of US operations?[34]

ZOMBIES AFTER 9/11

The zombie genre has taken a strong political turn since 2001, as a blood-soaked critique of America's foreign and domestic policy. The Bush administration, having learned the Vietnam lesson of broadcast war violence eroding public support for war efforts, imposed a journalism ban on showing flag-draped coffins, soldiers' funerals, and the effects of bombing campaigns.[35] In this absence, zombies have arisen in greater numbers than ever before. Joe Dante's *Masters of Horror* episode "Homecoming" (2005) was a direct critique of the Bush administration's ban on photographs of body bags and dead soldiers. It depicted flag-draped coffins bursting open to release undead American soldiers. Possessing the power of speech, these zombie veterans protested "dying for a lie" as they bloodily shambled their way to the polls with the singular purpose of voting the warmongering president out of office.[36] Romero's 2005 *Land of the Dead* was a direct indictment of the Bush administration.

According to Kyle William Bishop, "Because the aftereffects of war, terrorism, and natural disasters so closely resemble the scenarios depicted by zombie cinema, such images of death and destruction have all the more power to shock and terrify a population that has become otherwise jaded to more traditional horror films."[37] One may argue that the US public has also become jaded to war abroad, which in Rachel Maddow's analysis has become like background Muzak for much of the American public: "Kind of annoying when you tune in, but easy enough to tune out."[38] As US military power has become increasingly "unmoored," zombies have increasingly covered the planet and invaded our neighborhoods, bringing imaginary war home to our actual doorstep. Drone warfare, more technological forms of killing, and the absence of the portrayal of victims in establishment media render war both intangible and unending. And yet "Zombie Nation" plays out this very corporeal horror with an undead enemy who is everywhere. "Against a zombie enemy, the West can feel justified in ruthless extermination, in self-defense."[39] In the zombie war raging alongside our drifting and expanding global wars, lines are continually redrawn. The undead enemy does not require ethical consideration as to its humanity. We are not political allies with zombies one day and at war the next. Virtual victory is practiced.

The traumatic reality of actual global conflicts and disasters reappears in the genres of fantasy and horror. After a decade of war, with levels of posttraumatic stress syndrome among military veterans reaching staggering levels, zombies act as a cultural cipher, providing a place to interrogate social and political issues, and to engage the visceral realities of war that are all around but nevertheless typically hidden from mainstream view. "Since 9/11 and the proclamation of the 'War on Terror,' a new brand of explicitly violent horror movies has scored major box office hits. . . . But from the point of view of many directors, experts, and fans this 'reel' horror reflects the 'real' horror of our time: War, terrorism, economic decline, corporate greed, natural disasters, and social collapse."[40] Reel violence—which includes videogames, television, and graphic novels—mirrors real violence in times of political, social, and economic crisis. Commercially marketable dystopia may also draw audiences whose lives are not directly impacted by nonfiction violence, seeking terrifying experiences that actually pale against the myriad lived horrors of the present time.

The doomsday fascination with the zombie apocalypse surged in the first decade of the new millennium; popular infatuation with the undead reached new heights with the 2008 global economic crisis. Zombies' blood-splattered mark on mass culture became so clear during 2008–09 that *Time* magazine declared zombies "the official monster of the recession."[41] Citing the sheer volume of zombie narratives in media as indicative of something more compelling and complex than a superficial trend, Bishop observed, "Zombie cinema is among the most culturally revealing and resonant fictions of the recent decade of unrest."[42]

In "A Zombie Manifesto: The Nonhuman Condition in the Era of Advanced Capitalism," Sarah Juliet Lauro and Karen Embry noted that the ubiquitous zombie is a "pessimistic but . . . appropriate stand-in for our current moment, and specifically for America in a global economy, where we feed off the products of the rest of the planet, and, alienated from our own humanity, stumble forward, groping for immortality even as we decompose."[43] David McNally argued, "In the face of crumbling cities, soaring job loss, decaying social services and ecological destruction, impending doom can seem not only inevitable, but even preferable to the slow death march of late capitalism."[44]

UBIQUITOUS ENEMIES

On Halloween 2012, the US military partnered with the HALO Corporation, a private security firm, to stage a zombie apocalypse counterterrorism and emergency response training. Brad Barker, president of HALO, stated, "This is a very real exercise, this is not some type of big costume party."[45] Though skeptics might dismiss this as a publicity stunt, a recently released military document shows the stunning cross-fertilization of pop culture fantasy and official planning realities. As Gordon Lubold reported for *Foreign Policy*,

> Incredibly, the Defense Department has a response if zombies attacked and the armed forces had to eradicate flesh-eating walkers in order to "preserve the sanctity of human life" among all the "non-zombie humans."
>
> Buried on the military's secret computer network is an unclassified document, obtained by *Foreign Policy*, called "CONOP 8888." It's a zombie survival plan, a how-to guide for military planners trying to isolate the threat from a menu of the undead—from chicken zombies to vegetarian zombies and even "evil magic zombies"—and destroy them.
>
> "This plan fulfills fictional contingency planning guidance tasking for U.S. Strategic Command to develop a comprehensive [plan] to undertake military operations to preserve 'non-zombie' humans from the threats posed by a zombie horde," CONOP 8888's plan summary reads. "Because zombies pose a threat to all non-zombie human life, [Strategic Command] will be prepared to preserve the sanctity of human life and conduct operations in support of any human population—including traditional adversaries."[46]

CONOP 8888, otherwise known as "Counter-Zombie Dominance" and dated April 30, 2011, is no laughing matter, and yet of course it is. As its authors note in the document's "disclaimer section," this plan was not actually designed as a joke.[47] A recognizable mock-serious tone permeates zombie menace warnings. Call it Homeland Insecurity.

Concurrent with the "War on Terror," huge numbers of people have participated in zombie apocalypse scenarios, as our country experiences trauma at home and perpetrates it abroad in the name of self-defense against a morphing enemy who, under the condition of "endless" war, is "everywhere." An epidemic metaphor, the zombie apocalypse haunts America's post-9/11 imperial consciousness. It graphically depicts violent domination at home, while violent occupation abroad is abstractly justified as spreading freedom and democracy. Sociologist Avery Gordon observed, "Haunting is one way in which abusive systems of power make themselves known and their impacts felt in everyday life, especially when they are supposedly over and done with (slavery, for instance) or when their oppressive nature is denied (as in free labor or national security)."[48]

Zombies can be inserted anywhere.[49] Within the immense videogame culture industry, zombie survival horror games offer "pleasure found in violating social norms without fear of reprisal."[50] As Tanya Krzywinska analyzed, videogame zombies function as ideal antagonists: as the zombies are "strong, relentless, and already dead," players can "blow them away without guilt or a second thought."[51] All ambiguity about who is the enemy is burned away.

This first-person shooter rehearsal of zombie extermination, with increasingly realistic graphic representation, coincides with an era in which US warfare appears more and more like videogaming. Military bots and remote-controlled weaponized drones have become normal, owing partly to a tacit, mostly unspoken consensus that unmanned weapons are more "humane" because they reduce US casualties. Having learned that US drone operators refer to human fatalities as "bug splats," a group from the heavily drone-targeted region of Khyber Pakhtunkhwa in Pakistan organized as #NotABugSplat. They created a ninety-by-sixty–foot art image of a child's face and located it in a field, where it would be recognizable even to the long-range view of US drone operators. The group hoped that the image of the child, whose parents were killed in a drone strike, would humanize the victims of drone strikes and "create empathy and introspection amongst drone operators . . . dialogue amongst policy makers, eventually leading to decisions that will save innocent lives."[52]

In Pakistan, a community targeted by US drone strikes displays the large image of a child to humanize the victims of US drone strikes.

Zombie Industries sells shooting targets of zombie characters with bleeding torsos that can be repeatedly shot. Targets include zombie President Obama, zombie Osama bin Laden, a zombie gun control advocate, and—until a feminist campaign convinced Zombie Industries to discontinue it—the sexy "Ex Girlfriend Zombie."[53] Given that zombies function as the ultimate killable once-humans, it is crucial to pay attention to how the political category of zombies is wielded and by whom. Who are deemed not truly human, not fully alive, and thus monsters, undeserving of respect or protection?[54]

Through television programs like *The Walking Dead* and zombie-themed videogames, millions of people are becoming accustomed to zombie killing as a routine way of life. Fans and players witness graphic destruction of zombie heads and bodies hundreds of times, with cringing relief. We witness characters in varying degrees of trauma, the fight-or-flight response engaged at all times, against a post-apocalyptic backdrop.

The zombie pandemic serves as a rehearsal for an uncertain future, a mirror for the spectacular and mundane economic decay of the present. Native studies scholar Cutcha Risling Baldy uses *The*

Walking Dead series as critical pedagogy to explore American history with her students. In her article, "On Telling Native People to Just 'Get Over It' Or Why I Teach *The Walking Dead* in My Native Studies Classes . . . *Spoiler Alert*!" she described the power of the series to bring home the nonfiction reality that, for Native Americans, the apocalypse *did* happen and the world as they knew it *was* violently ended.[55] From this standpoint, viewers may begin to comprehend the depth of intergenerational trauma. "California Indians often refer to the Mission System and the Gold Rush as 'the end of the world.' What those who survived experienced was both the 'apocalypse' and 'post apocalypse.' It was nothing short of zombies running around trying to kill them."[56] She draws out the haunting question that arises multiple times in the series, "Do you think we can come back from this?"

PLAGUE NARRATIVES

The zombie pandemic is coming. It's not a matter of if but when.

—Zombie Research Society[57]

The zombie viral epidemic has endured to the present day, continually reincarnating fears of decimating, uncontainable disease. A dominant plague narrative of our times, it recycles and reanimates long Western histories of plague terror, a post-apocalyptic Black Death. In films such as *28 Days Later* and *World War Z*, zombie swarms move at speeds impossible to battle, which may speak to the rapid rates of global infection, whether a biological pandemic, or computer viruses that can travel the world in superhuman time.[58] *28 Days Later* vividly depicts London under quarantine from the "rage virus," its realism contributing to viewers' sense of how easily this *could* happen.

Zombie movies are almost always set during or shortly after the apocalypse: established infrastructures—and the reassurances they can bring—cease to exist or crumble quickly amid obligatory scenes of disorder, and authorities who are looked to for protection themselves fall victim to the erupting mayhem. Whether the birth of the virus is attributed to vague extraterrestrial origins, hazy pseudoscientific mistakes, a wonder drug gone spectacularly wrong, or evil government machinations, the rapid effects of societal collapse are consistent staples of the genre. Law enforcement, government, communications systems, family structures, and all supporting infrastructure are shown to be impermanent, forcing survivors to dive into deep reservoirs of resilience and self-reliance.[59]

Over and over we take in the ways that the zombie-wrought chaos metastasizes across the planet. The repeated message is that no one is in charge of the world any longer. The recurring theme of total disintegration of the consumer-based economic system as a necessary prerequisite for new growth does not immediately translate into optimism about that new growth. Attempts to rebuild the social order may be as problematic as what they replace. In zombie narratives, as a contemporary spin on ancient plague narratives, it may not be the specifics of an individual breakdown that are most important, but instead, "the very idea of breakdown, the dissolution of certainty and meaning that zombies represent."[60]

Blurring recent memory and real conditions of viral threats, myriad versions of the zombie virus tap into deep-seated fears of universal vulnerability, while holding them at a fictional, sometimes comical, distance. The narrator in Ruben Fleischer's *Zombieland* (2009) offers the simple explanation, "Mad cow became mad person became mad zombie." In the *Resident Evil* series, the root cause of the mutagenic t-Virus stems from the overreaching effects of corporate greed and militarism. Off the screen, the US Centers for Disease Control and Prevention have joined the undead trend, with their tongue-in-cheek emergency preparedness booklet called "Preparedness 101: Zombie Pandemic," which "demonstrates the importance of being prepared in an entertaining way that people of all ages will enjoy. Readers follow Todd, Julie, and their dog Max as a strange new disease begins spreading, turning ordinary people into zombies."[61] A sensationalist effort to prepare for the unforeseen, the CDC's jokingly serious educational outreach echoes that of survivalist groups, who appear to be invoking the day when their paranoia will be justified. For instance, Zombie Squad, whose motto is "Making Dead Things Deader," is armed and ready with detailed preparations. Numerous survival manuals and websites, akin to those Max Brooks parodies in his 2003 book *Zombie Survival Guide: Complete Protection From the Living Dead*, openly discuss the latest methodologies and gear needed for zombie killing, advertising zombie apocalypse readiness as full of transferable skills for natural disasters and human-caused destruction. Zombies cross over from media-produced dystopias into waking life through survivalist fantasies anticipating the end times, functioning simultaneously as an outlet for anxiety and a method for the dissemination of emergency response plans. Our nation is being regularly instructed and trained in how to meet this catastrophe.

The Walking Dead series puts forward the ontologically horrifying realization that we are all infected. The thin yet fundamental boundary between living self and undead other weakens to the point of erasure. What makes us biologically human recedes, bringing the fight to retain psychic integrity into stark relief. Functioning as another dimension of existential anxiety, the survivors' struggles challenge us to question what we are becoming or have already become.

Centuries-old plague narratives in Western history take a new spin in our techno-consumerist society. The inexorable zombie onslaught speaks particularly to a millennial generation whose identities are shaped by dependence on instantaneous technology. Collins and Bond have argued, "Accustomed to instant communication with virtual strangers, insulated from the natural world and dependent on fragile transportation, communication and power networks, millennial audiences have good reason to fear the chaotic anonymity of zombies."[62] Zombies are the physical shadow of the information era, and the apocalypse they bring with them is the specter of total unplugging. No longer networked, what are we connected to? Survivors use "single-function devices." There are no selfies.

In the 2006 book *World War Z: An Oral History of the Zombie War*, author Max Brooks paints a future portrait: As Collins and Bond summarized, "In the new post-plague world order, practical survival skills eclipse the more rarefied expertise associated with a sophisticated but highly fragile information-based society found in developed nations before the war."[63] Amid shifting notions of identity in the Internet age, the zombie serves as a critical meditation on what it means to be human. A shuffling, rotting corpse with no detectable intelligence and incapable of using a single tool seems a bizarre iconic villain for a technologically savvy, fast-paced generation. While films of robotic uprisings provide a forum to reflect on our techno-digital environment, the zombie hordes represent the eradication of both our off- and online selves. As millions inhabit virtual, immaterial realms, the figure of the zombie haunts the "evolved" cyborgian self-image of disembodied consciousness, forcing engagement with ravenous, wrecked bodies that are devoid of consciousness, depersonalized, wiped blank, left only with a hideous hunger drive.

Collective thought experiments of a near-future world left with a fraction of the human population, covered with decaying swarms of the undead, raise ethical, philosophical, and existential questions. With its common refrain "What would *you* do?" the zombie genre compels reflection on oneself as we witness human actors confront hellish choices. What would one do to survive? What unimaginable sacrifices might one have to make? Would I still be me? What holds humans together, without familiar societal structures? Will we retain our humanity in the face of the engulfing undead? Will I cannibalize or kill my loved ones? How will I find anything without the GPS tracking on my cell phone? What does single-tasking look like? What would it feel like to walk through empty, silent urban landscapes?

The zombie apocalypse is a glimpse of a radical, violent renewal of the social order. It is a massive Control-Alt-Delete. How will "the machine linger on"? On one level a mass hunter-gatherer fantasy, its sociohistorical popularity is significant at a time of unbridled corporate monopolies and seemingly inescapable privatization. In the new "zombie economy," money is useless, and everything is free to those who know how to forage for it. If early zombie fiction spoke to Western fears of racial leveling and reverse colonization, current zombie apocalypse visions illustrate a class leveling. Values are reprioritized with survival skills on top.

Zombie plague narratives are closely tied to post-apocalyptic landscapes of destruction and regeneration. Apocalyptic landscapes show us visions of a decaying built environment as nature takes it back, images of overgrowth and re-wilding, useless machines and technology, signaling the reduction of human control and predation. The earth continues on without us.[64] The "eco-zombie" may be the genre's most compelling emergent trend—the zombie reimagined as an avenger that refuses to accept environmental destruction and ultimately rids the earth of humans.[65] "Greening" the zombie reads it as an ecological figure, "encoding the rift between humans and their natural environment perpetrated by capitalism, an economic system that centrally depends on the 'downgrading or devaluing of nature.'"[66] A peculiar relationship exists between this repetitive rehearsal of the sci-fi post-apocalyptic future and our sci-non-fi apocalyptic present. Audiences of the zombie apocalypse continually witness the post-apocalypse succession of denial-breaking moments, situations, and realizations. This catharsis may alternately enable a turning away from present conditions or act as a means to shatter denial regarding troubling forecasts that, in Doyle Canning and Patrick Reinsborough's words, "the ecological crisis is already feeding the historic dynamics of militarism, entrenched corporate power, and the systems of racism and oppression that have haunted the human family for generations."[67]

SALT FOR A TWENTY-FIRST-CENTURY APOCALYPSE

Over forty years ago, Martin Luther King Jr. predicted, "A nation that continues year after year to spend more money on military defense than on programs of social uplift is approaching spiritual death."[68] It may be argued that we have long since arrived at this point, and that American empire has entered a state of spiritual *un-death*. Perhaps the zombie apocalypse is already here, now. What will anthropologists of future generations say about American culture's fixation on fighting zombies during this particular time? Our culture's use of an iconography of death and decay can be seen as a process to grapple with structural horror, climate destabilization, and accelerating change, as global capitalism is on a collision course with the earth's ecological limits. "In an America anxious over the fate of the social order, the zombie offers a talisman, a laughably horrific symbol about a fake apocalypse that keeps at bay real fears about social degeneration and collapse."[69] These past and present meanings, metaphors, and allegories of the reanimated dead invite re-cognition of our monster fixation with a critical edge. Historian of American monsters W. Scott Poole claimed, "Social justice can break the power of the monster, altering the structures of history and society so that the terror of history recedes."[70] What is the twenty-first–century equivalent of salt, the flavor that returns us to our sovereign embodied selves, releases humans from zombification, and allows the undead to rest?

The new millennium zombie apocalypse presents a humanizing challenge to audiences to become more fully "human," reflective, cooperative, and self-reliant. This more apocal-optimistic engagement is lucidly depicted in Brooks's *World War Z*, where ultimate human victory is not in doubt, and the zombie war serves as a horrific crucible out of which a surviving fraction of the human population emerges as warriors with profoundly renewed humanity. This fantasy is deployed to summon mass forces of humanity's highest qualities as we regroup to fight, brought into relief against the relentless, unthinking zombie hordes. The US is shown to have redeemed itself of the narcissistic features that left it ill-prepared for the zombie menace.[71] Brooks invites "zombie awareness" of what capacities nations currently possess to rise to such a vast challenge of potential annihilation. Hopeful regeneration follows the plague's scourging.

The original meaning of apocalypse derives from the Greek *apocalypsis*, "lifting a veil," "disclosure of knowledge," or "revelation." Lifting the veil that shrouds soul crushing and ecocidal business as usual, zombies' work is never done, it seems. As W. Scott Poole proclaimed in *Monsters in America*, "Imagining the world as we know it collapsing around us gives us the opportunity to take a long look at what that dead world values and call it into question."[72] A collective cultural autopsy of what is worth keeping from a dead or dying world informs prefigurative imagination, what future sustainability may look like, as sci-fi as those imaginings may be. Slavoj Žižek asked, "How come it is easier for us to imagine the end of all life on earth, an asteroid hitting the planet, than a modest change in our economic order?"[73] Overpopulation, income inequality, and climate destabilization, with grave realities in the present and dire predictions for the future, are all grimly reversed by the imagined undead destruction of humanity and its autopilot doomsday systems.

"Initially, zombie movies shocked audiences with their unfamiliar images; today, however, they are even more shocking because of their familiarity."[74] This normalized familiarity, alternating between laughable brain-eating horror and renewed power to terrify in various media genres, needs to be rendered shocking. Many cultural critics have interrogated the reasons for zombies' explosive popularity in the past decade. Longing for radical change and despairing of its potential, the paradoxes of the zombie obsession point to the entrenched hopelessness and profound desire at the heart of American empire. Ahmad states that the Z-generation popularity takes root in the zombie as a sign of "an unsated cultural appetite in the Global North for the type of radical transformations that a relatively affluent and politically complacent society cannot achieve."[75] In this view, the developed world's "zombification" depends on the absence of belief in the possibility of change and a corresponding lack of will to fight for civil and economic liberties. "They simply can't imagine," Werner de Gruijter has written, "that a more humane form of capitalism and democracy is attainable and that in this whole drama they could have a valuable role to play."[76]

Recent undead protests, featuring crowds dressed as zombies, hold up a monstrous mirror to economic systems that are devoid of consciousness, stumbling down a path of devastation. A fascinating proliferation of zombie demonstrations arose in response to the economic crash and age of austerity, with marches of the undead during the Occupy movement, a zombie invasion of the New York Stock Exchange, "hunger marches," and University of California students' "Rise of the Living Debt" protest against tuition hikes and student debt. As David McNally observed, "Revolt by the undead warns that the zombie laborers who sustain the twilight world of late capitalism might awaken and throw off their chains. These images offer the true counterpoint to the gloomy survivalism of the zombie apocalypse."[77] Embodying terrors of history and deadening social conditions, zombie rebellion calls for a destruction of reigning economic structures, a breakdown leading to possible breakthrough(s).

In *A Paradise Built in Hell*, Rebecca Solnit documented how communities have recurrently risen to their best in times of catastrophe. She offers a historian's intervention into the corporate media narrative that crises only bring out the worst in humans, who readily devolve to savagery and selfishness. Solnit reminds us that in disasters across North America throughout the twentieth century, the loss of electrical power sometimes allowed residents of disaster-struck cities to see stars otherwise obscured by urban light pollution.

> You can think of the current social order as something akin
> to this artificial light: another kind of power that fails in di-

saster. In its place appears a reversion to improvised, collaborative, cooperative, and local society. However beautiful the stars of a suddenly visible night sky, few nowadays could find their way by them. But the constellations of solidarity, altruism, and improvisation are within most of us and reappear at these times. People know what to do in a disaster. The loss of power, the disaster in the modern sense, is an affliction, but the reappearance of these old heavens is its opposite.[78]

Desperate times give rise to desperate fantasies. The temporal gap between near-future dystopian fiction and the present continues to shrink. Contemporary versions of the zombie narrative give evidence of a cultural desire to unplug and reboot, a traumatic liberation. The mythology of zombie apocalypse is a drastic "way out" of our contemporary systemic plagues. But we do not need to create more fantasies to shock us awake; we need only face the otherwise censored realities of survival in a time of global horror. With zombies, we have created humanoid monsters that repeatedly confront us with annihilation unless we radically shift. As Max Brooks states in *The Zombie Survival Guide*, "Conventional warfare is useless against these creatures, as is conventional thought."[79]

Zombie mobs devour individualism. This pop culture phenomenon can be seen both as a failure of the imagination and a summoning of the imagination in service of the mutual, collective effort required to challenge undead systems on a global scale. Rotting compost may become fertile soil. The most optimistic reading of the zombie apocalypse is the forced enacting of unconventional thought. The systemic "salt" of unconventional thought may be a return to diverse wisdom of how humans lived or could live outside these monstrous systems. The zombie threat musters crucial humanizing forces that spectators can tap into again and again. The bleakness of the genre tests us. The overwhelming threat of an inhuman future suggests our worst fears, while the promise of an alternative, in which human care and cooperation prevail, speaks to our unfulfilled yearnings. To face the truly monstrous challenges of our time, we may yet radically transform and de-zombify our society.

ZARA ZIMBARDO, MA, is a member of the interdisciplinary studies faculty at the California Institute of Integral Studies. She has a background in independent media as producer of an alternative current events television series highlighting grassroots movements for social and environmental justice, and has developed critical media literacy workshops, presentations, and curricula in collaboration with schools throughout the Bay Area. She is an anti-oppression facilitator and consultant, and cofounder of the antiracist feminist resource and training group, the White Noise Collective. Her ongoing research interests include the politics of representation, Islamophobia, collective memory, US militarism, and nonviolent social movements.

Notes

1. Umberto Eco, "Can Television Teach?," *Screen Education* 31 (1979), 15–24; quote at p. 15; republished in *The Screen Education Reader*, eds. Manuel Alvarado, Edward Buscombe and Richard Collins (New York: Columbia University Press, 1993).

2. Annalee Newitz, *Pretend We're Dead: Capitalist Monsters in American Pop Culture* (Durham NC: Duke University Press, 2006), 12.

3. For example, Seth Grahame-Smith's phenomenally popular 2009 parody, *Pride and Prejudice and Zombies*.

4. For example, "The only modern myth is the myth of the zombie." Gilles Deleuze and Felix Guattari, *Anti-Oedipus: Capitalism and Schizophrenia* (Minneapolis: University of Minnesota Press, 1983), 335.

5. Margo Collins and Elson Bond, "'Off the Page and into Your Brains!': New Millennium Zombies and the Scourge of Hopeful Apocalypses," in *Better off Dead: the Evolution of the Zombie as Post-human*, eds. Deborah Christie and Sarah Juliet Lauro (New York: Fordham University Press, 2011), 187–204, quotation at 187.

6. Newitz, *Pretend We're Dead*, 5.

7. Steven Shaviro, "Capitalist Monsters," *Historical Materialism* 10, no. 4 (2002), 281–90, at 288.

8. Quoted in Newitz, *Pretend We're Dead*, 7.

9. W. Scott Poole, *Monsters in America: Our Historical Obsession with the Hideous and The Haunting* (Waco, Texas: Baylor University Press, 2011), 202.

10. Sarah Juliet Lauro and Karen Embry, "A Zombie Manifesto: The Nonhuman Condition in the Era of Advanced Capitalism," *boundary 2* 35, no. 1 (Spring 2008), 85–108, at 86.

11. See, for example, Newitz, *Pretend We're Dead*, op cit.

12. Amy Wilentz, "A Zombie Is a Slave Forever," *New York Times*, October 30, 2012, http://www.nytimes.com/2012/10/31/opinion/a-zombie-is-a-slave-forever.html?_r=0.

13. "In the 1980s, with [François] Duvalier's son ousted from power and the moment ripe for reform, the literacy primer put out by the liberation theologians' wing of the Roman Catholic Church in Haiti was called 'A Taste of Salt,'" Wilentz, "A Zombie Is a Slave Forever," ibid.

14. David McNally, "Zombies: Apocalypse or Rebellion?," *Jacobin*, October 23, 2012, https://www.jacobinmag.com/2012/10/zombies-apocalypse-or-rebellion.

15. Kyle William Bishop, *American Zombie Gothic: The Rise and Fall (and Rise) of the Walking Dead in Popular Culture* (Jefferson: McFarland & Company, Inc., 2010), 13.

16. Chera Kee, "From Cannibal to Zombie and Back Again" in *Better Off Dead: The Evolution of the Zombie as Post-Human*, eds. Deborah Christie and Sarah Juliet Lauro (New York: Fordham University Press, 2011), 20.

17. Chris Vials, "The Origin of the Zombie in American Radio and Film: B-Horror, U.S. Empire, and the Politics of Disavowal" in *Generation Zombie: Essays on the Living Dead in Modern Culture*, eds. Stephanie Boluk and Wylie Lenz (Jefferson: McFarland & Company, Inc., 2011), 51. An anthropologist and ethnobotanist, Wade Davis wrote *The Serpent and the Rainbow* (New York: Simon & Schuster, 1985), a controversial account of the role played by pharmacological substances in Haitian zombification practices.

18. Chera Kee, "From Cannibal to Zombie and Back Again," 13.

19. Newitz, *Pretend We're Dead*, 90.

20. Joan Dayan describes how, during the 1804 massacre of whites led by Jean-Jacques Dessalines, the figure of Jean Zombi, "a mulatto of Port-au-Prince" who "earned a reputation for brutality" as "one of the fiercest slaughterers," became a prototype for subsequent zombie representations. See Joan Dayan, *Haiti, History, and the Gods* (Berkeley: University of California Press, 1998), 35–38.

21. Quoted by Kee, "From Cannibal to Zombie and Back Again," 17.

22. Bishop, *American Zombie Gothic*, 157. In the last few years, for example, Photoshopped images juxtapose fictional zombies clawing at mall windows and photos of actual shopping crowds on Black Friday, suggesting that, apart from make-up, the two groups are indistinguishable; meanwhile, Adbusters and other groups help to organize Black Friday anti-consumer protests with participants dressed as zombies. See, for example, "Apocalypse Now!: The Counter Black Friday Meme," *Adbusters*, November 28, 2013, https://www.adbusters.org/blogs/apocalypse-now-counter-black-friday-meme.html; and Abby Martin, "Black Friday's Rabid Zombie Shopping Stampede," Media Roots, November 29, 2013, http://www.mediaroots.org/black-fridays-rabid-zombie-shopping-stampede.

23. Aalya Ahmad, "Gray Is the New Black: Race, Class, and Zombies" in *Generation Zombie: Essays on the Living Dead in Modern Culture*, eds. Stephanie Boluk and Wylie Lenz (Jefferson, North Carolina: McFarland & Company, 2011), 137.

24. *Dawn of the Dead*, directed by George A. Romero, Laurel Production Inc, 1978.

25. Bishop, *American Zombie Gothic*, 112.

26. Zombie walks, organized public gatherings of people in zombie costume and gore make-up, originated in North America in 2001. They have since occurred with frequency in large cities throughout the world.

27. Wilentz, "A Zombie Is a Slave Forever."

28. David McNally, "Land of the Living Dead: Capitalism and the Catastrophes of Everyday Life," 108–27 in *Catastrophism: The Apocalyptic Politics of Collapse and Rebirth*, ed. Sasha Lilley, et al. (Oakland: PM Press, 2012); see especially 119ff. Also see his *Monsters of the Market: Zombies, Vampires and Global Capital* (Chicago: Haymarket Books, 2011) for an in depth analysis of how tales of undead monstrosity, disembodiment and enrichment, and obscure nighttime sites of forced labor circulate to describe the cultural economy of the global market system.

29. McNally, "Land of the Living Dead," 122.

30. On news coverage of Vietnam as a "living room war" see, for example, Daniel C. Hallin, *The Uncensored War: The Media and Vietnam* (New York: Oxford University Press, 1986).

31. Poole, *Monsters in America*, 198.

32. "George A. Romero's *Night of the Living Dead*," Museum of Modern Art, October 31, 2007, http://www.moma.org/visit/calendar/films/565; quoted by Deborah Christie, "A Dead New World: Richard Matheson and the Modern Zombie," 67–80, in *Better Off Dead*, ed. Christie and Lauro, 77.

33. Karen Randell, "Lost Bodies/Lost Souls: *Night of the Living Dead* and *Deathdream* as Vietnam Narrative," 67–76 in *Generation Zombie*, eds. Boluk and Lenz, 67.

34. On "ungrievable lives," see Judith Butler, *Frames of War: When Is Life Grievable?* (London and Brooklyn: Verso, 2009).

35. See Andrew Roth, Zoe Huffman, Jeffrey Huling, Kevin Stolle and Jocelyn Thomas, "Covering War's Victims: A Content Analysis of Iraq and Afghanistan War Photographs in the *New York Times* and the *San Francisco Chronicle*," 253–71 in *Censored 2008*, eds. Peter Phillips and Andrew Roth (New York: Seven Stories Press, 2007).

36. Dennis Lim, "Dante's Inferno," *Village Voice*, November 22, 2005, http://www.villagevoice.com/2005-11-22/film/dante-s-inferno.

37. Bishop, *American Zombie Gothic*, 11.

38. Rachel Maddow, *Drift: The Unmooring of American Military Power* (New York: Crown Publishers, 2012), 204.

39. Eric Hamako, "Zombie Orientals Ate My Brain!: Orientalism in Contemporary Zombie Stories," in *Race, Oppression and the Zombie: Essays on the Cross-Cultural Appropriations of the Caribbean Tradition*, eds. Christopher M. Moreman and Cory James Rushton (Jefferson North Carolina: McFarland & Company, 2011), 113.

40. Thomas Riegler, "The Connection between Real and Reel Horror," JGCinema, Cinema and Globalization, no date, http://www.jgcinema.com/single.php?sl=real-horror.

41. Lev Grossman, "Zombies Are the New Vampires," *Time*, April 9, 2009; quoted in McNally, "Zombies: Apocalypse or Rebellion?"

42. Bishop, *American Zombie Gothic*, 10.

43. Lauro and Embry, "Zombie Manifesto," 93.

44. McNally, "Zombies: Apocalypse or Rebellion?"

45. Julie Watson, "'Zombie Apocalypse' Training Drill Organized By Halo Corp. For Military, Police Set For Oct. 31 In San Diego," *Huffington Post*, October 27, 2012, http://www.huffington-post.com/2012/10/29/zombie-apocalypse-trainining-military-halo-corp-_n_2036996.html.

46. Gordon Lubold, "Exclusive: The Pentagon Has a Plan to Stop the Zombie Apocalypse. Seriously," *Foreign Policy*, May 13, 2014, http://www.foreignpolicy.com/articles/2014/05/13/exclusive_the_pentagon_has_a_plan_to_stop_the_zombie_apocalypse.

47. Ibid.

48. Avery Gordon, *Ghostly Matters: Haunting and the Sociological Imagination* (Minneapolis: University of Minnesota Press, 2008), xvi.

49. Shawn McIntosh, "The Evolution of the Zombie: The Monster That Keeps Coming Back," 1–17 in *Zombie Culture: Autopsies of Living Dead*, eds. Shawn McIntosh and Marc Leverette (Lanham, Maryland: Scarecrow Press, 2008).

50. Ibid., 13.

51. Tanya Krzywinska, "Zombies in Gamespace: Form, Context, and Meaning in Zombie-Based Video Games," 153–68 in *Generation Zombie*, eds. Boluk and Lenz, 153.

52. Rob Williams, "Giant 'Not A Bug Splat' Art Installation Takes Aim At Pakistan's Drone Operators," *Independent*, April 8, 2014, http://www.independent.co.uk/news/world/asia/giant-not-a-bug-splat-art-installation-takes-aim-at-pakistans-predator-drone-operators-9246768.html.

53. Maya, "Here's 'The Ex' Shooting Target That Zombie Industries Sells," *Feministing*, May 6, 2013, http://feministing.com/2013/05/06/heres-the-ex-shooting-target-that-zombie-industries-sells.

54. See Patricia J. Williams, "The Monsterization of Trayvon Martin," *Nation*, July 31, 2013, http://www.thenation.com/article/175547/monsterization-trayvon-martin.

55. Cutcha Risling Baldy, "On Telling Native People to Just 'Get Over It,' or Why I Teach the Walking Dead in my Native Studies Classes . . . *Spoiler alert*" http://cutchabaldy.weebly.com/1/post/2013/12/on-telling-native-people-to-just-get-over-it-or-why-i-teach-about-the-walking-dead-in-my-native-studies-classes-spoiler-alert.html.

56. Ibid.

57. "About Us," Zombie Research Society, no date, http://zombieresearchsociety.com/about-us.

58. For instance, in May 2000 the ILOVEYOU computer virus infected over fifty million computers within ten days. It is estimated that 10 percent of the world's internet-connected computers were affected, an outbreak which caused over $5 billion dollars in damages. See Kathleen Ohlson, "'Love' Virus Costs Approaching $7 Billion," *Computer World*, May 9, 2000, http://www.computerworld.com/s/article/44810/_Love_virus_costs_approaching_7B_research_firm_says.

59. "Knowledge is only part of the fight for survival. The rest must come from you. Personal choice, the will to live, must be paramount when the dead begin to rise. Without it, nothing will protect you." Max Brooks, *The Zombie Survival Guide: Complete Protection from the Living Dead* (New York: Three Rivers Press, 2003), xiv. Notably, Brooks's bestseller list handbook never acknowledges its status as fiction.

60. Steven Zani and Kevin Meaux, "Lucio Fulci and the Decaying Definition of Zombie Narratives," 98–115 in *Better Off Dead*, eds. Christie and Lauro, 101.

61. "Social Media: Zombie Apocalypse," Centers for Disease Control and Prevention, Emergency Preparedness and Response, March 12, 2014, http://emergency.cdc.gov/socialmedia/zombies.asp.

62. Collins and Bond, "Off the Page," 187.

63. Ibid., 188.

64. For a nonfiction effort to imagine a future without humans (or zombies), see Alan Weisman, *The World Without Us* (New York: Picador, 2007).

65. Sarah Juliet Lauro, "The Eco-Zombie: Environmental Critique in Zombie Narratives," 54–66, in *Generation Zombie*, eds. Boluk and Lenz.

66. Kerstin Oloff, "Greening the Zombie: Caribbean Gothic, World-Ecology, and Socio-Ecological Degradation," *Green Letters: Studies in Ecocriticism* 16, no. 1 (special issue on Global and Postcolonial Ecologies, Summer 2012), 31–45, quotation at 31.

67. Doyle Canning and Patrick Reinsborough, *Re:Imagining Change—How To Use Story-Based Strategy to Win Campaigns, Build Movements, and Change the World* (Oakland: PM Press, 2010), 101.

68. Martin Luther King, Jr., "Beyond Vietnam," Riverside Church, New York, April 4, 1967, http://mlk-kpp01.stanford.edu/index.php/encyclopedia/documentsentry/doc_beyond_vietnam.

69. Poole, *Monsters in America*, 203.

70. Ibid., 228.

71. Collins and Bond, "Off the Page," 192.

72. Poole, *Monsters in America*, 216.

73. *The Pervert's Guide to Ideology*, directed by Sophie Fiennes, 2013. Žižek's quote echoes the sentiment of the widely known saying attributed to Fredric Jameson, from which the title of this chapter is derived: "It is easier to imagine the end of the world than to imagine the end of capitalism."

74. Bishop, *American Zombie Gothic*, 36.

75. Ahmad, "Gray is the New Black," 131.

76. Werner de Gruijter, "The Zombification of the West," *Truthout*, March 15, 2014, http://www.truth-out.org/opinion/item/22451-the-zombification-of-the-west.

77. McNally, "Zombies: Apocalypse or Rebellion?"

78. Rebecca Solnit, *A Paradise Built in Hell: The Extraordinary Communities That Arise in Disaster.* (New York: Viking, 2009), 10.

79. Brooks, *Zombie Survival Guide*, xiii.

CHAPTER 10

Play it Again, (Uncle) Sam
A Brief History of US Imperialism, Propaganda, and the News

Deepa Kumar

President Barack Obama and his administration almost took the United States to war with Syria in 2013 over claims that Bashar Al-Assad had used chemical weapons on the Syrian opposition. In what seemed like a replay of history, Syrians were paraded on television screens in ways reminiscent of Iraqis under Saddam Hussein and a host of other such "worthy victims." In this essay, I examine some of the key wars that the US has engaged in over the last century and the part played by propaganda in winning public consent. With stunning consistency, the propaganda strategies used in one war are repeated and reproduced by the media with little critical scrutiny. I outline these strategies beginning with the 1898 Spanish–American War, which was pivotal in terms of setting up a framework that Uncle Sam would deploy repeatedly over the next century.

In the interest of brevity, I will only focus on what I consider are the key wars. Additionally, some of the historical detail and nuance of these wars has been excluded here in the interest of presenting a long view of US imperialism. I do, however, make space for moments when the news is contradictory and includes voices of dissent. Typically, this has happened wherever social movements have challenged the priorities and rhetoric of the political elite. I discuss these moments so as to offer hope to a new generation living under the tyranny of the "war on terror," and to make the point that antiwar movements have in the past, and can today, successfully forge an alternative agenda of peace and international solidarity.

THE POLITICS OF EMPIRE

In the late nineteenth and early twentieth centuries, the structure and organization of the world underwent a dramatic transformation. For instance in 1876, on the eve of the scramble for Africa, European powers controlled only 10 percent of the continent, namely Algeria, Cape Colony, Mozambique, and Angola. By the beginning of the twentieth century, however, virtually the entire continent was colonized. A similar picture emerges in the rest of the world. Whereas during the mid-nineteenth century many countries were independent and autonomous, by the beginning of the twentieth century, the world had been more or less divided up among the "great powers"— England, Germany, France, and the US. These countries were the most developed capitalist centers and each had their own empires. Yet, they also competed with each other to gain greater access to and control over the world's resources. Furthermore, these "great powers" were in competition not only among themselves, but also against older empires like Belgium, Spain, Portugal, Italy, Japan, and Russia.

The various wars that occurred during this period and up to the First World War were a product of this competition and the struggle over resources, new markets, and places for investment. In a nutshell, as theorists of imperialism have argued, imperial wars occur as a result of economic competition expressing itself in the military and political arena. Woodrow Wilson, writing in 1907 while president of Princeton University, made a similar observation:

> Since trade ignores national boundaries and the manufacturer insists on having the world as a market, the flag of his nation must follow him, and the doors of the nations which are closed against him must be battered down. Concessions obtained by financiers must be safeguarded by ministers of state, even if the sovereignty of unwilling nations be outraged in the process. Colonies must be obtained or planted, in order that no useful corner of the world may be overlooked or left unused.[1]

In order to ensure that "no useful corner" of the world be "left unused," under the leadership of presidents William McKinley, Theodore Roosevelt, William Howard Taft, and Woodrow Wilson, the US intervened in several countries between 1898 and 1920, from Nicaragua to Haiti and Mexico. These interventions occurred under both Democratic and Republican leaderships with both camps espousing a view that commerce follows the flag and that the flag follows commerce.

US Marine Corps Major General Smedley Butler, who participated in many of the aforementioned incursions into Central and South America, summarized the logic of imperial intervention as follows: "I spent most of my time being a high-class muscle man for Big Business, for Wall Street and the bankers. In short, I was a racketeer, a gangster for capitalism. I helped make Mexico and especially Tampico safe for American oil interests in 1914. I helped make Haiti and Cuba a decent place for the National City Bank boys to collect revenues in."[2] Butler, who had been quoted extensively by the news media for two decades when he was involved in various interventions, simply disappeared from the news after his 1935 book, *War is a Racket*, and a related article critical of US intervention cited above appeared in the magazine *Common Sense*.[3] Often quite consciously, the establishment media have tailored their narratives of US wars to suit the aims of empire.

1898: THE SPANISH–AMERICAN WAR

The first major war that launched the United States onto the imperial stage was war with Spain in 1898. The immediate context for this war was Cuba, one of the last vestiges of Spain's once vast empire in the Western hemisphere. The US had trade dealings with Cuba in the range of $100 million, and $35–$50 million in investments.[4] Thus, when the Cuban revolution against the Spanish broke out in 1895, the US saw this as an opportunity to rid Spain from its backyard.

At first, there was debate among members of the political elite about whether the US should go to war with Spain. Even sections of the business class were hesitant for fear of what war might do to the economy. Yet, a number of factors came together to propel the nation toward war.

Spain ruled Cuba with the utmost cruelty, and when the American public learned of this they were justifiably enraged. At the start of the revolution, Spain responded with a reign of terror to isolate the leaders. Thousands of peasants and agricultural workers were put into concentration camps and left to die of starvation and disease. The yellow journals, which specialized in sensational and unverified news—particularly Joseph Pulitzer's *New York World* and William Randolph Hearst's *New York Journal*—carried lurid stories of Spain's cruelty, and Hearst himself became a noted war hawk on the matter. This not only won public sympathy for the Cuban cause, but it also pushed a large section of the political elite to support Cuban independence, at least in spirit.

The advocacy journalism of the *Journal* and the *World* was bolstered by pro-imperialist voices such as Theodore Roosevelt, Henry Cabot Lodge, historian Brooks Adams, naval strategist Alfred T. Mahan, railroad tycoon James Hill and others.[5] But it was not until the *Maine* disaster that the country tipped in favor of war with Spain.

In February 1898, the *USS Maine*, stationed in Havana on a "friendly visit," exploded and sank.[6] There was no clear evidence at the time as to what caused the explosion, and historians even today argue that there is no proof of an attack. Yet, seeing this as an opportunity to inflame public opinion, Hearst's *Journal* argued that the *Maine* was deliberately attacked by Spain, even going so far as to produce a sketch showing how a mine or a torpedo had caused the explosion. With some exceptions, newspapers around the country at the time similarly gave a lot of space and attention to the *Maine* disaster, and beat the drums of war.[7] The slogan of the time was "Remember the *Maine*, to Hell with Spain."

In the two months following the *Maine* incident, there was a flurry of diplomatic engagement between the US and Spain. President McKinley took a position in favor of diplomacy rather than war. By April, it was clear that Spain was not only willing to give up Cuba but to concede to all of the US's demands. Yet, this was not enough for the jingoist section of the elite.[8] The US invaded Cuba under the guise of freeing the Cubans—a hollow justification given that Cuba would soon become a colony of the US in all but name. This was particularly evidenced by the Platt Amendment of 1901, which the US forced upon the Cubans, that inserted into their constitution that the US had the right to intervene unilaterally in Cuban affairs. The net result was that between May and August of 1898, the US annexed and occupied the last territories that Spain held in the Caribbean and the Pacific: Cuba, Puerto Rico, Guam, and the Philippines.

Despite the successes of these conquests, there was opposition toward imperialism. The opposition included figures such as former president Grover Cleveland and eight members of his cabinet, William Jennings Bryan, various senators and members of House, the wealthy industrialist Andrew Carnegie, the president of the American Federation of Labor (AFL) Samuel Gompers, prominent intellectuals and writers like Mark Twain, as well as educators, social workers, and others.[9] Close to half a million people joined the Anti-Imperialist League, first established in November 1898. While many opposed US imperialism on the grounds of democratic principles and antiracism, there were also those who opposed annexation because of the potential "degeneration" of the white race if it were to mix with people of "inferior" races.[10]

If the Spanish–American War is seen as an exemplar of sensationalist propaganda, it was also a moment when the classic ideology of imperialism began to gain ground in the US. As Ilia Rodriguez argued in her analysis of six metropolitan daily newspapers' coverage of the US occupation of Puerto Rico, the colonized were represented as the racialized "other" in need of colonial benevolence and administration. Puerto Ricans were described as being a "mixture of laziness and honesty—characteristics of an oppressed race—that render the Puerto Rican . . . a man to be carefully guided by wise hands."[11]

This rhetoric was not unique to the US but had it roots in European colonialism, best described by the English poet Rudyard Kipling as the "white man's burden." Kipling argued that the superior white race had a responsibility to bring civilization to the backward and inferior peoples of the world through colonization. The US adopted such a mission with zeal. The reluctant imperialist McKinley would later state that the natives should not be left to themselves as they were "unfit for self-government," and that such a course would only "expose them to the abuses of the other European powers and invite anarchy and chaos."[12] Similarly, the Philippine Commission report released in January 1900 stated that "the United States cannot withdraw from the Philippines. . . . The Filipinos are wholly unprepared for independence, and if independence were given to them they could not maintain it."[13]

Even though the US claimed to be liberating Spain's colonized people, this was not the reality. If Spain had used concentration camps to isolate revolutionaries and radicals from the general population, the US only reintroduced these methods. It is unclear how many people died in such US concentration camps. One estimate by General Bell is that in the Philippines, one-sixth of the population (about 600,000 people) on just one island (Luzon) was wiped out.[14] This process was referred to as "pacification." Various other methods of torture were also employed, such as forcibly pumping prisoners full of water up to five gallons at a time, so that the body became unrecognizable.[15] Commenting on the horrors committed in the Philippines, Mark Twain wrote that the American flag should have "the white stripes painted black and the stars replaced by the skull and cross bones."[16]

Overall, the Spanish–American War is instructive of how modern imperialist wars would be conducted and sold to the public. In particular, there are three narratives that would become a rubric for future wars. The first is the "rescue" narrative, wherein the US highlights the suffering of others in order to position itself as a savior. These "worthy victims," as Edward Herman and Noam Chomsky have argued, are given media attention in order to win public sympathy.[17] Yet, once the US intervenes the victims soon learn that the "rescue" narrative is apocryphal and that instead intervention was designed to further imperial ambitions. Second, a dramatic event such as the sinking of a ship often becomes the turning point in escalating jingoist rhetoric in the push for war. Third, after the initial incursion, occupation and colonization is justified on the grounds that, should the US leave, it would result in chaos because the native population is unable to govern itself. This is the White Man's Burden narrative, which advocates the necessity to civilize the native subject seen as "half devil, half child."

THE TWO WORLD WARS

Between 1876 and 1914, the six major imperial powers had grabbed twenty-five million square kilometers of the world and had colonized over *half a billion* (521 million) people. With almost the entire globe carved up, the dynamic of colonization from then on would be marked by a struggle among the great powers, between imperial "haves" and "have-nots," over a process of re-division. In the case of the First World War, the "haves" were Britain, France, and Russia, later joined by the US to form the "Allied" powers; and the "have-nots" were Germany, Austria-Hungary, Italy (which later switched sides), and Turkey.

The US did not initially join the war. Influential sections of the political elite and, by and large, the public did not want to intervene in the "European quarrel." The establishment news media reflected this opinion, and influential independent media such as *Appeal to Reason* and other radical newspapers took strong antiwar positions. Antiwar sentiment was so strong that in 1916, Woodrow Wilson's reelection campaign adopted the slogan, "He Kept Us Out of War." This sentiment continued such that, in 1920, when Eugene Debs, the Socialist candidate jailed for his antiwar views, ran for president from prison, he won over a million votes.[18]

Despite his promises, Wilson, who had rejected intervention in 1914, found himself in the war camp by 1915, and the US did enter the war in April 1917. A series of events precipitated the entry of the US into the war. First, the banking industry, led by the house of J. P. Morgan, initiated a campaign to intervene in the war as a way to enter foreign markets. In order to win the American public, they enlisted the help of twelve publishers and 197 newspapers.[19] Second, Britain sought to win the American public and initiated a massive propaganda campaign relying on 260,000 influential citizens to make its case, along with an inundation of newspapers, posters, cartoons, pictures, maps, and so forth. In essence, the propaganda concentrated on presenting Germany as the aggressor and as guilty of committing horrendous atrocities on innocent people. An inflammatory (and false) report, the Bryce report, provided grist for the mill by stating that German officers had raped Belgian girls, bayoneted a two-year-old child, and sliced off a woman's breast.[20] When the Germans sunk a British passenger liner, the *Lusitania*, which was also carrying rifle cartridges, it became a galvanizing moment. The ship attack triggered the rescue narrative, paving the way for US entry into the war.

As Philip Knightly argued in his book *The First Casualty*, the nationwide propaganda campaign sought to "rally the forces of good against the forces of evil."[21] The war was no longer a European affair but became a crusade, the duty of every "honorable" man. To further these efforts, in 1917, Wilson established the Creel Commission, named after former journalist George Creel, which was formally called the Committee on Public Information (CPI). The CPI was the first large-scale government propaganda office. Wilson argued that US intervention was in the "national interest," and the CPI furthered that notion using pamphlets, speakers, advertising, newspapers, and more.[22] As Knightly noted, people in the news business were some of the best recruits for the government's propaganda efforts and the "editors of the *Times*, the *Express*, the *Daily Mail*, the *Evening Post*, and the *Chronicle* and the managing director of Reuters all did their bit."[23] And if this wasn't enough, Creel mobilized some 75,000 citizens, called Four Minute Men, who volunteered to travel the country giving literally millions of pro-war public speeches, specifically targeting Germany as the enemy of democracy. Based in part on this propaganda blitz, sections of the American public changed their position on the war.

If the rescue narrative employed during World War I pertained to Belgian victimhood, during World War II it was the genocidal conditions that Jews faced at the hands of the Nazis that became central. The actual causes of the Second World War are similar to those of the first. While Britain and France sought to hold onto their empires, Germany and Japan pushed back against the greater powers' stranglehold. The US and Russia, in the meantime, attempted to take advantage of these conflicts to build their own empires. The immediate context was the economic crisis of the 1930s, known as the Great Depression. Various countries built protectionist blocs to defend their weakened economies. These economic struggles then turned into a military conflict to annex rivals' territories and markets. Yet, US intervention into this war was presented as one for democracy and against fascism. As the Council on Foreign Relations, an organization that worked closely with the US State Department, put it:

> If war aims are stated which seem to be concerned solely with Anglo-American imperialism, they would offer little to the people in the rest of the world and will be vulnerable to Nazi counter-promises. Such aims would also strengthen the most reactionary elements in the United States and the Brit-

ish Empire. The interests of other people should be stressed, not only those of Europe, but also of Asia, Africa, and Latin America. This would have a better propaganda effect.[24]

Indeed, there could not have been a more powerful rescue story than that involving the Nazi holocaust of Jews. Yet, these victims too would find the rescue story to be hollow. As Arthur Morse in *While Six Million Died* argued, the Allies "by a combination of political expediency, diplomatic evasion, indifference and raw bigotry . . . played directly into the hands of Adolf Hitler even as he set in motion the final plans for the greatest mass murder in history."[25]

From as early as 1933, the US knew of the conditions for Jews. Yet, it had strict immigration quotas and did not open up its border to Jews fleeing sure death. Even after the horrors of Kristalnacht in 1938, when the Nazis rounded up 20,000 Jews and sent them to concentration camps such as Dachau and Buchenwald, President Roosevelt failed to act. The US's immigration policies stayed the same. In 1939, the *St. Louis*, a ship carrying 936 Jews fleeing persecution, was turned back, forcing the passengers to return to Europe where many of them died in Hitler's gas chambers. The US refused to bomb the tracks to Auschwitz or its crematorium—even though Allied bombers flew over Auschwitz to bomb Nazi factories. Few people know this history, so well documented by Morse and other historians, thanks in large part to a pliant news media system that presented this war as the "good war." The galvanizing moment for the US's entry into the war was the attack on Pearl Harbor.

Replaying the motifs developed in 1898, the Second World War had both worthy victims and the drama of Pearl Harbor, just as the First World War had Belgian victims and the *Lusitania*. But the third element—the fate of the victims—is more varied. In the case of European Jews the US did not absorb the flood of immigrants but did support the plan to create a Jewish state in Palestine. This plan furthered the oil interests of Western nations in the Middle East. Thus, even though the US claimed to champion national self-determination, it did so only in cases where it advanced its own interests.

THE VIETNAM WAR

The dynamic of imperialism changed after the Second World War. Whereas the first two world wars involved inter-imperialist rivalry among a number of powerful nations, after 1945 the world would be dominated by the US and the USSR. Up until 1991, when the Soviet Union collapsed, this rivalry between the two superpowers, and their attempt to create "spheres of influence," characterized international politics in a bipolar world.

Vietnam had been a colony of France since the late nineteenth century. France appropriated the best farmland from the people, ran rubber plantations under slavery-like conditions, and raised illiteracy rates through ill-conceived colonial educational strategies.[26] On the eve of the Second World War, almost all of East Asia, with the exception of Japan, was ruled by colonial powers either directly or indirectly. Britain dominated the area, but the US and Japan challenged this. In 1945, a national liberation struggle led by Ho Chi Minh declared independence from France.

The US, despite its propaganda claims, was not prepared to recognize Vietnamese self-rule. It spent billions to finance France's war to retain control over Vietnam. After Vietnam was divided into two zones, the US pursued a policy of preventing national elections so that Ho Chi Minh would not come to power; instead it sought to establish an anticommunist state under US control in South Vietnam.[27] The puppet regime installed by the US was extremely unpopular, and the National Liberation Front (NLF) formed in 1960 launched a struggle for independence. It was in this context that policy makers in the US drew the conclusion that a military intervention would be the only way to squash the NLF. The public narrative was that the South needed to be defended from communist aggression. The so-called "domino theory" of Soviet expansion was developed in this context, and the policy of containment became the default US position on global communism.

In 1964, the Gulf of Tonkin incident served as the perfect justification for troop escalation and war. In a speech to the nation, President Lyndon B. Johnson stated that the destroyer, the *USS Maddox*, had been attacked by the North Vietnamese. The official story was that the *Maddox* was on "routine patrol" in the Tonkin Gulf and faced an "unprovoked attack" by Vietnamese torpedo boats. The truth, however, was that the *Maddox* was on an intelligence-gathering mission and, more importantly, was never fired upon. Eyewitness accounts state that the Vietnamese torpedo boats weren't even in the area.[28] Yet, the establishment media carried these claims without question. Even though information that contradicted the administration's propaganda was available to the press, they simply amplified the official propaganda line.[29] The key ingredients of the original war narrative were present—the drama of yet another attack on a ship (like the *Maine* and the *Lusitania* in decades past) combined with worthy South Vietnamese victims who needed to be rescued from the menacing communist threat. In fact, right up to 1968, the establishment media barely deviated from the government's propaganda.[30]

After 1968, however, antiwar voices would play a more prominent role. The three television networks now included an equal number of pro and antiwar guests. In fact, after 1970, antiwar guests outnumbered pro-war guests and editorials went from four to one in support of the war, to two to one against.[31] What precipitated this change? Several factors converged to shift media coverage. First, the Tet Offensive, a coordinated attack on the part of the NLF starting in January 1968, showed that the US was not winning the war in Vietnam. This pushed sections of the political elite to take a more public stance in opposition to the war. As Daniel Hallin argued, it was only when debates emerged in Congress over Vietnam policy that the establishment media created a space for dissenting views.[32] Second, the antiwar movement and the GI rebellion moved the public in an antiwar direction. The antiwar movement held teach-ins and demonstrations that educated the public on what the war really was about, and soldiers returning home would speak at these events and talk of atrocities committed by the US. But more importantly, soldiers refusing to fight an unjust war exerted powerful pressure on the establishment. Third, the sheer amount of death and destruction was starting to take a toll. Through the reports of investigative journalists like Seymour Hersh, Americans learned of incidents such as the My Lai massacre, during which hundreds of unarmed civilians—including women, children, and the elderly—were massacred in cold blood. Additionally, tens of thousands of US soldiers died in Vietnam, which led people to question whether the war was worth it.[33] It was in this context that the establishment media began to incorporate more dissenting viewpoints.

Eventually, the US lost the war in Vietnam and withdrew its troops. The Vietnam syndrome, which refers to the resistance on the part of the American public toward US engagement in wars and the commitment of troops, was its consequence. In order to counter this, the tactics of war and its corresponding propaganda strategies underwent a change.

PROPAGANDA AFTER VIETNAM

After Vietnam, sections of the political elite came to believe that it was media coverage of the war that led to US defeat. They argued that television distorted the war by showing graphic images of the dead, turning Americans against the war.[34] While television did show some images of casualties, it was nowhere near the claimed volume.

One study of evening news reports between 1965 and 1970 found that only about 3 percent showed heavy fighting with the dead or wounded.[35] Another study found that TV war stories featuring images of casualties—such as a soldier being lifted onto a helicopter—were brief and in the minority of all reports filed.[36]

Regardless of the reality, the myth that the media cost the US the war gained ground. Future war planners decided that they could never again risk uncensored media coverage of wars. The interventions in Granada in 1983 and Panama in 1989 were testing grounds for a new model of US propaganda that involved tight control over information. By the time of the Gulf War in 1991, the system of media censorship had been all but perfected. Then Secretary of Defense Dick Cheney, expressing his thoughts on the media, would say after the war: "Frankly, I looked on it as a problem to be managed. The information function was extraordinarily important. I did not have a lot of confidence that I could leave it to the press."[37] Cheney was drawing from his own experiences at skillfully managing the press during the Panama invasion, when the press had restricted access to the battlefield and were then provided stock images that aided the war effort.

The media pool system, formed after Granada, allowed the military to control the movement of journalists and to restrict where they went and what they saw. Journalists were taken to selected sites in Iraq during the first Gulf War of 1990–91 and were not allowed to interview soldiers without a military "minder" present. Additionally, reporters were not allowed to pass on stories until they were inspected by the military.

In the absence of direct access to the war, reporters were treated to press briefings with images of precision bombing and laser-guided missiles hitting their target. The military claimed that this was a new form of warfare in which civilians would not be harmed because "smart" technology allowed for "surgical strikes." This was not true. Only 7 percent of the ordinance was "smart." And the "smart" technology wasn't all that smart, as 70 percent missed their target.[38] Both smart and dumb bombs killed civilians and destroyed infrastructure, which included electrical power, water, sanitation, and communication facilities. This was not an accident, but an avowed goal of the campaign. Over 200,000 people died as a result of this war. When award-winning journalists Jon Alpert and Maryann DeLeo sent in video footage of the destruction and civilian casualties, NBC and CBS refused to air their videotapes. The media also squelched reports of "friendly fire."[39] Douglas Kellner noted of the 1991 Iraq War that such "control of press coverage was unprecedented in the history of US warfare."[40]

POST–COLD WAR IMPERIALISM

After the collapse of the Soviet Union in 1991, the US emerged as the lone "hyperpower" in a unipolar world and assumed the role of the global "protector" or "global cop" out to defend democracy and peace. At the time, there were at least two visions of US imperialism. The one, advanced by a section of the elite known as "neoconservatives," was that the US should take an aggressive approach in realizing its foreign policy objectives and not worry about appeasing its allies. The other vision was advanced by proponents of a more liberal imperialism that sought alliances and built multilateral ties in waging "humanitarian" wars.[41] Under President Bill Clinton, the latter won the day and it was the euphemistic "humanitarian" wars that would dominate during the 1990s.

The first display of humanitarian motivations was evidenced during the 1991 Gulf War, when it was argued that the US was rescuing the Kuwaitis from Iraqi aggression. One story that caught the imagination of the nation was the murder of Kuwaiti babies. Allegedly, Iraqi soldiers had snatched babies from their incubators and thrown them onto the floor or bayoneted them—a story reminiscent of German atrocities during World War I. Yet, like its predecessor, this claim was false. Instead, it was a public relations stunt planned by the PR firm Hill and Knowlton with the cooperation of the daughter of the Kuwaiti ambassador at the time, who testified to this before a congressional committee. Politicians, including President George Bush, cited this story as the truth and the media simply echoed them without checking the facts.[42] Certainly, it made for a more palatable excuse than control over oil resources—the real motivation for the Gulf War. Thus, in addition to tight control over media coverage, discussed above, the classic propaganda strategy involving worthy victims was resuscitated.

In fact, humanitarian wars are entirely based on the narrative of the US as protector of worthy victims around the world. Thus the interventions in Haiti, Rwanda, Bosnia, Yugoslavia, and so on in the 1990s were justified in these terms. However, in all these cases the conditions of the victims that the US claimed to alleviate either stayed the same or deteriorated. In 1999, for instance, the North Atlantic Treaty Organization (NATO) bombing of Serbia was meant to stop the "ethnic cleansing" of Albanians from Kosovo. Yet, the situation for the Kosovar Albanians only worsened after the NATO intervention. As if that were not bad enough, there is evidence to suggest that President Clinton and British Prime Minister Tony Blair knew beforehand that the war would exacerbate the conditions for Albanians but went ahead anyway.[43] The 1990s did not, however, have dramatic moments that would immediately fuel war, such as the bombing of naval vessels or cities like Pearl Harbor. Yet the attack on the World Trade Center in 1993, the bombings of US facilities in Saudi Arabia in 1995 and 1996, the embassy bombings in Kenya and Tanzania in 1998, then the attack on the *USS Cole* in 2000 all laid the groundwork for the War on Terror.

In September 2000, a full year before the events of September 11, 2001, a neoconservative document produced by the Project for a New American Century (PNAC) argued that the US should use overwhelming military force to take control of the gulf region. To realize this goal, the report stated that it was necessary to have "some catastrophic and catalyzing event—like a new Pearl Harbor."[44] Such an event presented itself with the attacks on the twin towers, and the neocons grabbed this opportunity to launch a propaganda campaign.

THE "WAR ON TERROR"

The rhetoric of the War on Terror shares some similarities with that of the Cold War in that both logics envision a powerful enemy against which the US must fight an ongoing war. Both also rely on a politics of fear and of what might happen should the US not act to stop its "enemies." In the case of the War on Terror, however, the enemy is a racialized "other"—the menacing Islamist terrorist. Drawing on older Orientalist stereotypes developed by Britain and France, and adding several new dimensions including the "clash of civilizations," the political elite demonized an entire religious group in order to advance an imperial agenda.[45]

The war on Afghanistan in 2001 was presented as a war of retaliation, one intended to capture and execute the purported mastermind of the 9/11 attacks, Osama bin Laden. Even though the vast majority of the 9/11 perpetrators were Saudi Arabian (as is bin Laden) the US chose to collectively punish the Afghan people while continuing to prop up its ally Saudi Arabia. Yet, the rescue narrative was not left out: the US claimed to be rescuing Muslim women from the brutal regime of the Taliban. All of a sudden, Afghan women who had been suffering under Taliban rule since 1996—when they were allies of the US—became the subject of numerous stories in the corporate media. Yet, like the other victims before them, Afghan women too found that their condition would only stay the same or deteriorate under US/NATO occupation.[46] In short, despite the passage of a century, the three central elements of war propaganda developed in 1898—the rescue narrative, the dramatic event (9/11), and paternalistic occupation—continue to hold sway.

The Iraq War would also reflect these elements. In the lead up to the war, the administration argued that Iraq had ties to al-Qaeda and 9/11, and that they possessed weapons of mass destruction. Even though they were lies, these two major justifications were developed with great skill, and before long the media were awash with stories that passed off propaganda as news.[47] Shortly after the war, real proof would emerge to confirm that Iraq neither possessed weapons of mass destruction nor had ties to al-Qaeda. It was then time to highlight the Kurdish victims who suffered chemical attacks, even though the worst chemical attacks occurred when the US still considered Saddam Hussein an ally. Through selective recollections of history, victims were again produced for heroes to rescue.

The real goal of intervention in Iraq was to advance the US's geopolitical aims in the region and to secure control over oil resources. Even mainstream figures such as the former Federal Reserve chair Alan Greenspan would admit to the oil motivation.[48] Yet, despite the revelation of the truth behind the propaganda, the US continued its occupation, a war and occupation that led to deaths of about a million Iraqis and over four thousand US soldiers. In order to justify occupation, the masters of spin argued that the US could not leave Iraq because the country would be thrown into chaos. The US therefore had a "responsibility" to stay the course for the sake of the Iraqis and in order to stabilize the country. We have come a full circle back to the Spanish–American War when the "white man's burden" argument was advanced to justify US colonization of Spain's territories. More than a century later, the American public was again told that the US needed to stay in Iraq because the natives weren't prepared for self-rule.

CONCLUSION

War propaganda has a habit of repeating itself. The all-too-real suffering of people at the hands of local or foreign oppressors has been used repeatedly to launch wars that advance an imperial agenda while forsaking the victims. Imagined attacks on ships like the *USS Maine* and the *Maddox* and real attacks like the ones on the *USS Cole*, Pearl Harbor, and the twin towers of the World Trade Center become moments to bolster patriotic fervor. And if slogans like "remember the *Maine*," were used by war makers over a century ago, today it is "remember 9/11." Then, as now, the establishment media act as the official propaganda arm of the war effort. Yesterday there was William Randolph Hearst, today there is Rupert Murdoch. But as previous wars show us, it is possible to resist the onslaught of propaganda and build an alternate agenda of peace. Students, soldiers, and investigative reporters who refused to accept the framework for Vietnam outlined by the political elite set themselves the task of uncovering the truth and then bringing that truth to the public. Today, this is exactly the burden and responsibility that a new generation must bear in relation to the ongoing, and seemingly endless, War on Terror.

DEEPA KUMAR, PHD, is an associate professor of media studies at Rutgers University. She is the author of *Outside the Box: Corporate Media, Globalization and the UPS Strike* and *Islamophobia and the Politics of Empire*. She has written dozens of articles that have appeared in scholarly journals as well as independent media. She has shared her expertise in numerous media outlets such as BBC, the *New York Times*, NPR, *USA Today*, *Philadelphia Inquirer*, Al Jazeera, and other national and international news media outlets.

Thanks to Marcelle Levine for additional assistance with citations.

Bibliography

Allen, J. *Vietnam: The (Last) War the US Lost*. Chicago: Haymarket Books, 2008.

Chomsky, N. *The New Military Humanism: Lessons from Kosovo*: Common Courage Press, 2000.

Hallin, D. *The "Uncensored War": The Media and Vietnam*. Berkeley, CA: University of California Press, 1989.

Herman, E. and Chomsky, N. *Manufacturing Consent: The Political Economy of Mass Media*. New York: Pantheon, 1988.

Kahin, G. H. *Intervention: How America Became Involved in Vietnam*. Garden City, New York: Anchor Press, 1987.

Karnow, S. *Vietnam: A History*. New York: The Viking Press, 1983.

Kellner, D. *The Persian Gulf TV War*. Boulder, CO: Westview Press, 1992.

Knightly, P. *The First Casualty*. Baltimore: John Hopkins University Press, 2004.

Kumar, D. "Media, War, and Propaganda: Strategies of Information Management during the 2003 Iraq War," *Communication and Critical/Cultural Studies* 3, no. 1 (2006).

Kumar, D. *Islamophobia and the Politics of Empire*. Chicago: Haymarket Books, 2012.

Lens, S. *The Forging of the American Empire*. Chicago: Haymarket Books, 2003.

McArthur, J. "An Orwellian Pitch: The Inner Workings of the War-Propaganda Machine Article." *LA Weekly*. March 21–27, 2003. http://www.laweekly.com/ink/03/18/features-mcarthur.php.

McArthur, J. *Second Front: Censorship and Propaganda in the Gulf War*. New York: Hill and Wang, 1992.

Morse, A. *While Six Million Died*. New York: Overlook Press, 1998.

Ngo, V. L. "Vietnam's Revolutionary Tradition in Vietnam and America" in *Vietnam and America: A Documented History*. Eds. M. Gettleman, J. Franklin, M. B. Young and H. B. Franklin. New York: Grove Press, 1995.

Rampton, S. and Stauber, J. *Weapons of Mass Deception: The Uses of Propaganda in Bush's War on Iraq*. New York: Jeremy Tarcher/Penguin, 2003.

Robinson, C. "Mass Media and the U.S. Presidency," in *Questioning the Media*. Eds. J. D. H. Downing, A. Mohammadi, and A. Sreberny. Thousand Oaks CA: Sage Publications, 1995.

Rodriguez, I. "News Reporting and Colonial Discourse: The Representation of Puerto Ricans in U.S. Press Coverage of the Spanish-American War." *Howard Journal of Communication* 9 (1998): 283–01.

Shoup, L. H. and Minter, W. *The Imperial Brain Trust: The Council on Foreign Relations and the United States Foreign Policy*. New York: Monthly Review Press, 1977.

Sloyan, P. "Hiding Bodies," *Rolling Stone*, March 20, 2003.

Solomon, N. *War Made Easy: How Presidents and Pundits Keep Spinning Us to Death*. Hoboken: Wiley & Sons, 2005.

Stabile, C. and Kumar, D. "Unveiling Imperialism: Media, Gender, and the War on Afghanistan," *Media, Culture and Society* 27, no. 5 (2005).

Thrall, T. *War in the Media Age*, New Jersey: Hampton Press, 2000.

Trent, B. and Kasper, D. *The Panama Deception*. Los Angeles: Rhine Home Video, 1993.

Notes

1. Sidney Lens, *The Forging of the American Empire* (Chicago: Haymarket Books, 2003), 195.

2. Ibid., 270–77; See also Smedley Butler, *War Is a Racket* (1935; reprint, Los Angeles: Feral House, 2003).

3. Cedric Robinson, "Mass Media and the U.S. Presidency," in *Questioning the Media*, ed. John D. H. Downing, Ali Mohammadi, and Annabelle Sreberny-Mohammadi (Thousand Oaks: Sage Publications, 1995).

4. Lens, *The Forging of the American Empire, 171*.

5. Ilia Rodriguez, "News Reporting and Colonial Discourse: The Representation of Puerto Ricans in U.S. Press Coverage of the Spanish-American War," *Howard Journal of Communication* 9 (1998): 283–301.

6. Phillip Knightly, *The First Casualty* (Baltimore: Johns Hopkins University Press, 2004), 100.

7. Ibid.

8. Lens, *The Forging of the American Empire.*
9. Ibid.
10. Rodriguez, "News Reporting and Colonial Discourse: The Representation of Puerto Ricans in U.S. Press Coverage of the Spanish-American War," 289.
11. Ibid., 297.
12. Ibid., 288.
13. Lens, 190.
14. Ibid., 188.
15. A similar practice is used today in Guantánamo and other US prisons and is known as "water boarding."
16. Lens, *The Forging of the American Empire,* 189.
17. Edward S. Herman and Noam Chomsky, *Manufacturing Consent: The Political Economy of the Mass Media* (New York: Pantheon Books, 1988).
18. See, for example, "People: Eugene Debs, 1855–1926," *The American Experience,* PBS, http://www.pbs.org/wgbh/amex/wilson/peopleevents/p_debs.html.
19. Lens, *The Forging of the American Empire,* 254.
20. Knightly, *The First Casualty,* 88.
21. Ibid. This theme resonates with the ways in which the Bush administration has referred to their enemies as "evil doers."
22. Richard Vaughn, "How Advertising Works: A Planning Model," *Journal of Advertising Research* 20, no. 5 (1980): 27–33.
23. Knightly, *The First Casualty,* 89.
24. Laurence H. Shoup and William Minter, *Imperial Brain Trust: The Council on Foreign Relations and the United States Foreign Policy* (New York: Monthly Review Press, 1977), 162–63.
25. Arthur Morse, *While Six Million Died* (New York: Overlook Press, 1998), 99.
26. Stanley Karnow, *Vietnam: A History* (New York: The Viking Press, 1983); Ngo Vinh Long, "Vietnam's Revolutionary Tradition," in *Vietnam and America: A Documented History,* eds. Marvin E. Gettleman, et al. (New York: Grove Press, 1995).
27. George Kahin, *Intervention: How America Became Involved in Vietnam* (Garden City, NY: Anchor Press, 1987).
28. Jeff Cohen and Norman Solomon, "30-year Anniversary: Tonkin Gulf Lie Launched Vietnam War," Fairness and Accuracy in Reporting, July 27, 1994, http://fair.org/media-beat-column/30-year-anniversary-tonkin-gulf-lie-launched-vietnam-war.
29. Daniel Hallin, *The "Uncensored War": The Media and Vietnam* (Berkeley: University of California Press, 1989).
30. Ibid.
31. John McArthur, "An Orwellian Pitch: The Inner Workings of the War-Propaganda Machine," *LA Weekly,* March 21–27, 2003, http://www.laweekly.com/ink/03/18/features-mcarthur.php.
32. Daniel C. Hallin, "The Media, the War in Vietnam, and Political Support: A Critique of the Thesis of an Oppositional Media," *Journal of Politics* 46, no. 1 (1984), 1–24.
33. Joe Allen, *Vietnam: The (Last) War the US Lost* (Chicago: Haymarket Books, 2008).
34. For a brief overview and bibliography on this topic, see the Museum of Broadcasting Communications, http://www.museum.tv/eotv/warontelevi.htm.
35. McArthur, "An Orwellian Pitch: The Inner Workings of the War-Propaganda Machine."
36. Hallin.
37. Patrick Sloyan, "Hiding Bodies," *Rolling Stone,* March 20, 2003, 47.
38. Douglas Kellner, *The Persian Gulf TV War* (Boulder: Westview Press, 1992).
39. Robinson, "Mass Media and the U.S. Presidency."
40. Kellner, 80.
41. Deepa Kumar, *Islamophobia and the Politics of Empire* (Chicago: Haymarket Books, 2012).
42. Robinson, "Mass Media and the U.S. Presidency."
43. Noam Chomsky, *The New Military Humanism: Lessons from Kosovo* (Monroe ME: Common Courage Press, 2002).

44. Project for the New American Century, "Rebuilding America's Defenses: Strategy, Forces, and Resources for a New Century," http://pnac.info/RebuildingAmericasDefenses.pdf, 51. The original site for the PNAC and this document is no longer available, so the above link is a backup site.

45. Kumar, *Islamophobia and the Politics of Empire*.

46. Carole Stabile and Deepa Kumar, "Unveiling Imperialism: Media, Gender, and the War on Afghanistan," *Media, Culture and Society* 27, no. 5 (2005).

47. Deepa Kumar, "Media, War, and Propaganda: Strategies of Information Management during the 2003 Iraq War," *Communication and Critical/Cultural Studies* 3, no. 1 (2006).

48. Peter Beaumont and Joanna Walters, "Greenspan Admits Iraq Was about oil, as Deaths Put at 1.2m," *Guardian*, September 15, 2007, http://www.theguardian.com/world/2007/sep/16/iraq.iraqtimeline.

Acknowledgments

Mickey Huff and Andy Lee Roth

We are pleased to thank everyone who has contributed to Project Censored over the past thirty-eight years. For those who contributed directly to this year's volume, we offer our sincere gratitude and pay our due respects:

To the courageous independent journalists who continue to investigate and report real news: without you, the Project would be impossible. To the faculty evaluators and student researchers at our college and university affiliates across the country: as the eyes and ears of Project Censored, you help us keep up with the cutting edge of independent journalism. To the authors in *Censored 2015*: your contributions inspire us to look ever deeper into the key issues covered in the Top 25 stories, and you help us grow and nurture a public discourse that is so lacking from our political and corporate media culture. To our national and international judges: your dedication and expertise assures that our Top 25 list includes only the best, most significant independent news stories each year.

To our stalwart allies at Seven Stories Press in New York, including Dan Simon, Veronica Liu, and Jon Gilbert. The entire Seven Stories crew—Stewart Cauley, Liz DeLong, Amy Hayden, Ruth Weiner, Silvia Stramenga, Ian Dreiblatt, Jesse Ruddock, and Heather McAdams, as well as interns Benjamin Rowen, Magali Roman, and Rio Santisban-Edwards—has our deepest respect and appreciation for your steadfast commitment to publishing the Project's research.

To Josh MacPhee of Just Seeds, whose artwork makes *Censored 2015* a book we would be pleased to have judged by its cover.

Carl Jensen, founder of the Project, continues to inspire us with his pioneering vision and critical questioning of the status quo. Peter Phillips stirs us to action, engaging everyone he meets—and especially those who work with him—in his ongoing and tireless efforts to promote media freedom and a people's democracy in service of human liberation. The members of the Media Freedom Foundation's board of directors (listed in the next section) continue to provide organizational structure and invaluable counsel. You keep us on course in pursuing Project Censored's mission.

Christopher Oscar and Doug Hecker, of Hole in the Media Productions, and Mike Fischer with the Fischtank Picture Company, have created a brilliant vehicle for sharing Project Censored's message with new audiences. *Project Censored: The Movie—Ending the Reign of Junk Food News* toured the film festival circuit last year, earning numerous awards. Through their ongoing efforts, the documentary is now available for download and purchase, making the film's crucial message even more accessible to communities and classrooms across the country and around the world.

We are grateful to our friends and supporters at Pacifica Radio, especially KPFA in Berkeley, California. *The Project Censored Show*, coming up on its fourth year on air, continues to broadcast live every Friday owing to the skills and dedication of our amazing producer Anthony Fest and control room operators Kirsten Thomas, Rod Akil, and Erica Bridgeman. We are also grateful to former Pacifica executive director Arlene Engelhardt and former KPFA interim general manager Andrew Phillips. Last but not least, we also wish to thank all the volunteers who support the overlapping missions of Project Censored and Pacifica.

Adam Armstrong is our extraordinary webmaster. He maintains our online presence at projectcensored.org, as well as our sister sites, including dailycensored.com and proyectocensurado.org. We could not reach our increasingly global Internet audience without his great skills and dedication to our shared cause. To Adam, we give our highest cyber salute.

Perhaps the most fun part of producing the book each year is looking over the volume's Top 25 stories and subsequent chapters and selecting editorial cartoons that further accentuate their significant yet underreported messages. We thank the inimitable Khalil Bendib, whose brilliant artwork and creativity again add vigor and edge to our annual volume.

We are grateful to Abby Martin, host of *Breaking the Set* on RT and founder of Media Roots; Michel Chossudovsky at Global Research; Rob Kall of Opednews.com; the good people of the Union for Democratic Communications; Stephen Lendman; Ken Jenkins; Allan Rees of No Lies Radio; the Social Justice Committee at the Berkeley Fellowship of Unitarian Universalists; and Jacob Van Vleet and everyone at Moe's Books in Berkeley, California—each of whom help the Project to reach a broader audience.

Colleagues and staff at Diablo Valley College provide Mickey with tremendous support and informed dialogue. Thanks to Hedy Wong, history department cochairs Matthew Powell and Melissa Jacobson, Greg Tilles, Manual Gonzales, Katie Graham, Nolan Higdon, Jacob Van Vleet, Adam Bessie, David Vela, Lyn Krause, Steve Johnson, Jeremy Cloward, Amer Araim, Mark Akiyama, and Dean Obed Vazquez, along with current and former teaching assistants and interns Marcelle Levine, Sam Park, Jen Eiden, Ellie Kim, Bryan Brennan, and Jagnoor Grewel. Mickey would also like to thank all of his classes for the inspiration they provide, as they are a constant reminder of the possibilities of the future, and of how privileged we are as educators to have such an amazing role in contributing to the public sphere.

The generous financial support of donors and subscribers, too numerous to mention here, literally sustain the Project. This year we are especially grateful to Chris Giuntoli, Sergio and Gaye Lub, Dave Nelson, Steve Outrim, Basja Samuelson, T. M. Scruggs, Mark and Debra Swedlund, John and Lyn Roth, Jonathan Ullman, and Elaine Wellin. A special grant from The Rex Foundation, received just as *Censored 2015* went to press, will help us consolidate and expand our campus affiliates program.

On a personal note, we are indebted to and thankful for the love and support of our families and close friends, as they oft make sacrifices behind the scenes so we can continue to do the work we do.

Finally, we are grateful to you, our readers, who cherish and demand a truly free press. Together, we can make a difference.

MEDIA FREEDOM FOUNDATION/PROJECT CENSORED
BOARD OF DIRECTORS

Project Censored 2013–14 National and International Judges

JULIE ANDRZEJEWSKI. Professor Emeritus of Human Relations and cofounder of the Social Responsibility Program, St. Cloud State University. Publications include *Social Justice, Peace, and Environmental Education* (2009).

ROBIN ANDERSEN. Professor of Communication and Media Studies at Fordham University. Author or editor of four books including *A Century of Media, A Century of War* (2006), and dozens of articles. She writes frequently for the media watch group Fairness and Accuracy in Reporting (FAIR).

OLIVER BOYD-BARRETT. Professor emeritus of Bowling Green State University–Ohio and of California State Polytechnic University–Pomona. Publications include *The International New Agencies* (1980), *Contra-Flow in Global News* (1994), *The Globalization of News* (1998), *Media in Global Context* (2009), *News Agencies in the Turbulent Era of the Internet* (2010), *Hollywood and the CIA* (2011), and *Media Imperialism* (2014).

KENN BURROWS. Faculty member for the Institute for Holistic Health Studies, Department of Health Education, San Francisco State University. Director of the Holistic Health Learning Center and producer of the biennial conference, Future of Health Care.

ERNESTO CARMONA. Journalist and writer. Chief correspondent, Telesur-Chile. Director, Santiago Circle of Journalists. President of the Investigation Commission on Attacks Against Journalists, Latin American Federation of Journalists (CIAP-FELAP).

ELLIOT D. COHEN. Professor and chair, Department of Humanities, Indian River State College. Editor and founder, *International Journal of Applied Philosophy*. Recent books include *Technology of Oppression: Preserving Freedom and Dignity in an Age of Mass, Warrantless Surveillance* (2014); *Theory and Practice of Logic-Based Therapy* (2013); and *Philosophy, Counseling, and Psychotherapy* (2013).

JOSÉ MANUEL DE-PABLOS. Professor, University of La Laguna (Tenerife, Canary Islands, Spain). Founder of *Revista Latina de Comunicación Social* (RLCS), a scientific journal based out of the Laboratory of Information Technologies and New Analysis of Communication.

GEOFF DAVIDIAN. Investigative journalist and editor, *The Putnam Pit* (Cookeville TN) and MilwaukeePress.net. Publications include the *Milwaukee Journal*, Reuters, the *Chicago Sun-Times*, the *Globe and Mail* (Toronto), the *New York Daily News*, *Albuquerque Journal*, *Seattle Post-Intelligencer*, and the *Vancouver Sun*.

LENORE FOERSTEL. Women for Mutual Security, facilitator of the Progressive International Media Exchange (PRIME).

ROBERT HACKETT. Professor, School of Communication, Simon Fraser University. Codirector of News Watch Canada since 1993; cofounder of Media Democracy Day (2001) and openmedia.ca (2007). Publications include *Expanding Peace Journalism* (coedited with I. S. Shaw and J. Lynch, 2011), and *Remaking Media: The Struggle To Democratize Public Communication* (with William K. Carroll, 2006).

KEVIN HOWLEY. Professor of Media Studies, DePauw University. Author of *Community Media: People, Places, and Communication Technologies* (2005); and editor of *Understanding Community Media* (2010) and *Media Interventions* (2013).

CARL JENSEN. Professor Emeritus, Communication Studies, Sonoma State University. Founder and former director of Project Censored. Author of *Censored: The News That Didn't Make the News and Why* (1990–96), *20 Years of Censored News* (1997), and *Stories that Changed America: Muckrakers of the 20th Century* (2002).

NICHOLAS JOHNSON.* Professor, College of Law, University of Iowa. Former commissioner, Federal Communications Commission (1966–73). Author of *How to Talk Back to Your Television Set*.

CHARLES L. KLOTZER. Founder, editor, and publisher emeritus of *St. Louis Journalism Review* and *FOCUS/Midwest.*

NANCY KRANICH. Lecturer, School of Communication and Information, and special projects librarian, Rutgers University. Past president of the American Library Association (ALA), convener of the ALA Center for Civic Life. Author of *Libraries and Democracy* (2001) and *Libraries and Civic Engagement* (2012).

DEEPA KUMAR. Associate professor, Media Studies at Rutgers University. Author of *Outside the Box: Corporate Media, Globalization and the UPS Strike* (2007) and *Islamophobia and the Politics of Empire* (2012). She is currently working on a book on the cultural politics of the war on terror.

MARTIN LEE. Investigative journalist and author. Cofounder of Fairness and Accuracy in Reporting, and former editor of FAIR's magazine, *Extra!* Director of Project CBD, a medical science information service. Author of *Smoke Signals: A Social History of Marijuana, The Beast Reawakens* and *Acid Dreams: The Complete Social History of LSD: The CIA, the Sixties and Beyond.*

DENNIS LOO. Associate professor of Sociology, California State University Polytechnic University–Pomona. Coeditor (with Peter Phillips) of *Impeach the President: The Case Against Bush and Cheney* (2006).

PETER LUDES. Professor of Mass Communication, Jacobs University Bremen. Founder in 1997 of German initiative on news enlightenment, publishing the most neglected German news (Project Censored, Germany); and editor of *Algorithms of Power: Key Invisibles* (2011).

WILLIAM LUTZ. Emeritus Professor of English, Rutgers University. Former editor of *The Quarterly Review of Doublespeak.* Author of *Doublespeak Defined* (1999); *The New Doublespeak: Why No One Knows What Anyone's Saying Anymore* (1996); *Doublespeak: From Revenue Enhancement to Terminal Living* (1989); *The Cambridge Thesaurus of American English* (1994).

SILVIA LAGO MARTINEZ. Professor of Sociology, Universidad de Buenos Aires; Codirector, Gino Germani Research Institute Program for Research on Information Society.

CONCHA MATEOS. Faculty in the Universidad Rey Juan Carlos (Madrid). Journalist for radio, television, and political organizations in Spain and Latin America. Coordinator for Project Censored Research in Europe and Latin America.

MARK CRISPIN MILLER. Professor of Media, Culture, and Communication, New York University, Steinhardt School of Culture, Education, and Human Development. Author, editor, activist.

JACK L. NELSON.* Distinguished Professor Emeritus, Graduate School of Education, Rutgers University. Former member, AAUP Academic Freedom Committee. Author of seventeen books, including *Critical Issues in Education*, 8th ed. (2013) and about 200 articles.

PETER PHILLIPS. Professor of Sociology, Sonoma State University. Director, Project Censored, 1996–2009. President, Media Freedom Foundation. Editor or coeditor of fourteen editions of *Censored*. Coeditor (with Dennis Loo) of *Impeach the President: The Case Against Bush and Cheney* (2006).

NANCY SNOW. Professor of Communications, California State University–Fullerton and adjunct professor of Communications and Public Diplomacy at the University of Southern California's Annenberg School for Communication and Journalism. Author/editor of seven books, including *Information War: American Propaganda, Free Speech, and Opinion Control Since 9/11* (2003).

SHEILA RABB WEIDENFELD.* President of D. C. Productions, Ltd. Emmy Award-winning television producer. Former press secretary to Betty Ford.

ROB WILLIAMS. President of the Action Coalition for Media Education (ACME), teaches media, communications, global studies, and journalism at the University of Vermont, Champlain College, and Saint Michael's College. He has authored numerous articles on media and media literacy education, as well as coedited an anthology entitled *Most Likely To Secede* (2013) about the Vermont independence movement.

*Indicates having been a Project Censored Judge since 1976

Report from the Media Freedom Foundation President

This report details some of Project Censored's daily work and highlights from the past year's efforts on behalf of media democracy in action.

The Media Freedom Foundation (MFF) is a nonprofit 501(c) (3) corporation that sponsors Project Censored and all its various programs. MFF has an eleven-person board of directors that is responsible for monitoring the budget and setting policy for our operations. Mickey Huff is director of Project Censored and has overall responsibility for its day-to-day management. Associate director Andy Lee Roth serves in a similar administrative capacity, with a focus on the development and maintenance of the campus affiliates program. Together they coordinated the production of *Censored 2015*.

Since its founding by Carl Jensen at Sonoma State University in 1976, Project Censored has worked with students and the public—through radio, television, film, books, and the Internet—to promote public understanding of the crucial roles that free speech and a free press play in making democratic government possible. Free speech and a free press are necessary to democracy. Without these, people cannot truly participate in making the decisions that shape our lives and our communities.

Project Censored has both critical and affirmative aspects. On the critical side, we expose and oppose news censorship. Affirmatively, we promote independent investigative journalism, media literacy, and critical thinking. We strive to achieve our mission in numerous ways.

Since 1993, we have researched and written an annual book of the top censored news stories and media analysis. Our book *Censored* is published annually by Seven Stories Press, an independent book publisher in New York City.

Since 2010, we have produced a weekly one-hour program, *The Project Censored Show*, for Pacifica Radio, which airs live from Berkeley, California, every Friday at 1:00 P.M. PST on KPFA 94.1 FM and online at KPFA.org. Our affiliate stations include WBAI (New York); WPFA (Washington DC); WPRR (Grand Rapids MI); KSKQ (Ashland OR); KFCF (Fresno CA); WRFN (Radio Free Nashville in Nashville TN); Progressive Radio Network; No Lies Radio; and various other Pacifica radio stations around the country. Please ask your local public/nonprofit radio station to air our weekly shows. See projectcensored. org/radio-archive for a listing of our shows and guests.

We currently have eighteen college and university campuses participating in the annual review of news stories. The network of professors, students, and community members who contribute to our affiliate research program is a cornerstone of the Project's mission to educate students and the public in media literacy and the crucial role that a free press plays in democracy. We started the affiliates program five years ago, as we began to separate the Project from its original home campus at Sonoma State University. Our affiliates program is not only a model of how we can all *be* the media, it is also a unique contribution of the Project: as far as we know, no other media watchdog organization in the US has a larger, more systematic student training program than Project Censored. Faculty from additional college and university campuses have expressed interest in joining our affiliates program, and with enhanced funding we anticipate expanding this program to include additional campuses. A generous grant from the Rex Foundation, awarded in May 2014, gives our campus affiliate program a welcome boost.

Throughout each year, students and faculty at our affiliate campuses produce Validated Independent News Stories (VINS), news stories from independent sources on topics ignored by corporate media. Students and faculty identify, research, and vet these stories. (For more on this, see the Note on Research and Evaluation in Chapter 1.) We post VINS that pass the vetting process on the Project Censored website. These stories become the nominees for the Project's annual Top 25 list of the most important censored or underreported news stories.

Teaching college classes and working with students to learn about alternative news outlets is a major part of our efforts to create a more media literate society. We invite faculty and students at campuses not yet affiliated with Project Censored to join us.

Adam Armstrong continues as webmaster for all of the MFF/Project Censored websites, including our Spanish-language site at proyectocensurado.org. Unique views on our sites run some 400,000 each month with millions of monthly hits. Adam also manages the *Daily Censored* blog—dailycensored.com—which now features more than fifty regular contributors, posting original news stories and opinion pieces. Adam is a vital member of our team.

We have also been touring communities around the nation screening our award-winning documentary film, *Project Censored The Movie: Ending the Reign of Junk Food News.* Six years in the making, the film was written, directed, and produced by Doug Hecker, a Project Censored alum, and Christopher Oscar, with editing by Mike Fischer. The film has won awards, including Best Director of a Documentary and Best Editing of a Documentary at the 2013 Madrid International Film Festival, as well as being honored as the Most Viewed Film at the 2013 Sonoma International Film Festival. The film is a vehicle through which we hope to engage people who do not already know about the Project from our books or website. The film is also is an excellent resource for high school and college teachers to use in their classrooms and is available to download, to own or rent, at projectcensoredthemovie.com. (See the final page of this book for more details.)

The Project Censored team is regularly invited as speakers to community events, college campuses, academic conferences, and independent bookstores worldwide. We address the issues of media censorship, propaganda, and the importance of truthful, independent media in society. To arrange for a member of our speaking team to come to your community or campus see projectcensored.org/speakers.

These efforts and others too numerous to list are part of our annual activities at Media Freedom Foundation/Project Censored. We currently do all of this on less than $100,000 a year. In addition to annual revenues from book sales and royalties, our primary financial support comes from individual donors around the world. A developing support option has been for donors to pledge five dollars or more per month. Currently, over 225 folks act as vital monthly contributors, giving five to thirty dollars a month online. Please consider making a monthly pledge at projectcensored.org. If you are affiliated with a nonprofit foundation or can make a larger gift in support of one or all of our activities, we would sincerely appreciate hearing from you.

At present, 90 percent of our operating budget comes from the support of individual donors, supplemented by book and DVD sales. We accomplish a lot with a little. Our modest budget—augmented by the tireless commitments of numerous volunteer supporters—allows us to maintain our current operations. However, as we hope to have communicated here, we are poised to expand our reach and our influence—via improved distribution of the new documentary, greater promotion of our annual book series, and, most of all, expansion of our campus affiliates program.

Promoting freedom of the press, highlighting media bias, and opposing news censorship—Project Censored is among the longest-running media watchdog organizations in the United States. Our track record and reputation is well established. Furthermore, we know of no other organization that systematically provides students the kind of direct and hands-on training in media literacy and critical thinking skills that Project Censored does.

We ask you to please support us financially as you are able, and to remember us in your estate planning.

Peter Phillips, PhD
President, Media Freedom Foundation/Project Censored
June 2014
PO Box 571
Cotati, CA 94931
(707) 874–2695
peter@projectcensored.org

How to Support Project Censored

NOMINATE A STORY

To nominate a Censored story, send us a copy of the article and include the name of the source publication, the date that the article appeared, and page number. For news stories published on the Internet, forward the URL to mickey@projectcensored.org; andy@projectcensored.org; and/or peter@projectcensored.org. The deadline for nominating Censored stories is March 15 of each year.

Criteria for Project Censored news story nominations:

▶ A censored news story reports information that the public has a right and need to know, but to which the public has had limited access.

▶ The news story is recent, having been first reported no later than one year ago. Censored 2015 the Top 25 list includes stories reported between April 2013 and March 2014. Thus, stories submitted for Censored 2016 should be no older than April 2014.

▶ The story has clearly defined concepts and solid, verifiable documentation. The story's claims should be supported by evidence—the more controversial the claims, the stronger the evidence necessary.

▶ The news story has been published, either electronically or in print, in a publicly circulated newspaper, journal, magazine, newsletter, or similar publication from either a domestic or foreign source.

MAKE A TAX-DEDUCTIBLE DONATION

Project Censored is supported by the Media Freedom Foundation, a 501(c)(3) nonprofit organization. We depend on tax-deductible donations to continue our work. To support our efforts on behalf of independent journalism and freedom of information, send checks to the address below or call (707) 874-2695.

Donations can also be made online at www.projectcensored.org.

Please consider helping us fight news censorship and promote media literacy.

Media Freedom Foundation
P.O. Box 571
Cotati, CA 94931
mickey@projectcensored.org
andy@projectcensored.org
peter@projectcensored.org
Phone: (707) 874-2695

About the Editors

ANDY LEE ROTH is the associate director of Project Censored. He has coedited four previous editions of Project Censored's yearbook, in addition to contributing chapters on Iceland and the commons (*Censored 2014*), the Military Commissions Act (*Censored 2009*) and news photographs depicting the human cost of war (*Censored 2008*). His research on topics ranging from ritual to broadcast news interviews and communities organizing for parklands has also appeared in journals including the *International Journal of Press/Politics; Social Studies of Science; Media, Culture & Society; City & Community; and Sociological Theory*. He reviews books for *YES! Magazine*. He earned a PhD in Sociology at the University of California–Los Angeles and a BA in Sociology and Anthropology at Haverford College. As of fall 2014, he teaches sociology at Pomona College and serves on the boards of the Media Freedom Foundation and the Claremont Wildlands Conservancy.

MICKEY HUFF is director of Project Censored and serves on the board of the Media Freedom Foundation. To date, he has edited or coedited six volumes of *Censored* and contributed numerous chapters to these works dating back to 2008. Additionally, he has coauthored several chapters on media and propaganda for other scholarly publications, most recently *Flashpoint in Ukraine* from Clarity Press (2014). He is currently professor of social science and history at Diablo Valley College in the San Francisco Bay Area, where he is cochair of the history department. Huff is cohost with former Project Censored director Dr. Peter Phillips of *The Project Censored Show*, the weekly syndicated public affairs program that originates from KPFA Pacifica Radio in Berkeley CA. For the past several years, Huff has worked on the national planning committee of Banned Books Week, working with the American Library Association and the National Coalition Against Censorship, of which Project Censored is a member. He is also a longtime musician and composer. He lives with his family in Northern California.

For more information about the editors, to invite them to speak at your school or in your community, or to conduct interviews, please visit projectcensored.org.

Index

C

C-SPAN, 214, 219
Canada, 41, 115, 117, 145, 168,
    212, 219, 223–226, 228–233,
    236–267, 319
Cape Colony, 296
Carnegie, Andrew, 299
Caspian basin, 55
*Catastrophism: The Apocalyptic
    Politics of Collapse and Rebirth,*
    276, 292
Cato Institute, 57, 157, 170
CBS Evening News, 51, 204
CBS, 51, 114, 132, 149, 163
Center for American Progress, 57
Center for Investigative Reporting,
    119, 120
Center for Media and Democracy,
    48, 50
Center for Media Justice, 45
Central Intelligence Agency (CIA),
    16, 19, 26, 27, 85, 101, 104, 105,
    109, 136, 139, 140, 144–146,
    148, 152, 161, 163, 167,
    203–207, 218
chaptering out, 80
Charter Schools, 73, 74
Chelsea Manning Support Network,
    102, 103
Cheney, Dick, 53, 307
Chevron, 55, 58
Chile, 41, 224, 318
China, 156, 157, 223, 284
Chomsky, Noam, 86, 301, 314
Church Committee hearings, 49

CitiGroup, 113
Citizens Trade Campaign, 42
Citizens United, 186
Clark, Bob, 277
Cleveland, Grover 299
climate change, 50–52, 57–59, 143,
    172
climate engineering, 52
Clinton, Bill 137, 201, 248, 308
clownfish, 38
CNN, 81, 114, 130–133, 142, 144, 156,
    157, 200
Coalition to Stop Police Brutality,
    Repression and the Criminal-
    ization of a Generation, 262
Cohen, Richard, 211
Colbert, Stephen, 133
Cold War, 55, 147, 148, 204, 207,
    210, 308, 309
collateral murder, 99
Commission on Protecting and Re-
    ducing Government Secrecy, 18
Committee on Public Information
    (CPI) 302
Common Dreams, 146, 157
Common Sense (magazine), 297
Congo, 272
Congressional Research Service, 39
CONOP 8888, 280
Coombs, David, 101–103
Cooperation Act, 1981, 247
corporate personhood, 186
Corporation for Public Broadcasting
    (CPB) 133
Council on Foreign Relations, 302,
    312
Courage to Resist, 102

Creel, George, 302
Crimea, 53
Cronkite, Walter 212
Cuba, 297, 298, 299

F

F-35 program, 60
Facebook, 16, 19, 148, 183, 189
Fairness and Accuracy in Reporting
     (FAIR), 51, 57, 58, 75, 102, 151,
     318
Farm Bill, 173
Farrakhan, Louis, 177
Fatal Encounters, 69
Federal Bureau of Investigation
     (FBI), 48–50, 88, 150, 189,
     206, 245, 246, 248
Federal Communications Commis-
     sion (FCC), 43–45, 64, 143
Feinstein, Diane, 108
First Amendment, 15–17, 21, 44, 98,
     100, 148, 158, 186, 188, 213
First Casualty, The, 301
First Nations, 227, 233, 236
First World War, 296, 301, 303
Fleischer, Ruben, 284
Forbes, 45
Foreign Intelligence Surveillance
     Act (FISA), 181, 190
Foreign Intelligence Surveillance
     Court, 189, 190
Foreign Policy, 144, 280
fossil fuel divestment, 52 fossil fuel
     emissions, 52
fossil fuels, 36, 50
Foucault, Michel, 25, 27
Four Minute Men, 302
Fourth Amendment, 17, 190
Fourth Estate, 13, 96, 204

Fox News, 81, 109, 114, 131–134, 142,
     145, 151, 152
France, 118, 296, 301, 302, 304, 305,
     309
Freedom of Information Act (FOIA),
     12, 49, 173, 174, 190
Freedom of the Press Foundation,
     107–109, 111
Freedom Summer, 176
French National Assembly, 116
Fujimori, Alberto, 228
Fukushima Daiichi nuclear power
     plant, 16, 23, 61, 62, 89, 96,
     121–125
Fundacion MEPI, 84

G

Gandhi, 200–203, 215
Gaza, 5, 67–69
Gazprom Company, 55
General Electric, 45, 61, 62
Germany, 52, 150, 296, 301, 302,
     320
Glass, Ira, 85
glioma, 62
global capitalism, 271, 287
global warming, 5, 22, 36, 50–52,
     59, 88, 235
GMO foods, 43, 172
Gompers, Samuel, 299
Google, 110, 116, 118, 183, 189, 245
Gordon, Avery, 281

Y

Z

PROJECT CENSORED THE MOVIE

ENDING THE REIGN OF JUNK FOOD NEWS

AVAILABLE ONLINE FOR RENTAL OR DOWNLOAD,
OR AS A PACKAGED DVD!

Determined to break the grip of Junk Food News on the American public, two California fathers uncover the true agenda of the corporate media while they investigate the importance of a free and independent press.

This new, award-winning documentary, six years in the making, takes an in-depth look at what is wrong with the news media in the US and what we can do about it. The film highlights the work of thirty-eight-year veteran media democracy organization Project Censored (PC) and their commitment to providing solutions through media literacy and critical thinking education while celebrating the best in underreported, independent journalism.

Project Censored The Movie, made by former PC Sonoma State University student Doug Hecker and longtime Project supporter Christopher Oscar, features original interviews and montages (edited by Mike Fischer) about PC and media censorship with Noam Chomsky, Howard Zinn, Daniel Ellsberg, Michael Parenti, Oliver Stone, Cynthia McKinney, Nora Barrows-Friedman, Peter Kuznick, Khalil Bendib, Abby Martin of RT's *Breaking the Set*, PC-affiliated faculty, students, as well as Project founder Dr. Carl Jensen, former director and president of the Media Freedom Foundation Dr. Peter Phillips, current director Prof. Mickey Huff, and associate director Dr. Andy Lee Roth. Plus much, much more!

See projectcensoredthemovie.com for details about how to screen this film in your community or at your school.

To stream, rent, or download the film now, please go to https://www.yekra.com/project-censored.